CCNA®
Routing and Switching
Review Guide

Todd Lammle

A Wiley Brand

Senior Acquisitions Editor: Jeff Kellum
Development Editor: Amy Breguet
Technical Editor: Isaac Valdez
Production Editor: Eric Charbonneau
Copy Editor: Judy Flynn
Editorial Manager: Pete Gaughan
Vice President and Executive Group Publisher: Richard Swadley
Associate Publisher: Chris Webb
Media Project Manager 1: Laura Moss-Hollister
Media Associate Producer: Marilyn Hummel
Media Quality Assurance: Josh Frank
Book Designer: Judy Fung
Compositor: Craig Woods, Happenstance Type-O-Rama
Proofreader: Kim Wimpsett
Indexer: Ted Laux
Project Coordinator, Cover: Katherine Crocker
Cover Designer: Ryan Sneed

Copyright © 2014 by John Wiley & Sons, Inc., Indianapolis, Indiana

Published simultaneously in Canada

ISBN: 978-1-118-78981-0

ISBN: 978-1-118-78962-9 (ebk.)

ISBN: 978-1-118-87686-2 (ebk.)

For general information on our other products and services or to obtain technical support, please contact our Customer Care Department within the U.S. at (877) 762-2974, outside the U.S. at (317) 572-3993 or fax (317) 572-4002.

Wiley publishes in a variety of print and electronic formats and by print-on-demand. Some material included with standard print versions of this book may not be included in e-books or in print-on-demand. If this book refers to media such as a CD or DVD that is not included in the version you purchased, you may download this material at http://booksupport.wiley.com. For more information about Wiley products, visit www.wiley.com.

Library of Congress Control Number: 2013954090

10 9 8 7 6 5 4 3 2

Dear Reader,

Thank you for choosing *CCNA Routing and Switching Review Guide*. This book is part of a family of premium-quality Sybex books, all of which are written by outstanding authors who combine practical experience with a gift for teaching.

Sybex was founded in 1976. More than 30 years later, we're still committed to producing consistently exceptional books. With each of our titles, we're working hard to set a new standard for the industry. From the paper we print on to the authors we work with, our goal is to bring you the best books available.

I hope you see all that reflected in these pages. I'd be very interested to hear your comments and get your feedback on how we're doing. Feel free to let me know what you think about this or any other Sybex book by sending me an email at contactus@sybex.com. If you think you've found a technical error in this book, please visit http://sybex.custhelp.com. Customer feedback is critical to our efforts at Sybex.

Best regards,

Chris Webb
Associate Publisher
Sybex, an Imprint of Wiley

Acknowledgments

First, a loud callout to Jim Frye, who was instrumental in putting this book together. He spent countless hours combining and summarizing my work from the CCENT and CCNA ICND2 study guides into what is a really nice review guide for the CCNA Routing and Switching certification. Thank you, Jim!

Thanks to Jeff Kellum, who always keeps me working hard and makes sure I am headed in the right direction. This is no easy task for Jeff!

And thanks to my production editor, Eric Charbonneau, for keeping the book on track, and Amy Breguet, for keeping all the edits in order and on time. And I can't forget Judy Flynn, the backbone of all my books, who reads every word over and over until the chapters are nearly flawless!

Last, thanks to Isaac Valdez, my tech editor for this edition of the review guide.

Thank you all!

About the Author

Todd Lammle is the authority on Cisco certification and internetworking and is Cisco certified in most Cisco certification categories. He is a world-renowned author, speaker, trainer, and consultant. Todd has three decades of experience working with LANs, WANs, and large enterprise licensed and unlicensed wireless networks, and lately he's been implementing large Cisco data centers worldwide. His years of real-world experience is evident in his writing; he is not just an author but an experienced networking engineer with very practical experience working on the largest networks in the world at such companies as Xerox, Hughes Aircraft, Texaco, AAA, Cisco, and Toshiba, among many others. Todd has published over 60 books, including the very popular *CCNA: Cisco Certified Network Associate Study Guide*, *CCNA Wireless Study Guide*, and *CCNA Data Center Study Guides*, all from Sybex. He runs an international consulting and training company based in Colorado, Texas, and San Francisco.

You can reach Todd through his forum and blog at www.lammle.com.

About the Contributor

Jim Frye has over 20 years of experience in the computing field and holds numerous IT industry certifications in computing and networking. Jim is employed with GlobalNet Training and Consulting, Inc., a network integration and training firm based in Colorado, Texas, and San Francisco. His technical expertise is a great value and asset to GlobalNet.

Contents at a Glance

Contents

Introduction

Welcome to the exciting world of Cisco certification! If you've picked up this book because you want to improve yourself and your life with a better, more satisfying and secure job, you've done the right thing. Whether you're striving to enter the thriving, dynamic IT sector or seeking to enhance your skillset and advance your position within it, being Cisco certified can seriously stack the odds in your favor to help you attain your goals!

Cisco certifications are powerful instruments of success that also markedly improve your grasp of all things internetworking. As you progress through this book, you'll gain a complete understanding of networking that reaches far beyond Cisco devices. By the end of this book, you'll comprehensively know how disparate network topologies and technologies work together to form the fully operational networks that are vital to today's very way of life in the developed world. The knowledge and expertise you'll gain here is essential for and relevant to every networking job and is why Cisco certifications are in such high demand—even at companies with few Cisco devices!

Although it's now common knowledge that Cisco rules routing and switching, the fact that it also rocks the voice, data center, and service provider world is also well recognized. And Cisco certifications reach way beyond the popular but less extensive certifications like those offered by CompTIA and Microsoft to equip you with indispensable insight into today's vastly complex networking realm. Essentially, by deciding to become Cisco certified, you're proudly announcing that you want to become an unrivaled networking expert—a goal that this book will get you well on your way to achieving. Congratulations in advance to the beginning of your brilliant future!

 For up-to-the-minute updates covering additions or modifications to the Cisco certification exams, as well as additional study tools, review questions, and bonus material, be sure to visit the Todd Lammle websites and forum at www.lammle.com, www.lammlesim.com, and www.lammle.com/forum.

Cisco's Network Certifications

It used to be that to secure the holy grail of Cisco certifications—the CCIE—you passed only one written test before being faced with a grueling, formidable hands-on lab. This intensely daunting, all-or-nothing approach made it nearly impossible to succeed and predictably didn't work out too well for most people. Cisco responded to this issue by creating a series of new certifications, which not only made it easier to eventually win the highly coveted CCIE prize, it gave employers a way to accurately rate and measure the skill levels of prospective and current employees. This exciting paradigm shift in Cisco's certification path truly opened doors that few were allowed through before!

Beginning in 1998, obtaining the Cisco Certified Network Associate (CCNA) certification was the first milestone in the Cisco certification climb as well as the official prerequisite to each of the more advanced levels. But that changed when Cisco announced the Cisco Certified Entry Network Technician (CCENT) certification. And then in March 2013, Cisco once again proclaimed that all-new CCENT and CCNA R/S tests will be required beginning in October of the same year; now the Cisco certification process looks like Figure I.1.

FIGURE I.1   The Cisco certification path

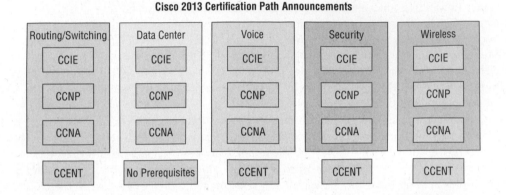

Cisco 2013 Certification Path Announcements

    I have included only the most popular tracks in Figure I.1. In addition to the ones in this image, there are also tracks for Design, Service Provider, Service Provider Operations, and Video. Also note that the CCIE Voice certification retirement will be announced shortly.

The Cisco Routing and Switching (R/S) path is by far the most popular and could very well remain so, but soon you'll see the Data Center path become more and more of a focus as companies migrate to data center technologies. The Voice track also actually does provide a good job opportunity. Still, understanding the foundation of R/S before attempting any other certification track is something I highly recommend.

Even so, and as the figure shows, you only need your CCENT certification to get underway for most of the tracks. Also, note that there are a few other certification tracks you can go down that are not shown in the figure, although they're not as popular as the ones shown. You can find information on all Cisco certification tracks at www.cisco.com.

Cisco Certified Entry Network Technician (CCENT)

Don't be fooled by the oh-so-misleading name of this first certification because it absolutely isn't entry level! Okay—maybe entry level for Cisco's certification path, but definitely not for someone without experience trying to break into the highly lucrative yet challenging IT job market! For the uninitiated, the CompTIA A+ and Network+ certifications aren't official prerequisites, but know that Cisco does expect you to have that type and level of experience before embarking on your Cisco certification journey.

All of this gets us to 2013, when the climb to Cisco supremacy just got much harder again. The innocuous-sounding siren's call of the CCENT can lure you to some serious trouble if you're not prepared, because it's actually much harder than the old CCNA ever was. This will rapidly become apparent once you start studying, but be encouraged! The fact that the certification process is getting harder really works better for you in the long run, because that which is harder to obtain only becomes that much more valuable when you finally do, right? Yes, indeed!

Another important factor to keep in mind is that the CCENT 100-101 exam, which is one of the exams this book was written for, costs $150 per attempt and it's anything but easy to pass! The good news is that this book will guide you step-by-step in building a strong foundation in routing and switching technologies. You really need to build on a strong technical foundation and stay away from exam cram type books, suspicious online material, and the like. They can help somewhat, but understand that you'll pass the Cisco certification exams only if you have a strong foundation and that you'll get that solid foundation only by reading as much as you can, performing the written labs and review questions in this book, and practicing lots and lots of hands-on labs. Additional practice exam questions, videos, and labs are offered on my website, and what seems like a million other sites offer additional material that can help you study.

However, there is one way to skip the CCENT exam and still meet the prerequisite required before moving on to any other certification track, and that path is through the CCNA Routing and Switching composite (CCNA R/S) exam. First, I'll discuss the Interconnecting Cisco Network Devices 2 (ICND2) exam and then tell you about the composite CCNA exam, which will provide you, when successful, with both the CCENT and the CCNA R/S certification.

Cisco Certified Network Associate Routing and Switching (CCNA R/S)

Once you have achieved your CCENT certification, you can take the ICND2 (200-101) exam in order to achieve your CCNA R/S certification. This is now the most popular certification Cisco has by far because it's the most sought-after certification of all employers.

As with the CCENT, this exam is also $150 per attempt—although thinking you can just skim a book and pass any of these exams would probably be a really expensive mistake! The CCENT/CCNA exams are extremely hard and cover a lot of material, so you have to really know your stuff. Taking a Cisco class or spending months with hands-on experience is definitely a requirement to succeed when faced with this monster!

And once you have your CCNA, you don't have to stop there—you can choose to continue and achieve an even higher certification, called the Cisco Certified Network Professional (CCNP). There are various ones, as shown in Figure I.1. The CCNP R/S is still the most popular, with Voice certifications coming in at a close second. And I've got to tell you that the Data Center certification will be catching up fast. Also good to know is that anyone with a CCNP R/S has all the skills and knowledge needed to attempt the notoriously dreaded but coveted CCIE R/S lab. But just becoming a CCNA R/S can land you that job you've dreamed about and that's what this book is all about: helping you to get and keep a great job!

Still, why take two exams to get your CCNA if you don't have to? Cisco still has the composite exam called CCNA 200-120 that, if passed, will land you with your CCENT and your CCNA R/S via only one test, priced accordingly at $300.

Why Become a CCENT and CCNA R/S?

Cisco, like Microsoft and other vendors that provide certification, has created the certification process to give administrators a set of skills and to equip prospective employers with a way to measure those skills or match certain criteria. And as you probably know, becoming a CCNA R/S is certainly the initial, key step on a successful journey toward a new, highly rewarding, and sustainable networking career.

The CCNA program was created to provide a solid introduction not only to the Cisco Internetwork Operating System (IOS) and Cisco hardware but also to internetworking in general, making it helpful to you in areas that are not exclusively Cisco's. And regarding today's certification process, it's not unrealistic that network managers—even those without Cisco equipment—require Cisco certifications for their job applicants.

Rest assured that if you make it through the CCNA and are still interested in Cisco and internetworking, you're headed down a path to certain success!

What Skills Do You Need to Become a CCENT?

The CCENT exam tests a candidate for the knowledge and skills required to successfully install, operate, and troubleshoot a small branch office network.

The exam includes questions on the operation of IP data networks, LAN switching technologies, IPv6, IP routing technologies, IP services network device security, and basic troubleshooting.

What Skills Do You Need to Become a CCNA R/S?

To be a CCNA R/S, you need to be able to successfully install, operate, and troubleshoot a small to medium-size enterprise branch network. Topics include LAN switching technologies, IP routing technologies, IP services (FHRP, syslog, SNMP v2 and v3), troubleshooting, and WAN technologies.

To become a CCNA R/S, as mentioned earlier, you have two options: take and pass the ICND1 and ICND2 exams, or pass one little test, the CCNA Composite exam (200-120), and then—poof!—you're a CCNA R/S. Oh, but don't you wish it were that easy? True, it's just one test, but it's a whopper, and to pass it you must possess enough knowledge to understand what the test writers are saying, and you need to know everything I mentioned previously! Hey, it's hard, but it can be done!

Candidates can prepare for the CCNA Composite exam by taking the Todd Lammle authorized Cisco bootcamps. This composite exam tests that a candidate has the knowledge and skills required to install, operate, and troubleshoot a small to medium-size enterprise branch network. The topics include all the areas covered under the 100-101 ICND1 and 200-101 ICND2 exams.

I can't stress this point enough: It's critical that you have some hands-on experience with Cisco routers. If you can get ahold of some basic routers and switches, you're set.

> For Cisco certification hands-on training with CCSI Todd Lammle, please see www.lammle.com. Each student will get hands-on experience by configuring at least three routers and two switches—no sharing of equipment!

How Is This Book Organized?

This book is organized according to the official objectives list prepared by Cisco for the CCNA exams.

> This book maps to the CCNA Composite (200-120) exam objectives, which is a composite of the CCENT/ICND1 (100-101) and ICND2 (200-101) exam objectives. Refer to the Cisco website (www.cisco.com/web/learning) for a detailed list of the exam objectives.

Within each chapter, the individual exam objectives are addressed. Each section of a chapter covers one exam objective. For each objective, the critical information is first presented, and then there are several Exam Essentials for each exam objective. Additionally, each chapter ends with a section of review questions. Here is a closer look at each of these components:

Exam Objectives   The individual exam objective sections present the greatest level of detail on information that is relevant to the CCNA exams. This is the place to start if you're unfamiliar with or uncertain about the technical issues related to the objective.

Exam Essentials   Here you are given a short list of topics that you should explore fully before taking the exam. Included in the Exam Essentials areas are notations of the key information you should take out of the corresponding exam objective section.

Review Questions   At the end of every chapter there are 10 questions to help you gauge your mastery of the material.

What's Available Online?

I have worked hard to provide some really great tools to help you with your certification process. All of the following tools, most of them available at www.sybex.com/go/ccnarsrg, should be loaded on your workstation when you're studying for the test:

Two CCNA Practice Exams   Online, you will find the Sybex test engine, with two exclusive CCNA bonus practice exams. Using this custom test engine, you can identify weak areas up front and then develop a solid studying strategy using each of these robust testing features. Our thorough readme file will walk you through the quick, easy installation process.

Electronic Flashcards   The companion study tools include 100 flashcards specifically written to hit you hard, so don't get discouraged if you don't ace your way through them at first! They're there to ensure that you're really ready for the exam. And no worries—armed with the review questions, practice exams, and flashcards, you'll be more than prepared when exam day comes!

Glossary   A complete glossary of CCENT, CCNA, and Cisco routing terms is available at www.sybex.com/go/ccnarsrg.

> Note that this book is designed to be a review of the exam topics and should be used in tandem with other study materials, including my *CCNA Routing and Switching Study Guide* (Sybex, 2013). The study guide includes a lot more additional tools, including more practice exam questions, a bonus LammleSim network simulator to provide hands-on experience, and samples from the Todd Lammle Video Training Series.

Where Do You Take the Exams?

You may take the ICND1, ICND2, or CCNA R/S Composite exam at any Cisco exam at any of the Pearson VUE authorized testing centers. For information, go to www.vue.com or call 877-404-EXAM (3926).

To register for a Cisco exam, follow these steps:

1. Determine the number of the exam you want to take. (The CCENT exam number is 100-101, ICND2 is 200-101, and CCNA R/S is 200-120.)

2. Register with the nearest Pearson VUE testing center. At this point, you will be asked to pay in advance for the exam.. You can schedule exams up to six weeks in advance or as late as the day you want to take it—but if you fail a Cisco exam, you must wait five days before you will be allowed to retake it. If something comes up and you need to cancel or reschedule your exam appointment, contact Pearson VUE at least 24 hours in advance.

3. When you schedule the exam, you'll get instructions regarding all appointment and cancellation procedures, the ID requirements, and information about the testing-center location.

Tips for Taking Your Cisco Exams

The Cisco exams contains about 50 questions and must be completed in about 90 minutes or less (the ICND2 exam is 75 minutes or less). This information can change per exam. You must get a score of about 85 percent to pass this exam, but again, each exam can be different.

Many questions on the exam have answer choices that at first glance look identical—especially the syntax questions! So remember to read through the choices carefully because close just doesn't cut it. If you get commands in the wrong order or forget one measly character, you'll get the question wrong.

Also, never forget that the right answer is the Cisco answer. In many cases, more than one appropriate answer is presented, but the *correct* answer is the one that Cisco recommends. On the exam, you will always be told to pick one, two, or three options, never "choose all that apply." The Cisco exam may include the following test formats:

- Multiple-choice single answer
- Multiple-choice multiple answer
- Drag-and-drop
- Router simulations

Cisco proctored exams will not show the steps to follow in completing a router interface configuration, but they do allow partial command responses. For example, show run or sho running or sh running-config would be acceptable.

Here are some general tips for exam success:

- Arrive early at the exam center so you can relax and review your study materials.

- Read the questions *carefully*. Don't jump to conclusions. Make sure you're clear about *exactly* what each question asks. "Read twice, answer once" is what I always tell my students.

- When answering multiple-choice questions that you're not sure about, use the process of elimination to get rid of the obviously incorrect answers first. Doing this greatly improves your odds if you need to make an educated guess.

- You can no longer move forward and backward through the Cisco exams, so double-check your answer before clicking Next since you can't change your mind.

After you complete an exam, you'll get immediate, online notification of your pass or fail status, a printed examination score report that indicates your pass or fail status, and your exam results by section. (The test administrator will give you the printed score report.) Test scores are automatically forwarded to Cisco within five working days after you take the test, so you don't need to send your score to them. If you pass the exam, you'll receive confirmation from Cisco, typically within two to four weeks, sometimes a bit longer.

Chapter 1

Operation of IP Data Networks

THE FOLLOWING CCNA ROUTING AND SWITCHING EXAM OBJECTIVES ARE COVERED IN THIS CHAPTER:

- ✓ Operation of IP Data Networks

- ✓ Recognize the purpose and functions of various network devices such as Routers, Switches, Bridges and Hubs.

- ✓ Select the components required to meet a given network specification.

- ✓ Identify common applications and their impact on the network.

- ✓ Describe the purpose and basic operation of the protocols in the OSI and TCP/IP models.

- ✓ Predict the data flow between two hosts across a network.

- ✓ Identify the appropriate media, cables, ports, and connectors to connect Cisco network devices to other network devices and hosts in a LAN.

In this chapter, I will review the basics of internetworking and what an internetwork is. I will go over some of the components that make up a network as well as some applications used in networking. I will also go over the OSI and TCP/IP models and, finally, explain how data flows across a network as well as discuss the various connectors used in a network.

Operation of IP Data Networks

Let's start by defining exactly what an internetwork is: You create an internetwork when you connect two or more networks via a router and configure a logical network addressing scheme with a protocol such as IPv4 or IPv6.

Why is it so important to learn Cisco internetworking anyway? Networks and networking have grown exponentially over the past 20 years, and understandably so. They've had to evolve at light speed just to keep up with huge increases in basic, mission-critical user needs (for example, simple sharing of data and printers) as well as greater burdens like multimedia remote presentations and conferencing. Unless everyone who needs to share network resources is located in the same office space—an increasingly uncommon situation—the challenge is to connect relevant networks so all users can share the wealth of whatever services and resources are required. Figure 1.1 shows a basic *local area network (LAN)* that's connected using a *hub*, which is basically just an antiquated device that connects wires together. Keep in mind that a simple network like this would be considered one collision domain and one broadcast domain.

FIGURE 1.1 A very basic network

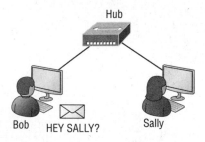

Figure 1.1 illustrates this scenario: Bob wants to send Sally a file, and to complete that goal in this kind of network, he'll simply broadcast that he's looking for her, which is basically just shouting out over the network. As networks grow and get more complex, a good network design is essential. Growth can be good, but growth can also hinder your network. LAN congestion can bring your network to a halt! The solution to this is to break up a large network into smaller networks, which is called *network segmentation*.

This concept is a lot like planning a new community or modernizing an existing one. More streets are added, complete with new intersections and traffic signals, plus post offices with official maps documenting all those street names and directions on how to get to each are built. You'll need to effect new laws to keep order to it all and provide a police station to protect this nice new neighborhood as well. In a networking neighborhood environment, all of this is carried out using devices like *routers*, *switches*, and *bridges*.

Exam Essentials

Understand what an internetwork is.   An internetwork consists of two or more networks that are connected together via a router. Networks are configured with a logical addressing schemes and segmented into smaller networks using routers, switches, and bridges.

Recognize the Purpose and Functions of Various Network Devices Such as Routers, Switches, Bridges, and Hubs

The scenario I just described brings me to the basic point of what this book and the Cisco certification objectives are really all about. My goal of showing you how to create efficient networks and segment them correctly in order to minimize all the chaotic yelling and screaming going on in them is a universal theme throughout my CCENT and CCNA series books. It's just inevitable that you'll have to break up a large network into a bunch of smaller ones at some point to match a network's equally inevitable growth, and as that expansion occurs, user response time simultaneously dwindles to a frustrating crawl. But if you master the vital technology and skills I have in store for you in this book, you'll be well equipped to rescue your network and its users by creating an efficient new network neighborhood to give them key amenities like the bandwidth they need to meet their evolving demands.

And this is no joke; most of us think of growth as good—and it can be—but as many of us experience daily when commuting to work, school, etc., it can also mean your LAN's traffic congestion can reach critical mass and grind to a complete halt!

So let's take a look at our new neighborhood now, because the word has gotten out; many more hosts have moved into it, so it's time to upgrade that new high-capacity infrastructure that we promised to handle the increase in population. Figure 1.2 shows a network that's been segmented with a switch, making each network segment that connects to the switch its own separate collision domain. Doing this results in a lot less yelling!

FIGURE 1.2   A switch can break up collision domains.

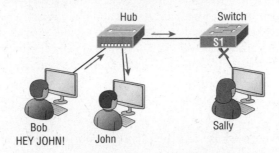

This is still one single broadcast domain. You can see that the hub used in Figure 1.2 just extended the one collision domain from the switch port. The result is that John received the data from Bob but, happily, Sally did not. This is good because Bob intended to talk with John directly, and if he had needed to send a broadcast instead, everyone, including Sally, would have received it, possibly causing unnecessary congestion.

Here's a list of some of the things that commonly cause LAN traffic congestion:

- Too many hosts in a collision or broadcast domain
- Broadcast storms
- Too much multicast traffic
- Low bandwidth
- Adding hubs for connectivity to the network
- A bunch of ARP broadcasts

Take another look at Figure 1.2 and make sure you see that I extended the main hub from Figure 1.1 to a switch in Figure 1.2. I did that because hubs don't segment a network; they just connect network segments.

As a network begins to grow, routers are used to connect networks and route packets of data from one network to another. Cisco became the de facto standard for routers because of its unparalleled selection of high-quality router products and fantastic service. So never forget that by default, routers are basically employed to efficiently break up a *broadcast domain*—the set of all devices on a network segment, which are allowed to "hear" all broadcasts sent out on that specific segment.

Figure 1.3 depicts a router in our growing network, creating an internetwork and breaking up broadcast domains.

FIGURE 1.3   Routers create an internetwork.

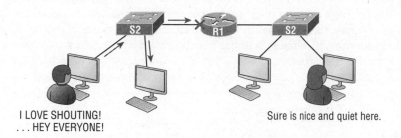

Each host is connected to its own collision domain because of the switch, and the router has created two broadcast domains. Routers also provide connections to wide area network (WAN) services as well as via a serial interface for WAN connections—specifically, a V.35 physical interface on a Cisco router.

Even though routers are known for breaking up broadcast domains by default, it's important to remember that they break up collision domains as well.

There are two advantages to using routers in your network:

- They don't forward broadcasts by default.
- They can filter the network based on layer 3, Network layer, information such as an IP address.

Here are four ways a router functions in your network:

- Packet switching
- Packet filtering
- Internetwork communication
- Path selection

It's helpful to think of routers as layer 3 switches. Unlike layer 2 switches, which forward or filter frames, routers (layer 3 switches) use logical addressing and provide an important capacity called *packet switching*. Routers can also provide packet filtering via access lists, and when routers connect two or more networks together and use logical addressing (IPv4 or IPv6), you then have an *internetwork*. Finally, routers use a routing table, which is essentially a map of the internetwork, to make best path selections for getting data to its proper destination and properly forward packets to remote networks.

Conversely, we don't use layer 2 switches to create internetworks because they don't break up broadcast domains by default. Instead, they're employed to add functionality to a network LAN. The main purpose of these switches is to make a LAN work better—to optimize its performance—providing more bandwidth for the LAN's users. Also, these switches don't forward packets to other networks like routers do. Instead, they only "switch" frames from one port to another within the switched network.

By default, switches break up collision domains, but what are these things? *Collision domain* is an Ethernet term used to describe a network scenario in which one device sends a packet out on a network segment and every other device on that same segment is forced to pay attention no matter what. This isn't very efficient because if a different device tries to transmit at the same time, a collision will occur, requiring both devices to retransmit, one at a time—not good! This happens a lot in a hub environment, where each host segment connects to a hub that represents only one collision domain and a single broadcast domain. By contrast, each and every port on a switch represents its own collision domain, allowing network traffic to flow much more smoothly.

Switches create separate collision domains within a single broadcast domain. Routers provide a separate broadcast domain for each interface. Don't let this ever confuse you!

You'll still hear Cisco and others refer to LAN switches as multiport bridges now and then.

Basically, switches are multiport bridges with more brain power and more ports!

You would use a bridge in a network to reduce collisions within broadcast domains and to increase the number of collision domains in your network. Doing this provides more bandwidth for users. And never forget that using hubs in your Ethernet network can contribute to congestion. As always, plan your network design carefully!

Exam Essentials

Describe the difference between a collision domain and a broadcast domain.   *Collision domain* is an Ethernet term used to describe a network collection of devices in which one particular device sends a packet on a network segment, forcing every other device on that same segment to pay attention to it. With a broadcast domain, a set of all devices on a network hears all broadcasts sent on all segments.

Understand the difference between a hub, a bridge/switch, and a router.   All ports on a hub are in one collision domain. When data is received on a port, it is sent out to all ports simultaneously. Each port on a switch is a separate collision domain. When data is received on a switchport, it is sent only to the receiving host that needs it. Routers are used to create internetworks and provide connections to WAN services. Routers break up broadcast and collision domains as well.

Select the Components Required to Meet a Given Network Specification

The term *bridging* was introduced before routers and switches were implemented, so it's pretty common to hear people referring to switches as bridges. That's because bridges and switches basically do the same thing—break up collision domains on a LAN. Note to self that you cannot buy a physical bridge these days, only LAN switches, which use bridging technologies. This means that you'll still hear Cisco and others refer to LAN switches as multiport bridges now and then.

But does it mean that a switch is just a multiple-port bridge with more brainpower? Well, pretty much, only there are still some key differences. Switches do provide a bridging function, but they do that with greatly enhanced management ability and features. Plus, most bridges had only 2 or 4 ports, which is severely limiting. Of course, it was possible to get your hands on a bridge with up to 16 ports, but that's nothing compared to the hundreds of ports available on some switches!

Figure 1.4 shows how a network would look with various internetwork devices in place. Remember, a router doesn't just break up broadcast domains for every LAN interface; it breaks up collision domains too.

Looking at Figure 1.4, did you notice that the router has the center stage position and connects each physical network together? I'm stuck with using this layout because of the ancient bridges and hubs involved. I really hope you don't run across a network like this, but it's still really important to understand the strategic ideas that this figure represents!

See that bridge up at the top of the internetwork shown in Figure 1.4? It's there to connect the hubs to a router. The bridge breaks up collision domains, but all the hosts connected to both hubs are still crammed into the same broadcast domain. That bridge also created only three collision domains, one for each port, which means that each device connected to a hub is in the same collision domain as every other device connected to that same hub. This is really lame and to be avoided if possible, but it's still better than having one collision domain for all hosts! So don't do this at home; it's a great museum piece and a wonderful example of what not to do, but this inefficient design would be terrible for use in today's networks! It does show us how far we've come though, and again, the foundational concepts it illustrates are really important for you to get.

The three interconnected hubs at the bottom of the figure also connect to the router. This setup creates one collision domain and one broadcast domain and makes that bridged network, with its two collision domains, look much better by contrast!

The best network connected to the router is the LAN switched network on the left. Why? Because each port on that switch breaks up collision domains. But it's not all good— all devices are still in the same broadcast domain. This can be bad because all devices must listen to all broadcasts transmitted. And if your broadcast domains are too large, the users have less bandwidth and are required to process more broadcasts. Network response time eventually will slow to a level that could cause your users to riot and strike, so it's important to keep your broadcast domains small in the vast majority of networks today.

FIGURE 1.4   Internetworking devices

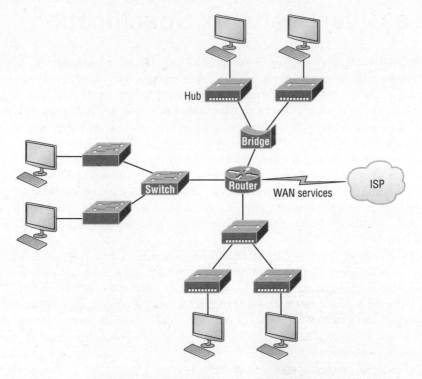

Figure 1.5 demonstrates a network you'll typically stumble upon today.

LAN switches are at the center of this network, with the routers connecting the logical networks. If I went ahead and implemented this design, I've created something called virtual LANs, or VLANs, which are used when you logically break up broadcast domains in a layer 2 switched network. It's really important to understand that even in a switched network environment, you still need a router to provide communication between VLANs.

FIGURE 1.5   Switched networks creating an internetwork

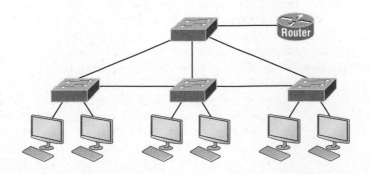

Still, clearly the best network design is the one that's perfectly configured to meet the business requirements of the specific company or client it serves, and it's usually one in which LAN switches exist in harmony with routers strategically placed in the network.

Let's look at Figure 1.4 again. How many collision domains and broadcast domains are really there in this internetwork?

The all-hub network at the bottom is one collision domain; the bridge network on top equals three collision domains. Add in the switch network of five collision domains—one for each switch port—and you get a total of nine!

In Figure 1.5, each port on the switch is a separate collision domain, and each VLAN would be a separate broadcast domain. So how many collision domains do you see here? I'm counting 12—remember that connections between the switches are considered a collision domain! Since the figure doesn't show any VLAN information, we can assume that the default of one VLAN, or one broadcast domain, is in place.

Exam Essentials

Understand the importance of essential network design.   Placing routers and switches in a properly designed network configuration will fulfill the needs of a specific company or client and will operate with optimal performance.

Identify the functions and advantages of routers.   Routers perform packet switching, filtering, and path selection, and they facilitate internetwork communication. One advantage of routers is that they reduce broadcast traffic.

Identify Common Applications and Their Impact on the Network

In this section, we'll go over the different applications and services typically used in IP networks, and although there are many more protocols defined here, we'll focus on the protocols most relevant to the CCNA objectives. Here's a list of the protocols and applications we'll cover in this section:

- Telnet
- SSH
- FTP
- TFTP
- SNMP
- HTTP
- HTTPS

- ▪ NTP
- ▪ DNS
- ▪ DHCP/BootP

Telnet

Telnet was one of the first Internet standards, developed in 1969, and is the chameleon of protocols—its specialty is terminal emulation. It allows a user on a remote client machine, called the Telnet client, to access the resources of another machine, the Telnet server, in order to access a command-line interface. Telnet achieves this by pulling a fast one on the Telnet server and making the client machine appear as though it were a terminal directly attached to the local network. This projection is actually a software image—a virtual terminal that can interact with the chosen remote host. A drawback is that there are no encryption techniques available within the Telnet protocol, so everything must be sent in clear text, including passwords! Figure 1.6 shows an example of a Telnet client trying to connect to a Telnet server.

FIGURE 1.6 Telnet

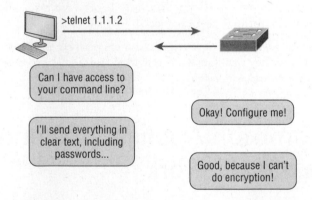

These emulated terminals are of the text-mode type and can execute defined procedures such as displaying menus that give users the opportunity to choose options and access the applications on the duped server. Users begin a Telnet session by running the Telnet client software and then logging into the Telnet server. Telnet uses an 8-bit, byte-oriented data connection over TCP, which makes it very thorough. It's still in use today because it is so simple and easy to use, with very low overhead, but again, with everything sent in clear text, it's not recommended in production.

Secure Shell (SSH)

Secure Shell (SSH) protocol sets up a secure session that's similar to Telnet over a standard TCP/IP connection and is employed for doing things like logging into systems, running programs on remote systems, and moving files from one system to another. And it does all of this while maintaining an encrypted connection. Figure 1.7 shows an SSH client trying to connect to an SSH server. The client must send the data encrypted!

FIGURE 1.7   Secure Shell

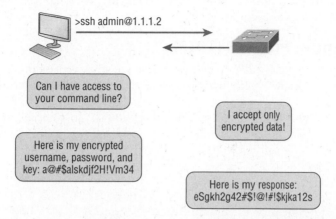

FIGURE 1.7   Secure Shell

You can think of it as the new-generation protocol that's now used in place of the antiquated and very unused rsh and rlogin—even Telnet.

File Transfer Protocol (FTP)

File Transfer Protocol (FTP) actually lets us transfer files, and it can accomplish this between any two machines using it. But FTP isn't just a protocol; it's also a program. Operating as a protocol, FTP is used by applications. As a program, it's employed by users to perform file tasks by hand. FTP also allows for access to both directories and files and can accomplish certain types of directory operations, such as relocating into different ones (Figure 1.8).

But accessing a host through FTP is only the first step. Users must then be subjected to an authentication login that's usually secured with passwords and usernames implemented by system administrators to restrict access. You can get around this somewhat by adopting the username *anonymous*, but you'll be limited in what you'll be able to access.

FIGURE 1.8   FTP

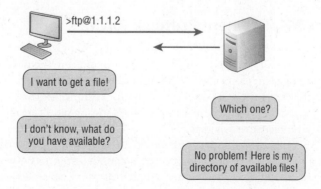

Even when employed by users manually as a program, FTP's functions are limited to listing and manipulating directories, typing file contents, and copying files between hosts. It can't execute remote files as programs.

Trivial File Transfer Protocol (TFTP)

Trivial File Transfer Protocol (TFTP) is the stripped-down, stock version of FTP, but it's the protocol of choice if you know exactly what you want and where to find it because it's fast and so easy to use!

But TFTP doesn't offer the abundance of functions that FTP does because it has no directory-browsing abilities, meaning that it can only send and receive files (Figure 1.9).

FIGURE 1.9   TFTP

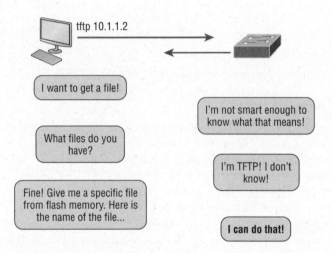

This compact little protocol also skimps in the data department, sending much smaller blocks of data than FTP. Also, there's no authentication as with FTP, so it's even more insecure, and few sites support it because of the inherent security risks.

Simple Network Management Protocol (SNMP)

Simple Network Management Protocol (SNMP) collects and manipulates valuable network information, as you can see in Figure 1.10. It gathers data by polling the devices on the network from a network management station (NMS) at fixed or random intervals, requiring them to disclose certain information, or even by asking for certain information from the device. In addition, network devices can inform the NMS station about problems as they occur so the network administrator is alerted.

When all is well, SNMP receives something called a *baseline*—a report delimiting the operational traits of a healthy network. This protocol can also stand as a watchdog over the network, quickly notifying managers of any sudden turn of events. These network watchdogs are called *agents*, and when aberrations occur, agents send an alert called a *trap* to the management station.

FIGURE 1.10   SNMP

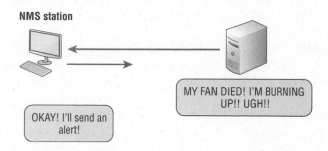

Hypertext Transfer Protocol (HTTP)

All those snappy websites comprising a mélange of graphics, text, links, ads, and so on, rely on the *Hypertext Transfer Protocol (HTTP)* to make it all possible (Figure 1.11). It's used to manage communications between web browsers and web servers and opens the right resource when you click a link, wherever that resource may actually reside.

In order for a browser to display a web page, it must find the exact server that has the right web page, plus the exact details that identify the information requested. This information must then be sent back to the browser. Nowadays, it's highly doubtful that a web server would have only one page to display!

FIGURE 1.11   HTTP

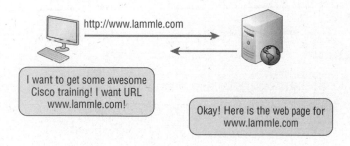

Your browser can understand what you need when you enter a Uniform Resource Locator (URL), which we usually refer to as a web address, such as, for example, www.lammle.com/forum and www.lammle.com/blog.

So basically, each URL defines the protocol used to transfer data, the name of the server, and the particular web page on that server.

Hypertext Transfer Protocol Secure (HTTPS)

Hypertext Transfer Protocol Secure (HTTPS) is also known as Secure Hypertext Transfer Protocol. It uses Secure Sockets Layer (SSL) or Transport Layer Security (TLS). Sometimes you'll see it referred to as SHTTP or S-HTTP, which were slightly different protocols, but since Microsoft supported HTTPS, it became the de facto standard for securing web communication. But no matter—as indicated, it's a secure version of HTTP that arms you with a whole bunch of security tools for keeping transactions between a web browser and a server secure.

It's what your browser needs to fill out forms, sign in, authenticate, and encrypt an HTTP message when you do things online like make a reservation, access your bank account, or buy something.

Network Time Protocol (NTP)

Kudos to professor David Mills of the University of Delaware for coming up with this handy protocol that's used to synchronize the clocks on our computers to one standard time source (typically, an atomic clock). *Network Time Protocol (NTP)* works by synchronizing devices to ensure that all computers on a given network agree on the time (Figure 1.12).

This may sound pretty simple, but it's very important because so many of the transactions done today are time and date stamped. Think about databases—a server can get messed up pretty badly and even crash if it's out of sync with the machines connected to it by even mere seconds! You can't have a transaction entered by a machine at, say, 1:50 a.m. when the server records that transaction as having occurred at 1:45 a.m. So basically, NTP works to prevent a "back to the future *sans* DeLorean" scenario from bringing down the network—very important indeed!

FIGURE 1.12   NTP

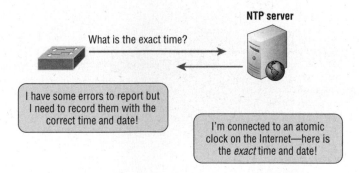

Domain Name Service (DNS)

Domain Name Service (DNS) resolves hostnames—specifically, Internet names, such as www.lammle.com. But you don't have to actually use DNS. You just type in the IP address of any device you want to communicate with and find the IP address of a URL by using the Ping program. For example, >ping www.cisco.com will return the IP address resolved by DNS.

An IP address identifies hosts on a network and the Internet as well, but DNS was designed to make our lives easier. Think about this: What would happen if you wanted to move your web page to a different service provider? The IP address would change and no one would know what the new one was. DNS allows you to use a domain name to specify an IP address. You can change the IP address as often as you want and no one will know the difference.

To resolve a DNS address from a host, you'd typically type in the URL from your favorite browser, which would hand the data to the Application layer interface to be transmitted on the network. The application would look up the DNS address and send a UDP request to your DNS server to resolve the name (Figure 1.13).

FIGURE 1.13   DNS

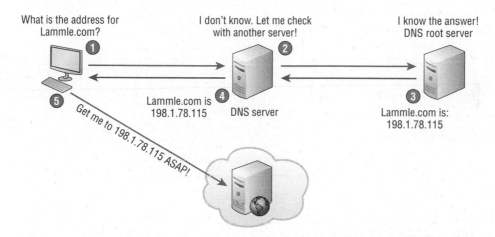

If your first DNS server doesn't know the answer to the query, then the DNS server forwards a TCP request to its root DNS server. Once the query is resolved, the answer is transmitted back to the originating host, which means the host can now request the information from the correct web server.

DNS is used to resolve a *fully qualified domain name (FQDN)*—for example, www.lammle.com or todd.lammle.com. An FQDN is a hierarchy that can logically locate a system based on its domain identifier.

If you want to resolve the name *todd*, you must either type in the FQDN of todd.lammle .com or have a device such as a PC or router add the suffix for you. For example, on a Cisco router, you can use the command ip domain-name lammle.com to append each request with the lammle.com domain. If you don't do that, you'll have to type in the FQDN to get DNS to resolve the name.

An important thing to remember about DNS is that if you can ping a device with an IP address but cannot use its FQDN, then you might have some type of DNS configuration failure.

Dynamic Host Configuration Protocol (DHCP)/Bootstrap Protocol (BootP)

Dynamic Host Configuration Protocol (DHCP) assigns IP addresses to hosts. It allows for easier administration and works well in small to very large network environments. Many types of hardware can be used as a DHCP server, including a Cisco router.

DHCP differs from BootP in that BootP assigns an IP address to a host but the host's hardware address must first be entered manually in a BootP table on the BootP server. You can think of DHCP as a dynamic BootP. But remember that BootP is also used to send an operating system to a host and the host can boot from it. DHCP can't do that.

But there's still a lot of information a DHCP server can provide to a host when the host is requesting an IP address from the DHCP server. Here's a list of the most common types of information a DHCP server can provide:

- IP address
- Subnet mask
- Domain name
- Default gateway (routers)
- DNS server address
- WINS server address

A client that sends out a DHCP Discover message in order to receive an IP address sends out a broadcast at both layer 2 and layer 3:

- The layer 2 broadcast is all *f*s in hex, which looks like this: ff:ff:ff:ff:ff:ff.
- The layer 3 broadcast is 255.255.255.255, which means all networks and all hosts.

DHCP is connectionless, which means it uses User Datagram Protocol (UDP) at the Transport layer, also known as the Host-to-Host layer.

Seeing is believing, so here's an example of output from my analyzer showing the layer 2 and layer 3 broadcasts:

```
Ethernet II, Src: 0.0.0.0 (00:0b:db:99:d3:5e),Dst: Broadcast(ff:ff:ff:ff:ff:ff)
Internet Protocol, Src: 0.0.0.0 (0.0.0.0),Dst: 255.255.255.255(255.255.255.255)
```

The Data Link and Network layers are both sending out "all hands" broadcasts saying, "Help—I don't know my IP address!"

Figure 1.14 shows the process of a client-server relationship using a DHCP connection. This is the four-step process a client takes to receive an IP address from a DHCP server:

1. The DHCP client broadcasts a DHCP Discover message looking for a DHCP server (UDP port 67).

2. The DHCP server that received the DHCP Discover message sends a layer 2 unicast DHCP Offer (UDP port 68) message back to the host.

3. The client then broadcasts to the server a DHCP Request message asking for the offered IP address and possibly other information.

4. The server finalizes the exchange with a unicast DHCP Acknowledgment message.

FIGURE 1.14   DHCP client four-step process

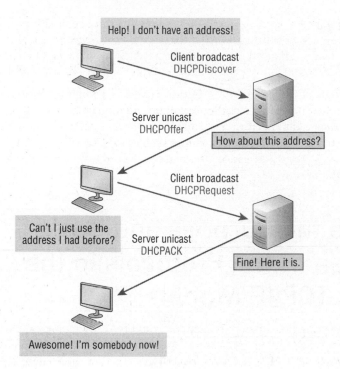

DHCP Conflicts

A DHCP address conflict occurs when two hosts use the same IP address. This sounds bad, and it is!

During IP address assignment, a DHCP server checks for conflicts using the Ping program to test the availability of the address before it's assigned from the pool. If no host replies, then the DHCP server assumes that the IP address is not already allocated. This helps the server know that it's providing a good address, but what about the host? To provide extra protection against that terrible IP conflict issue, the host can broadcast for its own address!

A host uses something called a gratuitous ARP to help avoid a possible duplicate address. A gratuitous ARP is an ARP response made to all devices on the network when there was never an original ARP request. Using this gratuitous ARP, the DHCP client sends an ARP broadcast out on the local LAN or VLAN using its newly assigned address to solve conflicts before they occur.

So, if an IP address conflict is detected, the address is removed from the DHCP pool (scope), and it's really important to remember that the address will not be assigned to a host until the administrator resolves the conflict by hand!

Exam Essentials

Identify Process/Application layer protocols.   Telnet is a terminal emulation program that allows you to log into a remote host and run programs. File Transfer Protocol (FTP) is a connection-oriented service that allows you to transfer files. Trivial FTP (TFTP) is a connectionless file transfer program. Simple Mail Transfer Protocol (SMTP) is a sendmail program.

Describe the functions of DNS and DHCP in the network.   Dynamic Host Configuration Protocol (DHCP) provides network configuration information (including IP addresses) to hosts, eliminating the need to perform the configurations manually. Domain Name Service (DNS) resolves hostnames—both Internet names such as www.lammle.com and device names such as Workstation 2—to IP addresses, eliminating the need to know the IP address of a device for connection purposes.

Describe the Purpose and Basic Operation of the Protocols in the OSI and TCP/IP Models

When networks first came into being, computers could typically communicate only with computers from the same manufacturer. For example, companies ran either a complete DECnet solution or an IBM solution, never both together. In the late 1970s, the *Open Systems Interconnection (OSI) reference model* was created by the International Organization for Standardization (ISO) to break through this barrier.

The OSI model was meant to help vendors create interoperable network devices and software in the form of protocols so that different vendor networks could work in peaceable accord with each other.

The Layered Approach

A *reference model* is a conceptual blueprint of how communications should take place. It addresses all the processes required for effective communication and divides them into logical groupings called *layers*. When a communication system is designed in this manner, it's known as a *layered architecture* because it's hierarchical.

Models happen to be really important to software developers too. They often use a reference model to understand computer communication processes so they can determine which functions should be accomplished on a given layer. This means that if someone is creating a protocol for a certain layer, they need to be concerned only with their target layer's function. Software that maps to another layers' protocols and is specifically designed to be deployed there will handle additional functions. The technical term for this idea is *binding*. The communication processes that are related to each other are bound, or grouped together, at a particular layer.

Advantages of Reference Models

The OSI model is hierarchical, and there are many advantages that can be applied to any layered model, but as I said, the OSI model's primary purpose is to allow different vendors' networks to interoperate.

Here's a list of some of the more important benefits for using the OSI layered model:

- It divides the network communication process into smaller and simpler components, facilitating component development, design, and troubleshooting.

- It allows multiple-vendor development through the standardization of network components.

- It encourages industry standardization by clearly defining what functions occur at each layer of the model.

- It allows various types of network hardware and software to communicate.

- It prevents changes in one layer from affecting other layers to expedite development.

- It eases the learning process by allowing you to understand the functions, benefits, and considerations of one layer at a time instead of having to overcome one large and complex subject.

The OSI Reference Model

One of best gifts the OSI specifications gives us is paving the way for the data transfer between disparate hosts running different operating systems, like Unix hosts, Windows machines, Macs, smartphones, and so on.

The OSI is a logical model, not a physical one. It's essentially a set of guidelines that developers can use to create and implement applications to run on a network. It also provides a framework for creating and implementing networking standards, devices, and internetworking schemes.

The OSI has seven different layers, divided into two groups. The top three layers (known as the upper layers) define how the applications within the end stations will communicate with each other as well as with users. The bottom four layers define how data is transmitted end to end.

Figure 1.15 shows the three upper layers and their functions.

FIGURE 1.15 The upper layers

Application	• Provides a user interface
Presentation	• Presents data • Handles processing such as encryption
Session	• Keeps different applications' data separate

When looking at Figure 1.15, understand that users interact with the computer at the Application layer and also that the upper layers are responsible for applications communicating between hosts. None of the upper layers knows anything about networking or network addresses because that's the responsibility of the four bottom layers.

Figure 1.16 shows the four lower layers and their functions. You can see that it's these four bottom layers that define how data is transferred through physical media like wire, cable, fiber optics, switches, and routers. These bottom layers also determine how to rebuild a data stream from a transmitting host to a destination host's application.

FIGURE 1.16   The lower layers

Transport	• Provides reliable or unreliable delivery • Performs error correction before retransmit
Network	• Provides logical addressing, which routers use for path determination
Data Link	• Combines packets into bytes and bytes into frames • Provides access to media using MAC address • Performs error detection not correction
Physical	• Moves bits between devices • Specifies voltage, wire speed, and pin-out of cables

The following network devices and protocols operate at all seven layers of the OSI model:

- Network management stations (NMSs)
- Web and application servers
- Gateways (not default gateways)
- Servers
- Network hosts

Basically, the ISO is pretty much the Emily Post of the network protocol world. Just as Ms. Post wrote the book setting the standards—or protocols—for human social interaction, the ISO developed the OSI reference model as the precedent and guide for an open network protocol set. Defining the etiquette of communication models, it remains the most popular means of comparison for protocol suites today.

As you've just seen, the OSI reference model has the following seven layers:

- Application layer (layer 7)
- Presentation layer (layer 6)
- Session layer (layer 5)
- Transport layer (layer 4)
- Network layer (layer 3)
- Data Link layer (layer 2)
- Physical layer (layer 1)

Some people like to use a mnemonic to remember the seven layers, such as **All People Seem To Need Data Processing**. Figure 1.17 shows a summary of the functions defined at each layer of the OSI model.

FIGURE 1.17   OSI layer functions

Application	• File, print, message, database, and application services
Presentation	• Data encryption, compression, and translation services
Session	• Dialog control

Transport	• End-to-end connection
Network	• Routing

Data Link	• Framing
Physical	• Physical topology

I've separated the seven-layer model into three different functions: the upper layers, the middle layers, and the bottom layers. The upper layers communicate with the user interface and application, the middle layers do reliable communication and routing to a remote network, and the bottom layers communicate to the local network.

With this in hand, you're now ready to explore each layer's function in detail!

The Application Layer

The *Application layer* of the OSI model marks the spot where users actually communicate to the computer and comes into play only when it's clear that access to the network will be needed soon. Take the case of Internet Explorer (IE). You could actually uninstall every trace of networking components like TCP/IP, the NIC card, and so on, and still use IE to view a local HTML document. But things would get ugly if you tried to do things like view a remote HTML document that must be retrieved because IE and other browsers act on these types of requests by attempting to access the Application layer. So basically, the Application layer is working as the interface between the actual application program and the next layer down by providing ways for the application to send information down through the protocol stack. This isn't actually part of the layered structure because browsers don't live in the Application layer, but they interface with it as well as the relevant protocols when asked to access remote resources.

The Presentation Layer

The *Presentation layer* gets its name from its purpose: It presents data to the Application layer and is responsible for data translation and code formatting. Think of it as the OSI model's translator, providing coding and conversion services. One very effective way of ensuring a successful data transfer is to convert the data into a standard format before transmission. Computers are configured to receive this generically formatted data and then reformat it back into its native state to read it. An example of this type of translation service occurs when translating old IBM Extended Binary Coded Decimal Interchange Code (EBCDIC) data to PC ASCII, the American Standard Code for Information Interchange (often pronounced "askee"). So just remember that by providing translation services, the Presentation layer ensures that data transferred from the Application layer of one system can be read by the Application layer of another one.

The Session Layer

The *Session layer* is responsible for setting up, managing, and dismantling sessions between Presentation layer entities and keeping user data separate. Dialog control between devices also occurs at this layer.

The Transport Layer

The *Transport layer* segments and reassembles data into a single data stream. Services located at this layer take all the various data received from upper-layer applications and then combine it into the same, concise data stream. These protocols provide end-to-end data transport services and can establish a logical connection between the sending host and destination host on an internetwork.

A pair of well-known protocols called TCP and UDP are integral to this layer, and understand that although both work at the Transport layer, TCP is known as a reliable service but UDP is not. This distinction gives application developers more options because they have a choice between the two protocols when they are designing products for this layer.

The Transport layer is responsible for providing mechanisms for multiplexing upper-layer applications, establishing sessions, and tearing down virtual circuits. It can also hide the details of network-dependent information from the higher layers as well as provide transparent data transfer.

 The term *reliable networking* can be used at the Transport layer. Reliable networking requires that acknowledgments, sequencing, and flow control will all be used.

The Transport layer can be either connectionless or connection-oriented, but because Cisco really wants you to understand the connection-oriented function of the Transport layer, I'm going to go into that in more detail here.

Connection-Oriented Communication

For reliable transport to occur, a device that wants to transmit must first establish a connection-oriented communication session with a remote device (its peer system), known as a *call setup* or a *three-way handshake*. Once this process is complete, the data transfer occurs, and when it's finished, a call termination takes place to tear down the virtual circuit.

Figure 1.18 depicts a typical reliable session taking place between sending and receiving systems. In it, you can see that both hosts' application programs begin by notifying their individual operating systems that a connection is about to be initiated. The two operating systems communicate by sending messages over the network confirming that the transfer is approved and that both sides are ready for it to take place. After all of this required synchronization takes place, a connection is fully established and the data transfer begins. And by the way, it's really helpful to understand that this virtual circuit setup is often referred to as overhead!

FIGURE 1.18   Establishing a connection-oriented session

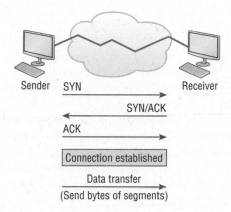

While the information is being transferred between hosts, the two machines periodically check in with each other, communicating through their protocol software to ensure that all is going well and that the data is being received properly.

Here's a summary of the steps in the connection-oriented session—that three-way handshake—pictured in Figure 1.18:

- The first "connection agreement" segment is a request for *synchronization (SYN)*.

- The next segments *acknowledge (ACK)* the request and establish connection parameters—the rules—between hosts. These segments request that the receiver's sequencing is synchronized here as well so that a bidirectional connection can be formed.

- The final segment is also an acknowledgment, which notifies the destination host that the connection agreement has been accepted and that the actual connection has been established. Data transfer can now begin.

Flow Control

Since floods and losing data can both be tragic, we have a fail-safe solution in place known as *flow control*. Its job is to ensure data integrity at the Transport layer by allowing applications to request reliable data transport between systems. Flow control prevents a sending host on one side of the connection from overflowing the buffers in the receiving host. Reliable data transport employs a connection-oriented communications session between systems, and the protocols involved ensure that the following will be achieved:

- The segments delivered are acknowledged back to the sender upon their reception.
- Any segments not acknowledged are retransmitted.
- Segments are sequenced back into their proper order upon arrival at their destination.
- A manageable data flow is maintained in order to avoid congestion, overloading, or worse, data loss.

Because of the transport function, network flood control systems really work well. Instead of dumping and losing data, the Transport layer can issue a "not ready" indicator to the sender, or potential source of the flood. This mechanism works kind of like a stop-light, signaling the sending device to stop transmitting segment traffic to its overwhelmed peer. After the peer receiver processes the segments already in its memory reservoir—its buffer—it sends out a "ready" transport indicator. When the machine waiting to transmit the rest of its datagrams receives this "go" indicator, it resumes its transmission. The process is pictured in Figure 1.19.

In a reliable, connection-oriented data transfer, datagrams are delivered to the receiving host hopefully in the same sequence they're transmitted. A failure will occur if any data segments are lost, duplicated, or damaged along the way—a problem solved by having the receiving host acknowledge that it has received each and every data segment.

A service is considered connection-oriented if it has the following characteristics:

- A virtual circuit, or "three-way handshake" is set up.
- It uses sequencing.
- It uses acknowledgments.
- It uses flow control.

FIGURE 1.19   Transmitting segments with flow control

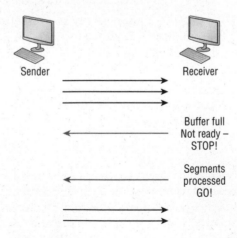

Windowing

Ideally, data throughput happens quickly and efficiently. And as you can imagine, it would be painfully slow if the transmitting machine had to actually wait for an acknowledgment after sending each and every segment! The quantity of data segments, measured in bytes, that the transmitting machine is allowed to send without receiving an acknowledgment is called a *window*.

The size of the window controls how much information is transferred from one end to the other before an acknowledgment is required. While some protocols quantify information depending on the number of packets, TCP/IP measures it by counting the number of bytes.

As you can see in Figure 1.20, there are two window sizes—one set to 1 and one set to 3.

If you've configured a window size of 1, the sending machine will wait for an acknowledgment for each data segment it transmits before transmitting another one but will allow three to be transmitted before receiving an acknowledgment if the window size is set to 3.

In this simplified example, both the sending and receiving machines are workstations. Remember that in reality, the transmission isn't based on simple numbers but in the amount of bytes that can be sent!

FIGURE 1.20   Windowing

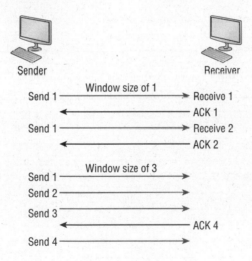

Acknowledgments

Reliable data delivery ensures the integrity of a stream of data sent from one machine to the other through a fully functional data link. It guarantees that the data won't be duplicated or lost. This is achieved through something called *positive acknowledgment with retransmission*—a technique that requires a receiving machine to communicate with the transmitting source by sending an acknowledgment message to the sender when it receives data. The sender documents each segment measured in bytes and then sends and waits for this acknowledgment before sending the next segment. Also important is that when it sends a segment, the transmitting machine starts a timer and will retransmit if it expires before it gets an acknowledgment from the receiving end. Figure 1.21 shows the process I just described.

In the figure, the sending machine transmits segments 1, 2, and 3. The receiving node acknowledges that it has received them by requesting segment 4 (what it is expecting next). When it receives the acknowledgment, the sender then transmits segments 4, 5, and 6. If segment 5 doesn't make it to the destination, the receiving node acknowledges that event with a request for the segment to be resent. The sending machine will then resend the lost segment and wait for an acknowledgment, which it must receive in order to move on to the transmission of segment 7.

The Transport layer, working in tandem with the Session layer, also separates the data from different applications, an activity known as *session multiplexing*, and it happens when a client connects to a server with multiple browser sessions open. This is exactly what's taking place when you go someplace online like Amazon and click multiple links, opening them simultaneously to get information when comparison shopping. The client data from each browser session must be separate when the server application receives it, which is pretty slick technologically speaking, and it's the Transport layer to the rescue for that juggling act!

FIGURE 1.21   Transport layer reliable delivery

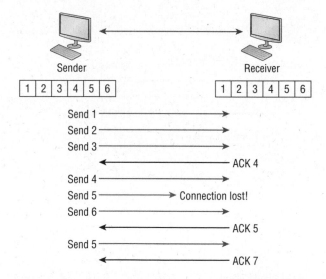

The Network Layer

The *Network layer*, or layer 3, manages device addressing, tracks the location of devices on the network, and determines the best way to move data. This means that it's up to the Network layer to transport traffic between devices that aren't locally attached. Routers, which are layer 3 devices, are specified at this layer and provide the routing services within an internetwork.

Here's how that works: First, when a packet is received on a router interface, the destination IP address is checked. If the packet isn't destined for that particular router, it will look up the destination network address in the routing table. Once the router chooses an exit interface, the packet will be sent to that interface to be framed and sent out on the local network. If the router can't find an entry for the packet's destination network in the routing table, the router drops the packet.

Data and route update packets are the two types of packets used at the Network layer:

Data packets   These are used to transport user data through the internetwork. Protocols used to support data traffic are called routed protocols, and IPv4 and IPv6 are key examples.

Route update packets   These packets are used to update neighboring routers about the networks connected to all routers within the internetwork. Protocols that send route update packets are called routing protocols; the most critical ones for CCNA are RIP, RIPv2, EIGRP, and OSPF. Route update packets are used to help build and maintain routing tables.

Figure 1.22 shows an example of a routing table. The routing table each router keeps and refers to includes the following information.

FIGURE 1.22   Routing table used in a router

Routing table		
NET	INT	Metric
1	E0	0
2	S0	0
3	S0	1

Routing table		
NET	INT	Metric
1	S0	1
2	S0	0
3	E0	0

Network addresses   Protocol-specific network addresses. A router must maintain a routing table for individual routing protocols because each routed protocol keeps track of a network with a different addressing scheme. For example, the routing tables for IPv4, IPv6, and IPX are completely different, so the router keeps a table for each one. Think of it as a street sign in each of the different languages spoken by the American, Spanish, and French people living on a street; the street sign would read Cat/Gato/Chat.

Interface   The exit interface a packet will take when destined for a specific network.

Metric   The distance to the remote network. Different routing protocols use different ways of computing this distance. Routing protocols like the Routing Information Protocol, or RIP, use hop count, which refers to the number of routers a packet passes through en route to a remote network. Others use bandwidth, delay of the line, or even tick count (1/18 of a second) to determine the best path for data to get to a given destination.

And as I mentioned earlier, routers break up broadcast domains, which means that by default, broadcasts aren't forwarded through a router. Do you remember why this is a good thing? Routers also break up collision domains, but you can also do that using layer 2, Data Link layer, switches. Because each interface in a router represents a separate network, it must be assigned unique network identification numbers, and each host on the network connected to that router must use the same network number. Figure 1.23 shows how a router works in an internetwork. Note that in the figure, each router LAN interface is a broadcast domain. Routers break up broadcast domains by default and provide WAN services.

FIGURE 1.23   A router in an internetwork

Here are some router characteristics that you should never forget:

- Routers, by default, will not forward any broadcast or multicast packets.
- Routers use the logical address in a Network layer header to determine the next-hop router to forward the packet to.
- Routers can use access lists, created by an administrator, to control security based on the types of packets allowed to enter or exit an interface.
- Routers can provide layer 2 bridging functions if needed and can simultaneously route through the same interface.
- Layer 3 devices—in this case, routers—provide connections between *virtual LANs (VLANs)*.
- Routers can provide *quality of service (QoS)* for specific types of network traffic.

The Data Link Layer

The *Data Link layer* provides for the physical transmission of data and handles error notification, network topology, and flow control. This means that the Data Link layer will ensure that messages are delivered to the proper device on a LAN using hardware addresses and will translate messages from the Network layer into bits for the Physical layer to transmit.

The Data Link layer formats the messages, each called a *data frame*, and adds a customized header containing the hardware destination and source address. This added information forms a sort of capsule that surrounds the original message in much the same way that engines, navigational devices, and other tools were attached to the lunar modules of the Apollo project. These various pieces of equipment were useful only during certain stages of space flight and were stripped off the module and discarded when their designated stage was completed. The process of data traveling through networks is similar. I like this analogy!

Figure 1.24 shows the Data Link layer with the Ethernet and IEEE specifications. When you check it out, notice that the IEEE 802.2 standard is used in conjunction with and adds functionality to the other IEEE standards.

It's important for you to understand that routers, which work at the Network layer, don't care at all about where a particular host is located. They're only concerned about where networks are located and the best way to reach them—including remote ones. Routers are totally obsessive when it comes to networks, which in this case is a good thing! It's the Data Link layer that's responsible for the actual unique identification of each device that resides on a local network.

FIGURE 1.24   Data Link layer

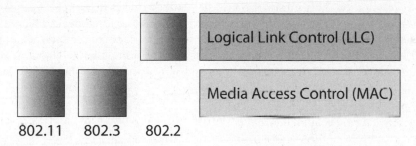

For a host to send packets to individual hosts on a local network as well as transmit packets between routers, the Data Link layer uses hardware addressing. Each time a packet is sent between routers, it's framed with control information at the Data Link layer, but that information is stripped off at the receiving router and only the original packet is left completely intact. This framing of the packet continues for each hop until the packet is finally delivered to the correct receiving host. It's really important to understand that the packet itself is never altered along the route; it's only encapsulated with the type of control information required for it to be properly passed on to the different media types.

The IEEE Ethernet Data Link layer has two sub-layers:

Media Access Control (MAC)   This first sub-layer is just above the Physical layer and defines how packets are placed on the media. Contention media access is "first come, first served" access where everyone shares the same bandwidth—hence the name. Physical addressing is defined here as well as logical topologies. What's a logical topology? It's the signal path through a physical topology. Line discipline, error notification (but not correction), the ordered delivery of frames, and optional flow control can also be used at this sub-layer.

Logical Link Control (LLC)   The second sub-layer sits between the MAC sub-layer and the Network layer and is responsible for identifying Network layer protocols and then encapsulating them. An LLC header tells the Data Link layer what to do with a packet once a frame is received. It works like this: a host receives a frame and looks in the LLC header to find out where the packet is destined—for instance, the IP protocol at the Network layer. The LLC can also provide flow control and sequencing of control bits.

The switches and bridges I talked about near the beginning of the chapter both work at the Data Link layer and filter the network using hardware (MAC) addresses. I'll talk about these next.

Switches and Bridges at the Data Link Layer

Layer 2 switching is considered hardware-based bridging because it uses specialized hardware called an *application-specific integrated circuit (ASIC)*. ASICs can run up to high gigabit speeds with very low latency rates.

Bridges and switches read each frame as it passes through the network. The layer 2 device then puts the source hardware address in a filter table and keeps track of which port the frame was received on. This information (logged in the bridge's or switch's filter table) is what helps the machine determine the location of the specific sending device. Figure 1.25 shows a switch in an internetwork and how John is sending packets to the Internet and Sally doesn't hear his frames because she is in a different collision domain. The destination frame goes directly to the default gateway router, and Sally doesn't see John's traffic, much to her relief.

FIGURE 1.25   A switch in an internetwork

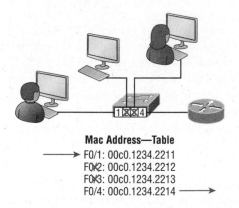

Mac Address—Table
F0/1: 00c0.1234.2211
F0/2: 00c0.1234.2212
F0/3: 00c0.1234.2213
F0/4: 00c0.1234.2214 ⟶

The real estate business is all about location, location, location, and it's the same way for both layer 2 and layer 3 devices. Though both need to be able to negotiate the network, it's crucial to remember that they're concerned with very different parts of it. Primarily, layer 3 machines (such as routers) need to locate specific networks, whereas layer 2 machines (switches and bridges) need to eventually locate specific devices. So, networks are to routers what individual devices are to switches and bridges. And routing tables that "map" the internetwork are for routers, just as filter tables that "map" individual devices are for switches and bridges.

After a filter table is built on the layer 2 device, it will forward frames only to the segment where the destination hardware address is located. If the destination device is on the same segment as the frame, the layer 2 device will block the frame from going to any other segments. If the destination is on a different segment, the frame can be transmitted only to that segment. This is called *transparent bridging*.

When a switch interface receives a frame with a destination hardware address that isn't found in the device's filter table, it will forward the frame to all connected segments. If the unknown device that was sent the "mystery frame" replies to this forwarding action, the switch updates its filter table regarding that device's location. But in the event the destination address of the transmitting frame is a broadcast address, the switch will forward all broadcasts to every connected segment by default.

All devices that the broadcast is forwarded to are considered to be in the same broadcast domain. This can be a problem because layer 2 devices propagate layer 2 broadcast storms that can seriously choke performance, and the only way to stop a broadcast storm from propagating through an internetwork is with a layer 3 device—a router!

The biggest benefit of using switches instead of hubs in your internetwork is that each switch port is actually its own collision domain. Remember that a hub creates one large collision domain, which is not a good thing! But even armed with a switch, you still don't get to just break up broadcast domains by default because neither switches nor bridges will do that. They'll simply forward all broadcasts instead.

Another benefit of LAN switching over hub-centered implementations is that each device on every segment plugged into a switch can transmit simultaneously. Well, at least they can as long as there's only one host on each port and there isn't a hub plugged into a switch port! As you might have guessed, this is because hubs allow only one device per network segment to communicate at a time.

The Physical Layer

Finally arriving at the bottom, we find that the *Physical layer* does two things: it sends bits and receives bits. Bits come only in values of 1 or 0—a Morse code with numerical values. The Physical layer communicates directly with the various types of actual communication media. Different kinds of media represent these bit values in different ways. Some use audio tones, while others employ *state transitions*—changes in voltage from high to low and low to high. Specific protocols are needed for each type of media to describe the proper bit patterns to be used, how data is encoded into media signals, and the various qualities of the physical media's attachment interface.

The Physical layer specifies the electrical, mechanical, procedural, and functional requirements for activating, maintaining, and deactivating a physical link between end systems. This layer is also where you identify the interface between the *data terminal equipment (DTE)* and the *data communication equipment (DCE)*. (Some old phone-company employees still call DCE "data circuit-terminating equipment.") The DCE is usually located at the service provider, while the DTE is the attached device. The services available to the DTE are most often accessed via a modem or *channel service unit/data service unit (CSU/DSU)*.

The Physical layer's connectors and different physical topologies are defined by the OSI as standards, allowing disparate systems to communicate. The Cisco exam objectives are interested only in the IEEE Ethernet standards.

Hubs at the Physical Layer

A hub is really a multiple-port repeater. A repeater receives a digital signal, reamplifies or regenerates that signal, and then forwards the signal out the other port without looking at any data. A hub does the same thing across all active ports: any digital signal received from a segment on a hub port is regenerated or reamplified and transmitted out all other ports on the hub. This means all devices plugged into a hub are in the same collision domain as well as in the same broadcast domain. Figure 1.26 shows a hub in a network and how when one host transmits, all other hosts must stop and listen.

FIGURE 1.26   A hub in a network

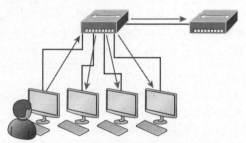

I love it when everyone has to listen to everything I say!

Hubs, like repeaters, don't examine any of the traffic as it enters or before it's transmitted out to the other parts of the physical media. And every device connected to the hub, or hubs, must listen if a device transmits. A physical star network, where the hub is a central device and cables extend in all directions out from it, is the type of topology a hub creates. Visually, the design really does resemble a star, whereas Ethernet networks run a logical bus topology, meaning that the signal has to run through the network from end to end.

Hubs and repeaters can be used to enlarge the area covered by a single LAN segment, but I really do not recommend going with this configuration! LAN switches are affordable for almost every situation and will make you much happier.

Exam Essentials

Define the OSI layers, understand the function of each, and describe how devices and networking protocols can be mapped to each layer.   You must remember the seven layers of the OSI model and what function each layer provides. The Application, Presentation, and Session layers are upper layers and are responsible for communicating from a user interface to an application. The Transport layer provides segmentation, sequencing, and virtual circuits. The Network layer provides logical network addressing and routing through an internetwork. The Data Link layer provides framing and placing of data on the network medium. The Physical layer is responsible for taking 1s and 0s and encoding them into a digital signal for transmission on the network segment.

Differentiate connection-oriented and connectionless network services and describe how each is handled during network communications.   Connection-oriented services use acknowledgments and flow control to create a reliable session. More overhead is used than in a connectionless network service. Connectionless services are used to send data with no acknowledgments or flow control. This is considered unreliable.

Predict the Data Flow between Two Hosts across a Network

Once you create an internetwork by connecting your WANs and LANs to a router, you'll need to configure logical network addresses, like IP addresses, to all hosts on that internetwork for them to communicate successfully throughout it.

The term *routing* refers to taking a packet from one device and sending it through the network to another device on a different network. Routers don't really care about hosts—they only care about networks and the best path to each one of them. The logical network address of the destination host is key to get packets through a routed network. It's the hardware address of the host that's used to deliver the packet from a router and ensure that it arrives at the correct destination host.

Routing is irrelevant if your network has no routers because their job is to route traffic to all the networks in your internetwork, but rarely will your network have no routers! So here's an important list of the minimum factors a router must know to be able to effectively route packets:

- Destination address
- Neighbor routers from which it can learn about remote networks
- Possible routes to all remote networks
- The best route to each remote network
- How to maintain and verify routing information

The router learns about remote networks from neighboring routers or from an administrator. The router then builds a routing table, which is basically a map of the internetwork, and it describes how to find remote networks. If a network is directly connected, then the router already knows how to get to it.

But if a network isn't directly connected to the router, the router must use one of two ways to learn how to get to the remote network. The *static routing* method requires someone to hand-type all network locations into the routing table, which can be a pretty daunting task when used on all but the smallest of networks!

Conversely, when *dynamic routing* is used, a protocol on one router communicates with the same protocol running on neighboring routers. The routers then update each other about all the networks they know about and place this information into the routing table. If a change occurs in the network, the dynamic routing protocols automatically inform all routers about the event. If static routing is used, the administrator is responsible for updating all changes by hand onto all routers. Most people usually use a combination of dynamic and static routing to administer a large network.

Before we jump into the IP routing process, let's take a look at a very simple example that demonstrates how a router uses the routing table to route packets out of an interface. We'll be going into a more detailed study of the process soon, but I want to show you something called the "longest match rule" first. With it, IP will scan a routing table to find the longest match as compared to the destination address of a packet. Let's take a look at Figure 1.27 to get a picture of this process.

FIGURE 1.27   A simple routing example

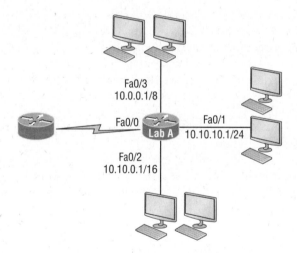

Figure 1.27 shows a simple network. Lab_A has four interfaces. Can you see which interface will be used to forward an IP datagram to a host with a destination IP address of 10.10.10.30?

By using the command show ip route on a router, we can see the routing table (map of the internetwork) that Lab A has used to make its forwarding decisions:

```
Lab_A#sh ip route
Codes: L - local, C - connected, S - static,
[output cut]
```

```
         10.0.0.0/8 is variably subnetted, 6 subnets, 4 masks
C        10.0.0.0/8 is directly connected, FastEthernet0/3
L        10.0.0.1/32 is directly connected, FastEthernet0/3
C        10.10.0.0/16 is directly connected, FastEthernet0/2
L        10.10.0.1/32 is directly connected, FastEthernet0/2
C        10.10.10.0/24 is directly connected, FastEthernet0/1
L        10.10.10.1/32 is directly connected, FastEthernet0/1
S*       0.0.0.0/0 is directly connected, FastEthernet0/0
```

The C in the routing table output means that the networks listed are "directly connected," and until we add a routing protocol like RIPv2, OSPF, and so on, to the routers in our internetwork, or enter static routes, only directly connected networks will show up in our routing table. But wait—what about that L in the routing table—that's new, isn't it? Yes it is, because in the new Cisco IOS 15 code, Cisco defines a different route, called a local route. Each has a /32 prefix defining a route just for the one address. So in this example, the router has relied upon these routes that list their own local IP addresses to more efficiently forward packets to the router itself.

So let's get back to the original question: By looking at the figure and the output of the routing table, can you determine what IP will do with a received packet that has a destination IP address of 10.10.10.30? The answer is that the router will packet-switch the packet to interface FastEthernet 0/1, which will frame the packet and then send it out on the network segment. Based upon the longest match rule, IP would look for 10.10.10.30, and if that isn't found in the table, then IP would search for 10.10.10.0, then 10.10.0.0, and so on, until a route is discovered.

The IP Routing Process

The IP routing process is fairly simple and doesn't change, regardless of the size of your network. For a good example of this fact, I'll use Figure 1.28 to describe step-by-step what happens when Host A wants to communicate with Host B on a different network.

FIGURE 1.28   IP routing example using two hosts and one router

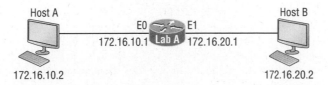

In Figure 1.28 a user on Host A pinged Host B's IP address. Routing doesn't get any simpler than this, but it still involves a lot of steps, so let's work through them now:

1. Internet Control Message Protocol (ICMP) creates an echo request payload, which is simply the alphabet in the data field.

2. ICMP hands that payload to Internet Protocol (IP), which then creates a packet. At a minimum, this packet contains an IP source address, an IP destination address, and a Protocol field with 01h. Don't forget that Cisco likes to use *0x* in front of hex characters, so this could also look like 0x01. This tells the receiving host to whom it should hand the payload when the destination is reached—in this example, ICMP.

3. Once the packet is created, IP determines whether the destination IP address is on the local network or a remote one.

4. Since IP has determined that this is a remote request, the packet must be sent to the default gateway so it can be routed to the remote network. The Registry in Windows is parsed to find the configured default gateway.

5. The default gateway of Host A is configured to 172.16.10.1. For this packet to be sent to the default gateway, the hardware address of the router's interface Ethernet 0, which is configured with the IP address of 172.16.10.1, must be known. Why? So the packet can be handed down to the Data Link layer, framed, and sent to the router's interface that's connected to the 172.16.10.0 network. Because hosts communicate only via hardware addresses on the local LAN, it's important to recognize that for Host A to communicate to Host B, it has to send packets to the Media Access Control (MAC) address of the default gateway on the local network.

> **NOTE**   MAC addresses are always local on the LAN and never go through and past a router.

6. Next, the Address Resolution Protocol (ARP) cache of the host is checked to see if the IP address of the default gateway has already been resolved to a hardware address.

   If it has, the packet is then free to be handed to the Data Link layer for framing. Remember that the hardware destination address is also handed down with that packet. To view the ARP cache on your host, use the following command:

```
C:\>arp -a
Interface: 172.16.10.2 --- 0x3
  Internet Address      Physical Address      Type
  172.16.10.1           00-15-05-06-31-b0     dynamic
```

   If the hardware address isn't already in the ARP cache of the host, an ARP broadcast will be sent out onto the local network to search for the 172.16.10.1 hardware address. The router then responds to the request and provides the hardware address of Ethernet 0, and the host caches this address.

7. Once the packet and destination hardware address are handed to the Data Link layer, the LAN driver is used to provide media access via the type of LAN being used, which is Ethernet in this case. A frame is then generated, encapsulating the packet with control information. Within that frame are the hardware destination and source addresses plus,

in this case, an Ether-Type field, which identifies the specific Network layer protocol that handed the packet to the Data Link layer. In this instance, it's IP. At the end of the frame is something called a Frame Check Sequence (FCS) field that houses the result of the cyclic redundancy check (CRC). The frame would look something like what I've detailed in Figure 1.29. It contains Host A's hardware (MAC) address and the destination hardware address of the default gateway. It does not include the remote host's MAC address—remember that!

FIGURE 1.29   Frame used from Host A to the Lab A router when Host B is pinged

Destination MAC (router's E0 MAC address)	Source MAC (Host A MAC address)	Ether-Type field	Packet	FCS CRC

8. Once the frame is completed, it's handed down to the Physical layer to be put on the physical medium (in this example, twisted-pair wire) one bit at a time.

9. Every device in the collision domain receives these bits and builds the frame. They each run a CRC and check the answer in the FCS field. If the answers don't match, the frame is discarded.

  - If the CRC matches, then the hardware destination address is checked to see if it matches (which, in this example, is the router's interface Ethernet 0).

  - If it's a match, then the Ether-Type field is checked to find the protocol used at the Network layer.

10. The packet is pulled from the frame, and what is left of the frame is discarded. The packet is handed to the protocol listed in the Ether-Type field—it's given to IP.

11. IP receives the packet and checks the IP destination address. Since the packet's destination address doesn't match any of the addresses configured on the receiving router itself, the router will look up the destination IP network address in its routing table.

12. The routing table must have an entry for the network 172.16.20.0 or the packet will be discarded immediately and an ICMP message will be sent back to the originating device with a destination network unreachable message.

13. If the router does find an entry for the destination network in its table, the packet is switched to the exit interface—in this example, interface Ethernet 1. The following output displays the Lab A router's routing table. The C means "directly connected." No routing protocols are needed in this network since all networks (all two of them) are directly connected.

```
Lab_A>sh ip route
C       172.16.10.0 is directly connected,    Ethernet0
L       172.16.10.1/32 is directly connected, Ethernet0
C       172.16.20.0 is directly connected,    Ethernet1
L       172.16.20.1/32 is directly connected, Ethernet1
```

14. The router packet-switches the packet to the Ethernet 1 buffer.

15. The Ethernet 1 buffer needs to know the hardware address of the destination host and first checks the ARP cache.

  - If the hardware address of Host B has already been resolved and is in the router's ARP cache, then the packet and the hardware address will be handed down to the Data Link layer to be framed. Let's take a look at the ARP cache on the Lab A router by using the show ip arp command:

```
Lab_A#sh ip arp
Protocol  Address       Age(min)  Hardware Addr   Type   Interface
Internet  172.16.20.1    -         00d0.58ad.05f4  ARPA   Ethernet1
Internet  172.16.20.2    3         0030.9492.a5dd  ARPA   Ethernet1
Internet  172.16.10.1    -         00d0.58ad.06aa  ARPA   Ethernet0
Internet  172.16.10.2    12        0030.9492.a4ac  ARPA   Ethernet0
```

  The dash (-) signifies that this is the physical interface on the router. This output shows us that the router knows the 172.16.10.2 (Host A) and 172.16.20.2 (Host B) hardware addresses. Cisco routers will keep an entry in the ARP table for 4 hours.

  - Now if the hardware address hasn't already been resolved, the router will send an ARP request out E1 looking for the 172.16.20.2 hardware address. Host B responds with its hardware address, and the packet and destination hardware addresses are then both sent to the Data Link layer for framing.

16. The Data Link layer creates a frame with the destination and source hardware addresses, Ether-Type field, and FCS field at the end. The frame is then handed to the Physical layer to be sent out on the physical medium one bit at a time.

17. Host B receives the frame and immediately runs a CRC. If the result matches the information in the FCS field, the hardware destination address will be then checked next. If the host finds a match, the Ether-Type field is then checked to determine the protocol that the packet should be handed to at the Network layer—IP in this example.

18. At the Network layer, IP receives the packet and runs a CRC on the IP header. If that passes, IP then checks the destination address. Since a match has finally been made, the Protocol field is checked to find out to whom the payload should be given.

19. The payload is handed to ICMP, which understands that this is an echo request. ICMP responds to this by immediately discarding the packet and generating a new payload as an echo reply.

20. A packet is then created including the source and destination addresses, Protocol field, and payload. The destination device is now Host A.

21. IP then checks to see whether the destination IP address is a device on the local LAN or on a remote network. Since the destination device is on a remote network, the packet needs to be sent to the default gateway.

22. The default gateway IP address is found in the Registry of the Windows device, and the ARP cache is checked to see if the hardware address has already been resolved from an IP address.

23. Once the hardware address of the default gateway is found, the packet and destination hardware addresses are handed down to the Data Link layer for framing.

24. The Data Link layer frames the packet of information and includes the following in the header:

    ▪ The destination and source hardware addresses

    ▪ The Ether-Type field with 0x0800 (IP) in it

    ▪ The FCS field with the CRC result in tow

25. The frame is now handed down to the Physical layer to be sent out over the network medium one bit at a time.

26. The router's Ethernet 1 interface receives the bits and builds a frame. The CRC is run, and the FCS field is checked to make sure the answers match.

27. Once the CRC is found to be okay, the hardware destination address is checked. Since the router's interface is a match, the packet is pulled from the frame and the Ether-Type field is checked to determine which protocol the packet should be delivered to at the Network layer.

28. The protocol is determined to be IP, so it gets the packet. IP runs a CRC check on the IP header first and then checks the destination IP address.

IP does not run a complete CRC as the Data Link layer does—it only checks the header for errors.

Since the IP destination address doesn't match any of the router's interfaces, the routing table is checked to see whether it has a route to 172.16.10.0. If it doesn't have a route over to the destination network, the packet will be discarded immediately. I want to take a minute to point out that this is exactly where the source of confusion begins for a lot of administrators because when a ping fails, most people think the packet never reached the destination host. But as we see here, that's not *always* the case. All it takes for this to happen is for even just one of the remote routers to lack a route back to the originating host's network and—*poof!*—the packet is dropped on the *return trip*, not on its way to the host!

Just a quick note to mention that when (and if) the packet is lost on the way back to the originating host, you will typically see a request timed-out message because it is an unknown error. If the error occurs because of a known issue, such as if a route is not in the routing table on the way to the destination device, you will see a destination unreachable message. This should help you determine if the problem occurred on the way to the destination or on the way back.

29. In this case, the router happens to know how to get to network 172.16.10.0—the exit interface is Ethernet 0—so the packet is switched to interface Ethernet 0.

30. The router then checks the ARP cache to determine whether the hardware address for 172.16.10.2 has already been resolved.

31. Since the hardware address to 172.16.10.2 is already cached from the originating trip to Host B, the hardware address and packet are then handed to the Data Link layer.

32. The Data Link layer builds a frame with the destination hardware address and source hardware address and then puts IP in the Ether-Type field. A CRC is run on the frame and the result is placed in the FCS field.

33. The frame is then handed to the Physical layer to be sent out onto the local network one bit at a time.

34. The destination host receives the frame, runs a CRC, checks the destination hardware address, and then looks into the Ether-Type field to find out to whom to hand the packet.

35. IP is the designated receiver, and after the packet is handed to IP at the Network layer, it checks the Protocol field for further direction. IP finds instructions to give the payload to ICMP, and ICMP determines the packet to be an ICMP echo reply.

36. ICMP acknowledges that it has received the reply by sending an exclamation point (!) to the user interface. ICMP then attempts to send four more echo requests to the destination host.

You've just experienced Todd's 36 easy steps to understanding IP routing. The key point here is that if you had a much larger network, the process would be the *same*. It's just that the larger the internetwork, the more hops the packet goes through before it finds the destination host.

It's super-important to remember that when Host A sends a packet to Host B, the destination hardware address used is the default gateway's Ethernet interface. Why? Because frames can't be placed on remote networks—only local networks. So packets destined for remote networks must go through the default gateway.

Let's take a look at Host A's ARP cache now:

```
C:\ >arp -a
Interface: 172.16.10.2 --- 0x3
  Internet Address      Physical Address     Type
  172.16.10.1           00-15-05-06-31-b0    dynamic
  172.16.20.1           00-15-05-06-31-b0    dynamic
```

Did you notice that the hardware (MAC) address that Host A uses to get to Host B is the Lab A E0 interface? Hardware addresses are *always* local, and they never pass through a router's interface. Understanding this process is as important as air to you, so carve this into your memory!

The Cisco Router Internal Process

One more thing before we get to testing your understanding of my 36 steps of IP routing. I think it's important to explain how a router forwards packets internally. For IP to look up a destination address in a routing table on a router, processing in the router must take place, and if there are tens of thousands of routes in that table, the amount of CPU time would be enormous. It results in a potentially overwhelming amount of overhead—think about a router at your ISP that has to calculate millions of packets per second and even subnets to find the correct exit interface! Even with the little network I'm using in this book, lots of processing would need to be done if there were actual hosts connected and sending data.

Cisco uses three types of packet-forwarding techniques.

Process switching   This is actually how many people see routers to this day, because it's true that routers actually did perform this type of bare-bones packet switching back in 1990 when Cisco released its very first router. But those days when traffic demands were unimaginably light are long gone—not in today's networks! This process is now extremely complex and involves looking up every destination in the routing table and finding the exit interface for every packet. This is pretty much how I just explained the process in my 36 steps. But even though what I wrote was absolutely true in concept, the internal process requires much more than packet-switching technology today because of the millions of packets per second that must now be processed. So Cisco came up with some other technologies to help with the "big process problem."

Fast switching   This solution was created to make the slow performance of process switching faster and more efficient. Fast switching uses a cache to store the most recently used destinations so that lookups are not required for every packet. It is important to know that this "cache" is information from already processed packets, meaning that fast switching must "process switch" a packet first. Nevertheless, when the exit interface of the destination device was cached, as well as the layer 2 header, performance was dramatically improved, but as our networks evolved with the need for even more speed, Cisco created yet another technology!

Cisco Express Forwarding (CEF)   This is Cisco's newer creation, and it's the default packet-forwarding method used on all the latest Cisco routers. CEF proactively makes many different cache tables to help improve performance and is change triggered, not packet triggered. Translated, this means that when the network topology changes, the cache changes along with it.

Exam Essentials

Describe the basic IP routing process.   You need to remember that the frame changes at each hop but that the packet is never changed or manipulated in any way until it reaches the destination device (the TTL field in the IP header is decremented for each hop, but that's it!).

List the information required by a router to successfully route packets.   To be able to route packets, a router must know, at a minimum, the destination address, the location of neighboring routers through which it can reach remote networks, possible routes to all remote networks, the best route to each remote network, and how to maintain and verify routing information.

Identify the Appropriate Media, Cables, Ports, and Connectors to Connect Cisco Network Devices to Other Network Devices and Hosts in a LAN

The IEEE extended the 802.3 committee to three new committees known as 802.3u (Fast Ethernet), 802.3ab (Gigabit Ethernet on category 5), and then finally one more, 802.3ae (10 Gbps over fiber and coax). There are more standards evolving almost daily, such as the new 100 Gbps Ethernet (802.3ba)!

When designing your LAN, it's really important to understand the different types of Ethernet media available to you. Sure, it would be great to run Gigabit Ethernet to each desktop and 10 Gbps between switches, but you would need to figure out how to justify the cost of that network today! However, if you mix and match the different types of Ethernet media methods currently available, you can come up with a cost-effective network solution that works really great.

The *EIA/TIA* (Electronic Industries Alliance and the newer Telecommunications Industry Association) is the standards body that creates the Physical layer specifications for Ethernet. The EIA/TIA specifies that Ethernet use a *registered jack (RJ) connector* on *unshielded twisted-pair (UTP)* cabling (RJ45). But the industry is moving toward simply calling this an 8-pin modular connector.

Every Ethernet cable type that's specified by the EIA/TIA has inherent attenuation, which is defined as the loss of signal strength as it travels the length of a cable and is measured in decibels (dB). The cabling used in corporate and home markets is measured in categories. A higher-quality cable will have a higher-rated category and lower attenuation. For example, category 5 is better than category 3 because category 5 cables have more wire twists per foot and therefore less crosstalk. Crosstalk is the unwanted signal interference from adjacent pairs in the cable.

Here is a list of some of the most common IEEE Ethernet standards, starting with 10 Mbps Ethernet:

10Base-T (IEEE 802.3)   10 Mbps using category 3 unshielded twisted pair (UTP) wiring for runs up to 100 meters. Unlike with the 10Base-2 and 10Base-5 networks, each device must connect into a hub or switch, and you can have only one host per segment or wire. It uses an RJ45 connector (8-pin modular connector) with a physical star topology and a logical bus.

100Base-TX (IEEE 802.3u)   100Base-TX, most commonly known as Fast Ethernet, uses EIA/TIA category 5, 5E, or 6 UTP two-pair wiring. One user per segment; up to 100 meters long. It uses an RJ45 connector with a physical star topology and a logical bus.

100Base-FX (IEEE 802.3u)   Uses fiber cabling 62.5/125-micron multimode fiber. Point-to-point topology; up to 412 meters long. It uses ST and SC connectors, which are media-interface connectors.

1000Base-CX (IEEE 802.3z)   Copper twisted-pair, called twinax, is a balanced coaxial pair that can run only up to 25 meters and uses a special 9-pin connector known as the High Speed Serial Data Connector (HSSDC). This is used in Cisco's new Data Center technologies.

1000Base-T (IEEE 802.3ab)   Category 5, four-pair UTP wiring up to 100 meters long and up to 1 Gbps.

1000Base-SX (IEEE 802.3z)   The implementation of 1 Gigabit Ethernet running over multimode fiber-optic cable instead of copper twisted-pair cable, using short wavelength laser. Multimode fiber (MMF) using 62.5- and 50-micron core; uses an 850 nanometer (nm) laser and can go up to 220 meters with 62.5-micron, 550 meters with 50-micron.

1000Base-LX (IEEE 802.3z)   Single-mode fiber that uses a 9-micron core and 1300 nm laser and can go from 3 kilometers up to 10 kilometers.

1000Base-ZX (Cisco standard)   1000BaseZX, or 1000Base-ZX, is a Cisco specified standard for Gigabit Ethernet communication. 1000BaseZX operates on ordinary single-mode fiber-optic links with spans up to 43.5 miles (70 km).

10GBase-T (802.3.an)   10GBase-T is a standard proposed by the IEEE 802.3an committee to provide 10 Gbps connections over conventional UTP cables, (category 5e, 6, or 7 cables). 10GBase-T allows the conventional RJ45 used for Ethernet LANs and can support signal transmission at the full 100-meter distance specified for LAN wiring.

Armed with the basics covered so far in this chapter, you're equipped to go to the next level and put Ethernet to work using various Ethernet cabling.

Ethernet Cabling

A discussion about Ethernet cabling is an important one, especially if you are planning on taking the Cisco exams. You need to really understand the following three types of cables:

- Straight-through cable
- Crossover cable
- Rolled cable

We will look at each in the following sections, but first, let's take a look at the most common Ethernet cable used today, the category 5 enhanced unshielded twisted pair (UTP), shown in Figure 1.30.

The category 5 Enhanced UTP cable can handle speeds up to a gigabit with a distance of up to 100 meters. Typically we'd use this cable for 100 Mbps and category 6 for a gigabit, but the category 5 Enhanced is rated for gigabit speeds and category 6 is rated for 10 Gbps!

FIGURE 1.30   Category 5 enhanced UTP cable

Straight-Through Cable

The *straight-through cable* is used to connect the following devices:

▪ Host to switch or hub

▪ Router to switch or hub

Four wires are used in straight-through cable to connect Ethernet devices. It's relatively simple to create this type, and Figure 1.31 shows the four wires used in a straight-through Ethernet cable.

FIGURE 1.31   Straight-through Ethernet cable

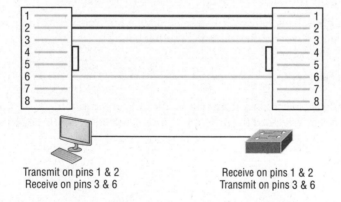

Transmit on pins 1 & 2
Receive on pins 3 & 6

Receive on pins 1 & 2
Transmit on pins 3 & 6

Notice that only pins 1, 2, 3, and 6 are used. Just connect 1 to 1, 2 to 2, 3 to 3, and 6 to 6 and you'll be up and networking in no time. However, remember that this would be a 10/100 Mbps Ethernet-only cable and wouldn't work with gigabit, voice, or other LAN or WAN technology.

Crossover Cable

The *crossover cable* can be used to connect the following devices:

▪ Switch to switch

▪ Hub to hub

- Host to host
- Hub to switch
- Router direct to host
- Router to router

The same four wires used in the straight-through cable are used in this cable—we just connect different pins together. Figure 1.32 shows how the four wires are used in a crossover Ethernet cable.

FIGURE 1.32   Crossover Ethernet cable

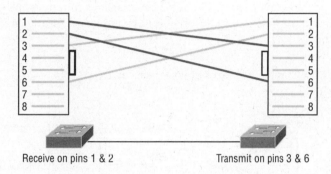

Receive on pins 1 & 2   Transmit on pins 3 & 6

Notice that instead of connecting 1 to 1, 2 to 2, and so on, here we connect pins 1 to 3 and 2 to 6 on each side of the cable. Figure 1.33 shows some typical uses of straight-through and crossover cables.

FIGURE 1.33   Typical uses for straight-through and crossover Ethernet cables

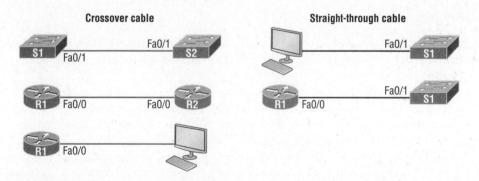

The crossover examples in Figure 1.33 are switch port to switch port, router Ethernet port to router Ethernet port, and PC Ethernet to router Ethernet port. For the straight-through examples I used PC Ethernet to switch port and router Ethernet port to switch port.

It's very possible to connect a straight-through cable between two switches, and it will start working because of autodetect mechanisms called auto-mdix. But be advised that the CCNA objectives do not typically consider autodetect mechanisms valid between devices!

UTP Gigabit Wiring (1000Base-T)

In 10Base-T and 100Base-T UTP wiring, only two wire pairs were used, but that is not good enough for Gigabit UTP transmission.

1000Base-T UTP wiring (Figure 1.34) requires four wire pairs and uses more advanced electronics so that each and every pair in the cable can transmit simultaneously. Even so, gigabit wiring is almost identical to my earlier 10/100 example, except that we'll use the other two pairs in the cable.

FIGURE 1.34   UTP Gigabit crossover Ethernet cable

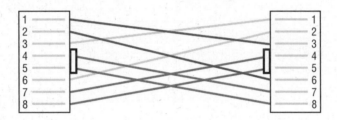

For a straight-through cable, it's still 1 to 1, 2 to 2, and so on, up to pin 8. And in creating the gigabit crossover cable, you'd still cross 1 to 3 and 2 to 6, but you would add 4 to 7 and 5 to 8—pretty straightforward!

Rolled Cable

Although *rolled cable* isn't used to connect any Ethernet connections together, you can use a rolled Ethernet cable to connect a host EIA-TIA 232 interface to a router console serial communication (COM) port.

If you have a Cisco router or switch, you would use this cable to connect your PC, Mac, or a device like an iPad to the Cisco hardware. Eight wires are used in this cable to connect serial devices, although not all eight are used to send information, just as in Ethernet networking. Figure 1.35 shows the eight wires used in a rolled cable.

These are probably the easiest cables to make because you just cut the end off on one side of a straight-through cable, turn it over, and put it back on—with a new connector, of course!

Okay, once you have the correct cable connected from your PC to the Cisco router or switch console port, you can start your emulation program such as putty or SecureCRT to create a console connection and configure the device. Set the configuration as shown in Figure 1.36.

FIGURE 1.35   Rolled Ethernet cable

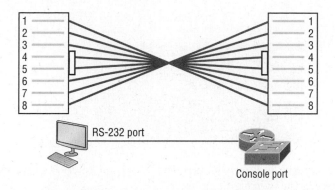

FIGURE 1.36   Configuring your console emulation program

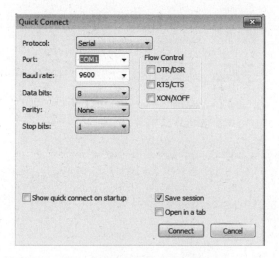

Notice that Bit Rate is set to 9600, Data Bits to 8, Parity to None, and Flow Control is set to None. At this point, you can click Connect and press the Enter key and you should be connected to your Cisco device console port.

Figure 1.37 shows a nice new 2960 switch with two console ports.

Notice that there are two console connections on this new switch—a typical original RJ45 connection and the newer mini type-B USB console. Remember that the new USB port supersedes the RJ45 port if you just happen to plug into both at the same time, and the USB port can have speeds up to 115,200 Kbps, which is awesome if you have to use Xmodem to update an IOS. I've even seen some cables that work on iPhones and iPads and allow them to connect to these mini USB ports!

FIGURE 1.37   Cisco 2960 console connections

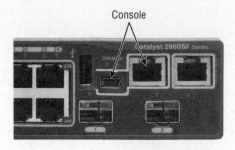

Now that you've seen the various RJ45 unshielded twisted-pair (UTP) cables, what type of cable is used between the switches in Figure 1.38?

FIGURE 1.38   RJ45 UTP cable question #1

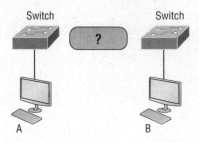

In order for host A to ping host B, you need a crossover cable to connect the two switches together. But what types of cables are used in the network shown in Figure 1.39?

FIGURE 1.39   RJ45 UTP cable question #2

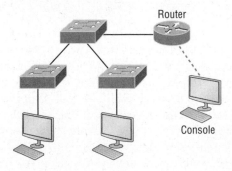

In Figure 1.39, there's a whole menu of cables in use. For the connection between the switches, we'd obviously use a crossover cable like we saw in Figure 1.34. The trouble is that you must understand that we have a console connection that uses a rolled cable. Plus, the connection from the router to the switch is a straight-through cable, as is true for the hosts to the switches. Keep in mind that if we had a serial connection, which we don't, we would use a V.35 to connect us to a WAN.

Fiber Optic

Fiber-optic cabling has been around for a long time and has some solid standards. The cable allows for very fast transmission of data, is made of glass (or even plastic!), is very thin, and works as a waveguide to transmit light between two ends of the fiber. Fiber optics has been used to go very long distances, as in intercontinental connections, but it is becoming more and more popular in Ethernet LAN networks due to the fast speeds available and because, unlike UTP, it's immune to interference like crosstalk.

Some main components of this cable are the core and the cladding. The core will hold the light and the cladding confines the light in the core. The tighter the cladding, the smaller the core, and when the core is small, less light will be sent but it can go faster and farther!

In Figure 1.40 you can see that there is a 9-micron core, which is very small and can be measured against a human hair, which is 50 microns.

FIGURE 1.40   Typical fiber cable. Dimensions are in um (10^{-6} meters). Not to scale.

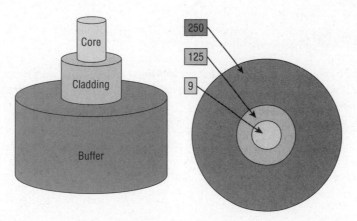

The cladding is 125 microns, which is actually a fiber standard that allows manufacturers to make connectors for all fiber cables. The last piece of this cable is the buffer, which is there to protect the delicate glass.

There are two major types of fiber optics: single-mode and multimode. Figure 1.41 shows the differences between multimode and single-mode fibers.

FIGURE 1.41   Multimode and single-mode fibers

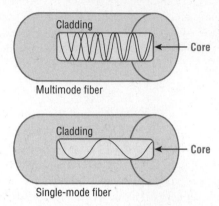

Single-mode is more expensive, has a tighter cladding, and can go much farther distances than multimode. The difference comes in the tightness of the cladding, which makes a smaller core, meaning that only one mode of light will propagate down the fiber. Multimode is looser and has a larger core so it allows multiple light particles to travel down the glass. These particles have to be put back together at the receiving end, so distance is less than that with single-mode fiber, which allows only very few light particles to travel down the fiber.

There are about 70 different connectors for fiber, and Cisco uses a few different types. Looking back at Figure 1.37, the two bottom ports are referred to as small form-factor pluggables, or SFPs.

Exam Essentials

Identify the IEEE physical standards for Ethernet cabling.   These standards describe the capabilities and physical characteristics of various cable types and include but are not limited to 10Base-2, 10Base-5, and 10Base-T.

Differentiate types of Ethernet cabling and identify their proper application.   The three types of cables that can be created from an Ethernet cable are straight-through (to connect a PC's or router's Ethernet interface to a hub or switch), crossover (to connect hub to hub, hub to switch, switch to switch, or PC to PC), and rolled (for a console connection from a PC to a router or switch).

Review Questions

1. What cable type is shown in the following image?

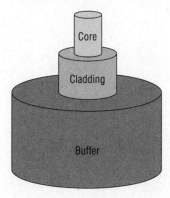

   A. Fiber optic

   B. Rollover

   C. Coaxial

   D. Full-duplex

2. Which of the following statements is/are true with regard to the device shown below?

   A. It includes one collision domain and one broadcast domain.

   B. It includes one collision domain and 10 broadcast domains.

   C. It includes 10 collision domains and one broadcast domain.

   D. It includes one collision domain and 10 broadcast domains.

   E. It includes 10 collision domains and 10 broadcast domains.

3. Which of the following Application layer protocols sets up a secure session that's similar to Telnet?

   A. FTP

   B. SSH

   C. DNS

   D. DHCP

4. What destination addresses will be used by HostA to send data to the HTTPS server as shown in the following network? (Choose two.)

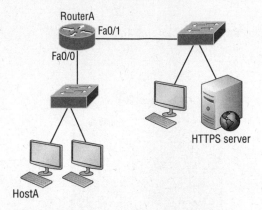

A. The IP address of the switch

B. The MAC address of the remote switch

C. The IP address of the HTTPS server

D. The MAC address of the HTTPS server

E. The IP address of RouterA's Fa0/0 interface

F. The MAC address of RouterA's Fa0/0 interface

5. In the following diagram, identify the cable types required for connections A and B.

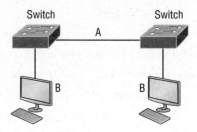

A. A crossover, B crossover

B. A crossover, B straight through

C. A straight through, B straight through

D. A straight through, B crossover

6. When a packet is routed across a network, the _____ in the frame changes at every hop while the _____ in the packet does not.

   A. MAC address, IP address

   B. IP address, MAC address

   C. Port number, IP address

   D. IP address, port number

7. What must happen if a DHCP IP conflict occurs?

   A. Proxy ARP will fix the issue.

   B. The client uses a gratuitous ARP to fix the issue.

   C. The administrator must fix the conflict by hand at the DHCP server.

   D. The DHCP server will reassign new IP addresses to both computers.

8. How many collision domains are present in the following diagram?

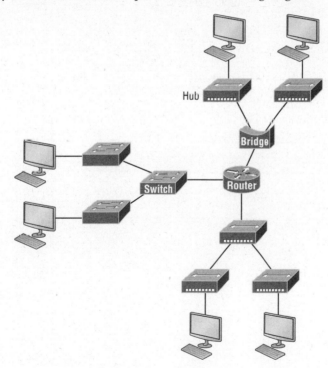

   A. 8

   B. 9

   C. 10

   D. 11

9. When a router looks up the destination in the routing table for every single packet it is called _____ .

   A. dynamic switching

   B. Fast switching

   C. Process switching

   D. Cisco Express Forwarding

10. What protocol is used to find the hardware address of a local device?

   A. RARP

   B. ARP

   C. IP

   D. ICMP

   E. BootP

Chapter 2

LAN Switching Technologies

✓ Determine the technology and media access control method for Ethernet networks.

✓ Identify basic switching concepts and the operation of Cisco switches.

- Collision Domains

- Broadcast Domains

- Types of switching

- CAM Table

✓ Configure and verify initial switch configuration including remote access management.

- Cisco IOS commands to perform basic switch setup

✓ Verify network status and switch operation using basic utilities such as ping, telnet and ssh.

✓ Identify enhanced switching technologies.

- RSTP

- PVSTP

- Etherchannels

✓ Describe how VLANs create logically separate networks and the need for routing between them.

- Explain network segmentation and basic traffic management concepts

✓ **Configure and verify VLANs.**

✓ **Configure and verify trunking on Cisco switches.**

- DTP

- Auto negotiation

✓ **Configure and verify PVSTP operation.**

- Describe root bridge election

- Spanning tree mode

In this chapter, we'll discuss Ethernet basics and how MAC addresses are used on an Ethernet LAN. We will also go over broadcast domains, collision domains, types of switching, and the CAM table.

I'm going to show you how to configure a Cisco IOS device using the Cisco IOS command-line interface (CLI). Once proficient with this interface, you'll be able to configure hostnames, banners, passwords, and more as well as troubleshoot skillfully using the Cisco IOS.

We'll also begin the journey to mastering the basics of router and switch configurations plus command verifications in this chapter.

We'll finish with some of the different switching technologies, such as RSTP and PVSTP.

Determine the Technology and Media Access Control Method for Ethernet Networks

Ethernet is a contention-based media access method that allows all hosts on a network to share the same link's bandwidth. It's so popular because it's really pretty simple to implement, and it makes troubleshooting fairly straightforward as well. Ethernet is readily scalable, meaning that it eases the process of integrating new technologies into an existing network infrastructure, such as upgrading from Fast Ethernet to Gigabit Ethernet.

CSMA/CD

Ethernet networking uses a protocol called *Carrier Sense Multiple Access with Collision Detection (CSMA/CD)*, which helps devices share the bandwidth evenly while preventing two devices from transmitting simultaneously on the same network medium. CSMA/CD was actually created to overcome the problem of the collisions that occur when packets are transmitted from different nodes at the same time. Good collision management is crucial. When a node transmits in a CSMA/CD network, all the other nodes on the network receive and examine that transmission. Only switches and routers can effectively prevent a transmission from propagating throughout the entire network!

Figure 2.1 shows how the CSMA/CD protocol works.

FIGURE 2.1   CSMA/CD

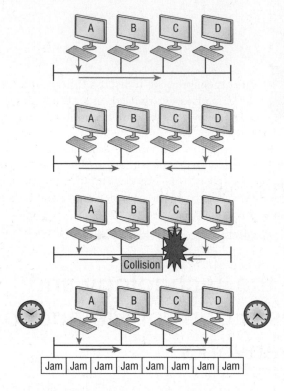

When a host wants to transmit over the network, it first checks for the presence of a digital signal on the wire. If all is clear and no other host is transmitting, the host will then proceed with its transmission.

But it doesn't stop there. The transmitting host constantly monitors the wire to make sure no other hosts begin transmitting. If the host detects another signal on the wire, it sends out an extended jam signal that causes all nodes on the segment to stop sending data—think busy signal.

The nodes respond to that jam signal by waiting a bit before attempting to transmit again. This is known as the backoff algorithm. The backoff algorithm determines when the colliding stations can retransmit. If collisions keep occurring after 15 tries, the nodes attempting to transmit will then time out. Half-duplex can be pretty messy!

When a collision occurs on an Ethernet LAN, the following happens:

1. A jam signal informs all devices that a collision occurred.

2. The collision invokes a random backoff algorithm.

3. Each device on the Ethernet segment stops transmitting for a short time until its backoff timer expires.

4. All hosts have equal priority to transmit after the timers have expired.

There are some ugly effects of having a CSMA/CD network sustain heavy collisions:

- Delay
- Low throughput
- Congestion

Backoff on an Ethernet network is the retransmission delay that's enforced when a collision occurs. When that happens, a host will resume transmission only after the forced time delay has expired. Keep in mind that after the backoff has elapsed, all stations have equal priority to transmit data.

Half- and Full-Duplex Ethernet

Half-duplex Ethernet is defined in the original IEEE 802.3 Ethernet specification, which differs a bit from how Cisco describes things. Cisco says Ethernet uses only one wire pair with a digital signal running in both directions on the wire.

Half-duplex also uses the CSMA/CD protocol to help prevent collisions and to permit retransmitting if one occurs. If a hub is attached to a switch, it must operate in half-duplex mode because the end stations must be able to detect collisions. Figure 2.2 shows a network with four hosts connected to a hub.

FIGURE 2.2   An example of half-duplex Ethernet

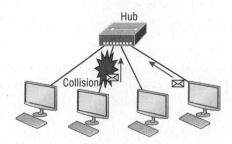

The problem here is that we can only run half-duplex, and if two hosts communicate at the same time, there will be a collision. Also, half-duplex Ethernet is only about 30 to 40 percent efficient because a large 100Base-T network will usually only give you 30 to 40 Mbps, at most, due to overhead of the CSMA/CD protocol.

Full-duplex Ethernet uses two pairs of wires at the same time instead of a single wire pair like half-duplex. And full-duplex uses a point-to-point connection between the transmitter of the transmitting device and the receiver of the receiving device. This means that full-duplex data transfers happen a lot faster when compared to half-duplex transfers. Also, because the transmitted data is sent on a different set of wires than the received data, collisions won't happen. Figure 2.3 shows four hosts connected to a switch, plus a hub. And by the way, definitely try not to use hubs if you can help it!

FIGURE 2.3 An example of full-duplex Ethernet

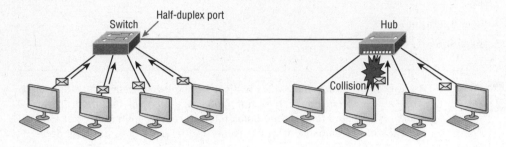

Theoretically, all hosts connected to the switch in Figure 2.3 can communicate at the same time because they can run full-duplex. Just keep in mind that the switch port connecting to the hub as well as the hosts connecting to that hub must run at half-duplex.

The reason you don't need to worry about collisions is that now it's like a freeway with multiple lanes instead of the single-lane road provided by half-duplex. Full-duplex Ethernet is supposed to offer 100 percent efficiency in both directions.

You can use full-duplex Ethernet in at least the following six situations:

- With a connection from a switch to a host
- With a connection from a switch to a switch
- With a connection from a host to a host
- With a connection from a switch to a router
- With a connection from a router to a router
- With a connection from a router to a host

Full-duplex Ethernet requires a point-to-point connection when only two nodes are present. You can run full-duplex with just about any device except a hub.

When a full-duplex Ethernet port is powered on, it first connects to the remote end and then negotiates with the other end of the Fast Ethernet link. This is called an *autodetect mechanism*. This mechanism first decides on the exchange capability, which means it checks to see if it can run at 10, 100, or even 1,000 Mbps. It then checks to see if it can run full-duplex, and if it can't, it will run half-duplex.

Remember that half-duplex Ethernet shares a collision domain and provides a lower effective throughput than full-duplex Ethernet, which typically has a private per-port collision domain plus a higher effective throughput.

Last, remember these important points:

- There are no collisions in full-duplex mode.
- A dedicated switch port is required for each full-duplex node.
- The host network card and the switch port must be capable of operating in full-duplex mode.
- The default behavior of 10Base-T and 100Base-T hosts is 10 Mbps half-duplex if the autodetect mechanism fails, so it is always good practice to set the speed and duplex of each port on a switch if you can.

Exam Essentials

Describe the operation of Carrier Sense Multiple Access with Collision Detection (CSMA/CD). CSMA/CD is a protocol that helps devices share the bandwidth evenly without having two devices transmit at the same time on the network medium. Although it does not eliminate collisions, it helps to greatly reduce them, which reduces retransmissions, resulting in a more efficient transmission of data for all devices.

Differentiate half-duplex and full-duplex communication and define the requirements to utilize each method. Full-duplex Ethernet uses two pairs of wires at the same time instead of one wire pair like half-duplex. Full-duplex allows for sending and receiving at the same time, using different wires to eliminate collisions, while half-duplex can send or receive but not at the same time and still can suffer collisions. For full-duplex, the devices at both ends of the cable must be capable of and configured to perform full-duplex.

Identify Basic Switching Concepts and the Operation of Cisco Switches

We rely on switching to break large collision domains into smaller ones. A collision domain is a network segment with two or more devices sharing the same bandwidth. A hub network is a typical example of this type of technology. But since each port on a switch is actually its own collision domain, we were able to create a much better Ethernet LAN by simply replacing our hubs with switches!

Switches truly have changed the way networks are designed and implemented. If a pure switched design is properly implemented, it absolutely will result in a clean, cost-effective, and resilient internetwork.

Collision Domains

Collision domain refers to a network scenario wherein one device sends a frame out on a physical network segment, forcing every other device on the same segment to pay attention to it. This is bad because if two devices on a single physical segment just happen to transmit simultaneously, it will cause a collision and require those devices to retransmit. Figure 2.4 shows an old, legacy network that's a single collision domain where only one host can transmit at a time.

FIGURE 2.4   Legacy collision domain design

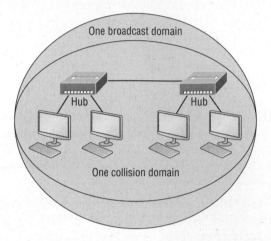

The hosts connected to each hub are in the same collision domain, so if one of them transmits, all the others must take the time to listen for and read the digital signal. It is easy to see how collisions can be a serious drag on network performance. It also has only one collision domain, but worse, it's also a single broadcast domain—what a mess!

Let's check out an example, in Figure 2.5, of a typical network design still used today.

FIGURE 2.5   A typical network you'd see today

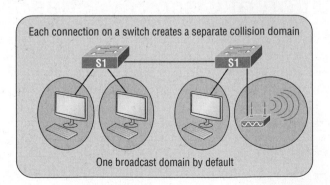

Because each port off a switch is a single collision domain, we gain more bandwidth for users, which is a great start. But switches don't break up broadcast domains by default, so this is still only one broadcast domain, which is not so good. This can work in a really small network, but to expand it at all, we would need to break up the network into smaller broadcast domains or our users won't get enough bandwidth!

And you're probably wondering about that device on the lower right. Well, that's a wireless access point, which is sometimes referred as an AP (which stands for access point). It's a wireless device that allows hosts to connect wirelessly using the IEEE 802.11 specification, and I added it to the figure to demonstrate how these devices can be used to extend a collision domain. But still, understand that APs don't actually segment the network; they only extend them, meaning our LAN just got a lot bigger, with an unknown amount of hosts that are all still part of one measly broadcast domain! This clearly demonstrates why it's so important to understand exactly what a broadcast domain is, and now is a great time to talk about them in detail.

Broadcast Domains

Broadcast domain refers to a group of devices on a specific network segment that hear all the broadcasts sent out on that specific network segment.

But even though a broadcast domain is usually a boundary delimited by physical media like switches and routers, it can also refer to a logical division of a network segment, where all hosts can communicate via a Data Link layer, hardware address broadcast.

Figure 2.6 shows how a router would create a broadcast domain boundary.

FIGURE 2.6   A router creates broadcast domain boundaries.

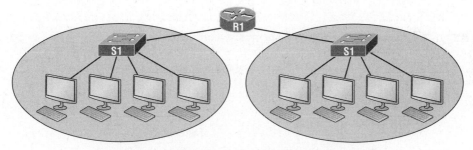

Two broadcast domains. How many collision domains do you see?

Here you can see that there are two router interfaces giving us two broadcast domains, and I count 10 switch segments, meaning we've got 10 collision domains.

The design depicted in Figure 2.5 is still in use today, and routers will be around for a long time, but in the latest, modern switched networks, it's important to create small broadcast domains. We achieve this by building virtual LANs (VLANs) within our switched networks, which I'll demonstrate shortly. Without employing VLANs in today's switched environments, there wouldn't be much bandwidth available to individual users. Switches break up collision domains with each port, which is awesome, but they're still only one broadcast domain by default! It's also one more reason why it's extremely important to design our networks very carefully.

And key to carefully planning your network design is to never allow broadcast domains to grow too large and get out of control. Both collision and broadcast domains can easily be controlled with routers and VLANs, so there's just no excuse to allow user bandwidth to slow to a painful crawl when there are plenty of tools in your arsenal to prevent the suffering!

Types of Switching

For coverage of this objective, please see the next section, "CAM Table."

CAM Table

Unlike old bridges, which used software to create and manage a content addressable memory (CAM) filter table, our new, fast switches use application-specific integrated circuits (ASICs) to build and maintain their MAC filter tables. But it's still okay to think of a layer 2 switch as a multiport bridge because their basic reason for being is the same: to break up collision domains.

Layer 2 switches and bridges are faster than routers because they don't take up time looking at the Network layer header information. Instead, they look at the frame's hardware addresses before deciding to forward, flood, or drop the frame.

Address Learning

When a switch is first powered on, the MAC forward/filter table (CAM) is empty, as shown in Figure 2.7.

FIGURE 2.7   Empty forward/filter table on a switch

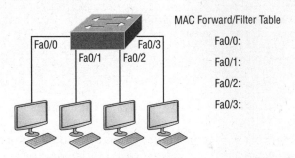

When a device transmits and an interface receives a frame, the switch places the frame's source address in the MAC forward/filter table, allowing it to refer to the precise interface the sending device is located on. The switch then has no choice but to flood the network with this frame out of every port except the source port because it has no idea where the destination device is actually located.

If a device answers this flooded frame and sends a frame back, then the switch will take the source address from that frame and place that MAC address in its database as well, associating this address with the interface that received the frame. Because the switch now has both of the relevant MAC addresses in its filtering table, the two devices can make a point-to-point connection. The switch doesn't need to flood the frame as it did the first time because now the frames can and will only be forwarded between these two devices. This is exactly why layer 2 switches are so superior to hubs. In a hub network, all frames are forwarded out all ports every time—no matter what. Figure 2.8 shows the processes involved in building a MAC database.

FIGURE 2.8 How switches learn hosts' locations

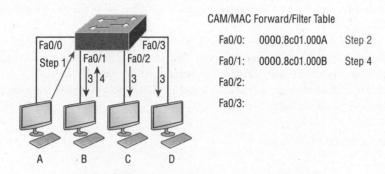

In this figure, you can see four hosts attached to a switch. When the switch is powered on, it has nothing in its MAC address forward/filter table, just as in Figure 2.7. But when the hosts start communicating, the switch places the source hardware address of each frame into the table along with the port that the frame's source address corresponds to.

Let me give you an example of how a forward/filter table is populated using Figure 2.8:

1. Host A sends a frame to Host B. Host A's MAC address is 0000.8c01.000A; Host B's MAC address is 0000.8c01.000B.

2. The switch receives the frame on the Fa0/0 interface and places the source address in the MAC address table.

3. Since the destination address isn't in the MAC database, the frame is forwarded out all interfaces except the source port.

4. Host B receives the frame and responds to Host A. The switch receives this frame on interface Fa0/1 and places the source hardware address in the MAC database.

5. Host A and Host B can now make a point-to-point connection and only these specific devices will receive the frames. Hosts C and D won't see the frames, nor will their MAC addresses be found in the database because they haven't sent a frame to the switch yet.

If Host A and Host B don't communicate to the switch again within a certain time period, the switch will flush their entries from the database to keep it as current as possible.

Forward/Filter Decisions

When a frame arrives at a switch interface, the destination hardware address is compared to the forward/filter MAC database. If the destination hardware address is known and listed in the database, the frame is sent only out of the appropriate exit interface. The switch won't transmit the frame out any interface except for the destination interface, which preserves bandwidth on the other network segments. This process is called *frame filtering.*

If the destination hardware address isn't listed in the MAC database, then the frame will be flooded out all active interfaces except the interface it was received on. If a device answers the flooded frame, the MAC database is then updated with the device's location—its correct interface.

If a host or server sends a broadcast on the LAN, by default, the switch will flood the frame out all active ports except the source port. Remember, the switch creates smaller collision domains, but it's always still one large broadcast domain by default.

In Figure 2.9, Host A sends a data frame to Host D. What do you think the switch will do when it receives the frame from Host A?

FIGURE 2.9   Forward/filter table

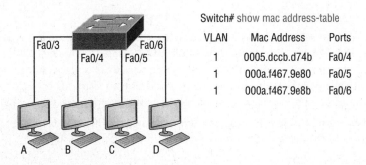

Let's examine Figure 2.10 to find the answer.

Since Host A's MAC address is not in the forward/filter table, the switch will add the source address and port to the MAC address table and then forward the frame to Host D. It's really important to remember that the source MAC is always checked first to make sure it's in the CAM table. After that, if Host D's MAC address wasn't found in the forward/filter table, the switch would've flooded the frame out all ports except for port Fa0/3 because that's the specific port the frame was received on.

Now let's take a look at the output that results from using a show mac address-table command:

```
Switch#sh mac address-table
Vlan    Mac Address      Type        Ports
----    -----------      --------    -----
   1    0005.dccb.d74b   DYNAMIC     Fa0/1
```

```
1    000a.f467.9e80    DYNAMIC    Fa0/3
1    000a.f467.9e8b    DYNAMIC    Fa0/4
1    000a.f467.9e8c    DYNAMIC    Fa0/3
1    0010.7b7f.c2b0    DYNAMIC    Fa0/3
1    0030.80dc.460b    DYNAMIC    Fa0/3
1    0030.9492.a5dd    DYNAMIC    Fa0/1
1    00d0.58ad.05f4    DYNAMIC    Fa0/1
```

FIGURE 2.10   Forward/filter table answer

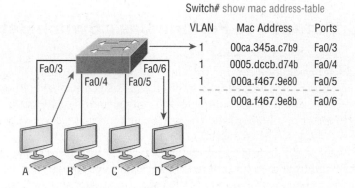

But let's say the preceding switch received a frame with the following MAC addresses:

Source MAC: **0005.dccb.d74b**

Destination MAC: **000a.f467.9e8c**

How will the switch handle this frame? The right answer is that the destination MAC address will be found in the MAC address table and the frame will be forwarded out only Fa0/3. Never forget that if the destination MAC address isn't found in the forward/filter table, the frame will be forwarded out all of the switch's ports except for the one on which it was originally received in an attempt to locate the destination device.

Exam Essentials

Remember the three switch functions.   Address learning, forward/filter decisions, and loop avoidance are the functions of a switch.

Remember the command show mac address-table.   The command show mac address-table will show you the forward/filter table used on the LAN switch.

Configure and Verify Initial Switch Configuration Including Remote Access Management

In the following sections, I'm going to show you how to configure a Cisco IOS device using the Cisco IOS command-line interface (CLI) and some command verifications.

I'll start with a basic IOS switch to begin building the network we'll use throughout this chapter for configuration examples.

Cisco IOS Commands to Perform Basic Switch Setup

When you first bring up a Cisco IOS device, it will run a power-on self-test—a POST. Upon passing that, the machine will look for and then load the Cisco IOS from flash memory if an IOS file is present, and then it will expand it into RAM. As you probably know, flash memory is electronically erasable programmable read-only memory—EEPROM. The next step is for the IOS to locate and load a valid configuration known as the startup-config that will be stored in *nonvolatile RAM (NVRAM)*.

Once the IOS is loaded and up and running, the startup-config will be copied from NVRAM into RAM and from then on referred to as the running-config.

But if a valid startup-config isn't found in NVRAM, your switch will enter setup mode, giving you a step-by-step dialog to help configure some basic parameters on it.

You can also enter setup mode at any time from the command line by typing the command **setup** from privileged mode, which I'll get to in a minute. Setup mode only covers some basic commands and generally isn't really all that helpful. Here's an example:

```
Would you like to enter the initial configuration dialog? [yes/no]: y


At any point you may enter a question mark '?' for help.
Use ctrl-c to abort configuration dialog at any prompt.
Default settings are in square brackets '[]'.


Basic management setup configures only enough connectivity
for management of the system, extended setup will ask you
to configure each interface on the system


Would you like to enter basic management setup? [yes/no]: y
Configuring global parameters:
```

```
Enter host name [Switch]: Ctrl+C
Configuration aborted, no changes made.
```

I highly recommend going through setup mode once and then never again because you should always use the CLI instead!

Entering the CLI

After the interface status messages appear and you press Enter, the Switch> prompt will pop up. This is called *user exec mode*, or user mode for short, and although it's mostly used to view statistics, it is also a stepping stone along the way to logging in to *privileged exec mode*, called privileged mode for short.

You can view and change the configuration of a Cisco switch only while in privileged mode, and you enter it via the enable command like this:

```
Switch>enable
Switch#
```

The Switch# prompt signals that you're in privileged mode, where you can both view and change the switch configuration. You can go back from privileged mode into user mode by using the disable command:

```
Switch#disable
Switch>
```

You can type **logout** from either mode to exit the console:

```
Switch>logout


Switch con0 is now available
Press RETURN to get started.
```

Next, I'll show how to perform some basic administrative configurations.

Overview of IOS Modes

To configure from a CLI, you can make global changes to the switch or device by typing **configure terminal**, or just **config t**. This will get you into global configuration mode where you can make changes to the running-config. Commands run from global configuration mode are predictably referred to as global commands, and they are typically set only once and affect the entire switch or device.

Type **config** from the privileged-mode prompt and then press Enter to opt for the default of terminal, like this:

```
Switch#config
Configuring from terminal, memory, or network [terminal]? [press enter]
```

```
Enter configuration commands, one per line.  End with CNTL/Z.
Switch(config)#
```

At this point, you make changes that affect the switch/device as a whole (globally), hence the term *global configuration mode*. For instance, to change the running-config—the current configuration running in dynamic RAM (DRAM)—use the configure terminal command, as I just demonstrated.

CLI Prompts

Let's explore the different prompts you'll encounter when configuring a switch or router.

 It's not important that you understand exactly what each of these command prompts accomplishes just yet. For now, relax and focus on just becoming familiar with the different prompts available.

Interfaces

To make changes to an interface, use the interface command from global configuration mode:

```
Switch(config)#interface ?
  Async              Async interface
  BVI                Bridge-Group Virtual Interface
  CTunnel            CTunnel interface
  Dialer             Dialer interface
  FastEthernet       FastEthernet IEEE 802.3
  Filter             Filter interface
  Filtergroup        Filter Group interface
  GigabitEthernet    GigabitEthernet IEEE 802.3z
  Group-Async        Async Group interface
  Lex                Lex interface
  Loopback           Loopback interface
  Null               Null interface
  Port-channel       Ethernet Channel of interfaces
  Portgroup          Portgroup interface
  Pos-channel        POS Channel of interfaces
  Tunnel             Tunnel interface
  Vif                PGM Multicast Host interface
  Virtual-Template   Virtual Template interface
  Virtual-TokenRing  Virtual TokenRing
  Vlan               Catalyst Vlans
```

```
fcpa              Fiber Channel
range             interface range command
```

```
Switch(config)#interface fastEthernet 0/1
Switch(config-if)#)
```

Notice that the prompt changed to Switch(config-if)#? This tells you that you're in *interface configuration mode*. And wouldn't it be nice if the prompt also gave you an indication of what interface you were configuring? Well, at least for now we'll have to live without the prompt information, because it doesn't. But it should already be clear to you that you really need to pay attention when configuring an IOS device!

Line Commands

To configure user-mode passwords, use the line command. The prompt then becomes Switch(config-line)#:

```
Switch(config)#line ?
  <0-16>   First Line number
  console  Primary terminal line
  vty      Virtual terminal
Switch(config)#line console 0
Switch(config-line)#
```

The line console 0 command is a global command, and sometimes you'll also hear people refer to global commands as major commands. In this example, any command typed from the (config-line) prompt is known as a subcommand.

Access List Configurations

To configure a standard named access list, you'll need to get to the prompt Switch(config-std-nacl)#:

```
Switch#config t
Switch(config)#ip access-list standard Todd
Switch(config-std-nacl)#
```

What you see here is a typical standard named ACL prompt. There are various ways to configure access lists, and the prompts are only slightly different from this particular example.

Routing Protocol Configurations

I need to point out that we don't use routing or routing protocols on 2960 switches, but we can and will use them on 3560 switches. Here is an example of configuring routing on a layer 3 switch:

```
Switch (config)#router rip
Switch(config-router)#
```

Did you notice that the prompt changed to Switch(config-router)#? To make sure you achieve the objectives specific to the Cisco exam and this book, I'll configure RIPv2, OSPF, and OSPFv3.

Editing and Help Features

The Cisco advanced editing features can also help you configure your router. If you type a question mark (?) at any prompt, you'll be given a list of all the commands available from that prompt:

```
Switch#?
Exec commands:
  access-enable    Create a temporary Access-List entry
  access-template  Create a temporary Access-List entry
  archive          manage archive files
  cd               Change current directory
  clear            Reset functions
  clock            Manage the system clock
  cns              CNS agents
  configure        Enter configuration mode
  connect          Open a terminal connection
  copy             Copy from one file to another
  debug            Debugging functions (see also 'undebug')
  delete           Delete a file
  diagnostic       Diagnostic commands
  dir              List files on a filesystem
  disable          Turn off privileged commands
  disconnect       Disconnect an existing network connection
  dot1x            IEEE 802.1X Exec Commands
  enable           Turn on privileged commands
  eou              EAPoUDP
  erase            Erase a filesystem
  exit             Exit from the EXEC
 --More-- ?
Press RETURN for another line, SPACE for another page, anything else to quit
```

And if this is not enough information for you, you can press the spacebar to get another whole page of information, or you can press Enter to go one command at a time. You can also press Q, or any other key for that matter, to quit and return to the prompt. Notice that I typed a question mark (?) at the more prompt and it told me what my options were from that prompt.

Here's a shortcut: to find commands that start with a certain letter, use the letter and the question mark with no space between them, like this:

```
Switch#c?
cd       clear  clock  cns  configure
connect  copy
Switch#c
```

By typing **c?**, I got a response listing all the commands that start with *c*. Also notice that the Switch#**c** prompt reappears after the list of commands is displayed. This can be really helpful when you happen to be working with long commands but you're short on patience and still need the next possible one. It would get old fast if you actually had to retype the entire command every time you used a question mark!

So with that, let's find the next command in a string by typing the first command and then a question mark:

```
Switch#clock ?
  set  Set the time and date


Switch#clock set ?
  hh:mm:ss  Current Time


Switch#clock set 2:34 ?
% Unrecognized command
Switch#clock set 2:34:01 ?
  <1-31>  Day of the month
  MONTH   Month of the year


Switch#clock set 2:34:01 21 july ?
  <1993-2035>  Year


Switch#clock set 2:34:01 21 july 2013
Switch#
00:19:45: %SYS-6-CLOCKUPDATE: System clock has been updated from 00:19:45 UTC Mon
 Mar 1 1993 to 02:34:01 UTC Wed Aug 21 2013, configured from console by console.
```

I entered the **clock ?** command and got a list of the next possible parameters plus what they do. Make note of the fact that you can just keep typing a command, a space, and then a question mark until <cr> (carriage return) is your only option left.

And if you're typing commands and receive

```
Switch#clock set 11:15:11
% Incomplete command.
```

no worries—that's only telling you that the command string simply isn't complete quite yet. All you need to do is to press the up arrow key to redisplay the last command entered and then continue with the command by using your question mark.

But if you get the error

```
Switch(config)#access-list 100 permit host 1.1.1.1 host 2.2.2.2
                                                  ^
% Invalid input detected at '^' marker.
```

all is not well because it means you actually have entered a command incorrectly. See that little caret—the ^? It's a very helpful tool that marks the exact point where you blew it and made a mess.

Here's another example of when you'll see that caret:

```
Switch#sh fastethernet 0/0
          ^
% Invalid input detected at '^' marker.
```

This command looks right, but be careful! The problem is that the full command is show interface fastethernet 0/0.

If you receive the error

```
Switch#sh cl
% Ambiguous command:  "sh cl"
```

you're being told that there are multiple commands that begin with the string you entered and it's not unique. Use the question mark to find the exact command you need:

```
Switch#sh cl?
class-map  clock  cluster
```

Case in point: There are three commands that start with show cl.

Table 2.1 lists the enhanced editing commands available on a Cisco router.

TABLE 2.1   Enhanced editing commands

Command	Meaning
Ctrl+A	Moves your cursor to the beginning of the line
Ctrl+E	Moves your cursor to the end of the line
Esc+B	Moves back one word

Command	Meaning
Ctrl+B	Moves back one character
Ctrl+F	Moves forward one character
Esc+F	Moves forward one word
Ctrl+D	Deletes a single character
Backspace	Deletes a single character
Ctrl+R	Redisplays a line
Ctrl+U	Erases a line
Ctrl+W	Erases a word
Ctrl+Z	Ends configuration mode and returns to EXEC
Tab	Finishes typing a command for you

Another really cool editing feature you need to know about is the automatic scrolling of long lines. In the following example, the command I typed reached the right margin and automatically moved 11 spaces to the left. How do I know this? Because the dollar sign [$] is telling me that the line has been scrolled to the left:

```
Switch#config t
Switch(config)#$ 100 permit ip host 192.168.10.1 192.168.10.0 0.0.0.255
```

You can review the router-command history with the commands shown in Table 2.2.

TABLE 2.2 Router-command history

Command	Meaning
Ctrl+P or up arrow	Shows last command entered
Ctrl+N or down arrow	Shows previous commands entered
show history	Shows last 20 commands entered by default
show terminal	Shows terminal configurations and history buffer size
terminal history size	Changes buffer size (max 256)

The following example demonstrates the show history command as well as how to change the history's size. It also shows how to verify the history with the show terminal command. First, use the show history command, which will allow you to see the last 20 commands that were entered on the router (even though my particular router reveals only 10 commands because that's all I've entered since rebooting it). Check it out:

```
Switch#sh history
  sh fastethernet 0/0
  sh ru
  sh cl
  config t
  sh history
  sh flash
  sh running-config
  sh startup-config
  sh ver
  sh history
```

Okay—now, we'll use the show terminal command to verify the terminal history size:

```
Switch#sh terminal
Line 0, Location: "", Type: ""
Length: 24 lines, Width: 80 columns
Baud rate (TX/RX) is 9600/9600, no parity, 2 stopbits, 8 databits
Status: PSI Enabled, Ready, Active, Ctrl-c Enabled, Automore On
  0x40000
Capabilities: none
Modem state: Ready
[output cut]
Modem type is unknown.
Session limit is not set.
Time since activation: 00:17:22
Editing is enabled.
History is enabled, history size is 10.
DNS resolution in show commands is enabled
Full user help is disabled
Allowed input transports are none.
Allowed output transports are telnet.
Preferred transport is telnet.
No output characters are padded
No special data dispatching characters
```

Administrative Configurations

Even though the following sections aren't critical to making a router or switch *work* on a network, they're still really important.

You can configure the following administrative functions on a router and switch:

- Hostnames
- Banners
- Passwords
- Interface descriptions

Remember, none of these will make your routers or switches work better or faster, but trust me, your life will be a whole lot better if you just take the time to set these configurations on each of your network devices.

Hostnames

We use the hostname command to set the identity of the router. This is only locally significant, meaning it doesn't affect how the router performs name lookups or how the device actually works on the internetwork. But the hostname is still important because it's often used for authentication in many wide area networks (WANs). Here's an example:

```
Switch#config t
Switch(config)#hostname Todd
Todd(config)#
```

Banners

A very good reason for having a *banner* is to give any and all who dare attempt to telnet or sneak into your internetwork a little security notice. And they're very cool because you can create and customize them so that they'll greet anyone who shows up on the router with exactly the information you want them to have!

Here are the three types of banners you need to be sure you're familiar with:

- Exec process creation banner
- Login banner
- Message of the day banner

And you can see them all illustrated in the following code:

```
Todd(config)#banner ?
  LINE        c banner-text c, where 'c' is a delimiting character
  exec        Set EXEC process creation banner
  incoming    Set incoming terminal line banner
  login       Set login banner
  motd        Set Message of the Day banner
```

```
  prompt-timeout  Set Message for login authentication timeout
  slip-ppp        Set Message for SLIP/PPP
```

Message of the day (MOTD) banners are the most widely used banners because they give a message to anyone connecting to the router via Telnet or an auxiliary port or even through a console port as seen here:

```
Todd(config)#banner motd ?
LINE c banner-text c, where 'c' is a delimiting character
Todd(config)#banner motd #
Enter TEXT message. End with the character '#'.
$ Acme.com network, then you must disconnect immediately.
#
Todd(config)#^Z (Press the control key + z keys to return to privileged mode)
Todd#exit
Router con0 is now available
Press RETURN to get started.
If you are not authorized to be in Acme.com network, then you
must disconnect immediately.
Todd#
```

You can set a banner on one line like this:

```
Todd(config)#banner motd x Unauthorized access prohibited! x
```

As mentioned earlier, there are a couple of other types of banners you should be aware of:

Exec banner   You can configure a line-activation (exec) banner to be displayed when EXEC processes such as a line activation or an incoming connection to a VTY line have been created. Simply initiating a user exec session through a console port will activate the exec banner.

Login banner   You can configure a login banner for display on all connected terminals. It will show up after the MOTD banner but before the login prompts. This login banner can't be disabled on a per-line basis, so to globally disable it you've got to delete it with the no banner login command.

Here's what a login banner output looks like:

```
!
banner login ^C
-----------------------------------------------------------------
Cisco Router and Security Device Manager (SDM) is installed on this device.
This feature requires the one-time use of the username "cisco"
with the password "cisco". The default username and password
have a privilege level of 15.
Please change these publicly known initial credentials using
```

```
SDM or the IOS CLI.
Here are the Cisco IOS commands.
username <myuser>  privilege 15 secret 0 <mypassword>
no username cisco
Replace <myuser> and <mypassword> with the username and
password you want to use.
For more information about SDM please follow the instructions
in the QUICK START GUIDE for your router or go to http://www.cisco.com/go/
sdm
-----------------------------------------------------------------
^C
!
```

The previous login banner should look pretty familiar to anyone who's ever logged into an ISR router because it's the banner Cisco has in the default configuration for its ISR routers.

NOTE   Remember that the login banner is displayed before the login prompts and after the MOTD banner.

Setting Passwords

There are five passwords you'll need to secure your Cisco routers: console, auxiliary, Telnet (VTY), enable, and enable secret. The enable secret and enable password are the ones used to set the password for securing privileged mode. Once the enable commands are set, users will be prompted for a password. The other three are used to configure a password when user mode is accessed through the console port, through the auxiliary port, or via Telnet.

Let's take a look at each of these now.

Enable Passwords

You set the enable passwords from global configuration mode like this:

```
Todd(config)#enable ?
  last-resort Define enable action if no TACACS servers
             respond
  password   Assign the privileged level password
  secret     Assign the privileged level secret
  use-tacacs Use TACACS to check enable passwords
```

Here's an example that shows how to set the enable passwords:

```
Todd(config)#enable secret todd
Todd(config)#enable password todd
The enable password you have chosen is the same as your
```

```
enable secret. This is not recommended. Re-enter the
enable password.
```

If you try to set the enable secret and enable passwords the same, the router will give you a polite warning to change the second password. Make a note to yourself that if there aren't any old legacy routers involved, you don't even bother to use the enable password!

User-mode passwords are assigned via the line command like this:

```
Todd(config)#line ?
  <0-16>   First Line number
  console  Primary terminal line
  vty      Virtual terminal
```

These two lines are especially important for the exam objectives:

console Sets a console user-mode password.

vty Sets a Telnet password on the router. If this password isn't set, then by default, Telnet can't be used.

To configure user-mode passwords, choose the line you want and configure it using the login command to make the switch prompt for authentication. Let's focus on the configuration of individual lines now.

Console Password

We set the console password with the line console 0 command, but look at what happened when I tried to type **line console ?** from the (config-line)# prompt—I received an error! Here's the example:

```
Todd(config-line)#line console ?
% Unrecognized command
Todd(config-line)#exit
Todd(config)#line console ?
  <0-0>   First Line number
Todd(config-line)#password console
Todd(config-line)#login
```

You can still type **line console 0** and that will be accepted, but the help screens just don't work from that prompt. Type **exit** to go back one level, and you'll find that your help screens now work.

Because there's only one console port, I can only choose line console 0. You can set all your line passwords to the same password, but doing this isn't exactly a brilliant security move!

And it's also important to remember to apply the login command or the console port won't prompt for authentication. The way Cisco has this process set up means you can't set the login command before a password is set on a line because if you set it but don't then set a password, that line won't be usable. You'll actually get prompted for a password that doesn't exist, so Cisco's method isn't just a hassle, it makes sense and is a feature after all!

Okay, there are a few other important commands you need to know regarding the console port.

For one, the `exec-timeout 0 0` command sets the time-out for the console EXEC session to zero, ensuring that it never times out. The default time-out is 10 minutes.

`Logging synchronous` is such a cool command that it should be a default, but it's not. It's great because it's the antidote for those annoying console messages that disrupt the input you're trying to type. The messages will still pop up, but at least you get returned to your router prompt without your input being interrupted! This makes your input messages oh so much easier to read!

Here's an example of how to configure both commands:

```
Todd(config-line)#line con 0
Todd(config-line)#exec-timeout ?
  <0-35791>  Timeout in minutes
Todd(config-line)#exec-timeout 0 ?
  <0-2147483>  Timeout in seconds
  <cr>
Todd(config-line)#exec-timeout 0 0
Todd(config-line)#logging synchronous
```

 You can set the console to go from never timing out (0 0) to timing out in 35,791 minutes and 2,147,483 seconds. Remember that the default is 10 minutes.

Telnet Password

To set the user-mode password for Telnet access into the router or switch, use the `line vty` command. IOS switches typically have 16 lines, but routers running the Enterprise edition have considerably more. The best way to find out how many lines you have is to use that handy question mark like this:

```
Todd(config-line)#line vty 0 ?
% Unrecognized command
Todd(config-line)#exit
Todd(config)#line vty 0 ?
  <1-15>  Last Line number
  <cr>
Todd(config)#line vty 0 15
Todd(config-line)#password telnet
Todd(config-line)#login
```

This output clearly shows that you cannot get help from your (config-line)# prompt. You must go back to global config mode in order to use the question mark (?).

So what will happen if you try to telnet into a device that doesn't have a VTY password set? You'll receive an error saying the connection has been refused because the password isn't set. So, if you telnet into a switch and receive a message like this one that I got from SwitchB, it means the switch doesn't have the VTY password set:

```
Todd#telnet SwitchB
Trying SwitchB (10.0.0.1)…Open


Password required, but none set
[Connection to SwitchB closed by foreign host]
Todd#
```

But you can still get around this and tell the switch to allow Telnet connections without a password by using the no login command:

```
SwitchB(config-line)#line vty 0 15
SwitchB(config-line)#no login
```

WARNING   I definitely do not recommend using the no login command to allow Telnet connections without a password, unless you're in a testing or classroom environment. In a production network, always set your VTY password!

After your IOS devices are configured with an IP address, you can use the Telnet program to configure and check your routers instead of having to use a console cable. You can use the Telnet program by typing **telnet** from any command prompt (DOS or Cisco).

Auxiliary Password

To configure the auxiliary password on a router, go into global configuration mode and type **line aux ?**. And by the way, you won't find these ports on a switch. This output shows that you only get a choice of 0–0, which is because there's only one port:

```
Todd#config t
Todd(config)#line aux ?
  <0-0>  First Line number
Todd(config)#line aux 0
Todd(config-line)#login
% Login disabled on line 1, until 'password' is set
Todd(config-line)#password aux
Todd(config-line)#login
```

Setting Up Secure Shell (SSH)

I strongly recommend using Secure Shell (SSH) instead of Telnet because it creates a more secure session. The Telnet application uses an unencrypted data stream, but SSH uses encryption keys to send data so your username and password aren't sent in the clear, vulnerable to anyone lurking around!

Here are the steps for setting up SSH:

1. Set your hostname:

```
Router(config)#hostname Todd
```

2. Set the domain name—both the hostname and domain name are required for the encryption keys to be generated:

```
Todd(config)#ip domain-name Lammle.com
```

3. Set the username to allow SSH client access:

```
Todd(config)#username Todd password Lammle
```

4. Generate the encryption keys for securing the session:

```
Todd(config)#crypto key generate rsa
The name for the keys will be: Todd.Lammle.com
Choose the size of the key modulus in the range of 360 to
4096 for your General Purpose Keys. Choosing a key modulus
Greater than 512 may take a few minutes.


How many bits in the modulus [512]: 1024
% Generating 1024 bit RSA keys, keys will be non-exportable...
[OK] (elapsed time was 6 seconds)


Todd(config)#
1d14h: %SSH-5-ENABLED: SSH 1.99 has been enabled*June 24
19:25:30.035: %SSH-5-ENABLED: SSH 1.99 has been enabled
```

5. Enable SSH version 2 on the router—not mandatory, but strongly suggested:

```
Todd(config)#ip ssh version 2
```

6. Connect to the VTY lines of the switch:

```
Todd(config)#line vty 0 15
```

7. Configure your access protocols:

```
Todd(config-line)#transport input ?
  all      All protocols
  none     No protocols
  ssh      TCP/IP SSH protocol
  telnet   TCP/IP Telnet protocol
```

Beware of this next line, and make sure you never use it in production because it's a horrendous security risk:

```
Todd(config-line)#transport input all
```

I recommend using the next line to secure your VTY lines with SSH:

```
Todd(config-line)#transport input ssh ?
  telnet   TCP/IP Telnet protocol
  <cr>
```

I actually do use Telnet once in a while when a situation arises that specifically calls for it. It just doesn't happen very often. But if you want to go with Telnet, here's how you do that:

```
Todd(config-line)#transport input ssh telnet
```

Know that if you don't use the keyword telnet at the end of the command string, then only SSH will work on the device. You can go with either, just so long as you understand that SSH is way more secure than Telnet.

Encrypting Your Passwords

Because only the enable secret password is encrypted by default, you'll need to manually configure the user-mode and enable passwords for encryption.

Notice that you can see all the passwords except the enable secret when performing a show running-config on an IOS device:

```
Todd#sh running-config
Building configuration...


Current configuration : 1020 bytes
!
! Last configuration change at 00:03:11 UTC Mon Mar 1 1993
!
version 15.0
no service pad
```

```
service timestamps debug datetime msec
service timestamps log datetime msec
no service password-encryption
!
hostname Todd
!
enable secret 4 ykw.3/tgsOuy9.6qmgG/EeYOYgBvfX4v.S8UNA9Rddg
enable password todd
!
[output cut]
!
line con 0
 password console
 login
line vty 0 4
 password telnet
 login
line vty 5 15
 password telnet
 login
!
end
```

To manually encrypt your passwords, use the `service password-encryption` command. Here's how:

```
Todd#config t
Todd(config)#service password-encryption
Todd(config)#exit
Todd#show run
Building configuration...
!
!
enable secret 4 ykw.3/tgsOuy9.6qmgG/EeYOYgBvfX4v.S8UNA9Rddg
enable password 7 1506040800
!
[output cut]
!
!
line con 0
 password 7 050809013243420C
 login
```

```
line vty 0 4
 password 7 06120A2D424B1D
 login
line vty 5 15
 password 7 06120A2D424B1D
 login
!
end
Todd#config t
Todd(config)#no service password-encryption
Todd(config)#^Z
Todd#
```

The passwords will now be encrypted. All you need to do is encrypt the passwords, perform a show run, and then turn off the command if you want. This output clearly shows us that the enable password and the line passwords are all encrypted.

Descriptions

Setting descriptions on an interface is another administratively helpful thing, and like the hostname, it's also only locally significant. One case where the description command comes in really handy is when you want to keep track of circuit numbers on a switch or a router's serial WAN port.

Here's an example on my switch:

```
Todd#config t
Todd(config)#int fa0/1
Todd(config-if)#description Sales VLAN Trunk Link
Todd(config-if)#^Z
Todd#
```

And on a router serial WAN:

```
Router#config t
Router(config)#int s0/0/0
Router(config-if)#description WAN to Miami
Router(config-if)#^Z
```

You can view an interface's description with either the show running-config command or the show interface—even with the show interface description command:

```
Todd#sh run
Building configuration...
```

```
Current configuration : 855 bytes
!
interface FastEthernet0/1
 description Sales VLAN Trunk Link
!
 [output cut]
```

```
Todd#sh int f0/1
FastEthernet0/1 is up, line protocol is up (connected)
  Hardware is Fast Ethernet, address is ecc8.8202.8282 (bia ecc8.8202.8282)
  Description: Sales VLAN Trunk Link
  MTU 1500 bytes, BW 100000 Kbit/sec, DLY 100 usec,
 [output cut]
```

```
Todd#sh int description
Interface                 Status       Protocol Description
Vl1                       up           up
Fa0/1                     up           up       Sales VLAN Trunk Link
Fa0/2                     up           up
```

Exam Essentials

List the options available to connect to a Cisco device for management purposes. The three options available are the console port, the auxiliary port, and in-band communication, such as Telnet, SSH and HTTP. Don't forget, a Telnet connection is not possible until an IP address has been configured and a Telnet password has been configured.

Recognize additional prompts available and describe their use. Additional modes are reached via the global configuration prompt, **routername(config)#**, and their prompts include interface, **router(config-if)#**, for making interface settings; line configuration mode, **router(config-line)#**, used to set passwords and make other settings to various connection methods; and lastly, routing protocol modes for various routing protocols, such as **router(config-router)#**, used to enable and configure routing protocols.

Access and utilize editing and help features. Make use of typing a question mark at the end of commands for help in using the commands. Additionally, understand how to filter command help with the same question mark and letters. Use the command history to retrieve commands previously utilized without retyping. Understand the meaning of the caret when an incorrect command is rejected. Finally, identify useful hot key combinations.

Know how to set the hostname of a router.   The command sequence to set the hostname of a router is as follows:

```
enable
config t
hostname Todd
```

Differentiate between the enable password and enable secret password.   Both of these passwords are used to gain access into privileged mode. However, the enable secret password is newer and is always encrypted by default. Also, if you set the enable password and then set the enable secret, only the enable secret will be used.

Describe the configuration and use of banners.   Banners provide information to users accessing a device and can be displayed at various login prompts. They are configured with the banner command and a keyword describing the specific type of banner.

Know how to set the enable secret on a router.   To set the enable secret, you use the global config command enable secret. Do not use enable secret password password or you will set your password to password password. Here is an example:

```
enable
config t
enable secret todd
```

Know how to set the console password on a router.   To set the console password, use the following sequence:

```
enable
config t
line console 0
password todd
login
```

Know how to set the Telnet password on a router.   To set the Telnet password, the sequence is as follows:

```
enable
config t
line vty 0 4
password todd
login
```

Describe the advantages of using Secure Shell and list its requirements.   Secure Shell (SSH) uses encrypted keys to send data so that usernames and passwords (as well as all information exchanged during the life of the connection) are not sent in the clear. It requires that a hostname and domain name be configured and that encryption keys be generated.

Verify Network Status and Switch Operation Using Basic Utilities Such as Ping, Telnet, and SSH

You can use the ping and traceroute commands to test connectivity to remote devices, and both of them can be used with many protocols, not just IP. But don't forget that the show ip route command is a great troubleshooting command for verifying your routing table and the show interfaces command will reveal the status of each interface to you.

I'm not going to get into the show interfaces commands here, but in addition to ping and traceroute, I am going to go over both the debug command and the show processes command that come in very handy when you need to troubleshoot a router.

ping Command

So far, you've seen lots of examples of pinging devices to test IP connectivity and name resolution using the DNS server. To see all the different protocols that you can use with the *ping* program, type **ping ?**:

```
SW-1#ping ?
  WORD  Ping destination address or hostname
  clns  CLNS echo
  ip    IP echo
  ipv6  IPv6 echo
  tag   Tag encapsulated IP echo
  <cr>
```

The ping output displays the minimum, average, and maximum times it takes for a ping packet to find a specified system and return. Here's an example:

```
SW-1#ping SW-3
Translating "SW-3"...domain server (4.4.4.4) [OK]
Type escape sequence to abort.
Sending 5, 100-byte ICMP Echos to 10.100.128.8, timeout is
  2 seconds:
!!!!!
Success rate is 100 percent (5/5), round-trip min/avg/max
  = 28/31/32 ms
```

This output tells us that the DNS server was used to resolve the name and the device was pinged in a minimum of 28 ms (milliseconds), an average of 31 ms, and up to 32 ms. This network has some latency!

The ping command can be used in user and privileged mode but not con-figuration mode!

traceroute Command

Traceroute—the traceroute command, or trace for short—shows the path a packet takes to get to a remote device. It uses time to live (TTL), time-outs, and ICMP error messages to outline the path a packet takes through an internetwork to arrive at a remote host.

The trace command, which you can deploy from either user mode or privileged mode, allows you to figure out which router in the path to an unreachable network host should be examined more closely as the probable cause of your network's failure.

To see the protocols that you can use with the traceroute command, type **traceroute ?**:

```
SW-1#traceroute ?
  WORD       Trace route to destination address or hostname
  appletalk  AppleTalk Trace
  clns       ISO CLNS Trace
  ip         IP Trace
  ipv6       IPv6 Trace
  ipx        IPX Trace
  mac        Trace Layer2 path between 2 endpoints
  oldvines   Vines Trace (Cisco)
  vines      Vines Trace (Banyan)
  <cr>
```

The traceroute command shows the hop or hops that a packet traverses on its way to a remote device.

Do not get confused! You can't use the tracert command; that's a Win-dows command. For a router, use the traceroute command!

Keep in mind that although it looks similar, tracert is a Windows command. Here's an example of using tracert on a Windows prompt:

```
C:\>tracert www.whitehouse.gov


Tracing route to a1289.g.akamai.net [69.8.201.107]
over a maximum of 30 hops:
```

```
1      *          *          *        Request timed out.
2    53 ms     61 ms     53 ms    hlrn-dsl-gw15-207.hlrn.qwest.net [207.225.112.207]
3    53 ms     55 ms     54 ms    hlrn-agw1.inet.qwest.net [71.217.188.113]
4    54 ms     53 ms     54 ms    hlr-core-01.inet.qwest.net [205.171.253.97]
5    54 ms     53 ms     54 ms    apa-cntr-01.inet.qwest.net [205.171.253.26]
6    54 ms     53 ms     53 ms    63.150.160.34
7    54 ms     54 ms     53 ms    www.whitehouse.gov [69.8.201.107]
```

Trace complete.

Okay, let's move on now and talk about how to troubleshoot your network using the debug command.

Debugging

Debug is a useful troubleshooting command that's available from the privileged exec mode of Cisco IOS. It's used to display information about various router operations and the related traffic generated or received by the router, and it displays error messages.

Because debugging output takes priority over other network traffic and because the debug all command generates more output than any other debug command, it can severely diminish the router's performance—even render it unusable! Because of this, it's nearly always best to use more specific debug commands.

As you can see from the following output, you can't enable debugging from user mode, only privileged mode:

```
SW-1>debug ?
% Unrecognized command
SW-1>en
SW-1#debug ?
  aaa                 AAA Authentication, Authorization and Accounting
  access-expression   Boolean access expression
  adjacency           adjacency
  aim                 Attachment Information Manager
  all                 Enable all debugging
  archive             debug archive commands
  arp                 IP ARP and HP Probe transactions
  authentication      Auth Manager debugging
  auto                Debug Automation
  beep                BEEP debugging
  bgp                 BGP information
  bing                Bing(d) debugging
```

```
call-admission      Call admission control
cca                 CCA activity
cdp                 CDP information
cef                 CEF address family independent operations
cfgdiff             debug cfgdiff commands
cisp                CISP debugging
clns                CLNS information
cluster             Cluster information
cmdhd               Command Handler
cns                 CNS agents
condition           Condition
configuration       Debug Configuration behavior
[output cut]
```

To disable debugging on a router, just use the command no in front of the debug command:

```
SW-1#no debug all
```

I typically just use the undebug all command since it is so easy when using the shortcut:

```
SW-1#un all
```

Remember that instead of using the debug all command, it's usually a much better idea to use specific commands—and only for short periods of time. Here's an example:

```
S1#debug ip icmp
ICMP packet debugging is on
S1#ping 192.168.10.17


Type escape sequence to abort.
Sending 5, 100-byte ICMP Echos to 192.168.10.17, timeout is 2 seconds:
!!!!!
Success rate is 100 percent (5/5), round-trip min/avg/max = 1/1/1 ms
S1#
1w4d: ICMP: echo reply sent, src 192.168.10.17, dst 192.168.10.17
1w4d: ICMP: echo reply rcvd, src 192.168.10.17, dst 192.168.10.17
1w4d: ICMP: echo reply sent, src 192.168.10.17, dst 192.168.10.17
1w4d: ICMP: echo reply rcvd, src 192.168.10.17, dst 192.168.10.17
1w4d: ICMP: echo reply sent, src 192.168.10.17, dst 192.168.10.17
1w4d: ICMP: echo reply rcvd, src 192.168.10.17, dst 192.168.10.17
1w4d: ICMP: echo reply sent, src 192.168.10.17, dst 192.168.10.17
1w4d: ICMP: echo reply rcvd, src 192.168.10.17, dst 192.168.10.17
1w4d: ICMP: echo reply sent, src 192.168.10.17, dst 192.168.10.17
```

```
1w4d: ICMP: echo reply rcvd, src 192.168.10.17, dst 192.168.10.17
SW-1#un all
```

I'm sure you can see that the debug command is one powerful command. And because of this, I'm also sure you realize that before you use any of the debugging commands, you should make sure you check the CPU utilization capacity of your router. This is important because in most cases, you don't want to negatively impact the device's ability to process the packets on your internetwork. You can determine a specific router's CPU utilization information by using the show processes command.

Remember, when you telnet into a remote device, you will not see console messages by default! For example, you will not see debugging output. To allow console messages to be sent to your Telnet session, use the terminal monitor command.

show processes Command

The show processes command (or show processes cpu) is a good tool for determining a given router's CPU utilization. Plus, it'll give you a list of active processes along with their corresponding process ID, priority, scheduler test (status), CPU time used, number of times invoked, and so on.

```
SW-1#sh processes
CPU utilization for five seconds: 5%/0%; one minute: 7%; five minutes: 8%
 PID QTy       PC Runtime(ms)  Invoked    uSecs    Stacks  TTY Process
   1 Cwe 29EBC58         0         22        0  5236/6000    0 Chunk Manager
   2 Csp 1B9CF10       241     206881        1  2516/3000    0 Load Meter
   3 Hwe 1F108D0         0          1        0  8768/9000    0 Connection Mgr
   4 Lst 29FA5C4   9437909     454026    20787  5540/6000    0 Check heaps
   5 Cwe 2A02468         0          2        0  5476/6000    0 Pool Manager
   6 Mst 1E98F04         0          2        0  5488/6000    0 Timers
   7 Hwe 13EB1B4      3686     101399       36  5740/6000    0 Net Input
   8 Mwe 13BCD84         0          1        0 23668/24000   0 Crash writer
   9 Mwe 1C591B4      4346      53691       80  4896/6000    0 ARP Input
  10 Lwe 1DA1504         0          1        0  5760/6000    0 CEF MIB API
  11 Lwe 1E76ACC         0          1        0  5764/6000    0 AAA_SERVER_DEADT
  12 Mwe 1E6F980         0          2        0  5476/6000    0 AAA high-capacit
  13 Mwe 1F56F24         0          1        0 11732/12000   0 Policy Manager
[output cut]
```

So basically, the output from the show processes command reveals that our router is happily able to process debugging commands without being overloaded—nice!

To see how to use Telnet and SSH to verify a network, please see the section "Configure and Verify Initial Switch Configuration Including Remote Access Management."

Exam Essentials

Describe the function of the `ping` command.   Packet Internet Groper (Ping) uses ICMP echo requests and ICMP echo replies to verify an active IP address on a network.

Understand the function of the `traceroute` command.   The traceroute command shows the path a packet takes to reach a remote device using time to live (TTL) and ICMP messages.

Identify Enhanced Switching Technologies

Spanning Tree Protocol (STP) was developed to put an end to loop issues in a layer 2 switched network. That's why we'll be thoroughly exploring the key features of this vital protocol as well as how it works within a switched network in this objective.

RSTP

Rapid Spanning Tree Protocol (RSTP), or IEEE 802.1w, is essentially an evolution of STP that allows for much faster convergence. But even though it does address all the convergence issues, it still permits only a single STP instance.

The good news is that Cisco IOS can run the Rapid PVST+ protocol—a Cisco enhancement of RSTP that provides a separate 802.1w spanning-tree instance for each VLAN configured within the network.

Keep in mind that Cisco documentation may say STP 802.1d and RSTP 802.1w, but it is referring to the PVST+ enhancement of each version.

Understand that RSTP wasn't meant to be something completely new and different. The protocol is more of an evolution than an innovation of the 802.1d standard, which offers faster convergence whenever a topology change occurs. Backward compatibility was a must when 802.1w was created.

So, RSTP helps with convergence issues that were the bane of traditional STP. Rapid PVST+ is based on the 802.1w standard in the same way that PVST+ is based on 802.1d.

The operation of Rapid PVST+ is simply a separate instance of 802.1w for each VLAN. Here's a list to clarify how this all breaks down:

- RSTP speeds the recalculation of the spanning tree when the layer 2 network topology changes.
- It's an IEEE standard that redefines STP port roles, states, and BPDUs.
- RSTP is extremely proactive and very quick, so it doesn't need the 802.1d delay timers.
- RSTP (802.1w) supersedes 802.1d while remaining backward compatible.
- Much of the 802.1d terminology and most parameters remain unchanged.
- 802.1w is capable of reverting to 802.1d to interoperate with traditional switches on a per-port basis.

And to clear up confusion, there are also five terminology adjustments between 802.1d's five port states to 802.1w's, compared here, respectively:

802.1d State		802.1w State
Disabled	=	Discarding
Blocking	=	Discarding
Listening	=	Discarding
Learning	=	Learning
Forwarding	=	Forwarding

Make note of the fact that RSTP basically just goes from discarding to learning to forwarding, whereas 802.1d requires five states to transition.

The task of determining the root bridge, root ports, and designated ports hasn't changed from 802.1d to RSTP, and understanding the cost of each link is still key to making these decisions well. Let's take a look at an example of how to determine ports using the newly revised IEEE cost specifications in Figure 2.11.

Can you figure out which is the root bridge? How about which port is the root and which ones are designated? Well, because SC has the lowest MAC address, it becomes the root bridge, and since all ports on a root bridge are forwarding designated ports, well, that's easy, right? Ports Gi0/1 and Gi0/10 become designated forwarding ports on SC.

But which one would be the root port for SA? To figure that out, we must first find the port cost for the direct link between SA and SC. Even though the root bridge (SC) has a Gigabit Ethernet port, it's running at 100 Mbps because SA's port is a 100 Mbps port, giving it a cost of 19. If the paths between SA and SC were both Gigabit Ethernet, their costs would be only 4, but because they're running 100 Mbps links instead, the cost jumps to a whopping 19!

FIGURE 2.11   RSTP example 1

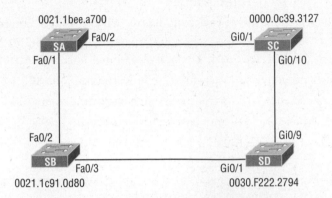

Can you find SD's root port? A quick glance at the link between SC and SD tells us that's a Gigabit Ethernet link with a cost of 4, so the root port for SD would be its Gi0/9 port.

The cost of the link between SB and SD is also 19 because it's also a Fast Ethernet link, bringing the full cost from SB to SD to the root (SC) to a total cost of 19 + 4 = 23. If SB were to go through SA to get to SC, then the cost would be 19 + 19, or 38, so the root port of SB becomes the Fa0/3 port.

The root port for SA would be the Fa0/1 port since that's a direct link with a cost of 19. Going through SB to SD would be 19 + 19 + 4 = 42, so we'll use that as a backup link for SA to get to the root just in case we need to.

Now, all we need is a forwarding port on the link between SA and SB. Because SA has the lowest bridge ID, Fa0/1 on SA wins that role. Also, the Gi0/1 port on SD would become a designated forwarding port. This is because the SB Fa0/3 port is a designated root port and you must have a forwarding port on a network segment! This leaves us with the Fa0/2 port on SB. Since it isn't a root port or designated forwarding port, it will be placed into blocking mode, which will prevent loops in our network.

Let's take a look at this example network when it has converged in Figure 2.12.

FIGURE 2.12   RSTP example 1 answer

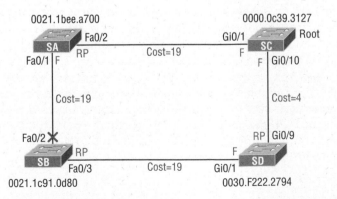

If this isn't clear and still seems confusing, just remember to always tackle this process following these three steps:

1. Find your root bridge by looking at bridge IDs.
2. Determine your root ports by finding the lowest path cost to the root bridge.
3. Find your designated ports by looking at bridge IDs.

PVSTP

Per-VLAN Spanning Tree Protocol+ (PVSTP+) is a Cisco proprietary extension to 801.2d STP that provides a separate 802.1 spanning-tree instance for each VLAN configured on your switches. All of the Cisco proprietary extensions were created to improve convergence times, which is 50 seconds by default. Cisco IOS switches run 802.1d PVST+ by default, which means you'll have optimal path selection, but the convergence time will still be slow.

Creating a per-VLAN STP instance for each VLAN is worth the increased CPU and memory requirements because it allows for per-VLAN root bridges. This feature allows the STP tree to be optimized for the traffic of each VLAN by allowing you to configure the root bridge in the center of each of them. Figure 2.13 shows how PVST+ would look in an optimized switched network with multiple redundant links.

FIGURE 2.13   PVST+ provides efficient root bridge selection.

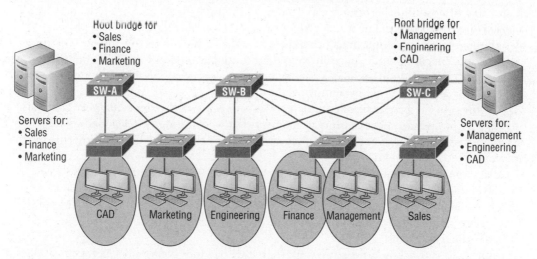

This root bridge placement clearly enables faster convergence as well as optimal path determination. This version's convergence is really similar to 802.1 CST's, which has one instance of STP no matter how many VLANs you have configured on your network. The difference is that with PVST+, convergence happens on a per-VLAN basis, with each VLAN running its own instance of STP, which shows us that we now have a nice, efficient root bridge selection for each VLAN.

To allow for PVST+ to operate, there's a field inserted into the BPDU to accommodate the extended system ID so that PVST+ can have a root bridge configured on a per-STP instance, shown in Figure 2.14. The bridge ID actually becomes smaller—only 4 bits—which means that we would configure the bridge priority in blocks of 4,096 rather than in increments of 1 as we did with CST. The extended system ID (VLAN ID) is a 12-bit field, and we can even see what this field is carrying via show spanning-tree command output, which I'll show you soon.

FIGURE 2.14   PVST+ unique bridge ID

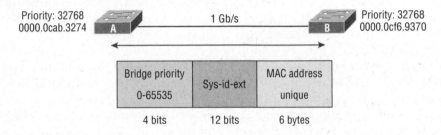

Etherchannels

Know that almost all Ethernet networks today will typically have multiple links between switches because this kind of design provides redundancy and resiliency. On a physical design that includes multiple links between switches, STP will do its job and put a port or ports into blocking mode. In addition to that, routing protocols like OSPF and EIGRP could see all these redundant links as individual ones, depending on the configuration, which can mean an increase in routing overhead.

We can gain the benefits from multiple links between switches by using port channeling. EtherChannel is a port channel technology that was originally developed by Cisco as a switch-to-switch technique for grouping several Fast Ethernet or Gigabit Ethernet ports into one logical channel.

Also important to note is that once your port channel (EtherChannel) is up and working, layer 2 STP and layer 3 routing protocols will treat those bundled links as a single one, which would stop STP from performing blocking. An additional nice result is that because the routing protocols now only see this as a single link, a single adjacency across the link can be formed—elegant!

Figure 2.15 shows how a network would look if we had four connections between switches, before and after configuring port channels.

There is a Cisco version and the IEEE version of port channel negotiation protocols. Cisco's version is called Port Aggregation Protocol (PAgP), and the IEEE 802.3ad standard is called Link Aggregation Control Protocol (LACP).

Cisco EtherChannel allows us to bundle up to eight active ports between switches. The links must have the same speed, duplex setting, and VLAN configuration—in other words, you can't mix interface types and configurations into the same bundle.

FIGURE 2.15   Before and after port channels

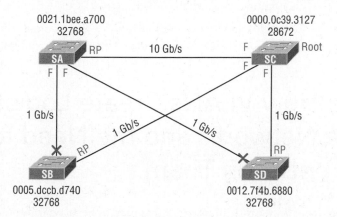

There are a few differences in configuring PAgP and LACP, but first, let's go over some terms so you don't get confused:

Port channeling   Refers to combining two to eight Fast Ethernet or two Gigabit Ethernet ports together between two switches into one aggregated logical link to achieve more band-width and resiliency.

EtherChannel   Cisco's proprietary term for port channeling.

PAgP   This is a Cisco proprietary port channel negotiation protocol that aids in the automatic creation of EtherChannel links. All links in the bundle must match the same parameters (speed, duplex, VLAN info), and when PAgP identifies matched links, it groups the links into an EtherChannel. This is then added to STP as a single bridge port. At this point, PAgP's job is to send packets every 30 seconds to manage the link for consistency, any link additions and modifications, and failures.

LACP (802.3ad)   This has the exact same purpose as PAgP but is nonproprietary so it can work between multi-vendor networks.

`Channel-group`   This is a command on Ethernet interfaces used to add the specified interface to a single EtherChannel. The number following this command is the port-channel ID.

`Interface port-channel`   This is a command that creates the bundled interface. Ports can be added to this interface with the `channel-group` command. Keep in mind that the interface number must match the group number.

Exam Essentials

Remember what RSTP and PVSTP are used for.   Rapid Spanning Tree Protocol (RSTP) is an evolution of Spanning Tree Protocol (STP) that allows much faster convergence in a single instance of STP. Per-VLAN Spanning Tree Protocol provides a separate spanning-tree instance for each VLAN configured on a switch.

Understand what EtherChannel is and how to configure it.   EtherChannel allows you to bundle links to get more bandwidth instead of allowing STP to shut down redundant ports.

Describe How VLANs Create Logically Separate Networks and the Need for Routing between Them

Figure 2.16 illustrates the flat network architecture that used to be so typical for layer 2 switched networks. With this configuration, every broadcast packet transmitted is seen by every device on the network regardless of whether the device needs to receive that data.

FIGURE 2.16   Flat network structure

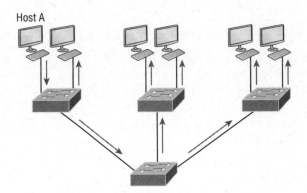

By default, routers allow broadcasts to occur only within the originating network, while switches forward broadcasts to all segments. The reason it's called a *flat network* is because it's one *broadcast domain*, not because the actual design is physically flat. In Figure 2.16, we see Host A sending out a broadcast and all ports on all switches forwarding it—all except the port that originally received it.

Now check out Figure 2.17. It pictures a switched network and shows Host A sending a frame with Host D as its destination. Clearly, the important factor here is that the frame is only forwarded out the port where Host D is located.

FIGURE 2.17   The benefit of a switched network

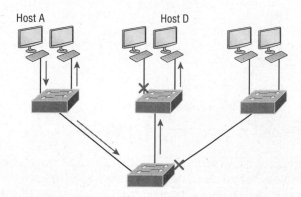

This is a huge improvement over the old hub networks, unless having one *collision domain* by default is what you really want for some reason!

The biggest benefit gained by having a layer 2 switched network is that it creates individual collision domain segments for each device plugged into each port on the switch.

The other big issue—security! This one is real trouble because within the typical layer 2 switched internetwork, all users can see all devices by default. And you can't stop devices from broadcasting, plus you can't stop users from trying to respond to broadcasts. This means your security options are dismally limited to placing passwords on your servers and other devices.

You can solve many of the problems associated with layer 2 switching with virtual LANs (VLANs).

Figure 2.18 shows all hosts in this very small company connected to one switch, meaning all hosts will receive all frames, which is the default behavior of all switches.

FIGURE 2.18   One switch, one LAN: before VLANs, there were no separations between hosts.

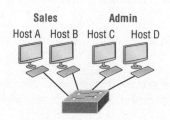

If we want to separate the host's data, we could either buy another switch or create VLANs, as shown in Figure 2.19.

FIGURE 2.19   One switch, two virtual LANs (*logical* separation between hosts): still physically one switch, but this switch acts as many separate devices.

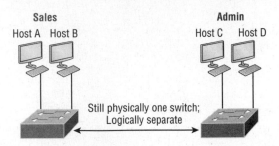

In Figure 2.19, I configured the switch to be two separate LANs, two subnets, two broadcast domains, two VLANs—they all mean the same thing—without buying another switch.

Notice that even though the separation is virtual and the hosts are all still connected to the same switch, the LANs can't send data to each other by default. This is because they are still separate networks.

VLANs simplify network management:

- Network adds, moves, and changes are achieved with ease by just configuring a port into the appropriate VLAN.

- A group of users that need an unusually high level of security can be put into its own VLAN so that users outside of that VLAN can't communicate with it.

- As a logical grouping of users by function, VLANs can be considered independent from their physical or geographic locations.

- VLANs greatly enhance network security if implemented correctly.

- VLANs increase the number of broadcast domains while decreasing their size.

Broadcast Control

Broadcasts occur in every protocol, but how often they occur depends upon three things:

- The type of protocol

- The application(s) running on the internetwork

- How these services are used

Some older applications have been rewritten to reduce their bandwidth consumption, but there's a new generation of applications that are so bandwidth greedy they'll consume any and all they can find.

Since switches have become more affordable, most everyone has replaced their flat hub networks with pure switched network and VLAN environments. All devices within a VLAN are members of the same broadcast domain and receive all broadcasts relevant to it. By default, these broadcasts are filtered from all ports on a switch that aren't members of the same VLAN.

Explain Network Segmentation and Basic Traffic Management Concepts

Switch ports are layer 2–only interfaces that are associated with a physical port that can belong to only one VLAN if it's an access port or all VLANs if it's a trunk port.

Switches are definitely pretty busy devices. As myriad frames are switched throughout the network, switches have to be able to keep track of all of them plus understand what to do with them depending on their associated hardware addresses. And remember, frames are handled differently according to the type of link they're traversing.

There are two different types of ports in a switched environment. Let's take a look at the first type in Figure 2.20.

FIGURE 2.20   Access ports

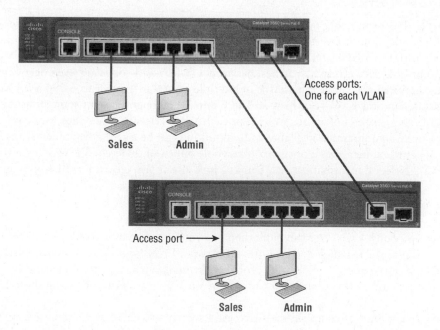

Notice there are access ports for each host and an access port between switches—one for each VLAN.

Access ports   An *access port* belongs to and carries the traffic of only one VLAN. Traffic is both received and sent in native formats with no VLAN information (tagging) whatsoever. Anything arriving on an access port is simply assumed to belong to the VLAN assigned to the port. Because an access port doesn't look at the source address, tagged traffic—a frame with added VLAN information—can be correctly forwarded and received only on trunk ports.

With an access link, this can be referred to as the *configured VLAN* of the port. Any device attached to an *access link* is unaware of a VLAN membership—the device just assumes it's part of some broadcast domain.

Voice access ports   Not to confuse you, but all that I just said about the fact that an access port can be assigned to only one VLAN is really only sort of true. Nowadays, most switches will allow you to add a second VLAN to an access port on a switch port for your voice traffic, called the voice VLAN. The voice VLAN used to be called the auxiliary VLAN, which allowed it to be overlaid on top of the data VLAN, enabling both types of traffic to travel through the same port. Even though this is technically considered to be a different type of link, it's still just an access port that can be configured for both data and voice VLANs. This allows you to connect both a phone and a PC device to one switch port but still have each device in a separate VLAN.

Trunk ports   The term *trunk port* was inspired by the telephone system trunks, which carry multiple telephone conversations at a time. So it follows that trunk ports can similarly carry multiple VLANs at a time as well. A *trunk link* is a 100, 1,000, or 10,000 Mbps point-to-point link between two switches, between a switch and router, or even between a switch and server, and it carries the traffic of multiple VLANs—from 1 to 4,094 VLANs at a time. But the amount is really only up to 1,001 unless you're going with something called extended VLANs. Instead of an access link for each VLAN between switches, you can create a trunk link, demonstrated in Figure 2.21. Trunking can be a real advantage because with it, you get to make a single port part of a whole bunch of different VLANs at the same time. All VLANs send information on a trunked link unless you clear each VLAN by hand.

Frame Tagging

You can set up your VLANs to span more than one connected switch. You can see that going on in Figure 2.21, which depicts hosts from two VLANs spread across two switches. This flexible, power-packed capability is probably the main advantage to implementing VLANs, and we can do this with up to a thousand VLANs and thousands upon thousands of hosts!

All this can get kind of complicated—even for a switch—so there needs to be a way for each one to keep track of all the users and frames as they travel the switch fabric and VLANs. When I say "switch fabric," I'm just referring to a group of switches that share the same VLAN information. And this just happens to be where *frame tagging* enters the scene. This frame identification method uniquely assigns a user-defined VLAN ID to each frame.

FIGURE 2.21   VLANs can span across multiple switches by using trunk links, which carry traffic for multiple VLANs.

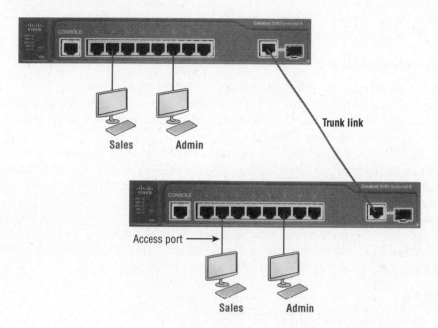

Here's how it works: Once within the switch fabric, each switch that the frame reaches must first identify the VLAN ID from the frame tag. It then finds out what to do with the frame by looking at the information in what's known as the filter table. If the frame reaches a switch that has another trunked link, the frame will be forwarded out of the trunk-link port.

Once the frame reaches an exit that's determined by the forward/filter table to be an access link matching the frame's VLAN ID, the switch will remove the VLAN identifier. This is so the destination device can receive the frames without being required to understand their VLAN identification information.

Another great thing about trunk ports is that they'll support tagged and untagged traffic simultaneously if you're using 802.1q trunking, which we will talk about next. The trunk port is assigned a default port VLAN ID (PVID) for a VLAN upon which all untagged traffic will travel. This VLAN is also called the native VLAN and is always VLAN 1 by default, but it can be changed to any VLAN number.

Similarly, any untagged or tagged traffic with a NULL (unassigned) VLAN ID is assumed to belong to the VLAN with the port default PVID. Again, this would be VLAN 1 by default. A packet with a VLAN ID equal to the outgoing port native VLAN is sent untagged and can communicate to only hosts or devices in that same VLAN. All other VLAN traffic has to be sent with a VLAN tag to communicate within a particular VLAN that corresponds with that tag.

VLAN Identification Methods

VLAN identification is what switches use to keep track of all those frames as they're traversing a switch fabric. It's how switches identify which frames belong to which VLANs, and there's more than one trunking method.

Inter-Switch Link (ISL)

Inter-Switch Link (ISL) is a way of explicitly tagging VLAN information onto an Ethernet frame. This tagging information allows VLANs to be multiplexed over a trunk link through an external encapsulation method. This allows the switch to identify the VLAN membership of a frame received over the trunked link.

By running ISL, you can interconnect multiple switches and still maintain VLAN information as traffic travels between switches on trunk links. ISL functions at layer 2 by encapsulating a data frame with a new header and by performing a new cyclic redundancy check (CRC).

ISL is proprietary to Cisco switches, and it's used for Fast Ethernet and Gigabit Ethernet links only. *ISL routing* is pretty versatile and can be used on a switch port, router interfaces, and server interface cards to trunk a server. Although some Cisco switches still support ISL frame tagging, Cisco is moving toward using only 802.1q.

IEEE 802.1q

Created by the IEEE as a standard method of frame tagging, IEEE 802.1q actually inserts a field into the frame to identify the VLAN. If you're trunking between a Cisco switched link and a different brand of switch, you've got to use 802.1q for the trunk to work.

Unlike ISL, which encapsulates the frame with control information, 802.1q inserts an 802.1q field along with tag control information, as shown in Figure 2.22.

FIGURE 2.22   IEEE 802.1q encapsulation with and without the 802.1q tag

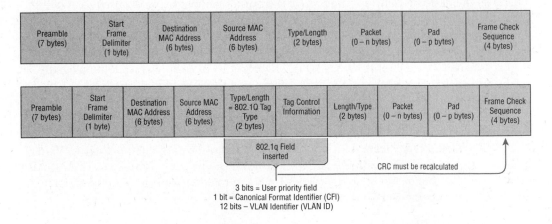

For the Cisco exam objectives, it's only the 12-bit VLAN ID that matters. This field identifies the VLAN and can be 2^{12}, minus 2 for the 0 and 4095 reserved VLANs, which means an 802.1q tagged frame can carry information for 4,094 VLANs.

It works like this: You first designate each port that's going to be a trunk with 802.1q encapsulation. The other ports must be assigned a specific VLAN ID in order for them to communicate. VLAN 1 is the default native VLAN, and when using 802.1q, all traffic for a native VLAN is untagged. The ports that populate the same trunk create a group with this native VLAN, and each port gets tagged with an identification number reflecting that. Again, the default is VLAN 1. The native VLAN allows the trunks to accept information that was received without any VLAN identification or frame tag.

Exam Essentials

Understand the term *frame tagging*.   *Frame tagging* refers to VLAN identification; this is what switches use to keep track of all those frames as they're traversing a switch fabric. It's how switches identify which frames belong to which VLANs.

Understand the 802.1q VLAN identification method.   This is a nonproprietary IEEE method of frame tagging. If you're trunking between a Cisco switched link and a different brand of switch, you have to use 802.1q for the trunk to work.

Configure and Verify VLANs

To configure VLANs on a Cisco Catalyst switch, use the global config vlan command. Remember that VLAN 1 is the native and management VLAN by default:

```
S1(config)#vlan ?
  WORD       ISL VLAN IDs 1-4094
  access-map Create vlan access-map or enter vlan access-map command mode
  dot1q      dot1q parameters
  filter     Apply a VLAN Map
  group      Create a vlan group
  internal   internal VLAN
S1(config)#vlan 2
S1(config-vlan)#name Sales
S1(config-vlan)#vlan 3
S1(config-vlan)#name Marketing
S1(config-vlan)#vlan 4
S1(config-vlan)#name Accounting
S1(config-vlan)#^Z
S1#
```

In this output, you can see that you can create VLANs from 1 to 4094. But this is only mostly true. As I said, VLANs can really only be created up to 1001, and you can't use, change, rename, or delete VLANs 1 or 1002 through 1005 because they're reserved. The VLAN numbers above 1005 are called extended VLANs and won't be saved in the database unless your switch is set to what is called VLAN Trunk Protocol (VTP) transparent mode. You won't see these VLAN numbers used too often in production. Here's an example of me attempting to set my S1 switch to VLAN 4000 when my switch is set to VTP server mode (the default VTP mode):

```
S1#config t
S1(config)#vlan 4000
S1(config-vlan)#^Z
% Failed to create VLANs 4000
Extended VLAN(s) not allowed in current VTP mode.
%Failed to commit extended VLAN(s) changes.
```

After you create the VLANs that you want, you can use the show vlan command to check them out. But notice that, by default, all ports on the switch are in VLAN 1. To change the VLAN associated with a port, you need to go to each interface and specifically tell it which VLAN to be a part of.

 Remember that a created VLAN is unused until it is assigned to a switch port or ports and that all ports are always assigned in VLAN 1 unless set otherwise.

Once the VLANs are created, verify your configuration with the show vlan command (sh vlan for short):

```
S1#sh vlan
```

VLAN	Name	Status	Ports
1	default	active	Fa0/1, Fa0/2, Fa0/3, Fa0/4
			Fa0/5, Fa0/6, Fa0/7, Fa0/8
			Fa0/9, Fa0/10, Fa0/11, Fa0/12
			Fa0/13, Fa0/14, Fa0/19, Fa0/20
			Fa0/21, Fa0/22, Fa0/23, Gi0/1
			Gi0/2
2	Sales	active	
3	Marketing	active	
4	Accounting	active	

[output cut]

I want you to remember that you can't change, delete, or rename VLAN 1 because it's the default VLAN and you just can't change that—period. It's also the native VLAN of all switches by default, and Cisco recommends that you use it as your management VLAN. If you're worried about security issues, then change it! Basically, any ports that aren't specifically assigned to a different VLAN will be sent down to the native VLAN—VLAN 1.

In the preceding S1 output, you can see that ports Fa0/1 through Fa0/14, Fa0/19 through 23, and Gi0/1 and Gi02 uplinks are all in VLAN 1. But where are ports 15 through 18? First, understand that the command show vlan only displays access ports, so now that you know what you're looking at with the show vlan command, where do you think ports Fa15–18 are? That's right! They are trunked ports. Cisco switches run a proprietary protocol called *Dynamic Trunking Protocol (DTP)*, and if there is a compatible switch connected, they will dynamically negotiate in hopes to start trunking automatically, which is precisely where my four ports are. You have to use the show interfaces trunk command to see your trunked ports like this:

```
S1# show interfaces trunk
Port        Mode          Encapsulation  Status     Native vlan
Fa0/15      desirable     n-isl          trunking   1
Fa0/16      desirable     n-isl          trunking   1
Fa0/17      desirable     n-isl          trunking   1
Fa0/18      desirable     n-isl          trunking   1


Port        Vlans allowed on trunk
Fa0/15      1-4094
Fa0/16      1-4094
Fa0/17      1-4094
Fa0/18      1-4094


[output cut]
```

This output reveals that the VLANs from 1 to 4094 are allowed across the trunk by default. Another helpful command, which is also part of the Cisco exam objectives, is the show interfaces *interface* switchport command:

```
S1#sh interfaces fastEthernet 0/15 switchport
Name: Fa0/15
Switchport: Enabled
Administrative Mode: dynamic desirable
Operational Mode: trunk
Administrative Trunking Encapsulation: negotiate
Operational Trunking Encapsulation: isl
Negotiation of Trunking: On
```

```
Access Mode VLAN: 1 (default)
Trunking Native Mode VLAN: 1 (default)
Administrative Native VLAN tagging: enabled
Voice VLAN: none
[output cut]
```

The underlined output shows us the administrative mode of dynamic desirable, that the port is a trunk port, and that DTP was used to negotiate the frame tagging method of ISL. It also predictably shows that the native VLAN is the default of 1.

Now that we can see the VLANs created, we can assign switch ports to specific ones. Each port can be part of only one VLAN, with the exception of voice access ports. Using trunking, you can make a port available to traffic from all VLANs. I'll cover that next.

Assigning Switch Ports to VLANs

You configure a port to belong to a VLAN by assigning a membership mode that specifies the kind of traffic the port carries plus the number of VLANs it can belong to. You can also configure each port on a switch to be in a specific VLAN (access port) by using the interface switchport command. You can even configure multiple ports at the same time with the interface range command.

In the next example, I'll configure interface Fa0/3 to VLAN 3. This is the connection from the S3 switch to the host device:

```
S3#config t
S3(config)#int fa0/3
S3(config-if)#switchport ?
  access        Set access mode characteristics of the interface
  autostate     Include or exclude this port from vlan link up calculation
  backup        Set backup for the interface
  block         Disable forwarding of unknown uni/multi cast addresses
  host          Set port host
  mode          Set trunking mode of the interface
  nonegotiate   Device will not engage in negotiation protocol on this
                interface
  port-security Security related command
  priority      Set appliance 802.1p priority
  private-vlan  Set the private VLAN configuration
  protected     Configure an interface to be a protected port
  trunk         Set trunking characteristics of the interface
  voice         Voice appliance attributes  voice
```

Let's start with setting an access port on S1, which is probably the most widely used type of port you'll find on production switches that have VLANs configured:

```
S3(config-if)#switchport mode ?
    access         Set trunking mode to ACCESS unconditionally
    dot1q-tunnel   set trunking mode to TUNNEL unconditionally
    dynamic        Set trunking mode to dynamically negotiate access or trunk mode
    private-vlan   Set private-vlan mode
    trunk          Set trunking mode to TRUNK unconditionally
```

```
S3(config-if)#switchport mode access
S3(config-if)#switchport access vlan 3
```

By starting with the switchport mode access command, you're telling the switch that this is a nontrunking layer 2 port. You can then assign a VLAN to the port with the switchport access command. Remember, you can choose many ports to configure simultaneously with the interface range command.

```
S3#show vlan
VLAN Name                        Status    Ports
---- -------------------------   --------- -------------------------------
1    default                     active    Fa0/4, Fa0/5, Fa0/6, Fa0/7
                                           Fa0/8, Fa0/9, Fa0/10, Fa0/11,
                                           Fa0/12, Fa0/13, Fa0/14, Fa0/19,
                                           Fa0/20, Fa0/21, Fa0/22, Fa0/23,
                                           Gi0/1 ,Gi0/2


2    Sales                       active
3    Marketing                   active    Fa0/3
```

Notice that port Fa0/3 is now a member of VLAN 3. But, can you tell me where ports 1 and 2 are? And why aren't they showing up in the output of show vlan? That's right, because they are trunk ports!

We can also see this with the show interfaces interface switchport command:

```
S3#sh int fa0/3 switchport
Name: Fa0/3
Switchport: Enabled
Administrative Mode: static access
Operational Mode: static access
Administrative Trunking Encapsulation: negotiate
Negotiation of Trunking: Off
Access Mode VLAN: 3 (Marketing)
```

The underlined output shows that Fa0/3 is an access port and a member of VLAN 3 (Marketing).

If you plug devices into each VLAN port, they can talk only to other devices in the same VLAN.

Exam Essentials

Remember to check a switch port's VLAN assignment when plugging in a new host.   If you plug a new host into a switch, then you must verify the VLAN membership of that port. If the membership is different than what is needed for that host, the host will not be able to reach the needed network services, such as a workgroup server or printer.

Configure and Verify Trunking on Cisco Switches

The 2960 switch only runs the IEEE 802.1q encapsulation method. To configure trunking on a Fast Ethernet port, use the interface command switchport mode trunk. It's a bit different on the 3560 switch.

The following switch output shows the trunk configuration on interfaces Fa0/15–18 as set to trunk:

```
S1(config)#int range f0/15-18
S1(config-if-range)#switchport trunk encapsulation dot1q
S1(config-if-range)#switchport mode trunk
```

If you have a switch that only runs the 802.1q encapsulation method, then you wouldn't use the encapsulation command as I did in the preceding output. Let's check out our trunk ports now:

```
S1(config-if-range)#do sh int f0/15 swi
Name: Fa0/15
Switchport: Enabled
Administrative Mode: trunk
Operational Mode: trunk
Administrative Trunking Encapsulation: dot1q
Operational Trunking Encapsulation: dot1q
Negotiation of Trunking: On
Access Mode VLAN: 1 (default)
Trunking Native Mode VLAN: 1 (default)
```

```
Administrative Native VLAN tagging: enabled
Voice VLAN: none
```

Notice that port Fa0/15 is a trunk and running 802.1q. Let's take another look:

```
S1(config-if-range)#do sh int trunk
Port        Mode              Encapsulation Status        Native vlan
Fa0/15      on                802.1q        trunking      1
Fa0/16      on                802.1q        trunking      1
Fa0/17      on                802.1q        trunking      1
Fa0/18      on                802.1q        trunking      1
Port        Vlans allowed on trunk
Fa0/15      1-4094
Fa0/16      1-4094
Fa0/17      1-4094
Fa0/18      1-4094
```

Take note of the fact that ports 15–18 are now in the trunk mode of on and the encapsulation is now 802.1q instead of the negotiated ISL. Here's a description of the different options available when configuring a switch interface:

switchport mode access   As discussed in the previous section, this puts the interface (access port) into permanent nontrunking mode and negotiates to convert the link into a nontrunk link. The interface becomes a nontrunk interface regardless of whether the neighboring interface is a trunk interface. The port would be a dedicated layer 2 access port.

switchport mode dynamic auto   This mode makes the interface able to convert the link to a trunk link. The interface becomes a trunk interface if the neighboring interface is set to trunk or desirable mode. The default is dynamic auto on a lot of Cisco switches, but that default trunk method is changing to dynamic desirable on most new models.

switchport mode dynamic desirable   This one makes the interface actively attempt to convert the link to a trunk link. The interface becomes a trunk interface if the neighboring interface is set to trunk, desirable, or auto mode. This is now the default switch port mode for all Ethernet interfaces on all new Cisco switches.

switchport mode trunk   Puts the interface into permanent trunking mode and negotiates to convert the neighboring link into a trunk link. The interface becomes a trunk interface even if the neighboring interface isn't a trunk interface.

switchport nonegotiate   This prevents the interface from generating DTP frames. You can use this command only when the interface switchport mode is access or trunk. You must manually configure the neighboring interface as a trunk interface to establish a trunk link.

Dynamic Trunking Protocol (DTP) is used for negotiating trunking on a link between two devices as well as negotiating the encapsulation type of either 802.1q or ISL. I use the nonegotiate command when I want dedicated trunk ports; no questions asked.

To disable trunking on an interface, use the switchport mode access command, which sets the port back to a dedicated layer 2 access switch port.

Defining the Allowed VLANs on a Trunk

Trunk ports send and receive information from all VLANs by default, and if a frame is untagged, it's sent to the native VLAN. Understand that this applies to the extended range VLANs too.

We can remove VLANs from the allowed list to prevent traffic from certain VLANs from traversing a trunked link. Notice that all VLANs are allowed across the trunk link by default:

```
S1#sh int trunk
[output cut]
Port       Vlans allowed on trunk
Fa0/15     1-4094
Fa0/16     1-4094
Fa0/17     1-4094
Fa0/18     1-4094


S1(config)#int f0/15
S1(config-if)#switchport trunk allowed vlan 4,6,12,15
S1(config-if)#do show int trunk
[output cut]
Port       Vlans allowed on trunk
Fa0/15     4,6,12,15
Fa0/16     1-4094
Fa0/17     1-4094
Fa0/18     1-4094
```

The preceding command affected the trunk link configured on S1 port F0/15, causing it to forward any traffic sent and received for only VLANs 4, 6, 12, and 15. You can try to remove VLAN 1 on a trunk link, but it will still send and receive management like CDP, DTP, and VTP.

To remove a range of VLANs, just use the hyphen:

```
S1(config-if)#switchport trunk allowed vlan remove 4-8
```

To set the trunk back to default:

```
S1(config-if)#switchport trunk allowed vlan all
```

Changing or Modifying the Trunk Native VLAN

You can change the trunk port native VLAN from VLAN 1, which many people do for security reasons. To change the native VLAN, use the following command:

```
S1(config)#int f0/15
S1(config-if)#switchport trunk native vlan ?
  <1-4094>  VLAN ID of the native VLAN when this port is in trunking mode


S1(config-if)#switchport trunk native vlan 4
1w6d: %CDP-4-NATIVE_VLAN_MISMATCH: Native VLAN mismatch discovered on
FastEthernet0/15 (4), with S3 FastEthernet0/1 (1).
```

So we've changed our native VLAN on our trunk link to 4, and by using the show running-config command, I can see the configuration under the trunk link:

```
S1#sh run int f0/15
Building configuration...


Current configuration : 202 bytes
!
interface FastEthernet0/15
 description 1st connection to S3
 switchport trunk encapsulation dot1q
 switchport trunk native vlan 4
 switchport trunk allowed vlan 4,6,12,15
 switchport mode trunk
end


S1#!
```

If all switches don't have the same native VLAN configured on the given trunk links, then we'll start to receive this error, which happened immediately after I entered the command:

```
1w6d: %CDP-4-NATIVE_VLAN_MISMATCH: Native VLAN mismatch discovered
on FastEthernet0/15 (4), with S3 FastEthernet0/1 (1).
```

This is a good, noncryptic error, so either we can go to the other end of our trunk link(s) and change the native VLAN or we set the native VLAN back to the default to fix it:

```
S1(config-if)#no switchport trunk native vlan
1w6d: %SPANTREE-2-UNBLOCK_CONSIST_PORT: Unblocking FastEthernet0/15
on VLAN0004. Port consistency restored.
```

Now our trunk link is using the default VLAN 1 as the native VLAN.

DTP

Many Cisco switches support the Cisco proprietary Dynamic Trunking Protocol (DTP), which is used to manage automatic trunk negotiation between switches. Cisco recommends that you don't allow this and to configure your switch ports manually instead.

Let's check out our switch port Gi0/13 on S1 and view its DTP status. I'll use the show dtp interface *interface* command to view the DTP statistics:

```
S1#sh dtp interface gi0/13
DTP information for GigabitEthernet0/13:
    TOS/TAS/TNS:                            ACCESS/AUTO/ACCESS
    TOT/TAT/TNT:                            NATIVE/NEGOTIATE/NATIVE
    Neighbor address 1:                     00211C910D8D
    Neighbor address 2:                     000000000000
    Hello timer expiration (sec/state):     12/RUNNING
    Access timer expiration (sec/state):    never/STOPPED
```

Auto Negotiation

Let's check out the different options available on the S1 switch with the switchport mode dynamic command:

```
S1(config-if)#switchport mode ?
  access        Set trunking mode to ACCESS unconditionally
  dot1q-tunnel  set trunking mode to TUNNEL unconditionally
  dynamic       Set trunking mode to dynamically negotiate access or trunk mode
  private-vlan  Set private-vlan mode
  trunk         Set trunking mode to TRUNK unconditionally
```

```
S1(config-if)#switchport mode dynamic ?
  auto       Set trunking mode dynamic negotiation parameter to AUTO
  desirable  Set trunking mode dynamic negotiation parameter to DESIRABLE
```

From interface mode, use the switch mode trunk command to turn trunking on. You can also use the switch mode dynamic command to set the port to auto or desirable trunking modes. To turn off DTP and any type of negotiation, use the switchport nonegotiate command.

Let's take a look at S2 and see if we can figure out why our two switches didn't create a trunk:

```
S2#sh int gi0/13 switchport
Name: Gi0/13
```

```
Switchport: Enabled
Administrative Mode: dynamic auto
Operational Mode: static access
Administrative Trunking Encapsulation: negotiate
Operational Trunking Encapsulation: native
Negotiation of Trunking: On
```

We can see that the port is in dynamic auto and that it's operating as an access port:

S2#**sh dtp interface gi0/13**
```
DTP information for GigabitEthernet0/3:
  DTP information for GigabitEthernet0/13:
  TOS/TAS/TNS:                        ACCESS/AUTO/ACCESS
  TOT/TAT/TNT:                        NATIVE/NEGOTIATE/NATIVE
  Neighbor address 1:                 000000000000
  Neighbor address 2:                 000000000000
  Hello timer expiration (sec/state): 17/RUNNING
  Access timer expiration (sec/state): never/STOPPED
```

Do you see the problem? Don't be fooled—it's not that they're running in access mode; it's because two ports in dynamic auto will not form a trunk! This is a really common problem to look for since most Cisco switches ship in dynamic auto. The other issue you need to be aware of, as well as check for, is the frame tagging method. Some switches run 802.1q, some run both 802.1q and *Inter-Switch Link (ISL) routing*, so be sure the tagging method is compatible between all of your switches!

It's time to fix our problem on the trunk ports between S1 and S2. All we need to do is to just fix one side of each link since dynamic auto will trunk with a port set to desirable or on:

S2(config)#**int gi0/13**
S2(config-if)#**switchport mode dynamic desirable**
23:11:37:%LINEPROTO-5-UPDOWN:Line protocol on Interface GigabitEthernet0/13, changed state to down
23:11:37:%LINEPROTO-5-UPDOWN:Line protocol on Interface Vlan1, changed state to down
23:11:40:%LINEPROTO-5-UPDOWN:Line protocol on Interface GigabitEthernet0/13, changed state to up
23:12:10:%LINEPROTO-5-UPDOWN:Line protocol on Interface Vlan1, changed state to up
S2(config-if)#**do show int trunk**

```
Port      Mode        Encapsulation  Status     Native vlan
Gi0/13    desirable   n-isl          trunking   1
[output cut]
```

Nice—it worked! With one side in auto and the other now in desirable, DTPs will be exchanged and they will trunk. Notice in the preceding output that the mode of S2's Gi0/13 link is desirable and that the switches actually negotiated ISL as a trunk encapsulation—go figure! But don't forget to notice the native VLAN. We'll work on the frame tagging method and native VLAN in a minute, but first, let's configure our other link:

```
S2(config-if)#int gi0/14
S2(config-if)#switchport mode dynamic desirable
23:12:%LINEPROTO-5-UPDOWN:Line protocol on Interface GigabitEthernet0/14,
changed state to down
23:12:%LINEPROTO-5-UPDOWN:Line protocol on Interface GigabitEthernet0/14,
changed state to up
S2(config-if)#do show int trunk


Port       Mode         Encapsulation  Status      Native vlan
Gi0/13     desirable    n-isl          trunking    1
Gi0/14     desirable    n-isl          trunking    1


Port       Vlans allowed on trunk
Gi0/13     1-4094
Gi0/14     1-4094
[output cut]
```

Great, we now have two trunked links between switches.

Exam Essentials

Remember how to set a trunk port on a 2960 switch.   To set a port to trunking on a 2960, use the switchport mode trunk command.

Configure and Verify PVSTP Operation

To verify spanning tree on a Cisco switch, just use the command show spanning-tree. From its output, we can determine our root bridge, priorities, root ports, and designated and blocking/discarding ports.

Let's use the same simple three-switch network we used earlier as the base to play around with the configuration of STP. Figure 2.23 shows the network we'll work with in this section.

FIGURE 2.23   Our simple three-switch network

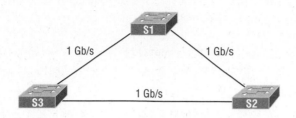

Let's start by taking a look at the output from S1:

```
S1#sh spanning-tree vlan 1
VLAN0001
  Spanning tree enabled protocol ieee
  Root ID    Priority    32769
             Address     0001.42A7.A603
             This bridge is the root
             Hello Time  2 sec  Max Age 20 sec  Forward Delay 15 sec


  Bridge ID  Priority    32769  (priority 32768 sys id ext 1)
             Address     0001.42A7.A603 him
             Hello Time  2 sec  Max Age 20 sec  Forward Delay 15 sec
             Aging Time  20


Interface        Role Sts Cost      Prio.Nbr Type
---------------- ---- --- --------- -------- --------------------------------

Gi1/1            Desg FWD 4         128.25   P2p
Gi1/2            Desg FWD 4         128.26   P2p
```

First, we can see that we're running the IEEE 802.1d STP version by default, and don't forget that this is really 802.1d PVST+! Looking at the output, we can see that S1 is the root bridge for VLAN 1. When you use this command, the top information is about the root bridge, and the bridge ID output refers to the bridge you're looking at. In this example, they are the one and the same. Notice the sys-id-ext 1 (for VLAN 1). This is the 12-bit PVST+ field that is placed into the BPDU so it can carry multiple-VLAN information. You add the priority and sys-id-ext to come up with the true priority for the VLAN. We can also see from the output that both Gigabit Ethernet interfaces are designated forwarding ports. You will not see a blocked/discarding port on a root bridge. Now let's take a look at S3's output:

```
S3#sh spanning-tree
VLAN0001
```

```
 Spanning tree enabled protocol ieee
 Root ID    Priority    32769
            Address     0001.42A7.A603
            Cost        4
            Port        26(GigabitEthernet1/2)
            Hello Time  2 sec  Max Age 20 sec  Forward Delay 15 sec


 Bridge ID  Priority    32769  (priority 32768 sys-id-ext 1)
            Address     000A.41D5.7937
            Hello Time  2 sec  Max Age 20 sec  Forward Delay 15 sec
            Aging Time  20


Interface       Role Sts Cost     Prio.Nbr Type
--------------- ---- --- -------- -------- --------------------------------
Gi1/1           Desg FWD 4        128.25   P2p
Gi1/2           Root FWD 4        128.26   P2p
```

Looking at the root ID, it's easy to see that S3 isn't the root bridge because the MAC addresses of the root bridge and this bridge are different and there is a root port. But the output tells us it's a cost of 4 to get to the root bridge and also that it's located out port 26 of the switch (Gi1/2). This tells us that the root bridge is one Gigabit Ethernet link away, which we already know is S1, but we can confirm this with the show cdp neighbors command:

```
Switch#sh cdp nei
Capability Codes: R - Router, T - Trans Bridge, B - Source Route Bridge
                  S - Switch, H - Host, I - IGMP, r - Repeater, P - Phone
Device ID    Local Intrfce   Holdtme    Capability   Platform   Port ID
S3           Gig 1/1         135             S        2960       Gig 1/1
S1           Gig 1/2         135             S        2960       Gig 1/1
```

That's how simple it is to find your root bridge if you don't have the nice figure as we do. Use the show spanning-tree command, find your root port, and then use the show cdp neighbors command. Let's see what S2's output has to tell us now:

```
S2#sh spanning-tree
VLAN0001
  Spanning tree enabled protocol ieee
  Root ID    Priority    32769
             Address     0001.42A7.A603
             Cost        4
             Port        26(GigabitEthernet1/2)
             Hello Time  2 sec  Max Age 20 sec  Forward Delay 15 sec
```

```
Bridge ID  Priority    32769  (priority 32768 sys-id-ext 1)
           Address     0030.F222.2794
           Hello Time  2 sec  Max Age 20 sec  Forward Delay 15 sec
           Aging Time  20


Interface        Role Sts Cost      Prio.Nbr Type
---------------- ---- --- --------- -------- -------------------------------
Gi1/1            Altn BLK 4         128.25   P2p
Gi1/2            Root FWD 4         128.26   P2p
```

We're certainly not looking at a root bridge since we're seeing a blocked port, which is S2's connection to S3!

Let's make S2 the root bridge for VLAN 2 and for VLAN 3:

```
S2#sh spanning-tree vlan 2
VLAN0002
  Spanning tree enabled protocol ieee
  Root ID    Priority    32770
             Address     0001.42A7.A603
             Cost        4
             Port        26(GigabitEthernet1/2)
             Hello Time  2 sec  Max Age 20 sec  Forward Delay 15 sec


  Bridge ID  Priority    32770  (priority 32768 sys-id-ext 2)
             Address     0030.F222.2794
             Hello Time  2 sec  Max Age 20 sec  Forward Delay 15 sec
             Aging Time  20


Interface        Role Sts Cost      Prio.Nbr Type
---------------- ---- --- --------- -------- -------------------------------
Gi1/1            Altn BLK 4         128.25   P2p
Gi1/2            Root FWD 4         128.26   P2p
```

We can see that the root bridge cost is 4, meaning that the root bridge is one gigabit link away. One more key factor I want to talk about before making S2 the root bridge for VLANs 2 and 3 is the sys-id-ext, which shows up as 2 in this output because this output is for VLAN 2. This sys-id-ext is added to the bridge priority, which in this case is 32768 + 2, which makes the priority 32770. Okay, now that you understand what that output is telling us, let's make S2 the root bridge:

```
S2(config)#spanning-tree vlan 2 ?
  priority  Set the bridge priority for the spanning tree
```

```
 root       Configure switch as root
 <cr>
S2(config)#spanning-tree vlan 2 priority ?
 <0-61440>  bridge priority in increments of 4096
S2(config)#spanning-tree vlan 2 priority 16384
```

You can set the priority to any value from 0 through 61440 in increments of 4096. Setting it to zero (0) means that the switch will always be a root as long as it has a lower MAC address than another switch that also has its bridge ID set to 0. If you want to set a switch to be the root bridge for every VLAN in your network, then you have to change the priority for each VLAN, with 0 being the lowest priority you can use. But trust me—it's never a good idea to set all switches to a priority of 0!

Furthermore, you don't actually need to change priorities because there is yet another way to configure the root bridge. Take a look:

```
S2(config)#spanning-tree vlan 3 root ?
 primary    Configure this switch as primary root for this spanning tree
 secondary  Configure switch as secondary root
S2(config)#spanning-tree vlan 3 root primary
```

Notice that you can set a bridge to either primary or secondary—very cool! Let's check to see if S2 is actually the root bridge for VLANs 2 and 3 now:

```
S2#sh spanning-tree vlan 2
VLAN0002
  Spanning tree enabled protocol ieee
  Root ID    Priority    16386
             Address     0030.F222.2794
             This bridge is the root
             Hello Time  2 sec  Max Age 20 sec  Forward Delay 15 sec


  Bridge ID  Priority    16386  (priority 16384 sys-id-ext 2)
             Address     0030.F222.2794
             Hello Time  2 sec  Max Age 20 sec  Forward Delay 15 sec
             Aging Time  20


Interface        Role Sts Cost      Prio.Nbr Type
---------------- ---- --- --------- -------- ------------------------------
Gi1/1            Desg FWD 4         128.25   P2p
Gi1/2            Desg FWD 4         128.26   P2p
```

Nice—S2 is the root bridge for VLAN 2, with a priority of 16386 (16384 + 2). Let's take a look to see the root bridge for VLAN 3. I'll use a different command for that this time. Check it out:

```
S2#sh spanning-tree summary
Switch is in pvst mode
Root bridge for: VLAN0002 VLAN0003
Extended system ID           is enabled
Portfast Default             is disabled
PortFast BPDU Guard Default  is disabled
Portfast BPDU Filter Default is disabled
Loopguard Default            is disabled
EtherChannel misconfig guard is disabled
UplinkFast                   is disabled
BackboneFast                 is disabled
Configured Pathcost method used is short
```

Name	Blocking	Listening	Learning	Forwarding	STP Active
VLAN0001	1	0	0	1	2
VLAN0002	0	0	0	2	2
VLAN0003	0	0	0	2	2
3 vlans	1	0	0	5	6

The preceding output tells us that S2 is the root for the two VLANs, but we can see we have a blocked port for VLAN 1 on S2, so it's not the root bridge for VLAN 1. This is because there's another bridge with a better bridge ID for VLAN 1 than S2's.

Here's how you enable RSTP on a Cisco switch:

```
S2(config)#spanning-tree mode rapid-pvst
```

It's a global command, not per VLAN. Let's verify we're running RSTP now:

```
S2#sh spanning-tree
VLAN0001
  Spanning tree enabled protocol rstp
  Root ID    Priority    32769
             Address     0001.42A7.A603
             Cost        4
             Port        26(GigabitEthernet1/2)
             Hello Time  2 sec  Max Age 20 sec  Forward Delay 15 sec
```

```
[output cut]
S2#sh spanning-tree summary
Switch is in rapid-pvst mode
Root bridge for: VLAN0002 VLAN0003
```

Looks like we're set! We're running RSTP, S1 is our root bridge for VLAN 1, and S2 is the root bridge for VLANs 2 and 3. I know this doesn't seem hard, and it really isn't, but you still need to practice what we've covered so far in this chapter to really get your skills solid!

Describe Root Bridge Election

The bridge ID is used to elect the root bridge in the STP domain and to determine the root port for each of the remaining devices when there's more than one potential root port available because they have equal-cost paths. This key bridge ID is 8 bytes long and includes both the priority and the MAC address of the device, as illustrated in Figure 2.24. Remember—the default priority on all devices running the IEEE STP version is 32,768.

FIGURE 2.24 STP operations

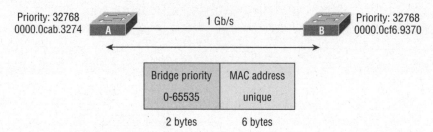

To determine the root bridge, you combine the priority of each bridge with its MAC address. If two switches or bridges happen to have the same priority value, the MAC address becomes the tiebreaker for figuring out which one has the lowest and, therefore, best ID. The two switches in Figure 2.24 are both using the default priority of 32,768, so the MAC address will be the determining factor instead.

And because Switch A's MAC address is 0000.0cab.3274 and Switch B's MAC address is 0000.0cf6.9370, Switch A wins and will become the root bridge.

Prior to the election of the root bridge, BPDUs are sent every 2 seconds out all active ports on a bridge/switch by default, and they're received and processed by all bridges. The root bridge is elected based on this information. You can change the bridge's ID by lowering its priority so that it will become a root bridge automatically. Being able to do that is important in a large switched network because it ensures that the best paths will actually be the ones chosen. Efficiency is always awesome in networking!

To verify spanning tree on a Cisco switch, just use the command show spanning-tree. From its output, we can determine our root bridge, priorities, root ports, and designated and blocking/discarding ports.

Let's use the same simple three-switch network we used earlier as the base to play around with the configuration of STP. Refer back to Figure 2.23, which shows the network we'll work with in this section.

Let's start by taking a look at the output from S1:

```
S1#sh spanning-tree vlan 1
VLAN0001
  Spanning tree enabled protocol ieee
  Root ID    Priority    32769
             Address     0001.42A7.A603
             This bridge is the root
             Hello Time   2 sec  Max Age 20 sec  Forward Delay 15 sec


  Bridge ID  Priority    32769  (priority 32768 sys-id-ext 1)
             Address     0001.42A7.A603 him
             Hello Time   2 sec  Max Age 20 sec  Forward Delay 15 sec
             Aging Time  20


Interface        Role Sts Cost      Prio.Nbr Type
---------------- ---- --- --------- -------- --------------------------------
Gi1/1            Desg FWD 4         128.25   P2p
Gi1/2            Desg FWD 4         128.26   P2p
```

First, we can see that we're running the IEEE 802.1d STP version by default, and don't forget that this is really 802.1d PVST+! Looking at the output, we can see that S1 is the root bridge for VLAN 1. When you use this command, the top information is about the root bridge, and the bridge ID output refers to the bridge you're looking at. In this example, they are the one and the same. Notice the sys-id-ext 1 (for VLAN 1). This is the 12-bit PVST+ field that is placed into the BPDU so it can carry multiple-VLAN information. You add the priority and sys-id-ext to come up with the true priority for the VLAN. We can also see from the output that both Gigabit Ethernet interfaces are designated forwarding ports. You will not see a blocked/discarding port on a root bridge. Now let's take a look at S3's output:

```
S3#sh spanning-tree
VLAN0001
  Spanning tree enabled protocol ieee
  Root ID    Priority    32769
             Address     0001.42A7.A603
             Cost        4
             Port        26(GigabitEthernet1/2)
             Hello Time   2 sec  Max Age 20 sec  Forward Delay 15 sec
```

```
Bridge ID  Priority    32769  (priority 32768 sys-id-ext 1)
           Address     000A.41D5.7937
           Hello Time  2 sec  Max Age 20 sec  Forward Delay 15 sec
           Aging Time  20


Interface         Role Sts Cost      Prio.Nbr Type
----------------  ---- --- --------- -------- -----------------------------
Gi1/1             Desg FWD 4         128.25   P2p
Gi1/2             Root FWD 4         128.26   P2p
```

Looking at the root ID, it's easy to see that S3 isn't the root bridge, because the MAC addresses of the root bridge and this bridge are different, and there is a root port. But the output tells us it's a cost of 4 to get to the root bridge and also that it's located out port 26 of the switch (Gi1/2). This tells us that the root bridge is one Gigabit Ethernet link away, which we already know is S1, but we can confirm this with the show cdp neighbors command:

```
Switch#sh cdp nei
Capability Codes: R - Router, T - Trans Bridge, B - Source Route Bridge
                  S - Switch, H - Host, I - IGMP, r - Repeater, P - Phone
Device ID   Local Intrfce   Holdtme    Capability   Platform   Port ID
S3          Gig 1/1         135            S        2960       Gig 1/1
S1          Gig 1/2         135            S        2960       Gig 1/1
```

That's how simple it is to find your root bridge if you don't have the nice figure as we do. Use the show spanning-tree command, find your root port, and then use the show cdp neighbors command. Let's see what S2's output has to tell us now:

```
S2#sh spanning-tree
VLAN0001
  Spanning tree enabled protocol ieee
  Root ID    Priority    32769
             Address     0001.42A7.A603
             Cost        4
             Port        26(GigabitEthernet1/2)
             Hello Time  2 sec  Max Age 20 sec  Forward Delay 15 sec


  Bridge ID  Priority    32769  (priority 32768 sys-id-ext 1)
             Address     0030.F222.2794
             Hello Time  2 sec  Max Age 20 sec  Forward Delay 15 sec
             Aging Time  20
```

```
Interface        Role Sts Cost      Prio.Nbr Type
---------------- ---- --- --------- -------- -------------------------------
Gi1/1            Altn BLK 4          128.25   P2p
Gi1/2            Root FWD 4          128.26   P2p
```

We're certainly not looking at a root bridge since we're seeing a blocked port, which is S2's connection to S3!

Let's make S2 the root bridge for VLAN 2 and for VLAN 3:

```
S2#sh spanning-tree vlan 2
VLAN0002
  Spanning tree enabled protocol ieee
  Root ID    Priority    32770
             Address     0001.42A7.A603
             Cost        4
             Port        26(GigabitEthernet1/2)
             Hello Time  2 sec  Max Age 20 sec  Forward Delay 15 sec


  Bridge ID  Priority    32770  (priority 32768 sys-id-ext 2)
             Address     0030.F222.2794
             Hello Time  2 sec  Max Age 20 sec  Forward Delay 15 sec
             Aging Time  20


Interface        Role Sts Cost      Prio.Nbr Type
---------------- ---- --- --------- -------- -------------------------------
Gi1/1            Altn BLK 4          128.25   P2p
Gi1/2            Root FWD 4          128.26   P2p
```

We can see that the root bridge cost is 4, meaning that the root bridge is one gigabit link away. One more key factor I want to talk about before making S2 the root bridge for VLANs 2 and 3 is the sys-id-ext, which shows up as 2 in this output because this output is for VLAN 2. This sys-id-ext is added to the bridge priority, which in this case is 32768 + 2, which makes the priority 32770.

```
S2(config)#spanning-tree vlan 2 ?
  priority  Set the bridge priority for the spanning tree
  root      Configure switch as root
  <cr>
S2(config)#spanning-tree vlan 2 priority ?
  <0-61440>  bridge priority in increments of 4096
S2(config)#spanning-tree vlan 2 priority 16384
```

You can set the priority to any value from 0 through 61440 in increments of 4096. Setting it to zero (0) means that the switch will always be a root as long as it has a lower MAC address than another switch that also has its bridge ID set to 0. If you want to set a switch to be the root bridge for every VLAN in your network, then you have to change the priority for each VLAN, with 0 being the lowest priority you can use. But trust me—it's never a good idea to set all switches to a priority of 0!

Furthermore, you don't actually need to change priorities because there is yet another way to configure the root bridge. Take a look:

```
S2(config)#spanning-tree vlan 3 root ?
  primary    Configure this switch as primary root for this spanning tree
  secondary  Configure switch as secondary root
S2(config)#spanning-tree vlan 3 root primary
```

Notice that you can set a bridge to either primary or secondary—very cool! Let's check to see if S2 is actually the root bridge for VLANs 2 and 3 now:

```
S2#sh spanning-tree vlan 2
VLAN0002
  Spanning tree enabled protocol ieee
  Root ID    Priority    16386
             Address     0030.F222.2794
             This bridge is the root
             Hello Time  2 sec  Max Age 20 sec  Forward Delay 15 sec


  Bridge ID  Priority    16386  (priority 16384 sys-id-ext 2)
             Address     0030.F222.2794
             Hello Time  2 sec  Max Age 20 sec  Forward Delay 15 sec
             Aging Time  20


Interface        Role Sts Cost      Prio.Nbr Type
---------------- ---- --- --------- -------- -------------------------------
Gi1/1            Desg FWD 4         128.25   P2p
Gi1/2            Desg FWD 4         128.26   P2p
```

Nice—S2 is the root bridge for VLAN 2, with a priority of 16386 (16384 + 2). Let's take a look to see the root bridge for VLAN 3. I'll use a different command for that this time. Check it out:

```
S2#sh spanning-tree summary
Switch is in pvst mode
Root bridge for: VLAN0002 VLAN0003
Extended system ID            is enabled
```

```
Portfast Default              is disabled
PortFast BPDU Guard Default   is disabled
Portfast BPDU Filter Default  is disabled
Loopguard Default             is disabled
EtherChannel misconfig guard  is disabled
UplinkFast                    is disabled
BackboneFast                  is disabled
Configured Pathcost method used is short
```

Name	Blocking	Listening	Learning	Forwarding	STP Active
VLAN0001	1	0	0	1	2
VLAN0002	0	0	0	2	2
VLAN0003	0	0	0	2	2
3 vlans	1	0	0	5	6

The preceding output tells us that S2 is the root for the two VLANs, but we can see we have a blocked port for VLAN 1 on S2, so it's not the root bridge for VLAN 1. This is because there's another bridge with a better bridge ID for VLAN 1 than S2's.

Here's how to enable RSTP on a Cisco switch.

```
S2(config)#spanning-tree mode rapid-pvst
```

Let's verify we're running RSTP now:

```
S2#sh spanning-tree
VLAN0001
  Spanning tree enabled protocol rstp
  Root ID    Priority    32769
             Address     0001.42A7.A603
             Cost        4
             Port        26(GigabitEthernet1/2)
             Hello Time  2 sec  Max Age 20 sec  Forward Delay 15 sec
[output cut
S2#sh spanning-tree summary
Switch is in rapid-pvst mode
Root bridge for: VLAN0002 VLAN0003
```

We're running RSTP, S1 is our root bridge for VLAN 1, and S2 is the root bridge for VLANs 2 and 3.

Spanning Tree Mode

It is important that you understand the various modes and terms that a bridge can perform and use with STP.

Root bridge　The *root bridge* is the bridge with the lowest, and therefore the best, bridge ID. The switches within the STP network elect a root bridge, which becomes the focal point in the network. All other decisions in the network, like which ports on the non-root bridges should be blocked or put in forwarding mode, are made from the perspective of the root bridge, and once it has been elected, all other bridges must create a single path to it. The port with the best path to the root bridge is called the root port.

Non-root bridges　These are all bridges that aren't the root bridge. Non-root bridges exchange BPDUs with all the other bridges and update the STP topology database on all switches. This prevents loops and helps defend against link failures.

BPDU　All switches exchange information to use for the subsequent configuration of the network. Each switch compares the parameters in the *Bridge Protocol Data Unit (BPDU)* that it sends to a neighbor with the parameters in the BPDU that it receives from other neighbors. Inside the BPDU is the bridge ID.

Bridge ID　The *bridge ID* is how STP keeps track of all the switches in the network. It's determined by a combination of the bridge priority, which is 32,768 by default on all Cisco switches, and the base MAC address. The bridge with the lowest bridge ID becomes the root bridge in the network. Once the root bridge is established, every other switch must make a single path to it. Most networks benefit by forcing a specific bridge or switch to be the root bridge by setting its bridge priority lower than the default value.

Port cost　*Port cost* determines the best path when multiple links are used between two switches. The cost of a link is determined by the bandwidth of a link, and this path cost is the deciding factor used by every bridge to find the most efficient path to the root bridge.

Path cost　A switch may encounter one or more switches on its path to the root bridge, and there may be more than one possible path. All unique paths are analyzed individually, and a *path cost* is calculated for each unique path by adding the individual port costs encountered on the way to the root bridge.

Bridge Port Roles

STP uses roles on each port connected between switches to determine how a port on a switch will act within the spanning-tree algorithm. Let's take a look at the roles each port between switches can play.

Root port　The *root port* is the link with the lowest path cost to the root bridge. If more than one link connects to the root bridge, then a port cost is found by checking the bandwidth of each link. The lowest-cost port becomes the root port. When multiple links connect to the same device, the port connected to the lowest port number on the upstream switch will be the one that's used. The root bridge can never have a root port designation, while every other switch in a network must have one and only one root port.

Designated port   A *designated port* is one that's been determined to have the best (lowest) cost to get to on a given network segment, compared to other ports on that segment. A designated port will be marked as a forwarding port, and you can have only one forwarding port per network segment.

Non-designated port   A *non-designated port* is one with a higher cost to the root bridge than the designated port. These are basically the ones left over after the root ports and designated ports have been determined. Non-designated ports are put in blocking or discarding mode—they are not forwarding ports!

Forwarding port   A *forwarding port* forwards frames and will be either a root port or a designated port.

Blocked port   A *blocked port* won't forward user frames in order to prevent loops. A blocked port will still always listen to BPDU frames from neighbor switches, but it will drop any and all other frames received and will never transmit a frame.

Alternate port   The *alternate port* corresponds to the blocking state of 802.1d. *Alternate* port is a term used with the newer 802.1w ([k]Rapid Spanning Tree Protocol). An alternative port is located on a switch connected to a LAN segment with two or more switches connected, and one of the other switches holds the designated port.

Backup port   The *backup port* corresponds to the blocking state of 802.1d. *Backup port* is a term now used with the newer 802.1w. A backup port is connected to a LAN segment where another port on that switch is acting as the designated port.

Exam Essentials

Understand the main purpose of the Spanning Tree Protocol in a switched LAN.   The main purpose of STP is to prevent switching loops in a network with redundant switched paths.

Remember the states of STP.   The purpose of the blocking state is to prevent the use of looped paths. A port in listening state prepares to forward data frames without populating the MAC address table. A port in learning state populates the MAC address table but doesn't forward data frames. A port in forwarding state sends and receives all data frames on the bridged port. Also, a port in the disabled state is virtually nonoperational.

Remember the command `show spanning-tree`.   You must be familiar with the command show spanning-tree and how to determine the root bridge of each VLAN. Also, you can use the show spanning-tree summary command to help you get a quick glimpse of your STP network and root bridges.

Review Questions

The following questions are designed to test your understanding of this chapter's material. For more information on how to get additional questions, please see this book's introduction.

1. In which of the following situations can you *not* use full-duplex?

   A. With a connection from a switch to a switch

   B. With a connection from a router to a router

   C. With a connection from a host to a host

   D. With a connection from a host to a hub

2. Which of the following is *not* one of the actions taken in the operation of CSMA/CD when a collision occurs?

   A. A jam signal informs all devices that a collision occurred.

   B. The collision invokes a random backoff algorithm on the systems involved in the collision.

   C. Each device on the Ethernet segment stops transmitting for a short time until their backoff timers expire.

   D. All hosts have equal priority to transmit after the timers have expired.

3. The output of the show running-config command comes from _____.

   A. NVRAM

   B. Flash

   C. RAM

   D. Firmware

4. Which two of the following commands are required when configuring SSH on your router? (Choose two.)

   A. enable secret *password*

   B. exec-timeout 0 0

   C. ip domain-name *name*

   D. username *name* password *password*

   E. ip ssh version 2

5. You are troubleshooting a connectivity problem in your corporate network and want to isolate the problem. You suspect that a route in a routing table with a path en route to an unreachable network is at fault. What IOS user exec command should you issue?

    A. `Router>ping`

    B. `Router>trace`

    C. `Router>show ip route`

    D. `Router>show interface`

    E. `Router>show cdp neighbors`

6. You telnet to a router and make your necessary changes; now you want to end the Telnet session. What command do you type in?

    A. `close`

    B. `disable`

    C. `disconnect`

    D. `exit`

7. Which if the following is *not* an issue addressed by STP?

    A. Broadcast storms

    B. Gateway redundancy

    C. A device receiving multiple copies of the same frame

    D. Constant updating of the MAC filter table

8. Which two of the following switch port violation modes will alert you via SNMP that a violation has occurred on a port? (Choose two.)

    A. Restrict

    B. Protect

    C. Shutdown

    D. Err-disable

9. Which of the following statements is true with regard to VLANs?

    A. VLANs greatly reduce network security.

    B. VLANs increase the number of collision domains while decreasing their size.

    C. VLANs decrease the number of broadcast domains while decreasing their size.

    D. Network adds, moves, and changes are achieved with ease by just configuring a port into the appropriate VLAN.

10. Which of the following statements is true with regard to ISL and 802.1q?

    A. 802.1q encapsulates the frame with control information; ISL inserts an ISL field along with tag control information.

    B. 802.1q is Cisco proprietary.

    C. ISL encapsulates the frame with control information; 802.1q inserts an 802.1q field along with tag control information.

    D. ISL is a standard.

Chapter

3

IP Addressing (IPv4 / IPv6)

THE FOLLOWING CCNA ROUTING AND SWITCHING EXAM OBJECTIVES ARE COVERED IN THIS CHAPTER:

✓ Describe the operation and necessity of using private and public IP addresses for IPv4 addressing.

✓ Identify the appropriate IPv6 addressing scheme to satisfy addressing requirements in a LAN/WAN environment.

✓ Identify the appropriate IPv4 addressing scheme using VLSM and summarization to satisfy addressing requirements in a LAN/WAN environment.

✓ Describe the technological requirements for running IPv6 in conjunction with IPv4 such as dual stack.

✓ Describe IPv6 addresses

- Global unicast
- Multicast
- Link local
- Unique local
- eui 64
- autoconfiguration

Once you understand the protocols and processes used at the various levels of the DoD model, you need to take the next logical step by delving into the world of IP addressing and the different classes of IP addresses used in networks today.

Because having a good grasp of the various IPv4 address types is critical to understanding IP addressing, subnetting, and variable length subnet masks (VLSMs), we'll explore these key topics in detail by discussing the various types of IPv4 addresses that you'll need to have down for the exam.

We'll end this chapter by covering IPv6 address types and explain the different routing protocols used in IPv6.

Describe the Operation and Necessity of Using Private and Public IP Addresses for IPv4 Addressing

An *IP address* is a numeric identifier assigned to each machine on an IP network. It designates the specific location of a device on the network.

An IP address is a software address, not a hardware address—the latter is hard-coded on a network interface card (NIC) and used for finding hosts on a local network. IP addressing was designed to allow hosts on one network to communicate with a host on a different network regardless of the type of LANs the hosts are participating in.

IP Terminology

Throughout this chapter you're being introduced to several important terms that are vital to understanding the Internet Protocol. Here are a few to get you started:

Bit A bit is one binary digit, either a 1 or a 0.

Byte A byte is 7 or 8 bits, depending on whether parity is used. For the rest of this chapter, always assume a byte is 8 bits.

Octet An octet, made up of 8 bits, is just an ordinary 8-bit binary number. In this chapter, the terms *byte* and *octet* are completely interchangeable.

Network address   This is the designation used in routing to send packets to a remote network—for example, 10.0.0.0, 172.16.0.0, and 192.168.10.0.

Broadcast address   The address used by applications and hosts to send information to all nodes on a network is called the broadcast address. Examples of layer 3 broadcasts include 255.255.255.255, which is any network, all nodes; 172.16.255.255, which is all subnets and hosts on network 172.16.0.0; and 10.255.255.255, which broadcasts to all subnets and hosts on network 10.0.0.0.

The Hierarchical IP Addressing Scheme

An IP address consists of 32 bits of information. These bits are divided into four sections, referred to as octets or bytes, with each containing 1 byte (8 bits). You can depict an IP address using one of three methods:

- Dotted-decimal, as in 172.16.30.56
- Binary, as in 10101100.00010000.00011110.00111000
- Hexadecimal, as in AC.10.1E.38

All these examples represent the same IP address.

The 32-bit IP address is a structured, or hierarchical, address as opposed to a flat, or nonhierarchical, address. Although either type of addressing scheme could have been used, *hierarchical addressing* was chosen for a good reason. The advantage of this scheme is that it can handle a large number of addresses, namely, 4.3 billion (a 32-bit address space with two possible values for each position—either 0 or 1   gives you 2^{32}, or 4,294,967,296). The disadvantage of the flat addressing scheme, and the reason it's not used for IP addressing, relates to routing. If every address were unique, all routers on the Internet would need to store the address of each and every machine on the Internet. This would make efficient routing impossible, even if only a fraction of the possible addresses were used!

The solution to this problem is to use a two- or three-level hierarchical addressing scheme that is structured by network and host or by network, subnet, and host.

This two- or three-level scheme can also be compared to a telephone number. The first section, the area code, designates a very large area. The second section, the prefix, narrows the scope to a local calling area. The final segment, the customer number, zooms in on the specific connection. IP addresses use the same type of layered structure. Rather than all 32 bits being treated as a unique identifier, as in flat addressing, a part of the address is designated as the network address and the other part is designated as either the subnet and host or just the node address.

Summary of the Network Addressing

The *network address* (which can also be called the network number) uniquely identifies each network. Every machine on the same network shares that network address as part of its IP address. For example, in the IP address 172.16.30.56, 172.16 is the network address.

The *node address* is assigned to, and uniquely identifies, each machine on a network. This part of the address must be unique because it identifies a particular machine—an individual—as opposed to a network, which is a group. This number can also be referred to as a *host address*. In the sample IP address 172.16.30.56, the 30.56 specifies the node address.

The designers of the Internet decided to create classes of networks based on network size. For the small number of networks possessing a very large number of nodes, they created the rank *Class A network*. At the other extreme is the *Class C network*, which is reserved for the numerous networks with a small number of nodes. The class distinction for networks between very large and very small is predictably called the *Class B network*.

Subdividing an IP address into a network and node address is determined by the class designation of one's network. Figure 3.1 summarizes the three classes of networks used to address hosts, as well as Class D and Class E, used for multicast addresses and scientific purposes, respectively.

FIGURE 3.1   Summary of the three classes of networks

	8 bits	8 bits	8 bits	8 bits
Class A:	Network	Host	Host	Host
Class B:	Network	Network	Host	Host
Class C:	Network	Network	Network	Host
Class D:	Multicast			
Class E:	Research			

To ensure efficient routing, Internet designers defined a mandate for the leading-bits section of the address for each different network class. For example, since a router knows that a Class A network address always starts with 0, the router might be able to speed a packet on its way after reading only the first bit of its address. This is where the address schemes define the difference between a Class A, a Class B, and a Class C address.

Network Address Range: Class A

The designers of the IP address scheme decided that the first bit (the most significant bit, or MSb) of the first byte in a Class A network address must always be off, or 0. This means a Class A address must be between 0 and 127 in the first byte, inclusive.

Consider the following network address:

0xxxxxxx

If we turn the other 7 bits all off and then turn them all on, we'll find the Class A range of network addresses:

```
00000000 = 0
01111111 = 127
```

So, a Class A network is defined in the first octet between 0 and 127, and it can't be less or more. Understand that 0 and 127 are not valid in a Class A network because they're reserved addresses.

Network Address Range: Class B

In a Class B network, the RFCs state that the first bit of the first byte must always be turned on but the second bit must always be turned off. Said another way, the MSb must always be 10. If you turn the other 6 bits all off and then all on, you will find the range for a Class B network:

```
10000000 = 128
10111111 = 191
```

As you can see, a Class B network is defined when the first byte is configured from 128 to 191.

Network Address Range: Class C

For Class C networks, the RFCs define the first 2 bits of the first octet as always turned on, but the third bit can never be on. Once again the MSb must be 110. Following the same process we used with the previous classes, convert from binary to decimal to find the range. Here's the range for a Class C network:

```
11000000 = 192
11011111 = 223
```

So, if you see an IP address with the first byte in the range 192 to 223, you'll know it is a Class C IP address.

Network Address Ranges: Classes D and E

The addresses between 224 to 255 are reserved for Class D and E networks. Class D (224–239) is used for multicast addresses and Class E (240–255) for scientific purposes, but I'm not going into these types of addresses because they are beyond the scope of knowledge you need to gain from this book.

Network Addresses: Special Purpose

Some IP addresses are reserved for special purposes, so network administrators can't ever assign these addresses to nodes. Table 3.1 lists the members of this exclusive little club and the reasons they're included in it.

TABLE 3.1   Reserved IP addresses

Address	Function
Network address of all 0s	Interpreted to mean "this network or segment."
Network address of all 1s	Interpreted to mean "all networks."

TABLE 3.1   Reserved IP addresses *(continued)*

Address	Function
Network 127.0.0.1	Reserved for loopback tests. Designates the local node and allows that node to send a test packet to itself without generating network traffic.
Node address of all 0s	Interpreted to mean "network address" or any host on a specified network.
Node address of all 1s	Interpreted to mean "all nodes" on the specified network; for example, 128.2.255.255 means "all nodes" on network 128.2 (Class B address).
Entire IP address set to all 0s	Used by Cisco routers to designate the default route. Could also mean "any network."
Entire IP address set to all 1s (same as 255.255.255.255)	Broadcast to all nodes on the current network; sometimes called an "all 1s broadcast" or local broadcast.

Class A Addresses

In a Class A network address, the first byte is assigned to the network address and the three remaining bytes are used for the node addresses. The Class A format is as follows:

network.node.node.node

For example, in the IP address 49.22.102.70, the 49 is the network address and 22.102.70 is the node address. Every machine on this particular network would have the distinctive network address of 49.

Class A network addresses are 1 byte long, with the first bit of that byte reserved and the 7 remaining bits available for manipulation (addressing). As a result, the maximum number of Class A networks that can be created is 128. Why? Because each of the 7 bit positions can be either a 0 or a 1, thus 2^7, or 128.

To complicate matters further, the network address of all 0s (0000 0000) is reserved to designate the default route (see Table 3.1 in the previous section). Additionally, the address 127, which is reserved for diagnostics, can't be used either, which means that you can really only use the numbers 1 to 126 to designate Class A network addresses. This means the actual number of usable Class A network addresses is 128 minus 2, or 126.

The IP address 127.0.0.1 is used to test the IP stack on an individual node and cannot be used as a valid host address. However, the loopback address creates a shortcut method for TCP/IP applications and services that run on the same device to communicate with each other.

Class A Valid Host IDs

Here's an example of how to figure out the valid host IDs in a Class A network address:

- All host bits off is the network address: 10.0.0.0.
- All host bits on is the broadcast address: 10.255.255.255.

The valid hosts are the numbers in between the network address and the broadcast address: 10.0.0.1 through 10.255.255.254. Notice that 0s and 255s can be valid host IDs. All you need to remember when trying to find valid host addresses is that the host bits can't all be turned off or on at the same time.

Class B Addresses

In a Class B network address, the first 2 bytes are assigned to the network address and the remaining 2 bytes are used for node addresses. The format is as follows:

network.network.node.node

For example, in the IP address 172.16.30.56, the network address is 172.16 and the node address is 30.56.

With a network address being 2 bytes (8 bits each), you get 2^{16} unique combinations. But the Internet designers decided that all Class B network addresses should start with the binary digit 1, then 0. This leaves 14 bit positions to manipulate, therefore 16,384, or 2^{14}, unique Class B network addresses.

A Class B address uses 2 bytes for node addresses. This is 2^{16} minus the two reserved patterns of all 0s and all 1s for a total of 65,534 possible node addresses for each Class B network.

Class B Valid Host IDs

Here's an example of how to find the valid hosts in a Class B network:

- All host bits turned off is the network address: 172.16.0.0.
- All host bits turned on is the broadcast address: 172.16.255.255.

The valid hosts would be the numbers in between the network address and the broadcast address: 172.16.0.1 through 172.16.255.254.

Class C Addresses

The first 3 bytes of a Class C network address are dedicated to the network portion of the address, with only 1 measly byte remaining for the node address. Here's the format:

network.network.network.node

Using the example IP address 192.168.100.102, the network address is 192.168.100 and the node address is 102.

In a Class C network address, the first three bit positions are always the binary 110. The calculation is as follows: 3 bytes, or 24 bits, minus 3 reserved positions leaves 21 positions. Hence, there are 2^{21}, or 2,097,152, possible Class C networks.

Each unique Class C network has 1 byte to use for node addresses. This leads to 2^8, or 256, minus the two reserved patterns of all 0s and all 1s, for a total of 254 node addresses for each Class C network.

Class C Valid Host IDs

Here's an example of how to find a valid host ID in a Class C network:

- All host bits turned off is the network ID: 192.168.100.0.
- All host bits turned on is the broadcast address: 192.168.100.255.

The valid hosts would be the numbers in between the network address and the broadcast address: 192.168.100.1 through 192.168.100.254.

Private IP Addresses (RFC 1918)

The people who created the IP addressing scheme also created private IP addresses. These addresses can be used on a private network, but they're not routable through the Internet. This is designed for the purpose of creating a measure of well-needed security, but it also conveniently saves valuable IP address space.

If every host on every network was required to have real routable IP addresses, we would have run out of IP addresses to hand out years ago. But by using private IP addresses, ISPs, corporations, and home users only need a relatively tiny group of bona fide IP addresses to connect their networks to the Internet. This is economical because they can use private IP addresses on their inside networks and get along just fine.

To accomplish this task, the ISP and the corporation—the end user, no matter who they are—need to use something called *Network Address Translation (NAT)*, which basically takes a private IP address and converts it for use on the Internet. Many people can use the same real IP address to transmit out onto the Internet. Doing things this way saves megatons of address space—good for us all!

The reserved private addresses are listed in Table 3.2.

TABLE 3.2 Reserved IP address space

Address Class	Reserved Address Space
Class A	10.0.0.0 through 10.255.255.255
Class B	172.16.0.0 through 172.31.255.255
Class C	192.168.0.0 through 192.168.255.255

IPv4 Address Types

Here are the address types and their definitions:

Loopback (localhost)   Used to test the IP stack on the local computer. Can be any address from 127.0.0.1 through 127.255.255.254.

Layer 2 broadcasts   These are sent to all nodes on a LAN.

Broadcasts (layer 3)   These are sent to all nodes on the network. Referred to as "one-to-all."

Unicast   This is an address for a single interface, and these are used to send packets to a single destination host. Referred to as "one-to-one."

Multicast   These are packets sent from a single source and transmitted to many devices on different networks. Referred to as "one-to-many."

Exam Essentials

Understand the classes of IP address ranges.   The Class A address range is 0–127. The Class B address range is 128–191. The Class C range is 192–223. The Class D range is 224–239. The Class E range is 240–255.

Understand the private IP address range.   The private Class A address range is 10.0.0.0–10.255.255.255. The private Class B address range is 172.16.0.0–172.31.255.255. The Class C range is 192.168.0.0–192.168.255.255.

Identify the Appropriate IPv6 Addressing Scheme to Satisfy Addressing Requirements in a LAN/WAN Environment

Understanding how IP addresses are structured and used is critical with IPv4 addressing, and it's also vital when it comes to IPv6. You probably already know that at 128 bits, an IPv6 address is much larger than an IPv4 address.

So let's take a look at Figure 3.2, which has a sample IPv6 address broken down into sections.

As you can clearly see, the address is definitely much larger. But what else is different? Well, first, notice that it has eight groups of numbers instead of four and also that those groups are separated by colons instead of periods. And hey, wait a second... there are letters in that address! Yep, the address is expressed in hexadecimal just like a MAC address is, so you could say this address has eight 16-bit hexadecimal colon-delimited blocks. That's already quite a mouthful, and you probably haven't even tried to say the address out loud yet!

FIGURE 3.2   IPv6 address example

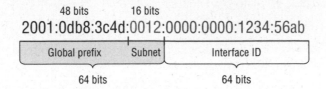

One other thing I want to point out is an important thing to keep in mind for when you set up your test network to actually experiment with IPv6. When you use a web browser to make an HTTP connection to an IPv6 device, you have to type the address into the browser with brackets around the literal address. Why? Well, a colon is already being used by the browser for specifying a port number, so basically, if you don't enclose the address in brackets, the browser will have no way to identify the information.

Here's an example of how this looks:

```
http://[2001:0db8:3c4d:0012:0000:0000:1234:56ab]/default.html
```

Now obviously if you can, you would rather use names to specify a destination (like www.lammle.com), but even though it's definitely going to be a pain, we just have to accept the fact that sometimes we have to bite the bullet and type in the address number. So it should be pretty clear that DNS is going to remain extremely important when implementing IPv6.

 There are four hexadecimal characters (16 bits) in each IPv6 field, and the fields are separated by colons.

Shortened Expression

The good news is that there are a few tricks to help rescue us when writing these monster addresses. For one thing, you can actually leave out parts of the address to abbreviate it, but to get away with doing that you have to follow a couple of rules. First, you can drop any leading zeros in each of the individual blocks. After you do that, the sample address from earlier would then look like this:

```
2001:db8:3c4d:12:0:0:1234:56ab
```

Okay, that's a definite improvement—at least we don't have to write all of those extra zeros! But what about whole blocks that don't have anything in them except zeros? Well, we can kind of lose those too—at least some of them. Again referring to our sample address, we can remove the two consecutive blocks of zeros by replacing them with a doubled colon, like this:

```
2001:db8:3c4d:12::1234:56ab
```

Cool—we replaced the blocks of all zeros with a doubled colon. The rule you have to follow to get away with this is that you can replace only one contiguous block of such zeros in an address. So if my address has four blocks of zeros and each of them were separated, I just don't get to replace them all because I can replace only one contiguous block with a doubled colon. Check out this example:

```
2001:0000:0000:0012:0000:0000:1234:56ab
```

And just know that you *can't* do this:

```
2001::12::1234:56ab
```

Instead, the best you can do is this:

```
2001::12:0:0:1234:56ab
```

The reason the preceding example is our best shot is that if we remove two sets of zeros, the device looking at the address will have no way of knowing where the zeros go back in. Basically, the router would look at the incorrect address and say, "Well, do I place two blocks into the first set of doubled colons and two into the second set, or do I place three blocks into the first set and one block into the second set?"

Exam Essentials

Understanding IPv6 addressing.   IPv6 addressing is not like IPv4 addressing. IPv6 addressing has much more address space, and an address is 128 bits long and represented in hexadecimal, unlike an IPv4 address, which is only 32 bits long and represented in decimal.

Identify the Appropriate IPv4 Addressing Scheme Using VLSM and Summarization to Satisfy Addressing Requirements in a LAN/WAN Environment

Teaching you a simple way to create many networks from a large single network using subnet masks of different lengths in various kinds of network designs is what my primary focus will be in this section. Doing this is called VLSM networking.

Older routing protocols like Routing Information Protocol version 1 (RIPv1) do not have a field for subnet information, so the subnet information gets dropped. This means that if a router running RIP has a subnet mask of a certain value, it assumes that *all* interfaces within the classful address space have the same subnet mask. This is called classful routing, and RIP is considered a classful routing protocol.

Classless routing protocols do support the advertisement of subnet information, which means you can use VLSM with routing protocols such as RIPv2, Enhanced Interior Gateway Protocol (EIGRP), and Open Shortest Path First (OSPF). The benefit of this type of network is that it saves a bunch of IP address space.

As the name suggests, VLSMs can use subnet masks with different lengths for different router interfaces. Check out Figure 3.3 to see an example of why classful network designs are inefficient.

FIGURE 3.3   Typical classful network

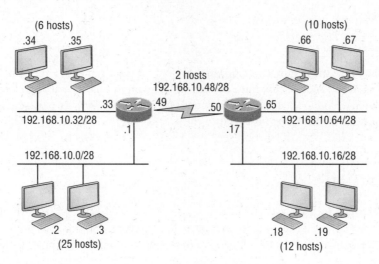

Looking at Figure 3.3, you can see that there are two routers, each with two LANs and connected together with a WAN serial link. In a typical classful network design that's running RIP, you could subnet a network like this:

192.168.10.0 = Network

255.255.255.240 (/28) = Mask

Our subnets would be 0, 16, 32, 48, 64, 80, etc., which allows us to assign 16 subnets to our internetwork. Each subnet provides only 14 hosts. This means that one LAN doesn't even have enough addresses needed for all the hosts, and this network as it is shown would not work as addressed in the figure! That's because the point-to-point WAN link also has 14 valid hosts.

All hosts and router interfaces have the same subnet mask—again, known as classful routing—and if we want this network to be efficient, we would definitely need to add different masks to each router interface.

But that's not our only problem—the link between the two routers will never use more than two valid hosts! This wastes valuable IP address space, and it's the big reason you need to learn about VLSM network design.

VLSM Design

Let's take Figure 3.3 and use a classless design instead, which will become the new network shown in Figure 3.4. In the previous example, we wasted address space—one LAN didn't have enough addresses because every router interface and host used the same subnet mask. Not so good. A better solution would be to provide for only the needed number of hosts on each router interface, and we're going to use VLSMs to achieve that goal.

FIGURE 3.4 Classless network design

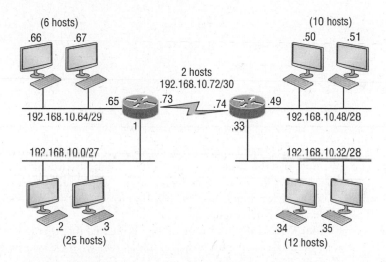

Now remember that we can use different size masks on each router interface. If we use a /30 on our WAN links and a /27, /28, and /29 on our LANs, we'll get 2 hosts per WAN interface and 30, 14, and 6 hosts per LAN interface—nice! This makes a huge difference—not only can we get just the right amount of hosts on each LAN, we still have room to add more WANs and LANs using this same network!

> To implement a VLSM design on your network, you need to have a routing protocol that sends subnet mask information with the route updates. The protocols that do that are RIPv2, EIGRP, and OSPF. Remember, RIPv1 will not work in classless networks, so it's considered a classful routing protocol.

Implementing VLSM Networks

To create VLSMs quickly and efficiently, you need to understand how block sizes and charts work together to create the VLSM masks. Table 3.3 shows you the block sizes used when creating VLSMs with Class C networks. For example, if you need 25 hosts, then you'll need a block size of 32. If you need 11 hosts, you'll use a block size of 16. Need 40 hosts? Then you'll need a block of 64. You cannot just make up block sizes—they've got to be the block sizes shown in Table 3.3. So memorize the block sizes in this table—it's easy. They're the same numbers we used with subnetting!

TABLE 3.3   Block sizes

Prefix	Mask	Hosts	Block Size
/25	128	126	128
/26	192	62	64
/27	224	30	32
/28	240	14	16
/29	248	6	8
/30	252	2	4

The next step is to create a VLSM table. Figure 3.5 shows you the table used in creating a VLSM network. The reason we use this table is so we don't accidentally overlap networks.

Based on what you've learned so far about block sizes and the VLSM table, let's create a VLSM network using a Class C network address 192.168.10.0 for the network in Figure 3.6 then fill out the VLSM table, as shown in Figure 3.7.

In Figure 3.6, we have four WAN links and four LANs connected together, so we need to create a VLSM network that will save address space. Looks like we have two block sizes of 32, a block size of 16, and a block size of 8, and our WANs each have a block size of 4. Take a look and see how I filled out our VLSM chart in Figure 3.7.

There are two important things to note here. The first is that we still have plenty of room for growth with this VLSM network design. The second point is that we could never achieve this goal with one subnet mask using classful routing.

Exam Essentials

Describe the benefits of variable length subnet masks (VLSMs).   VLSMs enable the creation of subnets of specific sizes and allow the division of a classless network into smaller networks that do not need to be equal in size. This makes use of the address space more efficient because many times IP addresses are wasted with classful subnetting.

FIGURE 3.5 The VLSM table

Subnet	Mask	Subnets	Hosts	Block
/25	128	2	126	128
/26	192	4	62	64
/27	224	8	30	32
/28	240	16	14	16
/29	248	32	6	8
/30	252	64	2	4

Network	Hosts	Block	Subnet	Mask
A				
B				
C				
D				
E				
F				
G				
H				
I				
J				
K				
L				

FIGURE 3.6   VLSM network example 1

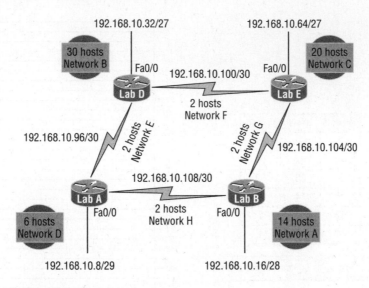

Describe the Technological Requirements for Running IPv6 in Conjunction with IPv4 Such as Dual Stack

Today's networks, as well as the Internet, have a ton of unforeseen requirements that simply weren't even considerations when IPv4 was created. We've tried to compensate with a collection of add-ons that can actually make implementing them more difficult than they would be if they were required by a standard. By default, IPv6 has improved upon and included many of those features as standard and mandatory. One of these sweet new standards is IPsec—a feature that provides end-to-end security.

The headers in an IPv6 packet have half the fields, and they are aligned to 64 bits, which gives us some seriously souped-up processing speed. Compared to IPv4, lookups happen at light speed! Most of the information that used to be bound into the IPv4 header was taken out, and now you can choose to put it, or parts of it, back into the header in the form of optional extension headers that follow the basic header fields.

FIGURE 3.7   VLSM table example 1

Subnet	Mask	Subnets	Hosts	Block
/25	128	2	126	128
/26	192	4	62	64
/27	224	8	30	32
/28	240	16	14	16
/29	248	32	6	8
/30	252	64	2	4

Network	Hosts	Block	Subnet	Mask
A	12	16	/28	240
B	20	32	/27	224
C	25	32	/27	224
D	4	8	/29	248
E	2	4	/30	252
F	2	4	/30	252
G	2	4	/30	252
H	2	4	/30	252

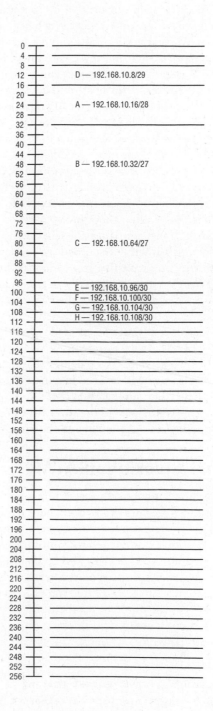

IPv6 gives us a substantially larger address space, meaning the address itself is a whole lot bigger—four times bigger as a matter of fact! An IPv6 address is actually 128 bits in length. All that additional room permits more levels of hierarchy inside the address space and a more flexible addressing architecture. It also makes routing much more efficient and scalable because the addresses can be aggregated a lot more effectively. IPv6 also allows multiple addresses for hosts and networks. This is especially important for enterprises veritably drooling for enhanced access and availability. Plus, the new version of IP now includes an expanded use of multicast communication—one device sending to many hosts or to a select group—that joins in to seriously boost efficiency on networks because communications will be more specific.

IPv4 uses broadcasts quite prolifically, causing a bunch of problems, the worst of which is of course the dreaded broadcast storm. This is an uncontrolled deluge of forwarded broadcast traffic that can bring an entire network to its knees and devour every last bit of bandwidth! Another nasty thing about broadcast traffic is that it interrupts each and every device on the network. When a broadcast is sent out, every machine has to stop what it's doing and respond to the traffic whether the broadcast is relevant to it or not.

There's no such thing as a broadcast in IPv6 because it uses multicast traffic instead. And there are two other types of communications as well: unicast, which is the same as it is in IPv4, and a new type called *anycast*. Anycast communication allows the same address to be placed on more than one device so that when traffic is sent to the device service addressed in this way, it's routed to the nearest host that shares the same address.

All of the routing protocols we've already discussed have been tweaked and upgraded for use in IPv6 networks, so it figures that many of the functions and configurations that you've already learned will be used in almost the same way as they are now. Knowing that broadcasts have been eliminated in IPv6, it's safe to conclude that any protocols relying entirely on broadcast traffic will go the way of the dodo. But unlike with the dodo, it'll be really nice to say goodbye to these bandwidth-hogging, performance-annihilating little gremlins!

Dual Stacking (ISATAP)

Intra-Site Automatic Tunnel Addressing Protocol (ISATAP) is an IPv6 transition mechanism meant to transmit IPv6 packets between dual-stack nodes on top of an IPv4 network.

This is the most common type of migration strategy because, well, it's the easiest on us—it allows our devices to communicate using either IPv4 or IPv6. *Dual stacking* lets you upgrade your devices and applications on the network one at a time. As more and more hosts and devices on the network are upgraded, more of your communication will happen over IPv6, and after you've arrived, everything's running on IPv6 and you get to remove all the old IPv4 protocol stacks you no longer need.

Plus, configuring dual stacking on a Cisco router is amazingly easy—all you have to do is enable IPv6 forwarding and apply an address to the interfaces already configured with IPv4. It'll look something like this:

```
Corp(config)#ipv6 unicast-routing
Corp(config)#interface fastethernet 0/0
```

```
Corp(config-if)#ipv6 address 2001:db8:3c4d:1::/64 eui-64
Corp(config-if)#ip address 192.168.255.1 255.255.255.0
```

To be honest, it's a good idea to understand the various tunneling techniques because it'll probably be awhile before everyone starts running IPv6 as a solo routed protocol.

6to4 Tunneling

6to4 tunneling is really useful for carrying IPv6 data over a network that's still IPv4. It's quite possible that you'll have IPv6 subnets or other portions of your network that are all IPv6, and those networks will have to communicate with each other. This isn't too complicated, but when you consider that you might find this happening over a WAN or some other network that you don't control, well, that could be a bit ugly. Even if you can't control the whole tamale, you can create a tunnel that will carry the IPv6 traffic across the IPv4 network.

The whole idea of tunneling isn't a difficult concept, and creating tunnels really isn't as hard as you might think. All it really comes down to is snatching the IPv6 packet that's happily traveling across the network and sticking an IPv4 header onto the front of it.

To get a picture of this, take a look at Figure 3.8.

FIGURE 3.8   Creating a 6to4 tunnel

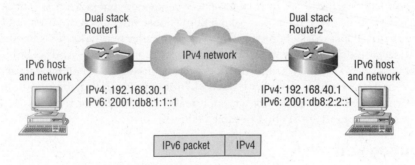

IPv6 packet encapsulated in an IPv4 packet

Now you have to add a little configuration to place a tunnel between those routers. Tunnels are pretty simple. You just have to tell each router where the tunnel begins and where you want it to end up. Referring again to Figure 3.8, here's how to configure the tunnel on each router:

```
Router1(config)#int tunnel 0
Router1(config-if)#ipv6 address 2001:db8:1:1::1/64
Router1(config-if)#tunnel source 192.168.30.1
Router1(config-if)#tunnel destination 192.168.40.1
Router1(config-if)#tunnel mode ipv6ip
```

```
Router2(config)#int tunnel 0
Router2(config-if)#ipv6 address 2001:db8:2:2::1/64
Router2(config-if)#tunnel source 192.168.40.1
Router2(config-if)#tunnel destination 192.168.30.1
Router2(config-if)#tunnel mode ipv6ip
```

With this in place, the IPv6 networks can now communicate over the IPv4 network. This is not meant to be a permanent configuration; your end goal should still be to run a total, complete IPv6 network end to end.

One important note here: If the IPv4 network that you're traversing in this situation has a NAT translation, it would absolutely break the tunnel encapsulation you've just created! Over the years, NAT has been upgraded a lot so that it can handle specific protocols and dynamic connections, and without one of these upgrades, NAT likes to demolish most connections. Because this transition strategy isn't present in most NAT implementations, that means trouble.

There is a way around this little problem, and it's a technology called *Teredo*; it allows all your tunnel traffic to be placed in UDP packets. NAT doesn't blast away at UDP packets, so they won't get broken as other protocols packets do. With Teredo in place and your packets disguised under their UDP cloak, the packets will easily slip by NAT alive and well.

IPv6 Routing

The routing protocols we'll still use in IPv6 have been renovated and given new names.

First on the list is the IPv6 RIPng (next generation). Those of you who've been in IT for a while know that RIP has worked pretty well for us on smaller networks. This happens to be the very reason it didn't get whacked and will still be around in IPv6. And we still have EIGRPv6 because EIGRP already had protocol-dependent modules and all we had to do was add a new one to it to fit in nicely with the IPv6 protocol. Rounding out our group of protocol survivors is OSPFv3—that's not a typo, it really is v3! OSPF for IPv4 was actually v2, so when it got its upgrade to IPv6, it became OSPFv3.

Static Routing with IPv6

To make static routing work, whether in IP or IPv6, you need these three tools:

▪ An accurate, up-to-date network map of your entire internetwork

▪ Next-hop address and exit interface for each neighbor connection

▪ All the remote subnet IDs

Of course, we don't need to have any of these for dynamic routing, which is why we mostly use dynamic routing.

Figure 3.9 shows a really good example of how to use static routing with IPv6. It really doesn't have to be that hard, but just as with IPv4, you absolutely need an accurate network map to make static routing work!

So here's what I did: First, I created a static route on the Corp router to the remote network 2001:1234:4321:1::/64 using the next-hop address. I could've just as easily used the Corp router's exit interface. Next, I just set up a default route for the Branch router with ::/0 and the Branch exit interface of Gi0/0—not so bad!

FIGURE 3.9 IPv6 static and default routing

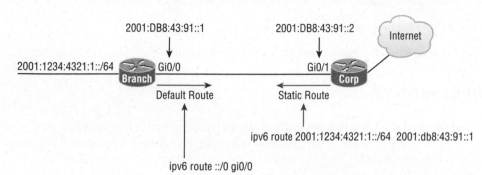

OSPFv3

The new version of OSPF continues with the trend of routing protocols being quite similar to their IPv4 versions. For instance, the foundation of OSPF remains the same—it's still a link-state routing protocol that divides an entire internetwork or AS into areas, creating a hierarchy. And just trust me on this one—be really thankful that multi-area OSPF is beyond the scope for the Cisco objectives covered in this chapter!

Anyway, in OSPF version 2, the router ID (RID) is determined by either the highest IP addresses assigned to the router or one you manually assigned. In version 3, you assign the RID and area ID, which are both still 32-bit values but aren't found via the IP address anymore because an IPv6 address is 128 bits. Changes in how these values are assigned, plus the removal of the IP address information from OSPF packet headers, make the new version of OSPF flexible enough to be used over almost any Network layer protocol.

Adjacencies and next-hop attributes now use link-local addresses. OSPFv3 still uses multicast traffic to send its updates and acknowledgments, with the addresses FF02::5 for OSPF routers and FF02::6 for OSPF-designated routers. These new addresses are the replacements for 224.0.0.5 and 224.0.0.6, respectively.

Other, less-flexible IPv4 protocols just can't compete with OSPFv2's ability to assign specific networks and interfaces into the OSPF process, but these are still configured during router configuration. In OSPFv3, and therefore the networks attached to them are simply configured directly on the interface in interface configuration mode instead.

Here's a sample of how the OSPFv3 configuration will look, starting with the optional configuration of the router ID in global configuration mode:

```
Router1(config)#ipv6 router osfp 10
Router1(config-rtr)#router-id 1.1.1.1
```

You get to execute some configurations from router configuration mode, like summarization and redistribution, but we don't even need to configure OSPFv3 from this prompt if we configure OSPFv3 from the interface!

This is because if we go with the interface configuration option, the router configuration process is added automatically. The interface configuration looks like this:

```
Router1(config-if)#ipv6 ospf 10 area 0
```

So, if we just go to each interface and assign a process ID and area—shazam, we're done!

Exam Essentials

Understand the dual stack mechanism.   The dual stack mechanism is meant to transmit IPv6 traffic over an IPv4 network. This allows you to upgrade network devices until the IPv4 devices are no longer needed.

Describe IPv6 Addresses

We're all familiar with IPv4's unicast, broadcast, and multicast addresses that basically define who or at least how many other devices we're talking to. But as I mentioned, IPv6 modifies that trio and introduces the anycast. Broadcasts, as we know them, have been eliminated in IPv6 because of their cumbersome inefficiency and basic tendency to drive us insane!

So let's find out what each of these types of IPv6 addressing and communication methods do for us.

Global Unicast

These are your typical publicly routable addresses and they're the same as in IPv4. Global addresses start at 2000::/3. Figure 3.10 shows how a unicast address breaks down. The ISP can provide you with a minimum /48 network ID, which in turn provides you 16 bits to create a unique 64-bit router interface address. The last 64-bits are the unique host ID.

FIGURE 3.10   IPv6 global unicast addresses

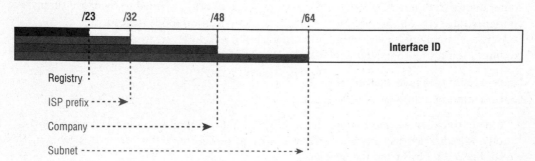

Multicast

Again, as in IPv4, packets addressed to a multicast address are delivered to all interfaces tuned into the multicast address. Sometimes people call them "one-to-many" addresses. It's really easy to spot a multicast address in IPv6 because they always start with FF.

Link Local

These are like the Automatic Private IP Address (APIPA) addresses that Microsoft uses to automatically provide addresses in IPv4 in that they're not meant to be routed. In IPv6, they start with FE80::/10, as shown in Figure 3.11. Think of these addresses as handy tools that give you the ability to throw a temporary LAN together for meetings or create a small LAN that's not going to be routed but still needs to share and access files and services locally.

FIGURE 3.11 IPv6 link-local FE80::/10: The first 10 bits define the address type.

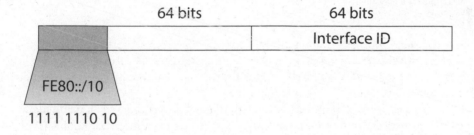

Unique Local

These addresses are also intended for nonrouting purposes over the Internet, but they are nearly globally unique, so it's unlikely you'll ever have one of them overlap. Unique local addresses were designed to replace site-local addresses, so they basically do almost exactly what IPv4 private addresses do: allow communication throughout a site while being routable to multiple local networks. Site-local addresses were deprecated as of September 2004.

eui 64

Autoconfiguration is an especially useful solution because it allows devices on a network to address themselves with a link-local unicast address as well as with a global unicast address. This process happens through first learning the prefix information from the router and then appending the device's own interface address as the interface ID. But where does it get that interface ID? Well, you know every device on an Ethernet network has a physical MAC address, which is exactly what's used for the interface ID. But since the interface ID in an IPv6 address is 64 bits in length and a MAC address is only 48 bits, where do the extra 16 bits come from? The MAC address is padded in the middle with the extra bits—it's padded with FFFE.

For example, let's say I have a device with a MAC address that looks like this: 0060:d673:1987. After it's been padded, it would look like this: 0260:d6FF:FE73:1987. Figure 3.12 illustrates what an EUI-64 address looks like.

FIGURE 3.12   EUI-64 interface ID assignment

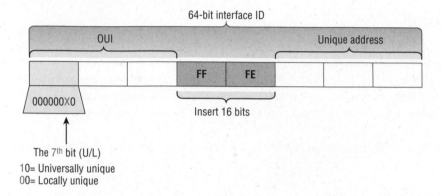

So where did that 2 in the beginning of the address come from? Another good question. You see that part of the process of padding, called modified EUI-64 format, changes a bit to specify if the address is locally unique or globally unique. And the bit that gets changed is the 7th bit in the address.

The reason for modifying the universal/local bit (the U/L bit) is that, when using manually assigned addresses on an interface, you can simply assign the address 2001:db8:1:9::1/64 instead of the much longer 2001:db8:1:9:0200::1/64. Also, if you are going to manually assign a link-local address, you can assign the short address FE80::1 instead of the long FE80::0200:0:0:1 or FE80:0:0:0:0200::1. So, even though at first glance it seems the IETF made this harder for you to simply understand IPv6 addressing by flipping the 7th bit, in reality this made addressing much simpler. Also, since most people don't typically override the burned-in address, the U/L bit is a 0, which means that you'll see this inverted to a 1 most of the time. But because you're studying the Cisco exam objectives, you'll need to look at inverting it both ways.

Here are a few examples:

- MAC address 0090:2716:fd0f

- IPv6 EUI-64 address: 2001:0db8:0:1:0290:27ff:fe16:fd0f

That one was easy! Too easy for the Cisco exam, so let's do another:

- MAC address aa12:bcbc:1234

- IPv6 EUI-64 address: 2001:0db8:0:1:a812:bcff:febc:1234

10101010 represents the first 8 bits of the MAC address (aa), which when inverting the 7th bit becomes 10101000. The answer becomes A8. I can't tell you how important this is for you to understand, so bear with me and work through a couple more!

- MAC address 0c0c:dede:1234

- IPv6 EUI-64 address: 2001:0db8:0:1:0e0c:deff:fede:1234

0c is 00001100 in the first 8 bits of the MAC address, which then becomes 00001110 when flipping the 7th bit. The answer is then 0e. Let's practice one more:

- MAC address 0**b**34:ba12:1234
- IPv6 EUI-64 address: 2001:0db8:0:1:0934:baff:fe12:1234

0b in binary is 00001011, the first 8 bits of the MAC address, which then becomes 00001001. The answer is 09.

autoconfiguration

To perform autoconfiguration, a host goes through a basic two-step process:

1. First, the host needs the prefix information, similar to the network portion of an IPv4 address, to configure its interface, so it sends a router solicitation (RS) request for it. This RS is then sent out as a multicast to all routers (FF02::2). The actual information being sent is a type of ICMP message, and like everything in networking, this ICMP message has a number that identifies it. The RS message is ICMP type 133.

2. The router answers back with the required prefix information via a router advertisement (RA). An RA message also happens to be a multicast packet that's sent to the all-nodes multicast address (FF02::1) and is ICMP type 134. RA messages are sent on a periodic basis, but the host sends the RS for an immediate response so it doesn't have to wait until the next scheduled RA to get what it needs.

These two steps are shown in Figure 3.13.

FIGURE 3.13   Two steps to IPv6 autoconfiguration

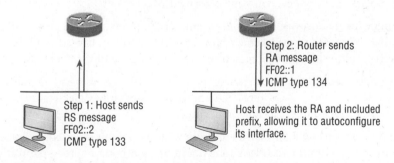

By the way, this type of autoconfiguration is also known as stateless autoconfiguration because it doesn't contact or connect to and receive any further information from the other device.

First take a look at Figure 3.14. In this figure, the Branch router needs to be configured, but I just don't feel like typing in an IPv6 address on the interface connecting to the Corp router. I also don't feel like typing in any routing commands, but I need more than a link-local address on that interface, so I'm going to have to do something! So basically, I want to have the Branch router work with IPv6 on the internetwork with the least amount of effort from me. Let's see if I can get away with that.

FIGURE 3.14   IPv6 autoconfiguration example

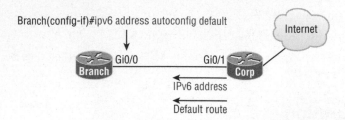

There is an easy way! IPv6 allows me to be relatively lazy when dealing with some parts of my network, yet it still works really well. When I use the command `ipv6 address autoconfig`, the interface will listen for RAs, and then, via the EUI-64 format, it will assign itself a global address.

Okay, this is all really great, but you're hopefully wondering what that `default` is doing there at the end of the command. If so, good catch! It happens to be a wonderful, optional part of the command that smoothly delivers a default route received from the Corp router, which will be automatically injected it into my routing table and set as the default route—so easy!

Exam Essentials

Understand why we need IPv6.   Without IPv6, the world would be depleted of IP addresses.

Understand link-local addresses.   A link-local address is like an IPv4 private IP address, but it can't be routed at all, not even in your organization.

Understand unique local addresses.   This, like a link-local address, is like a private IP address in IPv4 and cannot be routed to the Internet. However, the difference between link-local and unique local is that unique local can be routed within your organization or company.

Remember IPv6 addressing.   IPv6 addressing is not like IPv4 addressing. IPv6 addressing has much more address space, is 128 bits long, and represented in hexadecimal, unlike IPv4, which is only 32 bits long and represented in decimal.

Understand and be able to read an EUI-64 address with the 7th bit inverted.   Hosts can use autoconfiguration to obtain an IPv6 address, and one method of autoconfiguration is through what is called EUI-64. This takes the unique MAC address of a host and inserts FF:FE in the middle of the address to change a 48-bit MAC address to a 64-bit interface ID. In addition to the 16 bits begin inserted into the interface ID, the 7th bit of the first byte is inverted, typically from a 0 to a 1.

Review Questions

1. You want to ping the loopback address of your IPv6 local host. What will you type?

    A. `ping 127.0.0.1`

    B. `ping 0.0.0.0`

    C. `ping ::1`

    D. `trace 0.0.::1`

2. A host sends a type of NDP message providing the MAC address that was requested. Which type of NDP was sent?

    A. NA

    B. RS

    C. RA

    D. NS

3. What two multicast addresses does OSPFv3 use? (Choose two.)

    A. FF02::A

    B. FF02::9

    C. FF02::5

    D. FF02::6

4. Which of the following is true when describing a link-local address?

    A. Packets addressed to a broadcast address are delivered to a single interface.

    B. These are your typical publicly routable addresses, just like a regular publicly routable address in IPv4.

    C. These are like private addresses in IPv4 in that they are not meant to be routed over the Internet.

    D. These addresses are meant for nonrouting purposes, but they are almost globally unique, so it is unlikely they will have an address overlap.

5. Which of the following is true regarding OSPFv3? (Choose three.)

    A. Uses a wildcard to define interfaces

    B. Uses a network command under global configuration mode

    C. Uses a 32-bit router ID

    D. Uses link-state advertisements

    E. Uses an interface command to enable OSPF on an interface

6. A host sends a router solicitation (RS) on the data link. What destination address is sent with this request?

   A. FF02::A

   B. FF02::9

   C. FF02::2

   D. FF02::1

   E. FF02::5

7. Which of the following statements about IPv6 addresses are true? (Choose two.)

   A. Leading zeros are required.

   B. Two colons (::) are used to represent successive hexadecimal fields of zeros.

   C. Two colons (::) are used to separate fields.

   D. A single interface will have multiple IPv6 addresses of different types.

8. IPv6 unicast routing is running on the Corp router. Which of the following addresses would show up with the show ipv6 int brief command?

```
Corp#sh int f0/0
FastEthernet0/0 is up, line protocol is up
  Hardware is AmdFE, address is 000d.bd3b.0d80 (bia 000d.bd3b.0d80)
[output cut]
```

   A. FF02::3c3d:0d:bdff:fe3b:0d80

   B. FE80::3c3d:2d:bdff:fe3b:0d80

   C. FE80::3c3d:0d:bdff:fe3b:0d80

   D. FE80::3c3d:2d:ffbd:3bfe:0d80

9. Which of the following statements are true of IPv6 address representation? (Choose two.)

   A. The first 64 bits represent the dynamically created interface ID.

   B. A single interface may be assigned multiple IPv6 addresses of any type.

   C. Every IPv6 interface contains at least one loopback address.

   D. Leading zeroes in an IPv6 16-bit hexadecimal field are mandatory.

10. To enable OSPFv3, which of the following would you use?

   A. Router(config-if)#**ipv6 ospf 10 area 0.0.0.0**

   B. Router(config-if)#**ipv6 router rip 1**

   C. Router(config)#**ipv6 router eigrp 10**

   D. Router(config-rtr)#**no shutdown**

   E. Router(config-if)#**ospf ipv6 10 area 0**

Chapter

4

IP Routing Technologies

THE FOLLOWING CCNA ROUTING AND SWITCHING EXAM OBJECTIVES ARE COVERED IN THIS CHAPTER:

✓ **Describe basic routing concepts.**

- Packet forwarding
- CEF
- Router lookup process

✓ **Describe the boot process of Cisco IOS routers.**

- POST
- Router Bootup Process

✓ **Configure and verify utilizing the CLI to set basic Router configuration.**

- Cisco IOS commands to perform basic router setup

✓ **Configure and verify operation status of a device interface, both serial and ethernet.**

✓ **Verify router configuration and network connectivity.**

- Cisco IOS commands to review basic router information and network connectivity

✓ **Configure and verify routing configuration for a static or default route given specific routing requirements.**

✓ **Manage Cisco IOS Files.**

- Boot preferences
- Cisco IOS image(s)
- Licensing
  - Show license
  - Change license

✓ **Differentiate Methods of Routing and Routing Protocols.**

  - Static vs. Dynamic

  - Link state vs. Distance Vector

  - Administrative distance

  - split horizon

  - metric

  - next hop

  - ip routing table

  - Passive interfaces

✓ **Configure and verify OSPF (single area).**

  - Benefit of single area

  - neighbor adjacencies

  - OSPF states

  - Discuss Multi area

  - Configure OSPF v2

  - Configure OSPF v3

  - Router ID

  - Passive Interface

  - LSA types

✓ **Configure and verify EIGRP (single AS).**

  - Feasible Distance / Feasible Successors /Administrative distance

  - Feasibility condition

  - Metric composition

  - Router ID

  - Auto summary

  - Path selection

  - Load balancing

    - Equal

    - Unequal

  - Passive interface

✓ **Configure and verify interVLAN routing (Router on a stick).**

- sub interfaces
- upstream Routing
- encapsulation

✓ **Configure SVI interfaces.**

In this chapter, I will begin by covering some basic routing concepts, such as packet forwarding. I will go over the router boot process and how to configure a router interface. I will also cover how to ensure network connectivity and manage router IOS files. Finally, I will go over some routing protocols, such OSPF, EIGRP, and inter-VLAN routing.

Describe Basic Routing Concepts

The term *routing* refers to taking a packet from one device and sending it through the network to another device on a different network. Routers don't really care about hosts—they only care about networks and the best path to each one of them. The logical network address of the destination host is key to get packets through a routed network. It's the hardware address of the host that's used to deliver the packet from a router and ensure that it arrives at the correct destination host.

Routing is irrelevant if your network has no routers because their job is to route traffic to all the networks in your internetwork, but this is rarely the case! So here's an important list of the minimum factors a router must know to be able to affectively route packets:

- Destination address
- Neighbor routers from which it can learn about remote networks
- Possible routes to all remote networks
- The best route to each remote network
- How to maintain and verify routing information

The router learns about remote networks from neighboring routers or from an administrator. The router then builds a routing table, which is basically a map of the internetwork, and it describes how to find remote networks. If a network is directly connected, then the router already knows how to get to it.

But if a network isn't directly connected to the router, the router must use one of two ways to learn how to get to the remote network. The *static routing* method requires someone to hand-type all network locations into the routing table, which can be a pretty daunting task when used on all but the smallest of networks!

Conversely, when *dynamic routing* is used, a protocol on one router communicates with the same protocol running on neighboring routers. The routers then update each other about all the networks they know about and place this information into the routing table. If a change occurs in the network, the dynamic routing protocols automatically inform all routers about the event. If static routing is used, the administrator is responsible for updating all changes by hand onto all routers. Most people usually use a combination of dynamic and static routing to administer a large network.

Before we jump into the IP routing process, let's take a look at a very simple example that demonstrates how a router uses the routing table to route packets out of an interface. We'll be going into a more detailed study of the process soon, but I want to show you something called the "longest match rule" first. With it, IP will scan a routing table to find the longest match as compared to the destination address of a packet. Let's take a look at Figure 4.1 to get a picture of this process.

FIGURE 4.1 A simple routing example

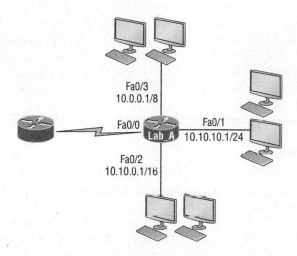

Figure 4.1 shows a simple network. Lab_A has four interfaces. Can you see which interface will be used to forward an IP datagram to a host with a destination IP address of 10.10.10.30?

By using the command show ip route on a router, we can see the routing table (map of the internetwork) that Lab_A has used to make its forwarding decisions:

```
Lab_A#sh ip route
Codes: L - local, C - connected, S - static,
[output cut]
        10.0.0.0/8 is variably subnetted, 6 subnets, 4 masks
C       10.0.0.0/8 is directly connected, FastEthernet0/3
L       10.0.0.1/32 is directly connected, FastEthernet0/3
C       10.10.0.0/16 is directly connected, FastEthernet0/2
L       10.10.0.1/32 is directly connected, FastEthernet0/2
C       10.10.10.0/24 is directly connected, FastEthernet0/1
L       10.10.10.1/32 is directly connected, FastEthernet0/1
S*      0.0.0.0/0 is directly connected, FastEthernet0/0
```

The C in the routing table output means that the networks listed are "directly connected," and until we add a routing protocol like RIPv2, OSPF, and so on, to the routers in our inter-network, or enter static routes, only directly connected networks will show up in our routing table. But wait—what about that L in the routing table—that's new, isn't it? Yes it is, because in the new Cisco IOS 15 code, Cisco defines a different route, called a local route. Each has a /32 prefix defining a route just for the one address. So in this example, the router has relied upon these routes that list their own local IP addresses to more efficiently forward packets to the router itself.

Packet Forwarding

For IP to look up a destination address in a routing table on a router, processing in the router must take place, and if there are tens of thousands of routes in that table, the amount of CPU time would be enormous. It results in a potentially overwhelming amount of overhead—think about a router at your ISP that has to calculate millions of packets per second and even subnet to find the correct exit interface! Even with the little network I'm using in this book, lots of processing would need to be done if there were actual hosts connected and sending data.

As explained in Chapter 1, Cisco uses three types of packet-forwarding techniques.

Process Switching

The first technique, process switching, is actually how many people see routers to this day because routers actually did perform this type of bare-bones packet switching back in 1990 when Cisco released its very first router. But those days when traffic demands were unimaginably light are long gone! This process is now extremely complex and involves looking up every destination in the routing table and finding the exit interface for every packet. This is pretty much how I explained the process in Chapter 1 in my 36 steps. But even though what I wrote was absolutely true in concept, the internal process requires much more than packet-switching technology today because of the millions of packets per second that must now be processed. So Cisco came up with some other technologies to help with the "big process problem."

Fast Switching

The second solution, fast switching, was created to make the slow performance of process switching faster and more efficient. Fast switching uses a cache to store the most recently used destinations so that lookups are not required for every packet. By caching the exit interface of the destination device, as well as the layer 2 header, performance was dramatically improved.

However, as our networks evolved with the need for even more speed, Cisco created yet another technology, Cisco Express Forwarding (CEF)!

CEF

Cisco Express Forwarding (CEF) is Cisco's newer creation, and it's the default packet-forwarding method used on all the latest Cisco routers. CEF makes many different cache tables to help improve performance and is change triggered, not packet triggered. Translated, this means that when the network topology changes, the cache changes along with it.

Router Lookup Process

Once a router has built its routing table from directly connected neighbors or from a static route entered by an administrator, it is ready to forward packets. When a packet is received on an interface, the router looks for a route that matches the packet's destination IP address. If the destination IP address matches similar remote networks, the router uses a longest match rule to determine the exit interface to send the packet. If a destination route cannot be found in the routing table, the packet is discarded.

Exam Essentials

List the information required by a router to successfully route packets.   To be able to route packets, a router must know, at a minimum, the destination address, the location of neighboring routers through which it can reach remote networks, possible routes to all remote networks, the best route to each remote network, and how to maintain and verify routing information.

View and interpret the routing table of a router.   Use the show ip route command to view the routing table. Each route will be listed along with the source of the routing information. A C to the left of the route will indicate directly connected routes, and other letters next to the route can also indicate a particular routing protocol that provided the information, such as, for example, R for RIP.

Compare and contrast static and dynamic routing.   Static routing creates no routing update traffic and creates less overhead on the router and network links, but it must be configured manually and does not have the ability to react to link outages. Dynamic routing creates routing update traffic and uses more overhead on the router and network links.

Describe the Boot Process of Cisco IOS Routers

Unless you happen to be really savvy about the inner and outer workings of all your car's systems and its machinery and how all of that technology works together, you'll take it to someone who *does* know how to keep it maintained, figure out what's wrong when it stops running, and get it up and running again. It's the same deal with Cisco networking devices— you need to know all about their major components, pieces, and parts as well as what they all do and why and how they all work together to make a network work. They more solid your knowledge, the more expert you are about these things and the better equipped you'll be to configure and troubleshoot a Cisco internetwork.

POST

The power-on self-test (POST) tests the hardware to verify that all components of the device are present and operational. For example, the POST checks for the different interfaces on the router. The POST is stored in and runs from read-only memory (ROM).

Router Bootup Process

When a router boots up, it performs a series of steps, called the boot sequence, to test the hardware and load the necessary software. The boot sequence consists of the following steps:

1. The router performs a POST.

2. The bootstrap then looks for and loads the Cisco IOS software. The bootstrap is a program in ROM that is used to execute programs. The bootstrap program is responsible for finding where each IOS program is located and then loading the file. By default, the IOS software is loaded from flash memory in all Cisco routers.

> The default order of an IOS loading from a Cisco device begins with flash, then TFTP server, and finally, ROM.

3. The IOS software looks for a valid configuration file stored in NVRAM. This file is called startup-config and is present in NVRAM only if an administrator copies the running-config file into NVRAM. (Cisco's new Integrated Services Router [ISR] has a small startup-config file preloaded.)

4. If a startup-config file is in NVRAM, the router will copy this file and place it in RAM and then call the file running-config. The router will use this file to run the router. The router should then be operational. If a startup-config file is not present in NVRAM, the router will attempt to locate a TFTP server that may contain this file. It will do so by broadcasting out any interface that detects carrier detect (CD), and if that fails, it will start the setup mode configuration process.

Exam Essentials

Identify the steps in the router boot sequence.   The steps in the boot sequence are POST, loading the IOS, and copying the startup configuration from NVRAM to RAM.

Configure and Verify Utilizing the CLI to Set Basic Router Configuration

In this section we'll go over the different router prompts as well as cover the basic administrative functions on a router.

Entering the CLI

After the interface status messages appear and you press Enter, the Router> prompt will pop up. This is called *user exec mode*, or user mode for short, and although it's mostly used to view statistics, it is also a stepping stone along the way to logging in to *privileged exec mode*, called privileged mode for short.

You can view and change the configuration of a Cisco router only while in privileged mode, and you enter it via the enable command like this:

```
Router>enable
Router#
```

The Router# prompt signals you're in privileged mode where you can both view and change the router configuration. You can go back from privileged mode into user mode by using the disable command:

```
Router#disable
Router>
```

You can type **logout** from either mode to exit the console:

```
Router>logout

Router con0 is now available
Press RETURN to get started.
```

Overview of Router Modes

To configure from a CLI, you can make global changes to the router by typing **configure terminal** or just **config t**. This will get you into global configuration mode where you can make changes to the running-config. Commands run from global configuration mode are predictably referred to as global commands, and they are typically set only once and affect the entire router.

Type **config** from the privileged-mode prompt and then press Enter to opt for the default of terminal like this:

```
Router#config
Configuring from terminal, memory, or network [terminal]? [press enter]
```

```
Enter configuration commands, one per line.  End with CNTL/Z.
Router(config)#
```

At this point, you make changes that affect the router as a whole (globally), hence the term *global configuration mode*. For instance, to change the running-config—the current configuration running in dynamic RAM (DRAM)—use the configure terminal command, as I just demonstrated.

CLI Prompts

Let's explore the different prompts you'll encounter when configuring a switch or router now, because knowing them well will really help you orient yourself and recognize exactly where you are at any given time while in configuration mode.

Interfaces

To make changes to an interface, you use the interface command from global configuration mode:

```
Router(config)#interface ?
  Async              Async interface
  BVI                Bridge-Group Virtual Interface
  CTunnel            CTunnel interface
  Dialer             Dialer interface
  FastEthernet       FastEthernet IEEE 802.3
  Filter             Filter interface
  Filtergroup        Filter Group interface
  GigabitEthernet    GigabitEthernet IEEE 802.3z
  Group-Async        Async Group interface
  Lex                Lex interface
  Loopback           Loopback interface
  Null               Null interface
  Port-channel       Ethernet Channel of interfaces
  Portgroup          Portgroup interface
  Pos-channel        POS Channel of interfaces
  Tunnel             Tunnel interface
  Vif                PGM Multicast Host interface
  Virtual-Template   Virtual Template interface
  Virtual-TokenRing  Virtual TokenRing
  Vlan               Catalyst Vlans
  fcpa               Fiber Channel
  range              interface range command
```

```
Switch(config)#interface fastEthernet 0/1
Switch(config-if)#)
```

The prompt changed to Router(config-if)#? This tells you that you're in *interface configuration mode*.

Line Commands

To configure user-mode passwords, use the line command. The prompt then becomes Router(config-line)#:

```
Router(config)#line ?
  <0-16>   First Line number
  console  Primary terminal line
  vty      Virtual terminal
Router(config)#line console 0
Router(config-line)#
```

The line console 0 command is a global command, and sometimes you'll also hear people refer to global commands as major commands. In this example, any command typed from the (config-line) prompt is known as a subcommand.

Access List Configurations

To configure a standard named access list, you'll need to get to the prompt Router(config-std-nacl)#:

```
Router#config t
Router(config)#ip access-list standard Todd
Router(config-std-nacl)#
```

What you see here is a typical basic standard ACL prompt. There are various ways to configure access lists, and the prompts are only slightly different from this particular example.

Routing Protocol Configurations

Here is an example of configuring routing on a router:

```
Router(config)#router rip
IP routing not enabled
Router(config)#ip routing
Router(config)#router rip
Router(config-router)#
```

Notice how the prompt changed to Router(config-router)#?

Defining Router Terms

Table 4.1 defines some of the terms I've used so far.

TABLE 4.1   Router terms

Mode	Definition
User exec mode	Limited to basic monitoring commands
Privileged exec mode	Provides access to all other router commands
Global configuration mode	Commands that affect the entire system
Specific configuration modes	Commands that affect interfaces/processes only
Setup mode	Interactive configuration dialog

Cisco IOS Commands to Perform Basic Router Setup

Even though the information in the following sections isn't critical to making a router or switch *work* on a network, it's still really important.

You can configure the following administrative functions on a router and switch:

- Hostnames
- Banners
- Passwords
- Interface descriptions

Hostnames

We use the hostname command to set the identity of the router. This is only locally significant, meaning it doesn't affect how the router performs name lookups or how the device actually works on the internetwork. But the hostname is still important because it's often used for authentication in many wide area networks (WANs). Here's an example:

```
Router#config t
Router(config)#hostname Todd
Todd(config)#hostname Chicago
Chicago(config)#hostname Todd
Todd(config)#
```

Banners

A very good reason for having a *banner* is to give any and all who dare attempt to telnet or sneak into your internetwork a little security notice. Here are the three types of banners you need to be sure you're familiar with:

- Exec process creation banner
- Login banner
- Message of the day banner

And you can see them all illustrated in the following code:

```
Todd(config)#banner ?
  LINE            c banner-text c, where 'c' is a delimiting character
  exec            Set EXEC process creation banner
  incoming        Set incoming terminal line banner
  login           Set login banner
  motd            Set Message of the Day banner
  prompt-timeout  Set Message for login authentication timeout
  slip-ppp        Set Message for SLIP/PPP
```

Message of the day (MOTD) banners are the most widely used banners because they give a message to anyone connecting to the router via Telnet or an auxiliary port or even through a console port as seen here:

```
Todd(config)#banner motd ?
LINE c banner-text c, where 'c' is a delimiting character
Todd(config)#banner motd #
Enter TEXT message. End with the character '#'.
$ Acme.com network, then you must disconnect immediately.
#
Todd(config)#^Z (Press the control key + z keys to return to privileged mode)
Todd#exit
Router con0 is now available
Press RETURN to get started.
If you are not authorized to be in Acme.com network, then you
must disconnect immediately.
Todd#
```

This MOTD banner essentially tells anyone connecting to the router to get lost if they're not on the guest list. The part to focus upon here is the delimiting character, which is what informs the router the message is done. Clearly, you can use any character you want for it except for the delimiting character in the message itself. Once the message is complete, press Enter, then press the delimiting character, and then press Enter again. Everything will still work if you don't follow this routine unless you have more than one banner. If that's the case, make sure you do follow it or your banners will all be combined into one message and put on a single line!

You can set a banner on one line like this:

```
Todd(config)#banner motd x Unauthorized access prohibited! x
```

Let's take a minute to go into more detail about the other two types of banners I mentioned:

Exec banner   You can configure a line-activation (exec) banner to be displayed when EXEC processes such as a line activation or an incoming connection to a VTY line have been created. Simply initiating a user exec session through a console port will activate the exec banner.

Login banner   You can configure a login banner for display on all connected terminals. It will show up after the MOTD banner but before the login prompts. This login banner can't be disabled on a per-line basis, so to globally disable it you've got to delete it with the no banner login command.

Here's what a login banner output looks like:

```
!
banner login ^C
----------------------------------------------------------------
Cisco Router and Security Device Manager (SDM) is installed on this device.
This feature requires the one-time use of the username "cisco"
with the password "cisco". The default username and password
have a privilege level of 15.
Please change these publicly known initial credentials using
SDM or the IOS CLI.
Here are the Cisco IOS commands.
username <myuser>  privilege 15 secret 0 <mypassword>
no username cisco
Replace <myuser> and <mypassword> with the username and
password you want to use.
For more information about SDM please follow the instructions
in the QUICK START GUIDE for your router or go to http://www.cisco.com/go/sdm
----------------------------------------------------------------
^C
!
```

This login banner should look pretty familiar to anyone who's ever logged into an ISR router because it's the banner Cisco has in the default configuration for its ISR routers.

Remember that the login banner is displayed before the login prompts and after the MOTD banner.

Setting Passwords

There are five passwords you'll need to secure your Cisco routers: console, auxiliary, telnet (VTY), enable password, and enable secret. The enable secret and enable password are the ones used to set the password for securing privileged mode. Once the `enable` commands are set, users will be prompted for a password. The other three are used to configure a password when user mode is accessed through the console port, through the auxiliary port, or via Telnet.

Let's take a look at each of these now.

Enable Passwords

You set the enable passwords from global configuration mode like this:

```
Todd(config)#enable ?
 last-resort Define enable action if no TACACS servers
            respond
 password   Assign the privileged level password
 secret     Assign the privileged level secret
 use-tacacs Use TACACS to check enable passwords
```

The following list describes the enable password parameters:

last-resort   This allows you to still enter the router if you set up authentication through a TACACS server and it's not available. It won't be used if the TACACS server is working.

password   This sets the enable password on older, pre-10.3 systems and isn't ever used if an enable secret is set.

secret   This sets the newer, encrypted password that overrides the enable password if it has been set.

use-tacacs   This tells the router to authenticate through a TACACS server. It comes in really handy when you have lots of routers because changing the password on a multitude of them can be insanely tedious. It's much easier to simply go through the TACACS server and change the password only once!

Here's an example that shows how to set the enable passwords:

```
Todd(config)#enable secret todd
Todd(config)#enable password todd
The enable password you have chosen is the same as your
  enable secret. This is not recommended. Re-enter the
  enable password.
```

If you try to set the enable secret and enable passwords the same, the router will give you a polite warning to change the second password. Make a note to yourself that if there aren't any old legacy routers involved, you don't even bother to use the enable password!

User-mode passwords are assigned via the line command like this:

```
Todd(config)#line ?
  <0-16>    First Line number
  console   Primary terminal line
  vty       Virtual terminal
```

And these two lines are especially important for the exam objectives:

console   Sets a console user-mode password.

vty   Sets a Telnet password on the router. If this password isn't set, then by default, Telnet can't be used.

To configure user-mode passwords, choose the line you want and configure it using the login command to make the switch prompt for authentication. Let's focus on the configuration of individual lines now.

Console Password

We set the console password with the line console 0 command, but look at what happened when I tried to type **line console ?** from the (config-line)# prompt—I received an error! Here's the example:

```
Todd(config-line)#line console ?
% Unrecognized command
Todd(config-line)#exit
Todd(config)#line console ?
  <0-0>  First Line number
Todd(config-line)#password console
Todd(config-line)#login
```

You can still type **line console 0** and that will be accepted, but the help screens just don't work from that prompt. Type **exit** to go back one level, and you'll find that your help screens now work.

And it's also important to remember to apply the login command or the console port won't prompt for authentication. The way Cisco has this process set up means you can't set the login command before a password is set on a line because if you set it but don't then set a password, that line won't be usable. You'll actually get prompted for a password that doesn't exist, so Cisco's method isn't just a hassle; it makes sense and is a feature after all!

> Definitely remember that although Cisco has this "password feature" on its routers starting with IOS 12.2 and above, it's not included in older IOSs.

Okay, there are a few other important commands you need to know regarding the console port.

For one, the exec-timeout 0 0 command sets the time-out for the console EXEC session to zero, ensuring that it never times out. The default time-out is 10 minutes.

Logging synchronous is such a cool command that it should be a default, but it's not. It's great because it's the antidote for those annoying console messages that disrupt the input you're trying to type. The messages will still pop up, but at least you get returned to your router prompt without your input being interrupted! This makes your input messages oh-so-much easier to read!

Here's an example of how to configure both commands:

```
Todd(config-line)#line con 0
Todd(config-line)#exec-timeout ?
  <0-35791>  Timeout in minutes
Todd(config-line)#exec-timeout 0 ?
  <0-2147483>  Timeout in seconds
  <cr>
Todd(config-line)#exec-timeout 0 0
Todd(config-line)#logging synchronous
```

> **NOTE** You can set the console to go from never timing out (0 0) to timing out in 35,791 minutes and 2,147,483 seconds. Remember that the default is 10 minutes.

Telnet Password

To set the user-mode password for Telnet access into the router or switch, use the line vty command. IOS switches typically have 16 lines, but routers running the Enterprise edition have considerably more. The best way to find out how many lines you have is to use that handy question mark like this:

```
Todd(config-line)#line vty 0 ?
% Unrecognized command
Todd(config-line)#exit
Todd(config)#line vty 0 ?
  <1-15>  Last Line number
  <cr>
Todd(config)#line vty 0 15
Todd(config-line)#password telnet
Todd(config-line)#login
```

This output clearly shows that you cannot get help from your (config-line)# prompt. You must go back to global config mode in order to use the question mark (?).

So what will happen if you try to telnet into a device that doesn't have a VTY password set? You'll receive an error saying the connection has been refused because the password isn't set. So, if you telnet into a switch and receive a message like this one that I got from Switch B, it means the switch doesn't have the VTY password set:

```
Todd#telnet SwitchB
Trying SwitchB (10.0.0.1)…Open

Password required, but none set
[Connection to SwitchB closed by foreign host]
Todd#
```

But you can still get around this and tell the switch to allow Telnet connections without a password by using the no login command:

```
SwitchB(config-line)#line vty 0 15
SwitchB(config-line)#no login
```

 WARNING I definitely do not recommend using the no login command to allow Telnet connections without a password, unless you're in a testing or classroom environment. In a production network, always set your VTY password!

After your IOS devices are configured with an IP address, you can use the Telnet program to configure and check your routers instead of having to use a console cable. You can use the Telnet program by typing **telnet** from any command prompt (DOS or Cisco).

Auxiliary Password

To configure the auxiliary password on a router, go into global configuration mode and type **line aux ?**. And by the way, you won't find these ports on a switch. This output shows that you only get a choice of 0–0, which is because there's only one port:

```
Todd#config t
Todd(config)#line aux ?
  <0-0>  First Line number
Todd(config)#line aux 0
Todd(config-line)#login
% Login disabled on line 1, until 'password' is set
Todd(config-line)#password aux
Todd(config-line)#login
```

Setting Up Secure Shell (SSH)

I strongly recommend using Secure Shell (SSH) instead of Telnet because it creates a more secure session. The Telnet application uses an unencrypted data stream, but SSH uses encryption keys to send data so your username and password aren't sent in the clear, vulnerable to anyone lurking around!

Here are the steps for setting up SSH:

1. Set your hostname:

```
Router(config)#hostname Todd
```

2. Set the domain name—both the hostname and domain name are required for the encryption keys to be generated:

```
Todd(config)#ip domain-name Lammle.com
```

3. Set the username to allow SSH client access:

```
Todd(config)#username Todd password Lammle
```

4. Generate the encryption keys for securing the session:

```
Todd(config)#crypto key generate rsa
The name for the keys will be: Todd.Lammle.com
Choose the size of the key modulus in the range of 360 to
4096 for your General Purpose Keys. Choosing a key modulus
Greater than 512 may take a few minutes.


How many bits in the modulus [512]: 1024
% Generating 1024 bit RSA keys, keys will be non-exportable...
[OK] (elapsed time was 6 seconds)


Todd(config)#
1d14h: %SSH-5-ENABLED: SSH 1.99 has been enabled*June 24
19:25:30.035: %SSH-5-ENABLED: SSH 1.99 has been enabled
```

5. Enable SSH version 2 on the router—not mandatory, but strongly suggested:

```
Todd(config)#ip ssh version 2
```

6. Connect to the VTY lines of the switch:

```
Todd(config)#line vty 0 15
```

7. Configure your access protocols:

```
Todd(config-line)#transport input ?
  all     All protocols
  none    No protocols
  ssh     TCP/IP SSH protocol
  telnet  TCP/IP Telnet protocol
```

Beware of this next line, and make sure you never use it in production because it's a horrendous security risk:

```
Todd(config-line)#transport input all
```

I recommend using the next line to secure your VTY lines with SSH:

```
Todd(config-line)#transport input ssh ?
  telnet  TCP/IP Telnet protocol
  <cr>
```

I actually do use Telnet once in a while when a situation arises that specifically calls for it. It just doesn't happen very often. But if you want to go with Telnet, here's how you do that:

```
Todd(config-line)#transport input ssh telnet
```

Know that if you don't use the keyword telnet at the end of the command string, then only SSH will work on the device. You can go with either, just so long as you understand that SSH is way more secure than Telnet.

Encrypting Your Passwords

Because only the enable secret password is encrypted by default, you'll need to manually configure the user-mode and enable passwords for encryption.

Notice that you can see all the passwords except the enable secret when performing a show running-config on a switch:

```
Todd#sh running-config
Building configuration...

Current configuration : 1020 bytes
!
! Last configuration change at 00:03:11 UTC Mon Mar 1 1993
!
version 15.0
no service pad
service timestamps debug datetime msec
service timestamps log datetime msec
no service password-encryption
!
hostname Todd
!
enable secret 4 ykw.3/tgsOuy9.6qmgG/EeYOYgBvfX4v.S8UNA9Rddg
```

```
enable password todd
!
[output cut]
!
line con 0
 password console
 login
line vty 0 4
 password telnet
 login
line vty 5 15
 password telnet
 login
!
end
```

To manually encrypt your passwords, use the service password-encryption command. Here's how:

```
Todd#config t
Todd(config)#service password-encryption
Todd(config)#exit
Todd#show run
Building configuration...
!
!
enable secret 4 ykw.3/tgsOuy9.6qmgG/EeYOYgBvfX4v.S8UNA9Rddg
enable password 7 1506040800
!
[output cut]
!
!
line con 0
 password 7 050809013243420C
 login
line vty 0 4
 password 7 06120A2D424B1D
 login
line vty 5 15
 password 7 06120A2D424B1D
 login
!
end
```

The passwords will now be encrypted. This output clearly shows us that the enable password and the line passwords are all encrypted.

Descriptions

Setting descriptions on an interface is another administratively helpful thing, and like the hostname, it's also only locally significant. One case where the description command comes in really handy is when you want to keep track of circuit numbers on a switch or a router's serial WAN port.

Here's an example on my switch:

```
Todd#config t
Todd(config)#int fa0/1
Todd(config-if)#description Sales VLAN Trunk Link
Todd(config-if)#^Z
Todd#
```

And on a router serial WAN:

```
Router#config t
Router(config)#int s0/0/0
Router(config-if)#description WAN to Miami
Router(config-if)#^Z
```

You can view an interface's description with either the show running-config command or the show interface—even with the show interface description command:

```
Todd#sh run
Building configuration...

Current configuration : 855 bytes
!
interface FastEthernet0/1
 description Sales VLAN Trunk Link
!
 [output cut]


Todd#sh int f0/1
FastEthernet0/1 is up, line protocol is up (connected)
  Hardware is Fast Ethernet, address is ecc8.8202.8282 (bia ecc8.8202.8282)
  Description: Sales VLAN Trunk Link
  MTU 1500 bytes, BW 100000 Kbit/sec, DLY 100 usec,
 [output cut]
```

```
Todd#sh int description
Interface                    Status        Protocol Description
Vl1                          up            up
Fa0/1                        up            up       Sales VLAN Trunk Link
Fa0/2                        up            up
```

Exam Essentials

Differentiate user, privileged, and global configuration modes, both visually and from a command capabilities perspective. User mode, indicated by the **routername>** prompt, provides a command-line interface with very few available commands by default. User mode does not allow the configuration to be viewed or changed. Privileged mode, indicated by the **routername#** prompt, allows a user to both view and change the configuration of a router. You can enter privileged mode by typing the command **enable** and entering the enable password or enable secret password, if set. Global configuration mode, indicated by the **routername(config)#** prompt, allows configuration changes to be made that apply to the entire router (as opposed to a configuration change that might affect only one interface, for example).

Recognize additional prompts available and describe their use. Additional modes are reached via the global configuration prompt, **routername(config)#**, and their prompts include interface mode, **router(config-if)#**, for making interface settings; line configuration mode, **router(config-line)#**, used to set passwords and make other settings to various connection methods; and routing protocol modes for various routing protocols, router(config-router)#, used to enable and configure routing protocols.

Access and utilize editing and help features. Make use of typing a question mark at the end of commands for help in using the commands. Additionally, understand how to filter command help with the same question mark and letters. Use the command history to retrieve commands previously utilized without retyping. Understand the meaning of the caret when an incorrect command is rejected. Finally, identify useful hot key combinations.

Identify the information provided by the show version command. The show version command will provide basic configuration for the system hardware as well as the software version, the names and sources of configuration files, the configuration register setting, and the boot images.

Set the hostname of a router. The command sequence to set the hostname of a router is as follows:

```
Router>enable
Router#config t
Router(config)#hostname Todd
```

Differentiate the enable password and enable secret password.   Both of these passwords are used to gain access into privileged mode. However, the enable secret password is newer and is always encrypted by default. Also, if you set the enable password and then set the enable secret, only the enable secret will be used.

Describe the configuration and use of banners.   Banners provide information to users accessing a device and can be displayed at various login prompts. They are configured with the banner command and a keyword describing the specific type of banner.

Set the enable secret on a router.   To set the enable secret, you use the global config command `enable secret`. Do not use `enable secret password password` or you will set your password to `password password`. Here is an example:

```
Router>enable
Router#config t
Router(config)#enable secret todd
```

Set the console password on a router.   To set the console password, use the following sequence:

```
Router>enable
Router#config t
Router(config)#line console 0
Router(confog-line)password todd
Router(config-line)#login
```

Set the Telnet password on a router.   To set the Telnet password, the sequence is as follows:

```
Router>enable
Router#config t
Router(config)#line vty 0 4
Router(confog-line)password todd
Router(config-line)#login
```

Configure and Verify Operation Status of a Device Interface, Both Serial and Ethernet

Interface configuration is arguably the most important router configuration because without interfaces, a router is a pretty useless object. Furthermore, interface configurations must be totally precise to enable communication with other devices. Network layer addresses, media type, bandwidth, and other administrator commands are all used to configure an interface.

On a layer 2 switch, interface configurations typically involve a lot less work than router interface configuration. Check out the output from the powerful verification command show ip interface brief, which reveals all the interfaces on my 3560 switch:

```
Todd#sh ip interface brief
Interface             IP-Address        OK? Method Status          Protocol
Vlan1                 192.168.255.8     YES DHCP   up                    up
FastEthernet0/1       unassigned        YES unset  up                    up
FastEthernet0/2       unassigned        YES unset  up                    up
FastEthernet0/3       unassigned        YES unset  down                down
FastEthernet0/4       unassigned        YES unset  down                down
FastEthernet0/5       unassigned        YES unset  up                    up
FastEthernet0/6       unassigned        YES unset  up                    up
FastEthernet0/7       unassigned        YES unset  down                down
FastEthernet0/8       unassigned        YES unset  down                down
GigabitEthernet0/1    unassigned        YES unset  down                down
```

The previous output shows the default routed port found on all Cisco switches (VLAN 1) plus nine layer-2 switch Fast Ethernet interface ports, with one port being a Gigabit Ethernet port used for uplinks to other switches.

Different routers use different methods to choose the interfaces used on them. For instance, the following command shows one of my 2800 ISR Cisco routers with two Fast Ethernet interfaces along with two serial WAN interfaces:

```
Router>sh ip int brief
Interface        IP-Address       OK? Method Status                     Protocol
FastEthernet0/0  192.168.255.11   YES DHCP   up                              up
FastEthernet0/1  unassigned       YES unset  administratively down     down
Serial0/0/0      unassigned       YES unset  administratively down     down
Serial0/1/0      unassigned       YES unset  administratively down     down
Router>
```

Previously, we always used the interface *type number* sequence to configure an interface, but the newer routers come with an actual physical slot and include a port number on the module plugged into it. So on a modular router, the configuration would be interface *type slot/port*, as demonstrated here:

```
Todd#config t
Todd(config)#interface GigabitEthernet 0/1
Todd(config-if)#
```

You can see that we are now at the Gigabit Ethernet slot 0, port 1 prompt, and from here we can make configuration changes to the interface. Make note of the fact that you can't just type **int gigabitethernet 0**. No shortcuts on the slot/port—you've got to type the slot/port variables in the command: *type slot/port* or, for example, **int gigabitethernet 0/1** (or just **int g0/1**).

Once in interface configuration mode, we can configure various options. Keep in mind that speed and duplex are the two factors to be concerned with for the LAN:

```
Todd#config t
Todd(config)#interface GigabitEthernet 0/1
Todd(config-if)#speed 1000
Todd(config-if)#duplex full
```

This command has shut off the autodetect mechanism on the port, forcing it to only run gigabit speeds at full duplex. For the ISR series router, it's basically the same, but you get even more options! The LAN interfaces are the same, but the rest of the modules are different—they use three numbers instead of two. The three numbers used here can represent slot/subslot/port, but this depends on the card used in the ISR router. For the exam, you just need to remember this: The first 0 is the router itself. You then choose the slot and then the port. Here's an example of a serial interface on my 2811:

```
Todd(config)#interface serial ?
  <0-2>  Serial interface number
Todd(config)#interface serial 0/0/?
  <0-1>  Serial interface number
Todd(config)#interface serial 0/0/0
Todd(config-if)#
```

View the output of the show ip interface brief command or a show running-config output first so you know the exact interfaces you have to deal with. Here's the output from one of my 2811s that has even more serial interfaces installed:

```
Todd(config-if)#do show run
Building configuration...
[output cut]
!
interface FastEthernet0/0
 no ip address
 shutdown
 duplex auto
 speed auto
!
interface FastEthernet0/1
 no ip address
 shutdown
 duplex auto
 speed auto
!
```

```
interface Serial0/0/0
 no ip address
 shutdown
 no fair-queue
!
interface Serial0/0/1
 no ip address
 shutdown
!
interface Serial0/1/0
 no ip address
 shutdown
!
interface Serial0/2/0
 no ip address
 shutdown
 clock rate 2000000
!
[output cut]
```

For the sake of brevity, I didn't include my complete running-config, but I've displayed all you really need. You can see the two built-in Fast Ethernet interfaces, the two serial interfaces in slot 0 (0/0/0 and 0/0/1), the serial interface in slot 1 (0/1/0), and the serial interface in slot 2 (0/2/0). And once you see the interfaces like this, it makes it a lot easier to understand how the modules are inserted into the router.

Just understand that if you type **interface e0** on an old 2500 series router, **interface fastethernet 0/0** on a modular router (such as the 2800 series router), or **interface serial 0/1/0** on a ISR router, all you're actually doing is choosing an interface to configure. Essentially, they're all configured the same way after that.

Bringing Up an Interface

You can disable an interface with the interface command shutdown and enable it with the no shutdown command. Just to remind you, all switch ports are enabled by default and all router ports are disabled by default, so we're going to talk more about router ports than switch ports in the next few sections.

If an interface is shut down, it'll display as administratively down when you use the show interfaces command (sh int for short):

```
Router#sh int f0/0
FastEthernet0/1 is administratively down, line protocol is down
[output cut]
```

Another way to check an interface's status is via the show running-config command. You can bring up the router interface with the no shutdown command (no shut for short):

```
Router(config)#int f0/0
Router(config-if)#no shutdown
*August 21 13:45:08.455: %LINK-3-UPDOWN: Interface FastEthernet0/0,
    changed state to up
Router(config-if)#do show int f0/0
FastEthernet0/0 is up, line protocol is up
[output cut]
```

Configuring an IP Address on an Interface

Even though you don't have to use IP on your routers, it's usually what everyone uses. To configure IP addresses on an interface, use the ip address command from interface configuration mode and remember that you do not set an IP address on a layer 2 switch port!

```
Todd(config)#int f0/1
Todd(config-if)#ip address 172.16.10.2 255.255.255.0
```

Also, don't forget to enable the interface with the no shutdown command. Remember to look at the show interface *int* output to see if the interface is administratively shut down or not. Show ip int brief and show running-config will also give you this information.

The ip address *address mask* command starts the IP processing on the router interface. Again, you do not configure an IP address on a layer 2 switch interface!

Okay—now if you want to add a second subnet address to an interface, you have to use the secondary parameter. If you type another IP address and press Enter, it will replace the existing primary IP address and mask. This is definitely one of the Cisco IOS's coolest features!

So let's try it. To add a secondary IP address, just use the secondary parameter:

```
Todd(config-if)#ip address 172.16.20.2 255.255.255.0 ?
  secondary  Make this IP address a secondary address
  <cr>
Todd(config-if)#ip address 172.16.20.2 255.255.255.0 secondary
Todd(config-if)#^Z
Todd(config-if)#do sh run
Building configuration...
[output cut]

interface FastEthernet0/1
 ip address 172.16.20.2 255.255.255.0 secondary
```

```
 ip address 172.16.10.2 255.255.255.0
 duplex auto
 speed auto
!
```

But I've got to stop here to tell you that I really wouldn't recommend having multiple IP addresses on an interface because it's really inefficient. I showed you how anyway just in case you someday find yourself dealing with an MIS manager who's in love with really bad network design and makes you administer it! And who knows? Maybe someone will ask you about it someday and you'll get to seem really smart because you know this.

Using the Pipe

This pipe (|) allows us to wade through all the configurations or other long outputs. Here's an example:

```
Router#sh run | ?
  append    Append redirected output to URL (URLs supporting append
            operation only)
  begin     Begin with the line that matches
  exclude   Exclude lines that match
  include   Include lines that match
  redirect  Redirect output to URL
  section   Filter a section of output
  tee       Copy output to URL

Router#sh run | begin interface
interface FastEthernet0/0
 description Sales VLAN
 ip address 10.10.10.1 255.255.255.248
 duplex auto
 speed auto
!
interface FastEthernet0/1
 ip address 172.16.20.2 255.255.255.0 secondary
 ip address 172.16.10.2 255.255.255.0
 duplex auto
 speed auto
!
interface Serial0/0/0
 description Wan to SF circuit number 6fdda 12345678
 no ip address
!
```

So basically, the pipe symbol is an output modifier. You can use it when scrutinizing a large routing table to find out whether a certain route is in it. Here's an example:

```
Todd#sh ip route | include 192.168.3.32
R       192.168.3.32 [120/2] via 10.10.10.8, 00:00:25, FastEthernet0/0
Todd#
```

First, you need to know that this routing table had over 100 entries, so without my trusty pipe, I'd probably still be looking through that output! It's a powerfully efficient tool that saves you major time and effort by quickly finding a line in a configuration—or as the preceding example shows, a single route within a huge routing table.

Serial Interface Commands

Before you just jump in and configure a serial interface, you need some key information, like knowing the interface will usually be attached to a CSU/DSU type of device that provides clocking for the line to the router. Check out Figure 4.2 for an example.

FIGURE 4.2   A typical WAN connection. Clocking is typically provided by a DCE network to routers. In nonproduction environments, a DCE network is not always present.

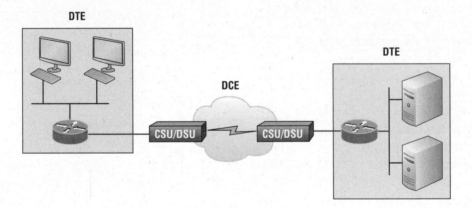

Here you can see that the serial interface is used to connect to a DCE network via a CSU/DSU that provides the clocking to the router interface. But if you have a back-to-back configuration, such as one that's used in a lab environment like the one in Figure 4.3, one end—the data communication equipment (DCE) end of the cable—must provide clocking!

By default, Cisco router serial interfaces are all data terminal equipment (DTE) devices, which means that you must configure an interface to provide clocking if you need it to act like a DCE device. Again, you would not provide clocking on a production T1 connection because you would have a CSU/DSU connected to your serial interface, as shown in Figure 4.2.

FIGURE 4.3   Providing clocking on a nonproduction network

Set clock rate if needed

Todd# config t
Todd(config)# interface serial 0
Todd(config-if)#clock rate 1000000

DCE

DTE

DCE side determined by the cable
Add clocking to DCE side only.

>**show controllers** *int* will show the cable connection type

You configure a DCE serial interface with the clock rate command:

```
Todd#config t
Enter configuration commands, one per line.  End with CNTL/Z.
Router(config)#int s0/0/0
Router(config-if)#clock rate ?
     Speed (bits per second)
 1200
 2400
 4800
 9600
 14400
 19200
 28800
 32000
 38400
 48000
 56000
 57600
 64000
-- output omitted --

Todd(config-if)#clock rate 1000000
```

The clock rate command is set in bits per second. Besides looking at the cable end to check for a label of DCE or DTE, you can see if a router's serial interface has a DCE cable connected with the show controllers *int* command:

```
Router#sh controllers s0/0/0
Interface Serial0/0/0
```

```
Hardware is GT96K
DTE V.35idb at 0x4342FCB0, driver data structure at 0x434373D4
```

Here is an example of an output depicting a DCE connection:

```
Router#sh controllers s0/2/0
Interface Serial0/2/0
Hardware is GT96K
DCE V.35, clock rate 1000000
```

The next command you need to get acquainted with is the bandwidth command. Every Cisco router ships with a default serial link bandwidth of T1 (1.544 Mbps). But this has nothing to do with how data is transferred over a link. The bandwidth of a serial link is used by routing protocols like EIGRP and OSPF to calculate the best cost path to a remote network. So if you're using RIP routing, the bandwidth setting of a serial link is irrelevant since RIP uses only hop count to determine this.

Here's an example of using the bandwidth command:

```
Router#config t
Router(config)#int s0/0/0
Router(config-if)#bandwidth ?
  <1-10000000>  Bandwidth in kilobits
  inherit       Specify that bandwidth is inherited
  receive       Specify receive-side bandwidth
Router(config-if)#bandwidth 1000
```

Did you notice that, unlike the clock rate command, the bandwidth command is configured in kilobits per second?

After going through all these configuration examples regarding the clock rate command, understand that the new ISR routers automatically detect DCE connections and set clock rate to 2000000. But know that you still need to understand the clock rate command for the Cisco exam, even though the new routers set it for you automatically!

Exam Essentials

Describe the process of preparing an interface for use.   To use an interface, you must configure it with an IP address and subnet mask in the same subnet of the hosts that will be connecting to the switch that is connected to that interface. It also must be enabled with the no shutdown command. A serial interface that is connected back to back with another router serial interface must also be configured with a clock rate on the DCE end of the serial cable.

Understand how to troubleshoot a serial link problem.   If you type **show interface serial 0/0** and see down, line protocol is down, this will be considered a Physical layer problem. If you see it as up, line protocol is down, then you have a Data Link layer problem.

Understand how to verify your router with the show interfaces **command.**   If you type **show interfaces**, you can view the statistics for the interfaces on the router, verify whether the interfaces are shut down, and see the IP address of each interface.

Verify Router Configuration and Network Connectivity

The show running-config command verifies your configuration and show startup-config verifies the configuration that'll be used the next time the router is reloaded.

Take a look at the running-config. If all appears well, you can verify your configuration with utilities like Ping and Telnet. Ping is a program that uses ICMP echo requests and replies.

Cisco IOS Commands to Review Basic Router Information and Network Connectivity

Did you know that you can ping with different protocols? Test this by typing **ping ?** at either the router user-mode or privileged-mode prompt:

```
Todd#ping ?
  WORD  Ping destination address or hostname
  clns  CLNS echo
  ip    IP echo
  ipv6  IPv6 echo
  tag   Tag encapsulated IP echo
  <cr>
```

If you want to find a neighbor's Network layer address, either you go straight to the router or switch itself or you can type **show cdp entry * protocol** to get the Network layer addresses you need for pinging.

You can also use an extended ping to change the default variables, as shown here:

```
Todd#ping
Protocol [ip]:
Target IP address: 10.1.1.1
Repeat count [5]:
```

```
% A decimal number between 1 and 2147483647.
Repeat count [5]: 5000
Datagram size [100]:
% A decimal number between 36 and 18024.
Datagram size [100]: 1500
Timeout in seconds [2]:
Extended commands [n]: y
Source address or interface: FastEthernet 0/1
Source address or interface: Vlan 1
Type of service [0]:
Set DF bit in IP header? [no]:
Validate reply data? [no]:
Data pattern [0xABCD]:
Loose, Strict, Record, Timestamp, Verbose[none]:
Sweep range of sizes [n]:
Type escape sequence to abort.
Sending 5000, 1500-byte ICMP Echos to 10.1.1.1, timeout is 2 seconds:
Packet sent with a source address of 10.10.10.1
```

Extended ping allows you to set the repeat count higher than the default of 5 and the datagram size larger. This raises the MTU and allows for a more accurate testing of throughput. The source interface is one last important piece of information I'll pull out of the output. You can choose which interface the ping is sourced from, which is really helpful in certain diagnostic situations. Using my switch to display the extended ping capabilities, I had to use my only routed port, which is named VLAN 1 by default.

Traceroute uses ICMP with IP time to live (TTL) time-outs to track the path a given packet takes through an internetwork. This is in contrast to Ping, which just finds the host and responds. Traceroute can also be used with multiple protocols. Check out this output:

```
Todd#traceroute ?
  WORD       Trace route to destination address or hostname
  aaa        Define trace options for AAA events/actions/errors
  appletalk  AppleTalk Trace
  clns       ISO CLNS Trace
  ip         IP Trace
  ipv6       IPv6 Trace
  ipx        IPX Trace
  mac        Trace Layer2 path between 2 endpoints
  oldvines   Vines Trace (Cisco)
  vines      Vines Trace (Banyan)
  <cr>
```

Telnet, FTP, and HTTP are really the best tools because they use IP at the Network layer and TCP at the Transport layer to create a session with a remote host. If you can telnet, ftp, or http into a device, you know that your IP connectivity just has to be solid!

```
Todd#telnet ?
  WORD IP address or hostname of a remote system
  <cr>
```

From the switch or router prompt, you just type a hostname or IP address and it will assume you want to telnet—you don't need to type the actual command, `telnet`.

Verifying with the *show interface* Command

Another way to verify your configuration is by typing show `interface` commands, the first of which is the `show interface ?` command. Doing this will reveal all the available interfaces to verify and configure.

> **NOTE**
> The show `interfaces` command, with an *s*, displays the configurable parameters and statistics of all interfaces on a router.

This command comes in really handy when you're verifying and troubleshooting router and network issues.

The following output is from my freshly erased and rebooted 2811 router:

```
Router#sh int ?
  Async             Async interface
  BVI               Bridge-Group Virtual Interface
  CDMA-Ix           CDMA Ix interface
  CTunnel           CTunnel interface
  Dialer            Dialer interface
  FastEthernet      FastEthernet IEEE 802.3
  Loopback          Loopback interface
  MFR               Multilink Frame Relay bundle interface
  Multilink         Multilink-group interface
  Null              Null interface
  Port-channel      Ethernet Channel of interfaces
  Serial            Serial
  Tunnel            Tunnel interface
  Vif               PGM Multicast Host interface
  Virtual-PPP       Virtual PPP interface
  Virtual-Template  Virtual Template interface
  Virtual-TokenRing Virtual TokenRing
  accounting        Show interface accounting
```

```
counters          Show interface counters
crb               Show interface routing/bridging info
dampening         Show interface dampening info
description       Show interface description
etherchannel      Show interface etherchannel information
irb               Show interface routing/bridging info
mac-accounting    Show interface MAC accounting info
mpls-exp          Show interface MPLS experimental accounting info
precedence        Show interface precedence accounting info
pruning           Show interface trunk VTP pruning information
rate-limit        Show interface rate-limit info
stats             Show interface packets & octets, in & out, by switching path
status            Show interface line status
summary           Show interface summary
switching         Show interface switching
switchport        Show interface switchport information
trunk             Show interface trunk information
|                 Output modifiers
<cr>
```

The only "real" physical interfaces are Fast Ethernet, Serial, and Async—the rest are all logical interfaces or commands you can use to verify with.

The next command is show interface fastethernet 0/0. It reveals the hardware address, logical address, and encapsulation method as well as statistics on collisions, as seen here:

```
Router#sh int f0/0
FastEthernet0/0 is up, line protocol is up
  Hardware is MV96340 Ethernet, address is 001a.2f55.c9e8 (bia 001a.2f55.c9e8)
  Internet address is 192.168.1.33/27
MTU 1500 bytes, BW 100000 Kbit, DLY 100 usec,
    reliability 255/255, txload 1/255, rxload 1/255
  Encapsulation ARPA, loopback not set
  Keepalive set (10 sec)
  Auto-duplex, Auto Speed, 100BaseTX/FX
  ARP type: ARPA, ARP Timeout 04:00:00
  Last input never, output 00:02:07, output hang never
  Last clearing of "show interface" counters never
  Input queue: 0/75/0/0 (size/max/drops/flushes); Total output drops: 0
  Queueing strategy: fifo
  Output queue: 0/40 (size/max)
```

```
 5 minute input rate 0 bits/sec, 0 packets/sec
 5 minute output rate 0 bits/sec, 0 packets/sec
    0 packets input, 0 bytes
    Received 0 broadcasts, 0 runts, 0 giants, 0 throttles
    0 input errors, 0 CRC, 0 frame, 0 overrun, 0 ignored
    0 watchdog
    0 input packets with dribble condition detected
    16 packets output, 960 bytes, 0 underruns
    0 output errors, 0 collisions, 0 interface resets
    0 babbles, 0 late collision, 0 deferred
    0 lost carrier, 0 no carrier
    0 output buffer failures, 0 output buffers swapped out
Router#
```

You probably guessed that we're going to go over the important statistics from this output, but first, just for fun, I've got to ask you, which subnet is FastEthernet 0/0 a member of and what's the broadcast address and valid host range?

The most important statistic of the show interface command is the output of the line and Data Link protocol status. If the output reveals that FastEthernet 0/0 is up and the line protocol is up, then the interface is up and running:

```
Router#sh int fa0/0
FastEthernet0/0 is up, line protocol is up
```

The first parameter refers to the Physical layer, and it's up when it receives carrier detect. The second parameter refers to the Data Link layer, and it looks for keepalives from the connecting end. Keepalives are important because they're used between devices to make sure connectivity hasn't been dropped.

Here's an example of where your problem will often be found—on serial interfaces:

```
Router#sh int s0/0/0
Serial0/0 is up, line protocol is down
```

If you see that the line is up but the protocol is down, as displayed here, you're experiencing a clocking (keepalive) or framing problem—possibly an encapsulation mismatch. Check the keepalives on both ends to make sure they match. Make sure that the clock rate is set, if needed, and that the encapsulation type is equal on both ends. The preceding output tells us that there's a Data Link layer problem.

If you discover that both the line interface and the protocol are down, it's a cable or interface problem. The following output would indicate a Physical layer problem:

```
Router#sh int s0/0/0
Serial0/0 is down, line protocol is down
```

As you'll see next, if one end is administratively shut down, the remote end would present as down and down:

```
Router#sh int s0/0/0
Serial0/0 is administratively down, line protocol is down
```

To enable the interface, use the command no shutdown from interface configuration mode.

The next show interface serial 0/0/0 command demonstrates the serial line and the maximum transmission unit (MTU)—1,500 bytes by default. It also shows the default bandwidth (BW) on all Cisco serial links, which is 1.544 Kbps. This is used to determine the bandwidth of the line for routing protocols like EIGRP and OSPF. Another important configuration to notice is the keepalive, which is 10 seconds by default. Each router sends a keepalive message to its neighbor every 10 seconds, and if both routers aren't configured for the same keepalive time, it won't work! Check out this output:

```
Router#sh int s0/0/0
Serial0/0 is up, line protocol is up
 Hardware is HD64570
 MTU 1500 bytes, BW 1544 Kbit, DLY 20000 usec,
   reliability 255/255, txload 1/255, rxload 1/255
 Encapsulation HDLC, loopback not set, keepalive set
 (10 sec)
 Last input never, output never, output hang never
 Last clearing of "show interface" counters never
 Queueing strategy: fifo
 Output queue 0/40, 0 drops; input queue 0/75, 0 drops
 5 minute input rate 0 bits/sec, 0 packets/sec
 5 minute output rate 0 bits/sec, 0 packets/sec
  0 packets input, 0 bytes, 0 no buffer
  Received 0 broadcasts, 0 runts, 0 giants, 0 throttles
  0 input errors, 0 CRC, 0 frame, 0 overrun, 0 ignored,
  0 abort
  0 packets output, 0 bytes, 0 underruns
  0 output errors, 0 collisions, 16 interface resets
  0 output buffer failures, 0 output buffers swapped out
  0 carrier transitions
  DCD=down DSR=down DTR=down RTS=down CTS=down
```

You can clear the counters on the interface by typing the command **clear counters**:

```
Router#clear counters ?
  Async            Async interface
  BVI              Bridge-Group Virtual Interface
  CTunnel          CTunnel interface
```

```
Dialer               Dialer interface
FastEthernet         FastEthernet IEEE 802.3
Group-Async          Async Group interface
Line                 Terminal line
Loopback             Loopback interface
MFR                  Multilink Frame Relay bundle interface
Multilink            Multilink-group interface
Null                 Null interface
Serial               Serial
Tunnel               Tunnel interface
Vif                  PGM Multicast Host interface
Virtual-Template     Virtual Template interface
Virtual-TokenRing    Virtual TokenRing
<cr>
```

```
Router#clear counters s0/0/0
Clear "show interface" counters on this interface
  [confirm][enter]
Router#
00:17:35: %CLEAR-5-COUNTERS: Clear counter on interface
  Serial0/0/0 by console
Router#
```

Troubleshooting with the *show interfaces* Command

Let's take a look at the output of the show interfaces command one more time before I move on. There are some important statistics in this output that are important for the Cisco exam:

```
275496 packets input, 35226811 bytes, 0 no buffer
   Received 69748 broadcasts (58822 multicasts)
   0 runts, 0 giants, 0 throttles
   0 input errors, 0 CRC, 0 frame, 0 overrun, 0 ignored
   0 watchdog, 58822 multicast, 0 pause input
   0 input packets with dribble condition detected
   2392529 packets output, 337933522 bytes, 0 underruns
   0 output errors, 0 collisions, 1 interface resets
   0 babbles, 0 late collision, 0 deferred
   0 lost carrier, 0 no carrier, 0 PAUSE output
   0 output buffer failures, 0 output buffers swapped out
```

Finding where to start when troubleshooting an interface can be the difficult part, but certainly we'll look for the number of input errors and CRCs right away.

Verifying with the *show ip interface* Command

The show ip interface command will provide you with information regarding the layer 3 configurations of a router's interfaces:

```
Router#sh ip interface
FastEthernet0/0 is up, line protocol is up
  Internet address is 1.1.1.1/24
  Broadcast address is 255.255.255.255
  Address determined by setup command
  MTU is 1500 bytes
  Helper address is not set
  Directed broadcast forwarding is disabled
  Outgoing access list is not set
  Inbound  access list is not set
  Proxy ARP is enabled
  Security level is default
  Split horizon is enabled
[output cut]
```

The status of the interface, the IP address and mask, information on whether an access list is set on the interface, and basic IP information are all included in this output.

Using the *show ip interface brief* Command

The show ip interface brief command is probably one of the best commands that you can ever use on a Cisco router. This command provides a quick overview of the router's interfaces, including the logical address and status:

```
Router#sh ip int brief
Interface        IP-Address    OK? Method Status           Protocol
FastEthernet0/0  unassigned    YES unset  up               up
FastEthernet0/1  unassigned    YES unset  up               up
Serial0/0/0      unassigned    YES unset  up               down
Serial0/0/1      unassigned    YES unset  administratively down down
Serial0/1/0      unassigned    YES unset  administratively down down
Serial0/2/0      unassigned    YES unset  administratively down down
```

Remember, administratively down means that you need to type **no shutdown** in order to enable the interface. Notice that Serial0/0/0 is up/down, which means that the Physical layer is good and carrier detect is sensed but no keepalives are being received from the remote end. In a nonproduction network, like the one I am working with, this tells us the clock rate hasn't been set.

Verifying with the *show protocols* Command

The show protocols command is also a really helpful command that you'd use in order to quickly see the status of layers 1 and 2 of each interface as well as the IP addresses used.

Here's a look at one of my production routers:

```
Router#sh protocols
Global values:
  Internet Protocol routing is enabled
Ethernet0/0 is administratively down, line protocol is down
Serial0/0 is up, line protocol is up
  Internet address is 100.30.31.5/24
Serial0/1 is administratively down, line protocol is down
Serial0/2 is up, line protocol is up
  Internet address is 100.50.31.2/24
Loopback0 is up, line protocol is up
  Internet address is 100.20.31.1/24
```

The show ip interface brief and show protocols commands provide the layer 1 and layer 2 statistics of an interface as well as the IP addresses. The next command, show controllers, only provides layer 1 information. Let's take a look.

Using the *show controllers* Command

The show controllers command displays information about the physical interface itself. It'll also give you the type of serial cable plugged into a serial port. Usually, this will only be a DTE cable that plugs into a type of data service unit (DSU).

```
Router#sh controllers serial 0/0
HD unit 0, idb = 0x1229E4, driver structure at 0x127E70
buffer size 1524 HD unit 0, V.35 DTE cable
```

```
Router#sh controllers serial 0/1
HD unit 1, idb = 0x12C174, driver structure at 0x131600
buffer size 1524 HD unit 1, V.35 DCE cable
```

Notice that serial 0/0 has a DTE cable, whereas the serial 0/1 connection has a DCE cable. Serial 0/1 would have to provide clocking with the clock rate command. Serial 0/0 would get its clocking from the DSU.

Let's look at this command again. In Figure 4.4, see the DTE/DCE cable between the two routers? Know that you will not see this in production networks!

FIGURE 4.4   Where do you configure clocking? Use the show controllers command on each router's serial interface to find out.

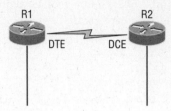

Router R1 has a DTE connection, which is typically the default for all Cisco routers. Routers R1 and R2 can't communicate. Check out the output of the show controllers s0/0 command here:

```
R1#sh controllers serial 0/0
HD unit 0, idb = 0x1229E4, driver structure at 0x127E70
buffer size 1524 HD unit 0, V.35 DCE cable
```

The show controllers s0/0 command reveals that the interface is a V.35 DCE cable. This means that R1 needs to provide clocking of the line to router R2. Basically, the interface has the wrong label on the cable on the R1 router's serial interface. But if you add clocking on the R1 router's serial interface, the network should come right up.

Let's check out another issue, shown in Figure 4.5, that you can solve by using the show controllers command. Again, routers R1 and R2 can't communicate.

FIGURE 4.5   The show controllers command reveals that R1 and R2 can't communicate.

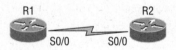

Here's the output of R1's show controllers s0/0 command and show ip interface s0/0:

```
R1#sh controllers s0/0
HD unit 0, idb = 0x1229E4, driver structure at 0x127E70
buffer size 1524 HD unit 0,
DTE V.35 clocks stopped
cpb = 0xE2, eda = 0x4140, cda = 0x4000
```

```
R1#sh ip interface s0/0
Serial0/0 is up, line protocol is down
  Internet address is 192.168.10.2/24
  Broadcast address is 255.255.255.255
```

If you use the show controllers command and the show ip interface command, you'll see that router R1 isn't receiving the clocking of the line. This network is a nonproduction network, so no CSU/DSU is connected to provide clocking for it. This means the DCE end of the cable will be providing the clock rate—in this case, the R2 router. The show ip interface indicates that the interface is up but the protocol is down, which means that no keepalives are being received from the far end. In this example, the likely culprit is the result of bad cable, or simply the lack of clocking.

Exam Essentials

Understand how to troubleshoot a serial link problem.   If you type **show interface serial 0/0** and see down, line protocol is down, this will be considered a Physical layer problem. If you see it as up, line protocol is down, then you have a Data Link layer problem.

Understand how to verify your router with the show interfaces **command.**   If you type **show interfaces**, you can view the statistics for the interfaces on the router, verify whether the interfaces are shut down, and see the IP address of each interface.

Configure and Verify Routing Configuration for a Static or Default Route Given Specific Routing Requirements

There are several ways to configure the routing tables to include all the networks in your internetwork so that packets will be properly forwarded. Understanding the different types of routing will be really helpful when choosing the best solution for your specific environment and business requirements.

Static Routing

Static routing is the process that ensues when you manually add routes in each router's routing table. Predictably, there are pros and cons to static routing, but that's true for all routing approaches.

Here are the pros:

- There is no overhead on the router CPU, which means you could probably make do with a cheaper router than you would need for dynamic routing.

- There is no bandwidth usage between routers, saving you money on WAN links as well as minimizing overhead on the router since you're not using a routing protocol.

- It adds security because you, the administrator, can be very exclusive and choose to allow routing access to certain networks only.

And here are the cons:

- Whoever the administrator is must have a vault-tight knowledge of the internetwork and how each router is connected in order to configure routes correctly. If you don't have a good, accurate map of your internetwork, things will get very messy quickly!

- If you add a network to the internetwork, you have to tediously add a route to it on all routers by hand, which only gets increasingly insane as the network grows.

- Due to the last point, it's just not feasible to use it in most large networks because maintaining it would be a full-time job in and of itself.

Here's the command syntax you use to add a static route to a routing table from global config:

```
ip route [destination_network] [mask] [next-hop_address or
    exitinterface] [administrative_distance] [permanent]
```

This list describes each command in the string:

ip route   The command used to create the static route.

destination_network   The network you're placing in the routing table.

mask   The subnet mask being used on the network.

next-hop_address   This is the IP address of the next-hop router that will receive packets and forward them to the remote network, which must signify a router interface that's on a directly connected network. You must be able to successfully ping the router interface before you can add the route. Important note to self is that if you type in the wrong next-hop address or the interface to the correct router is down, the static route will show up in the router's configuration but not in the routing table.

exitinterface   Used in place of the next-hop address if you want and shows up as a directly connected route.

administrative_distance   By default, static routes have an administrative distance of 1 or 0 if you use an exit interface instead of a next-hop address. You can change the default value by adding an administrative weight at the end of the command.

permanent   If the interface is shut down or the router can't communicate to the next-hop router, the route will automatically be discarded from the routing table by default. Choosing the permanent option keeps the entry in the routing table no matter what happens.

Before I guide you through configuring static routes, let's take a look at a sample static route to see what we can find out about it:

```
Router(config)#ip route 172.16.3.0 255.255.255.0 192.168.2.4
```

- The ip route command tells us simply that it's a static route.
- 172.16.3.0 is the remote network we want to send packets to.
- 255.255.255.0 is the mask of the remote network.
- 192.168.2.4 is the next hop, or router, that packets will be sent to.

But what if the static route looked like this instead?

```
Router(config)#ip route 172.16.3.0 255.255.255.0 192.168.2.4 150
```

That 150 at the end changes the default administrative distance (AD) of 1 to 150. As I said, I'll talk much more about AD when we get into dynamic routing, but for now, just remember that the AD is the trustworthiness of a route, where 0 is best and 255 is worst.

Default Routing

A *stub* network indicates that the networks in this design have only one way out to reach all other networks, which means that instead of creating multiple static routes, we can just use a single default route. This default route is used by IP to forward any packet with a destination not found in the routing table, which is why it is also called a gateway of last resort. Here's the configuration I could have done instead of typing in the static routes due to its stub status:

```
LA#config t
LA(config)#ip route 0.0.0.0 0.0.0.0 172.16.10.5
LA(config)#do sho ip route
[output cut]
Gateway of last resort is 172.16.10.5 to network 0.0.0.0
      172.16.0.0/30 is subnetted, 1 subnets
C        172.16.10.4 is directly connected, Serial0/0/1
L        172.16.10.6/32 is directly connected, Serial0/0/1
C     192.168.20.0/24 is directly connected, FastEthernet0/0
L     192.168.20.0/32 is directly connected, FastEthernet0/0
S*    0.0.0.0/0 [1/0] via 172.16.10.5
```

Configuring a default route is a lot easier than typing a bunch of static routes! The S*
shows the route as a candidate for the default route. Notice the gateway of last resort is
now set too. Everything the router receives with a destination not found in the routing table
will be forwarded to 172.16.10.5. You need to be careful where you place default routes
because you can easily create a network loop!

Verifying Your Configuration

Once all your routers' routing tables are configured, they must be verified. The best way
to do this, besides using the show ip route command, is via Ping. Start by pinging from
router to router.

```
Router1#ping 192.168.10.1
Type escape sequence to abort.
Sending 5, 100-byte ICMP Echos to 192.168.10.1, timeout is 2 seconds:
!!!!!
Success rate is 100 percent (5/5), round-trip min/avg/max = 4/4/4 ms
Corp#
```

Here you can see that I pinged from the Router1 router to the remote interface of the
Router2 router.

Since we can communicate from end to end and to each host without a problem, our
static and default route configurations have been a success!

Exam Essentials

Configure static routes at the CLI.   The command syntax to add a route is
ip route [*destination_network*] [*mask*] [*next-hop_address* or *exitinterface*]
[*administrative_distance*] [permanent].

Create a default route.   To add a default route, use the command syntax ip route
0.0.0.0 0.0.0.0 *ip-address* or the *exit interface* type and number.

Manage Cisco IOS Files

In the following sections, I'll cover the configuration register, which tells the router how to
boot; in addition, you can adjust this to recover a password on a Cisco device.

Boot Preferences

Cisco routers and switches have the capability of starting and loading the IOS from sources other than flash memory. In the following sections, I'll show you the methods you can use to configure a router to start and load an IOS other than the default setting of flash memory.

All Cisco routers have a 16-bit software register that's written into NVRAM. By default, the *configuration register* is set to load the Cisco IOS from *flash memory* and to look for and load the startup-config file from NVRAM. You can use the configuration register settings and to provide password recovery on your routers.

Understanding the Configuration Register Bits

The 16 bits (2 bytes) of the configuration register are read from 15 to 0, from left to right. The default configuration setting on Cisco routers is 0x2102. This means that bits 13, 8, and 1 are on, as shown in Table 4.2. Notice that each set of 4 bits (called a nibble) is read in binary with a value of 8, 4, 2, 1.

TABLE 4.2   The configuration register bit numbers

Configuration Register		2					1			0			2		
Bit number	15	14	13	12	11	10	9	8	7	6	5	4	3	2	1	0
Binary	0	0	1	0	0	0	0	1	0	0	0	0	0	0	1	0

Add the prefix *0x* to the configuration register address. The *0x* means that the digits that follow are in hexadecimal.

Table 4.3 lists the software configuration bit meanings. Notice that bit 6 can be used to ignore the NVRAM contents. This bit is used for password recovery.

Remember that in hex, the scheme is 0–9 and A–F (A = 10, B = 11, C = 12, D = 13, E = 14, and F = 15). This means that a 210F setting for the configuration register is actually 210(15), or 1111 in binary.

TABLE 4.3 Software configuration meanings

Bit	Hex	Description
0–3	0x0000–0x000F	Boot field (see Table 4.4).
6	0x0040	Ignore NVRAM contents.
7	0x0080	OEM bit enabled.
8	0x101	Break disabled.
10	0x0400	IP broadcast with all zeros.
5, 11–12	0x0800–0x1000	Console line speed.
13	0x2000	Boot default ROM software if network boot fails.
14	0x4000	IP broadcasts do not have net numbers.
15	0x8000	Enable diagnostic messages and ignore NVRAM contents.

The boot field, which consists of bits 0–3 in the configuration register (the last four bits), controls the router boot sequence and locates the Cisco IOS. Table 4.4 describes the boot field bits.

TABLE 4.4 The boot field (configuration register bits 00–03)

Boot Field	Meaning	Use
00	ROM monitor mode	To boot to ROM monitor mode, set the configuration register to 2100. You must manually boot the router with the b command. The router will show the rommon> prompt.
01	Boot image from ROM	To boot the mini-IOS image stored in ROM, set the configuration register to 2101. The router will show the Router(boot)> prompt. The mini-IOS is not available in all routers and is also referred to as RXBOOT.
02–F	Specifies a default boot filename	Any value from 2102 through 210F tells the router to use the boot commands specified in NVRAM.

Checking the Current Configuration Register Value

You can see the current value of the configuration register by using the show version command (sh version or show ver for short), as demonstrated here:

```
Router>sh version
Cisco IOS Software, 2800 Software (C2800NM-ADVSECURITYK9-M),
Version 15.1(4)M6, RELEASE SOFTWARE (fc2)
[output cut]
Configuration register is 0x2102
```

The last information given from this command is the value of the configuration register. In this example, the value is 0x2102—the default setting. The configuration register setting of 0x2102 tells the router to look in NVRAM for the boot sequence.

Notice that the show version command also provides the IOS version, and in the preceding example, it shows the IOS version as 15.1(4)M6.

The show version command will display system hardware configuration information, software version, and the names of the boot images on a router.

To change the configuration register, use the config-register command from global configuration mode:

```
Router(config)#config-register 0x2142
Router(config)#do sh ver
[output cut]
Configuration register is 0x2102 (will be 0x2142 at next reload)
```

It's important that you are careful when you set the configuration register!

If you save your configuration and reload the router and it comes up in setup mode, the configuration register setting is probably incorrect.

Boot System Commands

You can configure your router to boot another IOS if the flash is corrupted. You can also have all your routers boot from a TFTP host each time. This way, you'll never have to upgrade each router individually.

There are some boot commands you can play with that will help you manage the way your router boots the Cisco IOS—but please remember, we're talking about the router's IOS here, *not* the router's configuration!

```
Router>en
Router#config t
```

```
Enter configuration commands, one per line.  End with CNTL/Z.
Router(config)#boot ?
  bootstrap  Bootstrap image file
  config     Configuration file
  host       Router-specific config file
  network    Network-wide config file
  system     System image file
```

The boot command gives you several options. The typical settings that Cisco recommends using the boot system command will allow you to tell the router which system IOS file to boot from flash memory. Remember that the router, by default, boots the first system IOS file found in flash. You can change that with the following command as shown in the output:

```
Router(config)#boot system ?
  WORD   TFTP filename or URL
  flash  Boot from flash memory
  ftp    Boot from a server via ftp
  mop    Boot from a Decnet MOP server
  rcp    Boot from a server via rcp
  rom    Boot from rom
  tftp   Boot from a tftp server
Router(config)#boot system flash c2800nm-advsecurityk9-mz.151-4.M6.bin
```

Notice I could boot from flash, FTP, ROM, TFTP. The preceding command configures the router to boot the IOS listed in it. This is a helpful command for when you load a new IOS into flash and want to test it, or even when you want to totally change which IOS is loading by default.

The next command is considered a fall-back routine, but as I said, you can make it a permanent way to have your routers boot from a TFTP host. Personally, I wouldn't necessarily recommend doing this (single point of failure); I'm just showing you that it's possible:

```
Router(config)#boot system tftp ?
  WORD   System image filename
Router(config)#boot system tftp c2800nm-advsecurityk9-mz.151-4.M6.bin?
  Hostname or A.B.C.D  Address from which to download the file
  <cr>
Router(config)#boot system tftp c2800nm-advsecurityk9-mz.151-4.M6.bin 1.1.1.2
Router(config)#
```

As your last recommended fall-back option—the one to go to if the IOS in flash doesn't load and the TFTP host does not produce the IOS—load the mini-IOS from ROM like this:

```
Router(config)#boot system rom
Router(config)#do show run | include boot system
```

```
boot system flash c2800nm-advsecurityk9-mz.151-4.M6.bin
boot system tftp c2800nm-advsecurityk9-mz.151-4.M6.bin 1.1.1.2
boot system rom
Router(config)#
```

If the preceding configuration is set, the router will try to boot from the TFTP server if flash fails, and if the TFTP boot fails, the mini-IOS will load after six unsuccessful attempts of trying to locate the TFTP server.

Recovering Passwords

If you're locked out of a router because you forgot the password, you can change the configuration register to help you get back on your feet. As I said earlier, bit 6 in the configuration register is used to tell the router whether to use the contents of NVRAM to load a router configuration.

The default configuration register value is 0x2102, meaning that bit 6 is off. With the default setting, the router will look for and load a router configuration stored in NVRAM (startup-config). To recover a password, you need to turn on bit 6. Doing this will tell the router to ignore the NVRAM contents. The configuration register value to turn on bit 6 is 0x2142.

Here are the main steps to password recovery:

1. Boot the router and interrupt the boot sequence by performing a break, which will take the router into ROM monitor mode.

2. Change the configuration register to turn on bit 6 (with the value 0x2142).

3. Reload the router.

4. Enter privileged mode.

5. Copy the startup-config file to running-config, and don't forget to verify that your interfaces are re-enabled.

6. Change the password.

7. Reset the configuration register to the default value.

8. Save the router configuration.

9. Reload the router (optional).

I'm going to cover these steps in more detail in the following sections. I'll also show you the commands to restore access to ISR series routers.

You can enter ROM monitor mode by pressing Ctrl+Break, or Ctrl+Shift+6 then b, during router bootup.

The router will enter ROM by default in the following circumstances:

- The IOS is corrupt or missing.

- There's no network connectivity available to find a TFTP host.

- The mini-IOS from ROM doesn't load (meaning the default router fallback failed).

Interrupting the Router Boot Sequence

Your first step is to boot the router and perform a break. This is usually done by pressing the Ctrl+Break key combination when using HyperTerminal or puTTY while the router first reboots.

```
System Bootstrap, Version 15.1(4)M6, RELEASE SOFTWARE (fc2)
Copyright (c) 1999 by cisco Systems, Inc.
TAC:Home:SW:IOS:Specials for info
PC = 0xfff0a530, Vector = 0x500, SP = 0x680127b0
C2800 platform with 32768 Kbytes of main memory
PC = 0xfff0a530, Vector = 0x500, SP = 0x80004374
monitor: command "boot" aborted due to user interrupt
rommon 1 >
```

Notice the line that reads `monitor: command "boot" aborted due to user interrupt`. At this point, you will be at the `rommon 1>` prompt, which is called the ROM monitor mode.

Changing the Configuration Register

You can change the configuration register from within the IOS by using the `config-register` command. To turn on bit 6, use the configuration register value 0x2142.

> **NOTE** Remember that if you change the configuration register to 0x2142, the startup-config will be bypassed and the router will load into setup mode.

To change the bit value on a Cisco ISR series router, you just enter the following command at the `rommon 1>` prompt:

```
rommon 1 >confreg 0x2142
You must reset or power cycle for new config to take effect
rommon 2 >reset
```

Reloading the Router and Entering Privileged Mode

At this point, you need to reset the router like this:

- From the ISR series router, type **I** (for initialize) or **reset**.
- From an older series router, type **I**.

The router will reload and ask if you want to use setup mode (because no startup-config is used). Answer no to entering setup mode, press Enter to go into user mode, and then type **enable** to go into privileged mode.

Viewing and Changing the Configuration

Now you're past the point where you would need to enter the user-mode and privileged-mode passwords in a router. Copy the startup-config file to the running-config file:

```
copy startup-config running-config
```

Or use the shortcut:

```
copy start run
```

The configuration is now running in *random access memory (RAM)*, and you're in privileged mode, meaning that you can now view and change the configuration. But you can't view the enable secret setting for the password since it is encrypted. To change the password, do this:

```
config t
enable secret todd
```

Resetting the Configuration Register and Reloading the Router

After you're finished changing passwords, set the configuration register back to the default value with the config-register command:

```
config t
config-register 0x2102
```

It's important to remember to enable your interfaces after copying the configuration from NVRAM to RAM.

Finally, save the new configuration with a copy running-config startup-config and use reload to reload the router.

 If you save your configuration and reload the router and it comes up in setup mode, the configuration register setting is probably incorrect.

To sum this up, we now have Cisco's suggested IOS backup routine configured on our router: flash, TFTP host, ROM.

Cisco IOS Image(s)

Before you upgrade or restore a Cisco IOS, you really should copy the existing file to a TFTP host as a backup just in case the new image crashes and burns.

And you can use any TFTP host to accomplish this. By default, the flash memory in a router is used to store the Cisco IOS.

Before you back up an IOS image to a network server on your intranet, you've got to do these three things:

- Make sure you can access the network server.
- Ensure that the network server has adequate space for the code image.
- Verify the file naming and path requirement.

Connect your laptop or workstation's Ethernet port to a router's Ethernet interface, as shown in Figure 4.6.

FIGURE 4.6   Copying an IOS from a router to a TFTP host

Copy the IOS to a TFTP host.
Router# copy flash tftp
- IP address of the TFTP server
- IOS filename

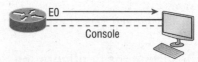

```
RouterX#copy flash tftp:
Source filename [] ?c2800nm-ipbase-mz.124-5a.bin
Address or name of remote host [] ? 10.1.1.1
Destination filename [c2800nm-ipbase-mz.124-5a.bin] [enter]
!!!!!!!!!!!!!!!!!!!!!!!!!!!!!!!!!!!!!!!!!!!!!!!!!!!!!!!!!!!!!!!<output omitted>
12094416 bytes copied in 98.858 secs (122341 bytes/sec)
RouterX#
```

- TFTP server software must be running on the PC.
- The PC must be on the same subnet as the router's E0 interface.
- The copy flash tftp command must be supplied the IP address of the PC.

Verify the following before attempting to copy the image to or from the router:

- TFTP server software must be running on the laptop or workstation.
- The Ethernet connection between the router and the workstation must be made with a crossover cable.
- The workstation must be on the same subnet as the router's Ethernet interface.
- The copy flash tftp command must be supplied the IP address of the workstation if you are copying from the router flash.
- And if you're copying "into" flash, you need to verify that there's enough room in flash memory to accommodate the file to be copied.

Verifying Flash Memory

Before you attempt to upgrade the Cisco IOS on your router with a new IOS file, it's a good idea to verify that your flash memory has enough room to hold the new image. You verify the amount of flash memory and the file or files being stored in flash memory by using the show flash command (sh flash for short):

```
Router#sh flash
-#- --length-- -----date/time------ path
1 45392400 Apr 14 2013 05:31:44 +00:00 c2800nm-advsecurityk9-mz.151-4.M6.bin

18620416 bytes available (45395968 bytes used)
```

There are about 45 MB of flash used, but there is still about 18 MB available. If you want to copy a file into flash that is more than 18 MB in size, the router will ask you if you want to erase flash. Be careful here!

 The show flash command will display the amount of memory consumed by the current IOS image as well as tell you if there's enough room available to hold both current and new images. You should know that if there's not enough room for both the old and new images you want to load, the old image will be erased!

The amount of RAM and flash is actually easy to tally using the show version command on routers:

```
Router#show version
[output cut]
System returned to ROM by power-on
System image file is "flash:c2800nm-advsecurityk9-mz.151-4.M6.bin"
[output cut]
Cisco 2811 (revision 1.0) with 249856K/12288K bytes of memory.
Processor board ID FTX1049A1AB
2 FastEthernet interfaces
2 Serial(sync/async) interfaces
1 Virtual Private Network (VPN) Module
DRAM configuration is 64 bits wide with parity enabled.
239K bytes of non-volatile configuration memory.
62720K bytes of ATA CompactFlash (Read/Write)
```

The first highlighted line shows us that this router has about 256 MB of RAM, and you can see that the amount of flash shows up on the last line. By rounding up, we get the amount of flash to 64 MB.

The main difference in the output of the show flash and show version commands is that the show flash command displays all files in flash memory and the show version command shows the actual name of the IOS file that the router is using.

Backing Up the Cisco IOS

To back up the Cisco IOS to a TFTP server, you use the copy flash tftp command. It's a straightforward command that requires only the source filename and the IP address of the TFTP server.

The key to success in this backup routine is to make sure you've got good, solid connectivity to the TFTP server. Check this by pinging the TFTP device from the router console prompt like this:

```
Router#ping 1.1.1.2
Type escape sequence to abort.
Sending 5, 100-byte ICMP Echos to 1.1.1.2, timeout
  is 2 seconds:
!!!!!
Success rate is 100 percent (5/5), round-trip min/avg/max
  = 4/4/8 ms
```

After you ping the TFTP server to make sure that IP is working, you can use the copy flash tftp command to copy the IOS to the TFTP server as shown next:

```
Router#copy flash tftp
Source filename []?c2800nm-advsecurityk9-mz.151-4.M6.bin
Address or name of remote host []?1.1.1.2
Destination filename [c2800nm-advsecurityk9-mz.151-4.M6.bin]?[enter]
!!!!!!!!!!!!!!!!!!!!!!!!!!!!!!!!!!!!!!!!!!!!!!!!!!!!!!!!!!!!!!!!!!!!!!!
!!!!!!!!!!!!
45395968 bytes copied in 123.724 secs (357532 bytes/sec)
Router#
```

Just copy the IOS filename from either the show flash or show version command and then paste it when prompted for the source filename.

In the preceding example, the contents of flash memory were copied successfully to the TFTP server. The address of the remote host is the IP address of the TFTP host, and the source filename is the file in flash memory.

WARNING   Many newer Cisco routers have removable memory. You may see names for this memory such as flash0:, in which case the command in the preceding example would be copy flash0: tftp:. Alternately, you may see it as usbflash0:.

Restoring or Upgrading the Cisco Router IOS

What happens if you need to restore the Cisco IOS to flash memory to replace an original file that has been damaged or if you want to upgrade the IOS? You can download the file from a TFTP server to flash memory by using the copy tftp flash command. This command requires the IP address of the TFTP host and the name of the file you want to download.

But before you begin, make sure the file you want to place in flash memory is in the default TFTP directory on your host. When you issue the command, TFTP won't ask you where the file is, so if the file you want to use isn't in the default directory of the TFTP host, this just won't work.

```
Router#copy tftp flash
Address or name of remote host []?1.1.1.2
Source filename []?c2800nm-advsecurityk9-mz.151-4.M6.bin
Destination filename [c2800nm-advsecurityk9-mz.151-4.M6.bin]?[enter]
%Warning: There is a file already existing with this name
Do you want to over write? [confirm][enter]
Accessing tftp://1.1.1.2/ c2800nm-advsecurityk9-mz.151-4.M6.bin...
Loading c2800nm-advsecurityk9-mz.151-4.M6.bin from 1.1.1.2 (via
    FastEthernet0/0): !!!!!!!!!!!!!!!!!!!!!!!!!!!!!!!!!!!!!!!!!!!!!!!!!!!!!!!!!!!!!
!!!!!!!!
[OK - 21710744 bytes]

45395968 bytes copied in 82.880 secs (261954 bytes/sec)
Router#
```

In the preceding example, I copied the same file into flash memory, so it asked me if I wanted to overwrite it. Remember that we are "playing" with files in flash memory. If I had just corrupted my file by overwriting it, I won't know for sure until I reboot the router. Be careful with this command! If the file is corrupted, you'll need to do an IOS restore from ROM monitor mode.

In the event of an error with restoring or upgrading an IOS on a router or switch, you are presented with this prompt: rommon>.

Follow these steps to recover from the error:

```
rommon 1 > tftpdnld

Missing or illegal ip address for variable IP_ADDRESS
Illegal IP address.

usage: tftpdnld [-hr]
  Use this command for disaster recovery only to recover an image via TFTP.
  Monitor variables are used to set up parameters for the transfer.
  (Syntax: "VARIABLE_NAME=value" and use "set" to show current variables.)
  "ctrl-c" or "break" stops the transfer before flash erase begins.

  The following variables are REQUIRED to be set for tftpdnld:
```

```
     IP_ADDRESS: The IP address for this unit
 IP_SUBNET_MASK: The subnet mask for this unit
DEFAULT_GATEWAY: The default gateway for this unit
    TFTP_SERVER: The IP address of the server to fetch from
      TFTP_FILE: The filename to fetch
```

```
  The following variables are OPTIONAL:
[uneeded output cut]
rommon 2 >set IP_Address:1.1.1.1
rommon 3 >set IP_SUBNET_MASK:255.0.0.0
rommon 4 >set DEFAULT_GATEWAY:1.1.1.2
rommon 5 >set TFTP_SERVER:1.1.1.2
rommon 6 >set TFTP_FILE: flash:c2800nm-advipservicesk9-mz.124-12.bin
rommon 7 >tftpdnld
```

From here, you can see all the variables you need to configure using the set command. Be sure you use ALL_CAPS, including the underscore (_).

You need to set the IP address, mask, and default gateway of your router, then the IP address of the TFTP host, which in this example is a directly connected router that I made a TFTP server with this command:

```
Router(config)#tftp-server flash:c2800nm-advipservicesk9-mz.124-12.bin
```

And finally, you set the IOS filename of the file on your TFTP server.

If you are loading a new file and you don't have enough room in flash memory to store both the new and existing copies, the router will ask to erase the contents of flash memory before writing the new file into flash memory, and if you are able to copy the IOS without erasing the old version, make sure you remember to use the boot system flash:IOS command.

There is one other way you can restore the IOS on a router, but it takes a while. You can use what is called the Xmodem protocol to actually upload an IOS file into flash memory through the console port. You'd use Xmodem through the console port procedure if you had no network connectivity to the router or switch.

Licensing

IOS licensing is now done quite differently than it was with previous versions of the IOS. Actually, there was no licensing before the new 15.0 IOS.

A new ISR router is pre-installed with the software images and licenses that you ordered.

Cisco does provide evaluation licenses for most software packages and features that are supported on the hardware you purchased. It is now called *Right-To-Use (RTU) licensing*. Once the temporary license expires after 60 days, you need to acquire a permanent license in order to continue to use the extended features that aren't available in your current version. This method of licensing allows you to enable a router to use different parts of the IOS.

Prior to the 15.0 code release, there were eight different software feature sets for each hardware router type. With the IOS 15.0 code, the packaging is now called a *universal image*, meaning all feature sets are available in one file with all features packed neatly inside.

To use the features in the IOS software, you must unlock them using the software activation process. Since all features available are inside the universal image already, you can just unlock the features you need as you need them—and of course pay for these features when you determine that they meet your business requirements. All routers come with something called the IP Base licensing, which is the prerequisite for installing all other features.

There are three different technology packages available for purchase that can be installed as additional feature packs on top of the prerequisite IP Base (default), which provides entry-level IOS functionality. These are as follows:

Data: MPLS, ATM, and multiprotocol support

Unified Communications: VoIP and IP telephony

Security: Cisco IOS Firewall, IPS, IPsec, 3DES, and VPN

For example, if you need MPLS and IPsec, you'll need the default IP Base, the Data, and the Security premium packages unlocked on your router.

To obtain the license, you'll need the unique device identifier (UDI), which has two components: the product ID (PID) and the serial number of the router. The show license UDI command provides this information in an output as shown:

```
Router#sh license udi
Device#   PID                SN              UDI
-----------------------------------------------------------------------
*0        CISC02901/K9       FTX1641Y07J     CISC02901/K9:FTX1641Y07J
```

After your 60-day evaluation period expires, you can either obtain the license file from the Cisco License Manager (CLM), which is an automated process, or use the manual process through the Cisco Product License Registration portal. Typically only larger companies will use the CLM because you'd need to install software on a server, which then keeps track of all your licenses for you.

When you purchase the software package with the features that you want to install, you need to permanently activate it using your UDI and the *product authorization key (PAK)* that you received with your purchase. This is essentially your receipt acknowledging that you purchased the license. You then need to connect the license with a particular router by combining the PAK and the UDI, which you do online at the Cisco Product License Registration portal. If you haven't already registered the license on a different router, and it is valid, Cisco will email you your permanent license, or you can download it from your account.

You now need to activate the license on the router. Staying with the manual method, you need to make the new license file available to the router either via a USB port on the router or through a TFTP server. Once it's available to the router, you'll use the license install command from privileged mode.

Assuming that you copied the file into flash memory, the command would look like something like this:

```
Router#license install ?
  archive:   Install from archive: file system
  flash:     Install from flash: file system
  ftp:       Install from ftp: file system
  http:      Install from http: file system
  https:     Install from https: file system
  null:      Install from null: file system
  nvram:     Install from nvram: file system
  rcp:       Install from rcp: file system
  scp:       Install from scp: file system
  syslog:    Install from syslog: file system
  system:    Install from system: file system
  tftp:      Install from tftp: file system
  tmpsys:    Install from tmpsys: file system
  xmodem:    Install from xmodem: file system
  ymodem:    Install from ymodem: file system
Router#license install flash:FTX1628838P_201302111432454180.lic
Installing licenses from "flash::FTX1628838P_201302111432454180.lic"
Installing...Feature:datak9...Successful:Supported
1/1 licenses were successfully installed
0/1 licenses were existing licenses
0/1 licenses were failed to install
April 12 2:31:19.786: %LICENSE-6-INSTALL: Feature datak9 1.0 was
installed in this device. UDI=CISCO2901/K9:FTX1628838P; StoreIndex=1:Primary
License Storage

April 12 2:31:20.078: %IOS_LICENSE_IMAGE_APPLICATION-6-LICENSE_LEVEL: Module
name =c2800 Next reboot level = datak9 and License = datak9
```

You need to reboot to have the new license take effect. Now that you have your license installed and running, how do you use Right-To-Use licensing to check out new features on your router?

Right-To-Use Licenses (Evaluation Licenses)

Originally called evaluation licenses, Right-To-Use (RTU) licenses are what you need when you want to update your IOS to load a new feature but either don't want to wait to get the license or just want to test if this feature will truly meet your business requirements.

Cisco's license model allows you to install the feature you want without a PAK. The Right-To-Use license works for 60 days before you would need to install your permanent license. To enable the Right-To-Use license, you use the license boot module command. The following demonstrates starting the Right-To-Use license on my 2900 series router, enabling the security module named securityk9:

```
Router(config)#license boot module c2900 technology-package securityk9
PLEASE READ THE FOLLOWING TERMS CAREFULLY. INSTALLING THE LICENSE OR LICENSE
KEY PROVIDED FOR ANY CISCO PRODUCT FEATURE OR USING
SUCHPRODUCT FEATURE CONSTITUTES YOUR FULL ACCEPTANCE OF THE
FOLLOWING TERMS. YOU MUST NOT PROCEED FURTHER IF YOU ARE NOT WILLING
TO BE BOUND BY ALL THE TERMS SET FORTH HEREIN.
[output cut]
Activation of the software command line interface will be evidence of
your acceptance of this agreement.

ACCEPT? [yes/no]: yes

% use 'write' command to make license boot config take effect on next boot
Feb 12 01:35:45.060: %IOS_LICENSE_IMAGE_APPLICATION-6-LICENSE_LEVEL:
Module name =c2900 Next reboot level = securityk9 and License = securityk9

Feb 12 01:35:45.524: %LICENSE-6-EULA_ACCEPTED: EULA for feature
securityk9 1.0 has been accepted. UDI=CISCO2901/K9:FTX1628838P; StoreIndex=0:
Built-In License Storage
```

Once the router is reloaded, you can use the security feature set. And it is really nice that you don't need to reload the router again if you choose to install a permanent license for this feature.

Show License

The show license command shows the licenses installed on the router:

```
Router#show license
Index 1 Feature: ipbasek9
     Period left: Life time
     License Type: Permanent
     License State: Active, In Use
     License Count: Non-Counted
     License Priority: Medium
Index 2 Feature: securityk9
     Period left: 8 weeks  2 days
     Period Used: 0  minute  0  second
     License Type: EvalRightToUse
```

```
    License State: Active, In Use
    License Count: Non-Counted
    License Priority: None
Index 3 Feature: uck9
    Period left: Life time
    License Type: Permanent
    License State: Active, In Use
    License Count: Non-Counted
    License Priority: Medium
Index 4 Feature: datak9
    Period left: Not Activated
    Period Used: 0  minute  0  second
    License Type: EvalRightToUse
    License State: Not in Use, EULA not accepted
    License Count: Non-Counted
    License Priority: None
Index 5 Feature: gatekeeper
 [output cut]
```

You can see in the preceding output that the ipbasek9 is permanent and the securityk9 has a license type of EvalRightToUse. The show license feature command provides the same information as show license, but it's summarized into one line as shown in the next output:

```
Router#sh license feature
```

Feature name	Enforcement	Evaluation	Subscription	Enabled	RightToUse
ipbasek9	no	no	no	yes	no
securityk9	yes	yes	no	no	yes
uck9	yes	yes	no	yes	yes
datak9	yes	yes	no	no	yes
gatekeeper	yes	yes	no	no	yes
SSL_VPN	yes	yes	no	no	yes
ios-ips-update	yes	yes	yes	no	yes
SNASw	yes	yes	no	no	yes
hseck9	yes	no	no	no	no
cme-srst	yes	yes	no	yes	yes
WAAS_Express	yes	yes	no	no	yes
UCVideo	yes	yes	no	no	yes

The show version command also shows the license information at the end of the command output:

```
Router#show version
[output cut]
```

```
License Info:

License UDI:

--------------------------------------------------
Device#   PID                 SN
--------------------------------------------------
*0        CISCO2901/K9        FTX1641Y07J


Technology Package License Information for Module:'c2900'

-----------------------------------------------------------------
Technology   Technology-package       Technology-package
             Current     Type         Next reboot
-----------------------------------------------------------------
ipbase       ipbasek9    Permanent    ipbasek9
security     None        None         None
uc           uck9        Permanent    uck9
data         None        None         None

Configuration register is 0x2102
```

The show version command shows if the license was activated. Don't forget, you'll need to reload the router to have the license features take effect if the license evaluation is not already active.

Change License

If your license is stored in flash and your flash files become corrupted, it's a good idea to always back up your IOS license!

If your license has been saved in a location other than flash, you can easily back it up to flash memory via the license save command:

Router#**license save flash:all_licenses.lic**

The preceding command will save your current license to flash. You can restore your license with the license install command I demonstrated earlier.

There are two steps to uninstalling the license on a router. First, to uninstall the license you need to disable the technology package, using the no license boot module command with the keyword disable at the end of the command line:

Router#**license boot module c2900 technology-package securityk9 disable**

The second step is to clear the license. To achieve this from the router, use the `license clear` command and then remove the license with the `no license boot module` command:

```
Router#license clear securityk9
Router#config t
Router(config)#no license boot module c2900 technology-package securityk9
disable
Router(config)#exit
Router#reload
```

After you run through the preceding commands, the license will be removed from your router.

Here's a summary of the license commands. These are important commands to have down, and you really need to understand them to meet the Cisco objectives:

- `show license` determines the licenses that are active on your system. It also displays a group of lines for each feature in the currently running IOS image along with several status variables related to software activation and licensing, both licensed and unlicensed features.

- `show license feature` allows you to view the technology package licenses and feature licenses that are supported on your router along with several status variables related to software activation and licensing. This includes both licensed and unlicensed features.

- `show license udi` displays the unique device identifier (UDI) of the router, which comprises the product ID (PID) and serial number of the router.

- `show version` displays various information about the current IOS version, including the licensing details at the end of the command's output.

- `license install` *url* installs a license key file into a router.

- `license boot module` installs a Right-To-Use license feature on a router.

Exam Essentials

Remember how to install a permanent and Right-To-Use license.   To install a permanent license on a router, use the `install license url` command. To install an evaluation feature, use the `license boot module` command.

Remember the verification commands used for licensing in the new ISR2 routers.   The `show license` command determines the licenses that are active on your system. The `show license feature` command allows you to view the technology package licenses and feature licenses that are supported on your router. The `show license udi` command displays the unique device identifier (UDI) of the router, which comprises the product ID (PID) and serial number of the router, and the `show version` command displays various information about the current IOS version, including the licensing details at the end of the command's output.

Differentiate Methods of Routing and Routing Protocols

In the following sections, I'll cover some of the different methods of routing, the different protocols used today, and some their features. It's important that you understand the differences and advantages as well as disadvantages of static routing compared to dynamic routing.

Static vs. Dynamic

In this section, I'll go over the differences between static routing and dynamic routing. I will also cover some of the aspects that are associated with the dynamic routing protocols, and a simple command to use to verify the routing table is correct.

With static routing, you manually add routes in each router's routing table. Predictably, there are pros and cons to static routing.

Here are the pros:

- There is no overhead on the router CPU, which means you could probably make do with a cheaper router than you would need for dynamic routing.

- There is no bandwidth usage between routers, saving you money on WAN links as well as minimizing overhead on the router since you're not using a routing protocol.

- It adds security because you, the administrator, can be very exclusive and choose to allow routing access to certain networks only.

Here are the cons:

- Whoever the administrator is must have a vault-tight knowledge of the internetwork and how each router is connected in order to configure routes correctly. If you don't have a good, accurate map of your internetwork, things will get very messy quickly!

- If you add a network to the internetwork, you have to tediously add a route to it on all routers by hand, which only gets increasingly insane as the network grows.

- Due to the last point, it's just not feasible to use it in most large networks because maintaining it would be a full-time job in and of itself.

Here is the command syntax you use to add a static route to a routing table from global config:

```
ip route [destination_network] [mask] [next-hop_address or
    exitinterface] [administrative_distance] [permanent]
Router(config)#ip route 172.16.3.0 255.255.255.0 192.168.2.4
```

Another type of static route is known as a default route. A default route is used by IP to forward any packet with a destination not found in the routing table, which is why it is also called a gateway of last resort. Default routes are generally placed on stub networks (networks with only one way in or out of the router).

The command syntax you use to add a static route to a routing table from global config is as follows:

```
Router(config)#ip route 0.0.0.0 0.0.0.0 172.16.10.5
```

With dynamic routing, protocols are used to find networks and update routing tables on routers. This is a whole lot easier than using static or default routing, but it will cost you in terms of router CPU processing and bandwidth on network links. A routing protocol defines the set of rules used by a router when it communicates routing information between neighboring routers. Common routing protocols include RIP, EIGRP, and OSPF.

Link State vs. Distance Vector

There are two types of routing protocols: distance-vector protocols and link-state protocols. Let's take a look.

Distance Vector

The distance-vector protocols in use today find the best path to a remote network by judging distance. In RIP routing, each instance where a packet goes through a router is called a hop, and the route with the least number of hops to the network will be chosen as the best one. The vector indicates the direction to the remote network. RIP is a distance-vector routing protocol and periodically sends out the entire routing table to directly connected neighbors.

Link State

In link-state protocols, also called shortest-path-first protocols, the routers each create three separate tables. One of these tables keeps track of directly attached neighbors, one determines the topology of the entire internetwork, and one is used as the routing table. Link-state routers know more about the internetwork than any distance-vector routing protocol ever could. OSPF is an IP routing protocol that's completely link state. Link-state protocols send updates containing the state of their own links to all other directly connected routers on the network. This is then propagated to their neighbors.

Administrative Distance

The *administrative distance (AD)* is used to rate the trustworthiness of routing information received on a router from a neighbor router. An administrative distance is represented by an integer from 0 to 255, where 0 is the most trusted and 255 means no traffic will be passed via this route.

If a router receives two updates listing the same remote network, the first thing the router checks is the AD. If one of the advertised routes has a lower AD than the other, then the route with the lowest AD will be chosen and placed in the routing table.

If both advertised routes to the same network have the same AD, then routing protocol metrics like *hop count* and/or bandwidth of the lines will be used to find the best path to the remote network. The advertised route with the lowest metric will be placed in the routing table, but if both advertised routes have the same AD as well as the same metrics, then the routing protocol will load-balance to the remote network, meaning the protocol will send data down each link.

Table 4.5 shows the default administrative distances that a Cisco router uses to decide which route to take to a remote network.

TABLE 4.5 Default administrative distances

Route Source	Default AD
Connected interface	0
Static route	1
EIGRP	90
OSPF	110
RIP	120
External EIGRP	170
Unknown	255 (This route will never be used.)

If a network is directly connected, the router will always use the interface connected to the network. If you configure a static route, the router will then believe that route over any other ones it learns about. You can change the administrative distance of static routes, but by default, they have an AD of 1.

Split Horizon

Split horizon is a type of distance-vector routing rule used to prevent routing loops in distant-vector routing protocols. When a router learns a route update from a neighbor, the router will not advertise the update back out the interface on which it was received.

Metric

Often referred to as routing metric, a metric is a measurement used by a routing protocol to calculate the best path to a remote network. Each routing protocol uses a different metric to calculate the best path.

Next Hop

Next hop refers to the next closest router a packet will go through on its way to its destination.

IP Routing Table

Routers learn about remote networks from neighboring routers or from an administrator. The router then builds a routing table, which is basically a map of the internetwork, and it describes how to find remote networks. If a network is directly connected, then the router already knows how to get to it.

Routing protocols will use an algorithm to find remote networks. Once the remote network is discovered, the best path to the remote network will be placed into the routing table.

By using the command show ip route on a router, we can see the routing table (map of the internetwork) that Lab_A has used to make its forwarding decisions:

```
Lab_A#sh ip route
Codes: L - local, C - connected, S - static,
[output cut]
        10.0.0.0/8 is variably subnetted, 6 subnets, 4 masks
C       10.0.0.0/8 is directly connected, FastEthernet0/3
L       10.0.0.1/32 is directly connected, FastEthernet0/3
C       10.10.0.0/16 is directly connected, FastEthernet0/2
L       10.10.0.1/32 is directly connected, FastEthernet0/2
C       10.10.10.0/24 is directly connected, FastEthernet0/1
L       10.10.10.1/32 is directly connected, FastEthernet0/1
S*      0.0.0.0/0 is directly connected, FastEthernet0/0
```

Passive Interfaces

The passive-interface command is used in routing protocols to prevent route updates from being sent out a specific interface but still allow updates to be received. Here's an example of how to configure the passive-interface command:

```
Router#config t
Router(config)#router rip
Router(config-router)#passive-interface FastEthernet 0/1
```

This command will stop RIP updates from being propagated out of FastEthernet interface 0/0, but it can still receive RIP updates.

Exam Essentials

Compare and contrast static and dynamic routing.   Static routing creates no routing update traffic and creates less overhead on the router and network links, but it must be configured manually and does not have the ability to react to link outages. Dynamic routing creates routing update traffic and uses more overhead on the router and network links.

Configure static routes at the CLI.   The command syntax to add a route is
`ip route [destination_network] [mask] [next-hop_address or  exitinterface] [administrative_distance] [permanent]`.

Create a default route.   To add a default route, use the command syntax `ip route 0.0.0.0 0.0.0.0 ip-address` or the *exit interface* type and number.

Understand administrative distance and its role in the selection of the best route.
Administrative distance (AD) is used to rate the trustworthiness of routing information received on a router from a neighbor router. Administrative distance is represented by an integer from 0 to 255, where 0 is the most trusted and 255 means no traffic will be passed via this route. All routing protocols are assigned a default AD, but it can be changed at the CLI.

Differentiate distance-vector, link-state, and hybrid routing protocols.   Distance-vector routing protocols make routing decisions based on hop count (think RIP), while link-state routing protocols are able to consider multiple factors such as bandwidth available and building a topology table. Hybrid routing protocols exhibit characteristics of both types.

Configure and Verify OSPF (Single Area)

Open Shortest Path First (OSPF) is an open standard routing protocol that's been implemented by a wide variety of network vendors, including Cisco. And it's that open standard characteristic that's the key to OSPF's flexibility and popularity.

Most people opt for OSPF, which works by using the Dijkstra algorithm to initially construct a shortest-path tree and follows that by populating the routing table with the resulting best paths. EIGRP's convergence time may be blindingly fast, but OSPF isn't that far behind, and its quick convergence is another reason it's a favorite. Another two great advantages OSPF offers are that it supports multiple, equal-cost routes to the same destination, and like EIGRP, it also supports both IP and IPv6 routed protocols.

Here's a list that summarizes some of OSPF's best features:

- Allows for the creation of areas and autonomous systems
- Minimizes routing update traffic
- Is highly flexible, versatile, and scalable
- Supports VLSM/CIDR
- Offers an unlimited hop count
- Is open standard and supports multi-vendor deployment

Because OSPF is the first link-state routing protocol that most people run into, it's a good idea to size it up against more traditional distance-vector protocols like RIPv2 and RIPv1. Table 4.6 presents a nice comparison of all three of these common protocols.

TABLE 4.6   OSPF and RIP Comparison

Characteristic	OSPF	RIPv2	RIPv1
Type of protocol	Link state	Distance vector	Distance vector
Classless support	Yes	Yes	No
VLSM support	Yes	Yes	No
Auto-summarization	No	Yes	Yes
Manual summarization	Yes	Yes	No
Noncontiguous support	Yes	Yes	No
Route propagation	Multicast on change	Periodic multicast	Periodic broadcast
Path metric	Bandwidth	Hops	Hops
Hop count limit	None	15	15
Convergence	Fast	Slow	Slow
Peer authentication	Yes	Yes	No
Hierarchical network requirement	Yes (using areas)	No (flat only)	No (flat only)
Updates	Event triggered	Periodic	Periodic
Route computation	Dijkstra	Bellman-Ford	Bellman-Ford

OSPF has many features beyond the few listed in Table 4.6, and all of them contribute to a fast, scalable, and robust protocol that can be actively deployed in thousands of production networks.

OSPF is designed to be implemented in a hierarchical fashion, which means separating the larger internetwork into smaller internetworks called areas. This is the best design for OSPF.

Here are some reasons for creating an OSPF hierarchically:

- To decrease routing overhead
- To speed up convergence
- To confine network instability to single areas of the network

These benefits make the additional configuration required by OSPF worth the effort.

Figure 4.7 shows a typical OSPF simple design. Notice how each router connects to the backbone—called area 0, or the backbone area. OSPF must have an area 0, and all other areas should connect to this area. Routers that connect other areas to the backbone area within an AS are called area border routers (ABRs). Still, at least one interface of the ABR must be in area 0.

FIGURE 4.7 OSPF design example. An OSPF hierarchical design minimizes routing table entries and keeps the impact of any topology changes contained within a specific area.

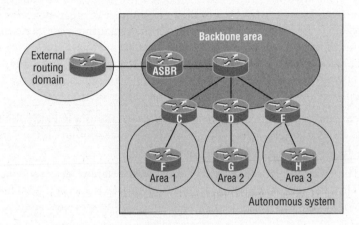

OSPF runs inside an autonomous system, but it can also connect multiple autonomous systems. The router that connects these ASs is called an autonomous system boundary router (ASBR).

Here are some vital terms to commit to memory:

Link   A *link* is a network or router interface assigned to any given network. When an interface is added to the OSPF process, it's considered to be a link. This link, or interface, will have up or down state information associated with it as well as one or more IP addresses.

Router ID   The *router ID (RID)* is an IP address used to identify the router. Cisco chooses the router ID by using the highest IP address of all configured loopback interfaces. If no loopback interfaces are configured with addresses, OSPF will choose the highest IP address out of all active physical interfaces. To OSPF, this is basically the "name" of each router.

Neighbor   *Neighbors* are two or more routers that have an interface on a common network, such as two routers connected on a point-to-point serial link. OSPF neighbors must have a number of common configuration options to be able to successfully establish a neighbor relationship, and all of these options must be configured exactly the same way:

- Area ID
- Stub area flag
- Authentication password (if using one)
- Hello and Dead intervals

Adjacency   An *adjacency* is a relationship between two OSPF routers that permits the direct exchange of route updates. Unlike EIGRP, which directly shares routes with all of its neighbors, OSPF is really picky about sharing routing information and will directly share routes only with neighbors that have also established adjacencies. And not all neighbors will become adjacent—this depends upon both the type of network and the configuration of the routers. In multi-access networks, routers form adjacencies with designated and backup designated routers. In point-to-point and point-to-multipoint networks, routers form adjacencies with the router on the opposite side of the connection.

Designated router   A *designated router (DR)* is elected whenever OSPF routers are connected to the same broadcast network to minimize the number of adjacencies formed and to publicize received routing information to and from the remaining routers on the broadcast network or link. Elections are won based upon a router's priority level, with the one having the highest priority becoming the winner. If there's a tie, the router ID will be used to break it. All routers on the shared network will establish adjacencies with the DR and the BDR, which ensures that all routers' topology tables are synchronized.

Backup designated router   A *backup designated router (BDR)* is a hot standby for the DR on broadcast, or multi-access, links. The BDR receives all routing updates from OSPF adjacent routers but does not disperse LSA updates.

Hello protocol   The OSPF Hello protocol provides dynamic neighbor discovery and maintains neighbor relationships. Hello packets and Link State Advertisements (LSAs) build and maintain the topological database. Hello packets are addressed to multicast address 224.0.0.5.

Neighborship database   The *neighborship database* is a list of all OSPF routers for which Hello packets have been seen. A variety of details, including the router ID and state, are maintained on each router in the neighborship database.

Topological database   The *topological database* contains information from all of the Link State Advertisement packets that have been received for an area. The router uses the information from the topology database as input into the Dijkstra algorithm that computes the shortest path to every network.

Link State Advertisement   A *Link State Advertisement (LSA)* is an OSPF data packet containing link-state and routing information that's shared among OSPF routers. An OSPF router will exchange LSA packets only with routers to which it has established adjacencies.

OSPF areas   An *OSPF area* is a grouping of contiguous networks and routers. All routers in the same area share a common area ID. Because a router can be a member of more than one area at a time, the area ID is associated with specific interfaces on the router. This would allow some interfaces to belong to area 1 while the remaining interfaces can belong to area 0. All of the routers within the same area have the same topology table. When configuring OSPF with multiple areas, you've got to remember that there must be an area 0 and that this is typically considered the backbone area. Areas also play a role in establishing a hierarchical network organization—something that really enhances the scalability of OSPF!

Broadcast (multi-access)   *Broadcast (multi-access) networks* such as Ethernet allow multiple devices to connect to or access the same network, enabling a *broadcast* ability in which a single packet is delivered to all nodes on the network. In OSPF, a DR and BDR must be elected for each broadcast multi-access network.

Nonbroadcast multi-access   *Nonbroadcast multi-access (NBMA)* networks are networks such as Frame Relay, X.25, and Asynchronous Transfer Mode (ATM). These types of networks allow for multi-access without broadcast ability as with Ethernet. NBMA networks require special OSPF configuration to function properly.

Point-to-point   *Point-to-point* refers to a type of network topology made up of a direct connection between two routers that provides a single communication path. The point-to-point connection can be physical—for example, a serial cable that directly connects two routers—or logical, where two routers thousands of miles apart are connected by a circuit in a Frame Relay network. Either way, point-to-point configurations eliminate the need for DRs or BDRs.

Point-to-multipoint   *Point-to-multipoint* refers to a type of network topology made up of a series of connections between a single interface on one router and multiple destination routers. All interfaces on all routers share the point-to-multipoint connection and belong to the same network. Point-to-multipoint networks can be further classified according to whether they support broadcasts or not. This is important because it defines the kind of OSPF configurations you can deploy.

All of these terms play a critical role when you're trying to understand how OSPF actually works.

Benefit of Single Area

The easiest and also least scalable way to configure OSPF is to just use a single area. Doing this requires a minimum of two commands.

The first command used to activate the OSPF routing process is as follows:

```
Router(config)#router ospf ?
<1-65535> Process ID
```

A value in the range from 1 to 65,535 identifies the OSPF process ID. It's a unique number on this router that groups a series of OSPF configuration commands under a specific running process. Different OSPF routers don't have to use the same process ID to communicate. It's a purely local value that doesn't mean a lot, but you still need to remember that it cannot start at 0; it has to start at a minimum of 1.

Neighbor Adjacencies

OSPF operation is basically divided into these three categories:

- Neighbor and adjacency initialization
- LSA flooding
- SPF tree calculation

The beginning neighbor/adjacency formation stage is a very big part of OSPF operation. When OSPF is initialized on a router, the router allocates memory for it as well as for the maintenance of both neighbor and topology tables. Once the router determines which interfaces have been configured for OSPF, it will then check to see if they're active and begin sending Hello packets.

The Hello protocol, illustrated in Figure 4.8, is used to discover neighbors, establish adjacencies, and maintain relationships with other OSPF routers. Hello packets are periodically sent out of each enabled OSPF interface and in environments that support multicast.

FIGURE 4.8 The Hello protocol

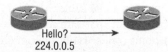

The address used for this is 224.0.0.5, and the frequency with which Hello packets are sent out depends upon the network type and topology. Broadcast and point-to-point networks send Hellos every 10 seconds, whereas non-broadcast and point-to-multipoint networks send them every 30 seconds.

OSPF States

When OSPF routers are initialized, they first start exchanging information using the Hello protocol via the multicast address 224.0.0.5. After the neighbor relationship is established between routers, the routers synchronize their link-state database (LSDB) by reliably exchanging LSAs. They actually exchange quite a bit of vital information when they start up.

The relationship that one router has with another consists of eight possible states. All OSPF routers begin in the DOWN state, and if all is well, they'll progress to either the 2WAY or FULL state with their neighbors. Figure 4.9 shows this neighbor state progression.

FIGURE 4.9 OSPF neighbor states, part 1

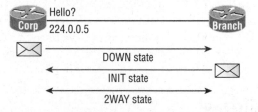

The process starts by sending out Hello packets. Every listening router will then add the originating router to the neighbor database. The responding routers will reply with all of their Hello information so that the originating router can add them to its own neighbor table. At this point, we will have reached the 2WAY state—only certain routers will advance beyond this to establish adjacencies.

Here are the first four possible relationship states:

DOWN   In the DOWN state, no Hello packets have been received on the interface. This does not imply that the interface itself is physically down.

ATTEMPT   In the ATTEMPT state, neighbors must be configured manually. It applies only to nonbroadcast multi-access (NBMA) network connections.

INIT   In the INIT state, Hello packets have been received from another router. Still, the absence of the router ID for the receiving router in the Neighbor field indicates that bidirectional communication hasn't been established yet.

2WAY   In the 2WAY state, Hello packets that include their own router ID in the Neighbor field have been received. Bidirectional communication has been established. In broadcast multi-access networks, an election can occur after this point.

After the DR and BDR have been selected, the routers will enter into the EXSTART state and are ready to discover the link-state information about the internetwork and create their LSDB. This process is illustrated in Figure 4.10.

FIGURE 4.10   OSPF router neighbor states, part 2

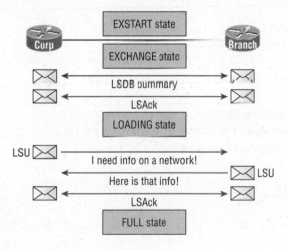

Here are the next four possible relationship states:

EXSTART   In the EXSTART state, the DR and BDR establish adjacencies with each router in the network. A master-slave relationship is created between each router and its adjacent DR and DBR. The router with the highest RID becomes the master, and the master-slave election dictates which router will start the exchange. Once routers exchange DBD packets, the routers will move into the EXCHANGE state.

EXCHANGE   In the EXCHANGE state, routing information is exchanged using Database Description (DBD or DD) packets, and Link State Request (LSR) and Link State Update packets may also be sent. When routers start sending LSRs, they're considered to be in the LOADING state.

LOADING   In the LOADING state, Link State Request (LSR) packets are sent to neighbors to request any Link-State Advertisements (LSAs) that may have been missed or corrupted while the routers were in the EXCHANGE state. Neighbors respond with Link State Update (LSU) packets, which are in turn acknowledged with Link State Acknowledgement (LSAck) packets. When all LSRs have been satisfied for a given router, the adjacent routers are considered synchronized and enter the FULL state.

FULL   In the FULL state, all LSA information is synchronized among neighbors, and adjacency has been established. OSPF routing can begin only after the FULL state has been reached!

It's important to understand that routers should be in the 2WAY and FULL states and the others are considered transitory. Routers shouldn't remain in any other state for extended period of times.

Discuss Multi Area

Multi-area OSPF is pretty straightforward, as is single area OSPF. The configuration is the same; just add the additional area statement into the configuration:

```
Corp#config t
Corp(config)#router ospf 1
Corp(config-router)#router-id 1.1.1.1
Corp(config-router)#Reload or use "clear ip ospf process" command, for this to
take effect

Corp(config-router)#network 10.10.0.0 0.0.255.255 area 0
Corp(config-router)#network 172.16.10.0 0.0.0.3 area 1
Corp(config-router)#network 172.16.10.4 0.0.0.3 area 2
```

Configure OSPF v2

The two factors that are foundational to OSPF configuration are enabling OSPF and configuring OSPF areas.

After identifying the OSPF process, you need to identify the interfaces on which you want to activate OSPF communications as well as the area in which each resides. This will also configure the networks you're going to advertise to others. Wildcards are used in the OSPF configuration.

Here's an example of a basic OSPF configuration for you, showing the second minimum command needed, the network command:

```
Router#config t
Router(config)#router ospf 1
Router(config-router)#network 10.0.0.0 0.255.255.255 area ?
  <0-4294967295>  OSPF area ID as a decimal value
```

```
A.B.C.D          OSPF area ID in IP address format
Router(config-router)#network 10.0.0.0 0.255.255.255 area 0
```

> The IDs for the areas can be any number from 0 to 4.2 billion. Don't get these numbers confused with the process ID, which ranges from 1 to 65,535.

Remember, the OSPF process ID number is irrelevant. It can be the same on every router on the network, or it can be different—doesn't matter. It's locally significant and just enables the OSPF routing on the router.

Wildcard Example

OSPF allows us to use wildcard masks in the configuration. This is very useful when you are using subnets.

You have a router with these four subnets connected to four different interfaces:

- 192.168.10.64/28
- 192.168.10.80/28
- 192.168.10.96/28
- 192.168.10.8/30

All interfaces need to be in area 0; the easiest configuration would look like this:

```
Test#config t
Test(config)#router ospf 1
Test(config-router)#network 192.168.10.0 0.0.0.255 area 0
```

The *show ip route* Command

There are several ways to verify proper OSPF configuration and operation.

First is the show ip route command:

```
O    192.168.10.0/24 [110/65] via 172.16.10.2, 1d17h, Serial0/0
     172.131.0.0/32 is subnetted, 1 subnets
    172.131.0.0/32 is subnetted, 1 subnets
C       172.131.1.1 is directly connected, Loopback0
    172.16.0.0/30 is subnetted, 4 subnets
C      172.16.10.4 is directly connected, Serial0/1
L      172.16.10.5/32 is directly connected, Serial0/1
C      172.16.10.0 is directly connected, Serial0/0
L      172.16.10.1/32 is directly connected, Serial0/0
O    192.168.20.0/24 [110/65] via 172.16.10.6, 1d17h, Serial0/1
    10.0.0.0/24 is subnetted, 2 subnets
C      10.10.10.0 is directly connected, FastEthernet0/0
L      10.10.10.1/32 is directly connected, FastEthernet0/0
```

This router shows only two dynamic routes for the internetwork, with the O representing OSPF internal routes. The Cs are directly connected networks, and two remote networks are showing up. Notice the 110/65, which is our administrative distance/metric.

The *show ip ospf* Command

The show ip ospf command will display OSPF information for one or all OSPF processes running on the router. Information contained therein includes the router ID, area information, SPF statistics, and LSA timer information.

```
Router#sh ip ospf
 Routing Process "ospf 1" with ID 223.255.255.254
 Start time: 00:08:41.724, Time elapsed: 2d16h
 Supports only single TOS(TOS0) routes
 Supports opaque LSA
 Supports Link-local Signaling (LLS)
 Supports area transit capability
 Router is not originating router-LSAs with maximum metric
 Initial SPF schedule delay 5000 msecs
 Minimum hold time between two consecutive SPFs 10000 msecs
 Maximum wait time between two consecutive SPFs 10000 msecs
 Incremental-SPF disabled
 Minimum LSA interval 5 secs
 Minimum LSA arrival 1000 msecs
 LSA group pacing timer 240 secs
 Interface flood pacing timer 33 msecs
 Retransmission pacing timer 66 msecs
 Number of external LSA 0. Checksum Sum 0x000000
 Number of opaque AS LSA 0. Checksum Sum 0x000000
 Number of DCbitless external and opaque AS LSA 0
 Number of DoNotAge external and opaque AS LSA 0
 Number of areas in this router is 1. 1 normal 0 stub 0 nssa
 Number of areas transit capable is 0
 External flood list length 0
 IETF NSF helper support enabled
 Cisco NSF helper support enabled
    Area BACKBONE(0)
        Number of interfaces in this area is 3
        Area has no authentication
        SPF algorithm last executed 00:11:08.760 ago
        SPF algorithm executed 5 times
        Area ranges are
        Number of LSA 6. Checksum Sum 0x03B054
```

```
        Number of opaque link LSA 0. Checksum Sum 0x000000
        Number of DCbitless LSA 0
        Number of indication LSA 0
        Number of DoNotAge LSA 0
        Flood list length 0
```

Notice the router ID (RID) of 223.255.255.254, which is the highest IP address configured on the router.

The *show ip ospf database* Command

Using the show ip ospf database command will give you information about the number of routers in the internetwork (AS) plus the neighboring router's ID—the topology database. Unlike the show ip eigrp topology command, this command reveals the OSPF routers, but not each and every link in the AS like EIGRP does.

The output is broken down by area. Here's a sample output:

```
Router#sh ip ospf database

              OSPF Router with ID (223.255.255.254) (Process ID 1)
Router Link States (Area 0)

Link ID         ADV Router      Age     Seq#        Checksum Link count
10.10.10.2      10.10.10.2      966     0x80000001 0x007162 1
172.31.1.4      172.31.1.4      885     0x80000002 0x00D27E 1
192.168.10.1    192.168.10.1    886     0x8000007A 0x00BC95 3
192.168.20.1    192.168.20.1    1133    0x8000007A 0x00E348 3
223.255.255.254 223.255.255.254 925     0x8000004D 0x000B90 5

              Net Link States (Area 0)

Link ID         ADV Router      Age     Seq#        Checksum
10.10.10.1      223.255.255.254 884     0x80000002 0x008CFE
```

You can see all the routers and the RID of each router—the highest IP address on each of them.

The router output shows the link ID—remember that an interface is also a link—and the RID of the router on that link under the ADV router, or advertising router.

The *show ip ospf interface* Command

The show ip ospf interface command reveals all interface-related OSPF information. Data is displayed about OSPF information for all OSPF-enabled interfaces or for specified interfaces.

```
Corp#sh ip ospf int f0/0
FastEthernet0/0 is up, line protocol is up
```

```
Internet Address 10.10.10.1/24, Area 0
Process ID 1, Router ID 223.255.255.254, Network Type BROADCAST, Cost: 1
Transmit Delay is 1 sec, State DR, Priority 1
Designated Router (ID) 223.255.255.254, Interface address 10.10.10.1
Backup Designated router (ID) 172.31.1.4, Interface address 10.10.10.2
Timer intervals configured, Hello 10, Dead 40, Wait 40, Retransmit 5
  oob-resync timeout 40
  Hello due in 00:00:08
Supports Link-local Signaling (LLS)
Cisco NSF helper support enabled
IETF NSF helper support enabled
Index 3/3, flood queue length 0
Next 0x0(0)/0x0(0)
Last flood scan length is 1, maximum is 1
Last flood scan time is 0 msec, maximum is 0 msec
Neighbor Count is 1, Adjacent neighbor count is 1
  Adjacent with neighbor 172.31.1.  Suppress hello for 0 neighbor(s)
```

This command has given us the following information:

- Interface IP address
- Area assignment
- Process ID
- Router ID
- Network type
- Cost
- Priority
- DR/BDR election information (if applicable)
- Hello and dead timer intervals
- Adjacent neighbor information

The show ip ospf interface f0/0 command is used when there would be a designated router elected on the Fast Ethernet broadcast multi-access network between two routers. A good question to ask here is, What are the hello and dead timers set to by default?

Use the show ip ospf interface command to receive this response:

```
Corp#sh ip ospf int f0/0
%OSPF: OSPF not enabled on FastEthernet0/0
```

This error occurs when OSPF is enabled on the router but not the interface. When this happens, you need to check your network statements because it means that the interface you're trying to verify is not in your OSPF process!

The *show ip ospf neighbor* Command

The show ip ospf neighbor command is super useful because it summarizes the pertinent OSPF information regarding neighbors and the adjacency state. If a DR or BDR exists, that information will also be displayed. Here's a sample:

```
Corp#sh ip ospf neighbor

Neighbor ID     Pri   State       Dead Time   Address      Interface
172.31.1.4       1    FULL/BDR    00:00:34    10.10.10.2   FastEthernet0/0
192.168.20.1     0    FULL/  -    00:00:31    172.16.10.6  Serial0/1
192.168.10.1     0    FULL/  -    00:00:32    172.16.10.2  Serial0/0
```

The *show ip protocols* Command

The show ip protocols command is also highly useful, whether you're running OSPF, EIGRP, RIP, BGP, IS-IS, or any other routing protocol that can be configured on your router. It provides an excellent overview of the actual operation of all currently running protocols!

```
Router#sh ip protocols
Routing Protocol is "ospf 1"
  Outgoing update filter list for all interfaces is not set
  Incoming update filter list for all interfaces is not set
  Router ID 223.255.255.254
  Number of areas in this router is 1. 1 normal 0 stub 0 nssa
  Maximum path: 4
  Routing for Networks:
      10.10.10.1 0.0.0.0 area 0
      172.16.10.1 0.0.0.0 area 0
      172.16.10.5 0.0.0.0 area 0
 Reference bandwidth unit is 100 mbps
  Routing Information Sources:
    Gateway         Distance      Last Update
    192.168.10.1        110       00:21:53
    192.168.20.1        110       00:21:53
  Distance: (default is 110) Distance: (default is 110)
```

From looking at this output, you can determine the OSPF process ID, OSPF router ID, type of OSPF area, networks and areas configured for OSPF, and the OSPF router IDs of neighbors.

Configure OSPF v3

The new version of OSPF continues the trend of routing protocols having a lot in common with their IPv4 versions. The foundation of OSPF remains the same—it's still a link-state routing protocol that divides an entire internetwork or autonomous system into areas, establishing a hierarchy.

Adjacencies and next-hop attributes now use link-local addresses, but OSPFv3 still uses multicast traffic to send its updates and acknowledgments. It uses the addresses FF02::5 for OSPF routers and FF02::6 for OSPF-designated routers. These new addresses are the replacements for 224.0.0.5 and 224.0.0.6, respectively.

The configuration of OSPFv3 starts by assigning the RID:

```
Router(config)#ipv6 router osfp 10
Router(config-rtr)#router-id 1.1.1.1
```

Go to each interface and enable it:

```
Router(config-if)#int s0/0/0
Router(config-if)#ipv6 ospf 1 area 0
Router(config-if)#int s0/0/1
Router(config-if)#ipv6 ospf 1 area 0
```

Router ID

It's really vital to configure loopback interfaces when using OSPF. In fact, Cisco suggests using them whenever you configure OSPF on a router for stability purposes.

Loopback interfaces are logical interfaces, which means they're virtual, software-only interfaces, not actual, physical router interfaces. A big reason we use loopback interfaces with OSPF configurations is because they ensure that an interface is always active and available for OSPF processes.

Loopback interfaces also come in very handy for diagnostic purposes as well as for OSPF configuration. Understand that if you don't configure a loopback interface on a router, the highest active IP address on a router will become that router's RID during bootup! Figure 4.11 illustrates how routers know each other by their router ID.

FIGURE 4.11   OSPF router ID (RID)

The RID is not only used to advertise routes, it's also used to elect the designated router (DR) and the backup designated router (BDR). These designated routers create adjacencies when a new router comes up and exchanges LSAs to build topological databases.

Passive Interface

You can stop unwanted network advertisements propagating throughout your network. One way to prevent this is with the `passive-interface` command. This command prevents OSPF updates from being sent out the particular interface it is configured for, but the interface will still receive them:

```
Router#config t
Router(config)#router ospf 2
Router(config-router)#passive-interface serial 0/0/0
```

LSA Types

A router's link-state database is made up of *Link-State Advertisements (LSAs)*. The LSA is used in the OSPF process to communicate a router's network topology to its neighbor. Here are the different types:

Type 1 LSA   Referred to as a router link advertisement (RLA), or just router LSA, a Type 1 LSA is sent by every router to other routers in its area. This advertisement contains the status of a router's link in the area to which it is connected. If a router is connected to multiple areas, then it will send separate Type 1 LSAs for each of the areas it's connected to. Type 1 LSAs contain the router ID (RID), interfaces, IP information, and current interface state.

Type 2 LSA   Referred to as a network link advertisement (NLA), a Type 2 LSA is generated by designated routers (DRs). Remember that a designated router is elected to represent other routers in its network, and it establishes adjacencies with them. The DR uses a Type 2 LSA to send out information about the state of other routers that are part of the same network. Note that the Type 2 LSA is flooded to all routers that are in the same area as the one containing the specific network but not to any outside of that area. These updates contain the DR and BDR IP information.

Type 3 LSA   Referred to as a summary link advertisement (SLA), a Type 3 LSA is generated by area border routers. These ABRs send Type 3 LSAs toward the area external to the one where they were generated. The Type 3 LSA advertises networks, and these LSAs advertise inter-area routes to the backbone area (area 0). Advertisements contain the IP information and RID of the ABR that is advertising an LSA Type 3.

Type 4 LSA   Type 4 LSAs are generated by area border routers. These ABRs send a Type 4 LSA toward the area external to the one in which they were generated. These are also summary LSAs like Type 3, but Type 4 LSAs are specifically used to inform the rest of the OSPF areas how to get to the ASBR.

Type 5 LSA   Referred to as AS external link advertisements, a Type 5 LSA is sent by autonomous system boundary routers to advertise routes that are external to the OSPF autonomous system and are flooded everywhere. A Type 5 LSA is generated for each individual external network advertised by the ASBR.

> The word *summary* often invokes images of a summarized network address that hides the details of many small subnets within the advertisement of a single large one. But in OSPF, summary link advertisements don't necessarily contain network summaries. Unless the administrator manually creates a summary, the full list of individual networks available within an area will be advertised by the SLAs.

Exam Essentials

Understand how to configure OSPFv3.   OSPFv3 uses the same basic mechanisms that OSPFv2 uses, but OSPFv3 is more easily configured by placing the configuring OSPFv3 on a per-interface basis with the `ipv6 ospf` *process-ID* `area` *area* command.

Know how OSPF routers become neighbors and/or adjacent.   OSPF routers become neighbors when each router sees the other's Hello packets.

Be able to configure single-area OSPF.   A minimal single-area configuration involves only two commands: `router ospf` *process-id* and `network` *x.x.x.x y.y.y.y* `area` *Z*.

Be able to verify the operation of OSPF.   There are many show commands that provide useful details on OSPF, and it is useful to be completely familiar with the output of each: `show ip ospf`, `show ip ospf database`, `show ip ospf interface`, `show ip ospf neighbor`, and `show ip protocols`.

Know the different types of LSA packets.   There are seven different types of LSA packets that Cisco uses, but here are the ones you need to remember: Type 1 LSAs (router link advertisements), Type 2 LSAs (network link advertisements), Type 3 and 4 LSAs (summary LSAs), and Type 5 LSAs (AS external link advertisements). Know how each functions.

Configure and Verify EIGRP (Single AS)

Enhanced Interior Gateway Routing Protocol (EIGRP) is a Cisco protocol that runs on Cisco routers and on some Cisco switches. In this part of the chapter, I'll cover the many features and functions of EIGRP, with added focus on the unique way that it discovers, selects, and advertises routes.

EIGRP has a number of features that make it especially useful within large, complex networks. A real standout among these is its support of VLSM, which is crucial to its ultra-efficient scalability. EIGRP even includes benefits gained through other common protocols like OSPF and RIPv2, such as the ability to create route summaries at any location we choose.

I'll also cover key EIGRP configuration details and give you examples of each, as well as demonstrate the various commands required to verify that EIGRP is working properly.

You can enter EIGRP commands using two modes: router configuration mode and interface configuration mode. Router configuration mode is used to enable the protocol, specify which networks will run EIGRP, and set global characteristics. Interface configuration mode is used to customize summaries, metrics, timers, and bandwidth.

To start an EIGRP session on a router, use the `router eigrp` command followed by the autonomous system number of your network. Then enter the network numbers connected to the router using the `network` command followed by the network number.

```
Router#config t
Router(config)#router eigrp 20
Router(config-router)#network 172.16.0.0
Router(config-router)#network 10.0.0.0
```

As with RIP, you use the classful network address (all subnet and host bits turned off) for EIGRP.

The AS number is irrelevant—as long as all routers use the same number. You can use any number from 1 to 65,535.

There are several commands that you can use on a router to troubleshoot and verify the EIGRP. Table 4.7 lists all of the most important commands that are used in conjunction with verifying EIGRP operation. It also offers a brief description of what each command does.

TABLE 4.7   EIGRP troubleshooting commands

Command	Description/Function
show ip route	Shows the entire routing table
show ip route eigrp	Shows only EIGRP entries in the routing table
show ip eigrp neighbors	Shows all EIGRP neighbors
show ip eigrp topology	Shows entries in the EIGRP topology table
debug eigrp packet	Shows Hello packets sent/received between adjacent routers
debug ip eigrp notification	Shows EIGRP changes and updates as they occur on your network

The following router output is from the show ip route example:

```
Router#sh ip route
      10.0.0.0/24 is subnetted, 12 subnets
D        10.1.11.0 [90/2172416] via 10.1.5.2, 00:01:05, Serial0/2/0
D        10.1.10.0 [90/2195456] via 10.1.5.2, 00:01:05, Serial0/2/0
D        10.1.9.0 [90/2195456] via 10.1.4.2, 00:01:05, Serial0/1/0
D        10.1.8.0 [90/2195456] via 10.1.4.2, 00:01:05, Serial0/1/0
D        10.1.12.0 [90/2172416] via 10.1.5.2, 00:01:05, Serial0/2/0
C        10.1.3.0 is directly connected, Serial0/0/1
C        10.1.2.0 is directly connected, Serial0/0/0
C        10.1.1.0 is directly connected, FastEthernet0/1
D        10.1.7.0 [90/2195456] via 10.1.2.2, 00:01:06, Serial0/0/0
D        10.1.6.0 [90/2195456] via 10.1.2.2, 00:01:06, Serial0/0/0
C        10.1.5.0 is directly connected, Serial0/2/0
C        10.1.4.0 is directly connected, Serial0/1/0
```

Notice that EIGRP routes are indicated with simply a *D* designation (DUAL) and that the default AD of these routes is 90. This represents internal EIGRP routes.

Let's see what's in the neighbor table:

```
Router#sh ip eigrp neighbors
IP-EIGRP neighbors for process 10
H   Address      Interface    Hold Uptime    SRTT  RTO Q  Seq
                              (sec)          (ms)  Cnt Num
1   10.1.3.2     Se0/0/1      14 00:35:10    1     200 0  81
3   10.1.5.2     Se0/2/0      10 02:51:22    1     200 0  31
2   10.1.4.2     Se0/1/0      13 03:17:20    1     200 0  20
0   10.1.2.2     Se0/0/0      10 03:19:37    1     200 0  80
```

Here is what this table tells us:

- The H field indicates the order in which the neighbor was discovered.

- The hold time is how long this router will wait for a Hello packet to arrive from a specific neighbor.

- The uptime indicates how long the neighborship has been established.

- The SRTT field is the smooth round-trip timer—an indication of the time it takes for a round trip from this router to its neighbor and back. This value is used to determine how long to wait after a multicast for a reply from this neighbor. If a reply isn't received in time, the router will switch to using unicasts in an attempt to complete the communication.

Now let's see what's in the topology table by using the show ip eigrp topology command:

```
Router#sh ip eigrp topology
IP-EIGRP Topology Table for AS(10)/ID(10.1.5.1)
Codes: P - Passive, A - Active, U - Update, Q - Query, R - Reply,
       r - reply Status, s - sia Status
P 10.1.11.0/24, 1 successors, FD is 2172416
        via 10.1.5.2 (2172416/28160), Serial0/2/0
P 10.1.10.0/24, 1 successors, FD is 2172416
        via 10.1.5.2 (2195456/281600), Serial0/2/0
P 10.1.9.0/24, 1 successors, FD is 2195456
        via 10.1.4.2 (2195456/281600), Serial0/1/0
P 10.1.8.0/24, 1 successors, FD is 2195456
        via 10.1.4.2 (2195456/72960), Serial0/1/0
P 10.1.12.0/24, 1 successors, FD is 2172416
        via 10.1.5.2 (2172416/28160), Serial0/2/0
P 10.1.3.0/24, 1 successors, FD is 76839936
        via Connected, Serial0/0/1
        via 10.1.2.2 (9849856/7719936), Serial0/0/0
P 10.1.2.0/24, 1 successors, FD is 2169856
        via Connected, Serial0/0/0
        via 10.1.2.2 (2681856/551936), Serial0/0/0
P 10.1.1.0/24, 1 successors, FD is 28160
        via Connected, FastEthernet0/1
P 10.1.7.0/24, 1 successors, FD is 793600
        via 10.1.2.2 (2195456/281600), Serial0/0/0
        via 10.1.3.2 (77081600/281600), Serial0/0/1
P 10.1.6.0/24, 1 successors, FD is 793600
        via 10.1.2.2 (2195456/281600), Serial0/0/0
        via 10.1.3.2 (77081600/281600), Serial0/0/1
P 10.1.5.0/24, 1 successors, FD is 2169856
        via Connected, Serial0/2/0
P 10.1.4.0/24, 1 successors, FD is 2169856
        via Connected, Serial0/1/0
```

Notice that every route is preceded by a *P*. This means that the route is in the passive state, which is a good thing because routes in the active state (*A*) indicate that the router has lost its path to this network and is searching for a replacement. Each entry also indicates the feasible distance, or FD, to each remote network plus the next-hop neighbor through which packets will travel to their destination. Plus, each entry also has two numbers in parentheses. The first indicates the feasible distance, and the second the advertised distance to a remote network.

Feasible Distance / Feasible Successors / Administrative Distance

Some terms are used with EIGRP to describe how a router measures the distance to a remote network. It's important that you learn these terms:

Feasible distance (FD)   This is the best metric among all paths to a remote network, including the metric to the neighbor that's advertising the remote network. The route with the lowest FD is the route that you'll find in the routing table because it's considered the best path. The feasible distance is calculated using the metric that's reported by the neighbor and referred to as the reported or advertised distance plus the metric to the neighbor reporting the route.

Feasible successor (FS)   A feasible successor is basically an entry in the topology table that represents a path that's inferior to the successor route(s). An FS is defined as a path whose advertised distance is less than the feasible distance of the current successor and considered a backup route. EIGRP will keep up to 32 feasible successors in the topology table in 15.0 code, but only up to 16 in previous IOS versions, which is still a lot! Only the path with the best metric—the successor—is copied and placed in the routing table. The show ip eigrp topology command will display all the EIGRP feasible successor routes known to the router.

> A feasible successor is a backup route and is stored in the topology table. A successor route is stored in the topology table and is copied and placed in the routing table.

Reported/advertised distance (AD)   This is the metric of a remote network, as reported by a neighbor. It's also the routing table metric of the neighbor and is the same as the second number in parentheses as displayed in the topology table. The first number is the administrative distance.

Feasibility Condition

Feasibility condition refers to the selection of successors and feasible successors that are guaranteed to be on a loop-free destination.

Metric Composition

EIGRP has a default hop count of 100, with a maximum of 255. In EIGRP, hop count refers to how many routers an EIGRP route update packet can go through before it will be discarded, which limits the size of the autonomous system (AS). Don't get confused, this isn't how metrics are calculated with EIGRP!

There are a bunch of powerful features that make EIGRP a real standout from other protocols. Here's a list of some of the major ones:

- Support for IP and IPv6 (and some other useless routed protocols) via protocol-dependent modules
- Considered classless (same as RIPv2 and OSPF)
- Support for VLSM/CIDR
- Support for summaries and discontiguous networks
- Efficient neighbor discovery
- Communication via Reliable Transport Protocol (RTP)
- Best path selection via Diffusing Update Algorithm (DUAL)
- Reduced bandwidth usage with bounded updates
- No broadcasts

Router ID

The EIGRP router ID is normally selected in the same manner as Open Shortest Path First (OSPF). The highest IP address assigned to a loopback interface is selected as the router ID. If there are not any loopback addresses configured, the highest IP address assigned to any other interface is chosen as the router ID. Here's an example:

```
Router#config t
Router(config)#router eigrp 10
Router(config-rtr)#eigrp router-id 1.1.1.1
```

Auto Summary

EIGRP automatically summarizes networks at their classful boundaries and supports the manual creation of summaries at any and all EIGRP routers.

This works well when all networks are contiguous (all networks are within the same network boundary). In the case where there are different network boundaries, the no auto-summary command would be needed.

Path Selection

EIGRP uses Diffusing Update Algorithm (DUAL) for selecting and maintaining the best path to each remote network. DUAL allows EIGRP to carry out these vital tasks:

- Figure out a backup route if there's one available.
- Support variable length subnet masks (VLSMs).

- Perform dynamic route recoveries.
- Query neighbors for unknown alternate routes.
- Send out queries for an alternate route.

DUAL enables EIGRP to converge amazingly fast! The key to the speed is twofold: First, EIGRP routers maintain a copy of all of their neighbors' routes to refer to for calculating their own cost to each remote network. So if the best path goes down, all it often takes to find another one is a quick scan of the topology table looking for a feasible successor. Second, if that quick table survey doesn't work out, EIGRP routers immediately ask their neighbors for help finding the best path.

Three critical conditions must be met for DUAL to work properly:

- Neighbors are discovered or noted as dead within a finite time.
- All transmitted messages are received correctly.
- All changes and messages are processed in the order in which they're detected.

Load Balancing

By default, EIGRP can provide equal-cost load balancing across up to 4 links. You can have EIGRP actually load-balance across up to 32 links with 15.0 code (equal or unequal) by using the following command:

```
Router(config)#router eigrp 10
Router(config-router)#maximum-paths ?
  <1-32>  Number of paths
```

Pre–15.0 code routers allowed up to 16 paths to remote networks. EIGRP has a default maximum hop count of 100 for route update packets, but it can be set up to 255. Here's how to change it:

```
Router(config)#router eigrp 10
Router(config-router)#metric maximum-hops ?
  <1-255>  Hop count
```

As you can see from this router output, EIGRP can be set to a maximum of 255 hops. Even though it doesn't use hop count in the path metric calculation, it still uses the maximum hop count to limit the scope of the AS.

Equal

With equal-cost load balancing, different paths to a remote network report the same routing metric. The maximum-paths command would determine the maximum number of routes EIGRP would use.

Unequal

With unequal-cost load balancing, different paths to a remote network report different routing metrics. The variance command would determine which route would be best to use:

```
Router(config)#router eigrp 10
Router(config-router)#variance 2
Router(config-router)#
```

Passive Interface

If you need to stop EIGRP from working on a specific interface, such as, for instance, a connection to your ISP, or if you didn't want to have a specific interface be part of the EIGRP process, you can use the passive-interface command. Here's how to do this from an EIGRP session:

```
passive-interface interface-type interface-number
```

This works because the interface-type portion defines the type of interface and the interface-number portion defines the number of the interface. The following command makes interface serial 0/0 into a passive interface:

```
Corp(config)#router eigrp 20
Corp(config-router)#passive-interface g0/0
```

Exam Essentials

Know the EIGRP features. EIGRP is a classless, advanced distance-vector protocol that supports IP, IPX, AppleTalk, and now IPv6. EIGRP uses a unique algorithm, called DUAL, to maintain route information and uses RTP to communicate with other EIGRP routers reliably.

Know how to configure EIGRP. Be able to configure basic EIGRP. This is configured the same as IGRP with classful addresses.

Know how to verify EIGRP operation. Know all of the EIGRP show commands and be familiar with their output and the interpretation of the main components of their output.

Configure and Verify InterVLAN Routing (Router on a Stick)

Hosts in a VLAN live in their own broadcast domain and can communicate freely. VLANs create network partitioning and traffic separation at layer 2 of the OSI, and as I said when I told you why we still need routers, if you want hosts or any other IP-addressable device to communicate between VLANs, you must have a layer 3 device to provide routing.

For this, you can use a router that has an interface for each VLAN or a router that supports ISL or 802.1q routing.

In Figure 4.12, each router interface is plugged into an access link. This means that each of the routers' interface IP addresses would then become the default gateway address for each host in each respective VLAN.

FIGURE 4.12   Router connecting three VLANs together for inter-VLAN communication, one router interface for each VLAN

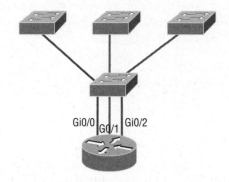

If you have more VLANs available than router interfaces, you can configure trunking on one Fast Ethernet interface or buy a layer 3 switch.

Instead of using a router interface for each VLAN, you can use one Fast Ethernet interface and run ISL or 802.1q trunking. Figure 4.13 shows how a Fast Ethernet interface on a router will look when configured with ISL or 802.1q trunking. This allows all VLANs to communicate through one interface. Cisco calls this a router on a stick (ROAS).

This configuration creates a potential bottleneck, as well as a single point of failure, so your host/VLAN count is limited.

Figure 4.14 shows how we would create a router on a stick using a router's physical interface by creating logical interfaces—one for each VLAN.

Here we see one physical interface divided into multiple subinterfaces, with one subnet assigned per VLAN, each subinterface being the default gateway address for each VLAN/subnet.

Configuring VLANs on your switch is pretty straightforward:

```
S1(config)#vlan 2
S1(config-vlan)#name Sales
S1(config-vlan)#vlan 3
S1(config-vlan)#name Marketing
S1(config-vlan)#vlan 4
S1(config-vlan)#name Accounting
S1(config-vlan)#^Z
S1#
```

FIGURE 4.13   Router on a stick: Single router interface connecting all three VLANs together for inter-VLAN communication

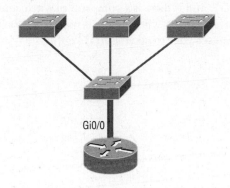

FIGURE 4.14   A router creates logical interfaces.

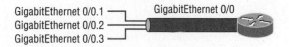

Once the VLANs are created, verify your configuration with the show vlan command (sh vlan for short):

S1#**sh vlan**

```
VLAN Name                        Status    Ports
---- -------------------------- --------- ------------------------------
1    default                    active    Fa0/1, Fa0/2, Fa0/3, Fa0/4
                                          Fa0/5, Fa0/6, Fa0/7, Fa0/8
```

```
                                           Fa0/9, Fa0/10, Fa0/11, Fa0/12
                                           Fa0/13, Fa0/14, Fa0/19, Fa0/20
                                           Fa0/21, Fa0/22, Fa0/23, Gi0/1
                                           Gi0/2
2    Sales                                 active
3    Marketing                             active
4    Accounting                            active
[output cut]
```

In the preceding S1 output, you can see that ports Fa0/1 through Fa0/14, Fa0/19 through 23, and Gi0/1 and Gi02 uplinks are all in VLAN 1. But where are ports 15 through 18? First, understand that the command show vlan only displays access ports, so now that you know what you're looking at with the show vlan command, where do you think ports Fa15–18 are? That's right! They are trunked ports. Cisco switches run a proprietary protocol called *Dynamic Trunk Protocol (DTP)*, and if there is a compatible switch connected, they will start trunking automatically, which is precisely where my four ports are. You have to use the show interfaces trunk command to see your trunked ports like this:

```
S1# show interfaces trunk
Port      Mode          Encapsulation  Status     Native vlan
Fa0/15    desirable     n-isl          trunking   1
Fa0/16    desirable     n-isl          trunking   1
Fa0/17    desirable     n-isl          trunking   1
Fa0/18    desirable     n-isl          trunking   1

Port      Vlans allowed on trunk
Fa0/15    1-4094
Fa0/16    1-4094
Fa0/17    1-4094
Fa0/18    1-4094

[output cut]
```

This output reveals that the VLANs from 1 to 4094 are allowed across the trunk by default. Another helpful command, which is also part of the Cisco exam objectives, is the show interfaces *interface* switchport command:

```
S1#sh interfaces fastEthernet 0/15 switchport
Name: Fa0/15
Switchport: Enabled
Administrative Mode: dynamic desirable
Operational Mode: trunk
Administrative Trunking Encapsulation: negotiate
```

```
Operational Trunking Encapsulation: isl
Negotiation of Trunking: On
Access Mode VLAN: 1 (default)
Trunking Native Mode VLAN: 1 (default)
Administrative Native VLAN tagging: enabled
Voice VLAN: none
[output cut]
```

The highlighted output shows us the administrative mode of dynamic desirable, that the port is a trunk port, and that DTP was used to negotiate the frame tagging method of ISL. It also predictably shows that the native VLAN is the default of 1.

You configure a port to belong to a VLAN by assigning a membership mode that specifies the kind of traffic the port carries plus the number of VLANs it can belong to. You can also configure each port on a switch to be in a specific VLAN (access port) by using the interface switchport command. You can even configure multiple ports at the same time with the interface range command.

Here's how to configure interface Fa0/3 to VLAN 3:

```
S1(config-if)#switchport mode ?
    access         Set trunking mode to ACCESS unconditionally
  dot1q-tunnel   set trunking mode to TUNNEL unconditionally
  dynamic        Set trunking mode to dynamically negotiate access or trunk mode
  private-vlan   Set private-vlan mode
  trunk          Set trunking mode to TRUNK unconditionally

S1(config-if)#switchport mode access
S1(config-if)#switchport access vlan 3
```

Look at our VLANs now:

```
S1#show vlan
VLAN Name                    Status    Ports
---- ------------------------ --------- -------------------------------
1    default                  active    Fa0/4, Fa0/5, Fa0/6, Fa0/7
                                        Fa0/8, Fa0/9, Fa0/10, Fa0/11,
                                        Fa0/12, Fa0/13, Fa0/14, Fa0/19,
                                        Fa0/20, Fa0/21, Fa0/22, Fa0/23,
                                        Gi0/1 ,Gi0/2


2    Sales                    active
3    Marketing                active    Fa0/3
```

Notice that port Fa0/3 is now a member of VLAN 3. But, can you tell me where ports 1 and 2 are? And why aren't they showing up in the output of show vlan? That's right, because they are trunk ports!

We can also see this with the show interfaces interface switchport command:

```
S1#sh int fa0/3 switchport
Name: Fa0/3
Switchport: Enabled
Administrative Mode: static access
Operational Mode: static access
Administrative Trunking Encapsulation: negotiate
Negotiation of Trunking: Off
Access Mode VLAN: 3 (Marketing)
```

To configure trunking on a Fast Ethernet port, use the interface command switchport mode trunk.

The following switch output shows the trunk configuration on interfaces Fa0/15–18 as set to trunk:

```
S1(config)#int range f0/15-18
S1(config-if-range)#switchport mode trunk
```

Sub Interfaces

To support ISL or 802.1q routing on a FastEthernet interface, the router's interface is divided into logical interfaces—one for each VLAN. These are called *subinterfaces*. From a Fast Ethernet or Gigabit interface, you can set the interface to trunk with the encapsulation command:

```
ISR#config t
ISR(config)#int f0/0.1
ISR(config-subif)#encapsulation ?
  dot1Q  IEEE 802.1Q Virtual LAN
ISR(config-subif)#encapsulation dot1Q ?
  <1-4094>  IEEE 802.1Q VLAN ID
```

The subinterface number is only locally significant, so it doesn't matter which subinterface numbers are configured on the router. Most of the time, I'll configure a subinterface with the same number as the VLAN I want to route. It's easy to remember that way since the subinterface number is used only for administrative purposes.

Upstream Routing

Upstream routing refers to the router used with a "router on a stick" configuration allowing routing upstream so hosts connected to the VLANs can get to remote services.

Encapsulation

VLAN identification is what switches use to keep track of all those frames as they're traversing a switch fabric. It's how switches identify which frames belong to which VLANs, and there's more than one trunking method.

Inter-Switch Link (ISL)

Inter-Switch Link (ISL) is a way of explicitly tagging VLAN information onto an Ethernet frame. This tagging information allows VLANs to be multiplexed over a trunk link through an external encapsulation method. This allows the switch to identify the VLAN membership of a frame received over the trunked link.

By running ISL, you can interconnect multiple switches and still maintain VLAN information as traffic travels between switches on trunk links. ISL functions at layer 2 by encapsulating a data frame with a new header and by performing a new cyclic redundancy check (CRC).

ISL is proprietary to Cisco switches and it's used for Fast Ethernet and Gigabit Ethernet links only. *ISL routing* is pretty versatile and can be used on a switch port, router interfaces, and server interface cards to trunk a server. Although some Cisco switches still support ISL frame tagging, Cisco is moving toward using only 802.1q.

IEEE 802.1q

Created by the IEEE as a standard method of frame tagging, IEEE 802.1q actually inserts a field into the frame to identify the VLAN. If you're trunking between a Cisco switched link and a different brand of switch, you've got to use 802.1q for the trunk to work.

Unlike ISL, which encapsulates the frame with control information, 802.1q inserts an 802.1q field along with tag control information, as shown in Figure 4.15.

For the Cisco exam objectives, it's only the 12-bit VLAN ID that matters. This field identifies the VLAN and can be 2^{12}, minus 2 for the 0 and 4,095 reserved VLANs, which means an 802.1q tagged frame can carry information for 4,094 VLANs.

FIGURE 4.15   IEEE 802.1q encapsulation with and without the 802.1q tag

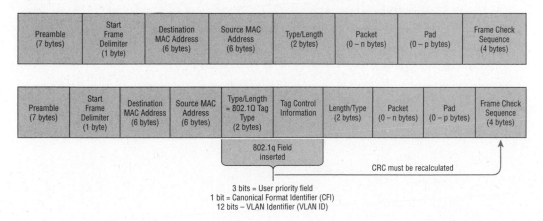

The basic purpose of ISL and 802.1q frame-tagging methods is to provide inter-switch VLAN communication. Remember that any ISL or 802.1q frame tagging is removed if a frame is forwarded out an access link—tagging is used internally and across trunk links only!

Exam Essentials

Understand the 802.1q VLAN identification method.   This is a nonproprietary IEEE method of frame tagging. If you're trunking between a Cisco switched-link and a different brand of switch, you have to use 802.1q for the trunk to work.

Remember how to create a Cisco router on a stick to provide inter-VLAN communication. You can use a Cisco Fast Ethernet or Gigabit Ethernet interface to provide inter-VLAN routing. The switch port connected to the router must be a trunk port; then you must create virtual interfaces (subinterfaces) on the router port for each VLAN connecting to it. The hosts in each VLAN will use this subinterface address as their default gateway address.

Configure SVI Interfaces

SVI, or switched virtual interface, is a method of inter-vlan routing without the aid of a router. Instead, a layer 3 switch is used to route packets from one VLAN to another. It can be configured in this manner:

1. Enable IP routing on the S1 switch.

   ```
   S1(config)#ip routing
   ```

2. Create two new interfaces on the S1 switch to provide inter-VLAN routing.

   ```
   S1(config)#interface vlan 10
   S1(config-if)#ip address 10.10.10.1 255.255.255.0
   S1(config-if)#interface vlan 20
   S1(config-if)#ip address 20.20.20.1 255.255.255.0
   ```

Exam Essentials

Remember how to provide inter-VLAN routing with a layer 3 switch.   You can use a layer 3 (multilayer) switch to provide inter-VLAN routing just as with a router on a stick, but using a layer 3 switch is more efficient and faster. First you start the routing process with the command `ip routing`, then create a virtual interface for each VLAN using the command `interface vlan` *vlan*, and then apply the IP address for that VLAN under that logical interface.

Review Questions

1. Which of the following statements is true with regard to ISL and 802.1q?

   A. 802.1q encapsulates the frame with control information; ISL inserts an ISL field along with tag control information.

   B. 802.1q is Cisco proprietary.

   C. ISL encapsulates the frame with control information; 802.1q inserts an 802.1q field along with tag control information.

   D. ISL is a standard.

2. What concept is depicted in the diagram?

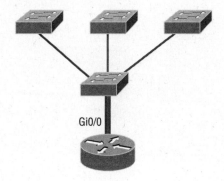

Gi0/0

   A. Multiprotocol routing

   B. Passive interface

   C. Gateway redundancy

   D. Router on a stick

3. In the following diagram, what command is missing to enable inter-VLAN routing between VLAN 2 and VLAN 3?

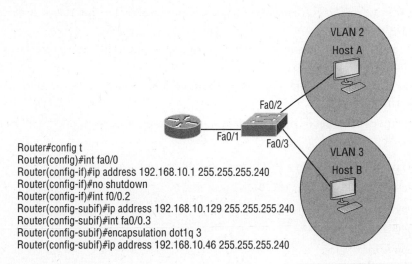

```
Router#config t
Router(config)#int fa0/0
Router(config-if)#ip address 192.168.10.1 255.255.255.240
Router(config-if)#no shutdown
Router(config-if)#int f0/0.2
Router(config-subif)#ip address 192.168.10.129 255.255.255.240
Router(config-subif)#int fa0/0.3
Router(config-subif)#encapsulation dot1q 3
Router(config-subif)#ip address 192.168.10.46 255.255.255.240
```

A. encapsulation dot1q 3 under int f0/0.2

B. encapsulation dot1q 2 under int f0/0.2

C. no shutdown under int f0/0.2

D. no shutdown under int f0/0.3

4. What command generated the following output?

```
172.31.1.4      1    FULL/BDR   00:00:34   10.10.10.2    FastEthernet0/0
192.168.20.1    0    FULL/  -   00:00:31   172.16.10.6   Serial0/1
192.168.10.1    0    FULL/  -   00:00:32   172.16.10.2   Serial0/0
```

A. show ip ospf neighbor

B. show ip ospf database

C. show ip route

D. show ip ospf interface

5. Which of the following describe the process identifier that is used to run OSPF on a router? (Choose two.)

A. It is locally significant.

B. It is globally significant.

C. It is needed to identify a unique instance of an OSPF database.

D. It is an optional parameter required only if multiple OSPF processes are running on the router.

E. All routes in the same OSPF area must have the same process ID if they are to exchange routing information.

6. Which two of the following are true regarding the distance-vector and link-state routing protocols? (Choose two.)

   A. Link state sends its complete routing table out of all active interfaces at periodic time intervals.

   B. Distance vector sends its complete routing table out of all active interfaces at periodic time intervals.

   C. Link state sends updates containing the state of its own links to all routers in the internetwork.

   D. Distance vector sends updates containing the state of its own links to all routers in the internetwork.

7. Which command will copy the IOS to a backup host on your network?

   A. `transfer IOS to 172.16.10.1`

   B. `copy run start`

   C. `copy tftp flash`

   D. `copy start tftp`

   E. `copy flash tftp`

8. If your routing table has a static, an RIP, and an EIGRP route to the same network, which route will be used to route packets by default?

   A. Any available route.

   B. RIP route.

   C. Static route.

   D. EIGRP route.

   E. They will all load-balance.

9. What command is used to permanently install a license on an ISR2 router?

   A. `install license`

   B. `license install`

   C. `boot system license`

   D. `boot license module`

10. CEF is Cisco's new packet-forwarding method in routing. It uses cache tables to help improve performance. How is this method performed?

   A. Packet triggered

   B. Chance triggered

   C. Table triggered

   D. Change triggered.

Chapter

5

IP Services

THE FOLLOWING CCNA ROUTING AND SWITCHING EXAM OBJECTIVES ARE COVERED IN THIS CHAPTER:

✓ **Configure and verify DHCP (IOS Router).**

- configuring router interfaces to use DHCP
- DHCP options
- excluded addresses
- lease time

✓ **Describe the types, features, and applications of ACLs.**

- Standard
  - Sequence numbers
  - Editing
- Extended
- Named
- Numbered
- Log option

✓ **Configure and verify ACLs in a network environment.**

- Named
- Numbered
- Log option

✓ **Identify the basic operation of NAT.**

- Purpose
- Pool
- Static
- 1 to 1
- Overloading

- Source addressing
- One way NAT

✓ **Configure and verify NAT for given network requirements.**

✓ **Configure and verify NTP as a client.**

✓ **Recognize High availability (FHRP).**

- VRRP
- HSRP
- GLBP

✓ **Configure and verify Syslog.**

- Utilize Syslog Output

✓ **Describe SNMP v2 & v3.**

In this chapter, I'll describe the DHCP process. I'll go over access control lists (ACLs) and Network Address Translation (NAT), and then I'll explain how to configure a router as an NTP client. In addition to covering FHRPs, I'll show you how to configure and verify syslog. Finally, I will go over SNMPv2 and v3.

Configure and Verify DHCP (IOS Router)

When we consider Dynamic Host Configuration Protocol (DHCP), we generally think this service is accomplished by a server. That is mostly true. But DHCP can also be configured on a router.

To configure a DHCP server for your hosts, you need the following information at minimum:

Network and mask for each LAN All addresses in a subnet can be leased to hosts by default.

Reserved/excluded addresses Reserved addresses for printers, servers, routers, and so on. These addresses will not be handed out to hosts. The first address of each subnet is usually reserved for the router, but you don't have to do this.

Default router This is the router's address for each LAN.

DNS address A list of DNS server addresses provided to hosts so they can resolve names.

Here are your configuration steps:

1. Exclude the addresses you want to reserve. The reason you do this step first is because as soon as you set a network ID, the DHCP service will start responding to client requests.

2. Create your pool for each LAN using a unique name.

3. Choose the network ID and subnet mask for the DHCP pool that the server will use to provide addresses to hosts.

4. Add the address used for the default gateway of the subnet.

5. Provide the DNS server address(es).

6. If you don't want to use the default lease time of 24 hours, you need to set the lease time in days, hours, and minutes, as in this example:

```
Router(config)#ip dhcp excluded-address 192.168.10.1 192.168.10.10
Router(config)#ip dhcp pool Sales_Wireless
Router(dhcp-config)#network 192.168.10.0 255.255.255.0
```

```
Router(dhcp-config)#default-router 192.168.10.1
Router(dhcp-config)#dns-server 4.4.4.4
Router(dhcp-config)#lease 3 12 15
```

Configuring Router Interfaces to Use DHCP

Configure the interface on the router the DHCP clients will use as their default gateway. If the correct address is not placed on the interface, no addresses from the DHCP pool will be handed out.

```
Router(config)#interface FastEthernet 0/0
Router(config-if)#ip address 192.168.10.1 255.255.255.0
Router(config-if)#no shutdown
```

DHCP Options

If you need to provide addresses from a DHCP server to hosts that aren't on the same LAN as the DHCP server, you can configure your router interface to relay or forward the DHCP client requests, as shown in Figure 5.1. If we don't provide this service, our router would receive the DHCP client broadcast, promptly discard it, and the remote host would never receive an address.

```
Router(config)#interface fa0/0
Router(config-if)#ip helper-address 10.10.10.254
```

FIGURE 5.1   Configuring a DHCP relay

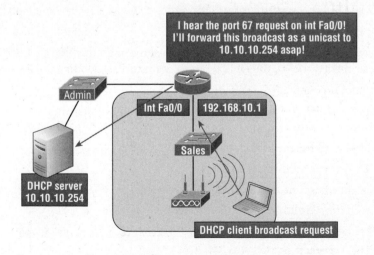

Excluded Addresses

Excluded addresses in a DHCP pool is pretty much required. In the pool of available addresses, you want to reserve addresses from the pool for hosts like the router interface, servers, and printers. If you have a switch in the network, you will want to reserve an IP address for switch management (VLAN 1).

Lease Time

By default, Cisco routers come with a 24-hour lease time. This can be changed to a desired lease time using the following syntax:

```
Router(dhcp-config)# lease {days [hours][minutes]
```

Use the show ip dhcp binding command to display the lease expiration time and date of the IP address of the host.

Exam Essentials

Understand how to configure DHCP on a router.   To configure the router as a DHCP server, first exclude the needed IP addresses. Next, define the pool name and range of addresses that will be available to hosts. Last, add the default-router configuration as well as options such as the ip-helper address and lease time.

Describe the Types, Features, and Applications of ACLs

Securing your network is essential. The proper use and configuration of access control lists (ACLs) is a vital part of router configuration because they are such versatile networking accessories. Contributing mightily to the efficiency and operation of your network, access lists give network managers a huge amount of control over traffic flow throughout the enterprise. With access lists, we can gather basic statistics on packet flow and security policies can be implemented. These dynamic tools also enable us to protect sensitive devices from the dangers of unauthorized access. Simply put, access lists help in implementing security policies by filtering unwanted packets.

Creating access lists is really a lot like programming a series of if-then statements—if a given condition is met, then a given action is taken. If the specific condition isn't met, nothing happens and the next statement is evaluated. Access list statements are basically packet filters that packets are compared against, categorized by, and acted upon accordingly. Once the lists are built, they can be applied to either inbound or outbound traffic on any interface. Applying an access list causes the router to analyze every packet crossing an interface in the specified direction and take the appropriate action.

There are three important rules involved when a packet is being compared with an access list:

- The packet is always compared with each line of the access list in sequential order—it will always start with the first line of the access list, move on to line 2, then line 3, and so on.

- The packet is compared with lines of the access list only until a match is made. Once it matches the condition on a line of the access list, the packet is acted upon and no further comparisons take place.

- There is an implicit "deny" at the end of each access list—this means that if a packet doesn't match the condition on any of the lines in the access list, the packet will be discarded.

Each of these rules has some powerful implications when filtering IP packets with access lists, so keep in mind that creating effective access lists definitely takes some practice.

Standard

These ACLs use only the source IP address in an IP packet as the condition test. All decisions are made based on the source IP address. This means that standard access lists basically permit or deny an entire suite of protocols. They don't distinguish between any of the many types of IP traffic such as Web, Telnet, UDP, and so on.

Standard IP access lists filter network traffic by examining the source IP address in a packet. You create a *standard IP access list* by using the access list numbers 1–99 or numbers in the expanded range of 1300–1999.

```
Router(config)#access-list 10 ?
  deny    Specify packets to reject
  permit  Specify packets to forward
  remark  Access list entry comment
```

Sequence Numbers

Sequence numbers allow you to specify a particular position of entry within the ACL. You can insert an ACL statement into a desired position within the existing list.

Editing

Editing an ACL is a matter of resequencing the ACL statements into a desired position or order. Sequencing values start at 10 and then increment by 10 (10, 20, 30, etc.). If an entry does not have a sequence number, it is given a sequence number of 10 more than the last entry.

Extended

Extended access lists can evaluate many of the other fields in the layer 3 and layer 4 headers of an IP packet. They can evaluate source and destination IP addresses, the Protocol field in the Network layer header, and the port number at the Transport layer header. This gives extended access lists the ability to make much more granular decisions when controlling traffic.

Extended access list numbers range from 100 to 199. The 2000–2699 range is also available for extended IP access lists. In the following example, Telnet access is being denied to host 172.16.30.2:

```
Router(config)#access-list 110 deny tcp any host 172.16.30.2 eq 23
```

Named

Named access lists are either standard or extended and not actually a distinct type. They are created and referred to differently than standard and extended access lists are, but they're still functionally the same.

Numbered

The following output displays a good example of the many access list number ranges that you can use to filter traffic on your network. The IOS version delimits the protocols you can specify access for:

```
Router(config)#access-list ?
  <1-99>            IP standard access list
  <100-199>         IP extended access list
  <1000-1099>       IPX SAP access list
  <1100-1199>       Extended 48-bit MAC address access list
  <1200-1299>       IPX summary address access list
  <1300-1999>       IP standard access list (expanded range)
  <200-299>         Protocol type-code access list
  <2000-2699>       IP extended access list (expanded range)
  <300-399>         DECnet access list
  <600-699>         Appletalk access list
  <700-799>         48-bit MAC address access list
  <800-899>         IPX standard access list
  <900-999>         IPX extended access list
  dynamic-extended  Extend the dynamic ACL absolute timer
  rate-limit        Simple rate-limit specific access list
```

Log Option

The log command is used to log messages every time the access list entry is hit. This can monitor inappropriate access attempts.

Exam Essentials

Remember the standard and extended IP access list number ranges.   The number ranges you can use to configure a standard IP access list are 1–99 and 1300–1999. The number ranges for an extended IP access list are 100–199 and 2000–2699.

Configure and Verify ACLs in a Network Environment

In this part of the chapter, I'll show you how to configure a named access list and a numbered access list and how to use the log feature. I'll also go over some verification commands used in ACLs.

Once you create an access list, it's not really going to do anything until you apply it. To use an access list as a packet filter, you need to apply it to an interface on the router where you want the traffic filtered. And you've got to specify which direction of traffic you want the access list applied to. By specifying the direction of traffic, you can and must use different access lists for inbound and outbound traffic on a single interface:

Inbound access lists   When an access list is applied to inbound packets on an interface, those packets are processed through the access list before being routed to the outbound interface. Any packets that are denied won't be routed because they're discarded before the routing process is invoked.

Outbound access lists   When an access list is applied to outbound packets on an interface, packets are routed to the outbound interface and then processed through the access list before being queued.

There are some general access list guidelines that you should keep in mind when creating and implementing access lists on a router:

▪ You can assign only one access list per interface per protocol per direction. This means that when applying IP access lists, you can have only one inbound access list and one outbound access list per interface.

▪ Organize your access lists so that the more specific tests are at the top.

- Anytime a new entry is added to the access list, it will be placed at the bottom of the list, which is why I highly recommend using a text editor for access lists.
- You can't remove one line from an access list. If you try to do this, you will remove the entire list. This is why it's best to copy the access list to a text editor before trying to edit the list. The only exception is when you're using named access lists.

 You can edit, add, or delete a single line from a named access list.

- Unless your access list ends with a permit any command, all packets will be discarded if they do not meet any of the list's tests. This means every list should have at least one permit statement or it will deny all traffic.
- Create access lists and then apply them to an interface. Any access list applied to an interface without access list test statements present will not filter traffic.
- Access lists are designed to filter traffic going through the router. They will not filter traffic that has originated from the router.
- Place IP standard access lists as close to the destination as possible. This is the reason we don't really want to use standard access lists in our networks. You can't put a standard access list close to the source host or network because you can filter based only on source address and all destinations would be affected as a result.
- Place IP extended access lists as close to the source as possible. Since extended access lists can filter on very specific addresses and protocols, you don't want your traffic to traverse the entire network just to be denied. By placing this list as close to the source address as possible, you can filter traffic before it uses up precious bandwidth.

Named

Named access lists are just another way to create standard and extended access lists. In large companies or corporations, a named access list can be very beneficial, especially when dealing with numerous ACLs.

```
Routerconfig t
Router(config)# ip access-list ?
  extended    Extended Access List
  log-update  Control access list log updates
  logging     Control access list logging
  resequence  Resequence Access List
  standard    Standard Access List
```

Notice that I used the ip access-list command instead of the access-list command. Doing this allows me to enter a named access list.

```
Router(config)#ip access-list standard ?
  <1-99>       Standard IP access-list number
  <1300-1999>  Standard IP access-list number (expanded range)
  WORD         Access-list name
```

```
Router(config)#ip access-list standard BlockSales
Router(config-std-nacl)#
```

You have more flexibility when creating named ACLs. You can apply sequence numbers to the permit or deny statements and reorder, add, or even remove statements from a named ACL.

Here's a sample configuration:

```
Router#show access-list 100
Extended IP access list 100
10 permit ip host x.x.x.x host x.x.x.x
20 permit tcp any host x.x.x.x
30 permit ip host x.x.x.x host x.x.x.x
40 permit icmp any any
50 permit ip any any
```

```
Router(config)# ip access-list extended 100
Router(config)# ip access-list resequence 150 1 2
Router(config)# end
```

Log Option

The Log option gives you the ability to log events each time an ACL is acted upon. If you have a deny statement in your ACL that denies a particular application service such as Telnet, a log event will be created when someone on the network attempts to telnet into a device. Here's an example:

```
Router(config)#access-list 110 deny tcp any host 172.16.30.2 eq 23 log
```

It's always good to be able to verify a router's configuration. Table 5.1 lists the various commands for verifying ACLs.

TABLE 5.1   Commands used to verify access list configuration

Command	Effect
show access-list	Displays all access lists configured on the router and their parameters. Also shows statistics about how many times a line either permitted or denied a packet. This command does not show you which interface the list is applied on.
show access-list 110	Reveals only the parameters for access list 110. Again, this command will not reveal the specific interface the list is set on.
show ip access-list	Shows only the IP access lists configured on the router.
show ip interface	Displays which interfaces have access lists set on them.
show running-config	Shows the access lists and the specific interfaces that have ACLs applied on them.

Exam Essentials

Understand the term *implicit deny*.   At the end of every access list is an *implicit deny*. What this means is that if a packet does not match any of the lines in the access list, it will be discarded. Also, if you have nothing but deny statements in your list, the list will not permit any packets.

Understand the standard IP access list configuration command.   To configure a standard IP access list, use the access list numbers 1–99 or 1300–1999 in global configuration mode. Choose permit or deny, and then choose the source IP address you want to filter on.

Understand the extended IP access list configuration command.   To configure an extended IP access list, use the access list numbers 100–199 or 2000–2699 in global configuration mode. Choose permit or deny, the Network layer protocol field, the source IP address you want to filter on, the destination address you want to filter on, and finally, the Transport layer port number if TCP or UDP has been specified as the protocol.

Remember the command to verify an access list on a router interface.   To see whether an access list is set on an interface and in which direction it is filtering, use the show ip interface command. This command will not show you the contents of the access list, merely which access lists are applied on the interface.

Remember the command to verify the access list configuration.   To see the configured access lists on your router, use the show access-list command. This command will not show you which interfaces have an access list set.

Identify the Basic Operation of NAT

In the following sections, I'm going to cover Network Address Translation (NAT) and Port Address Translation (PAT), also known as NAT overload. I will also go over of the types of NAT.

It's important to understand the Cisco objectives for this section. They are very straight-forward: you have hosts on your inside corporate network using RFC 1918 addresses and you need to allow those hosts access to the Internet by configuring NAT translations.

Because we'll be using access control lists (ACLs) in our NAT configurations, it's important that you're really comfortable with them.

Purpose

Network Address Translation (NAT) is similar to Classless Inter-Domain Routing (CIDR) in that the original intention for NAT was to slow the depletion of available IP address space by allowing multiple private IP addresses to be represented by a much smaller number of public IP addresses.

Since then, it's been discovered that NAT is also a useful tool for network migrations and mergers, server load sharing, and creating "virtual servers."

Because NAT really decreases the overwhelming amount of public IP addresses required in a networking environment, it comes in really handy when two companies that have duplicate internal addressing schemes merge. NAT is also a great tool to use when an organization changes its Internet service provider (ISP) but the networking manager needs to avoid the hassle of changing the internal address scheme.

NAT can be especially helpful in the following situations:

▪ When you need to connect to the Internet and your hosts don't have globally unique IP addresses

▪ When you've changed to a new ISP that requires you to renumber your network

▪ When you need to merge two intranets with duplicate addresses

You typically use NAT on a border router. For example, in Figure 5.2, NAT is used on the Corporate router connected to the Internet.

There are some advantages and disadvantages to using NAT, as shown in Table 5.2.

TABLE 5.2 Advantages and disadvantages of implementing NAT

Advantages	Disadvantages
Conserves legally registered addresses.	Translation results in switching path delays.
Remedies address overlap events.	Causes loss of end-to-end IP traceability.

Advantages	Disadvantages
Increases flexibility when connecting to the Internet.	Certain applications will not function with NAT enabled.
Eliminates address renumbering as a network evolves.	

FIGURE 5.2   Where to configure NAT

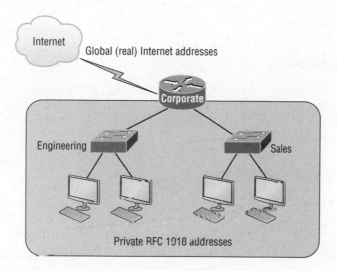

Pool

Dynamic NAT gives you the ability to map an unregistered IP address to a registered IP address from out of a pool of registered IP addresses. You don't have to statically configure your router to map each inside address to an individual outside address as you would using static NAT, but you do have to have enough real, bona fide IP addresses for everyone who's going to be sending packets to and receiving them from the Internet at the same time.

Static

Static NAT is designed to allow one-to-one mapping between local and global addresses. Keep in mind that the static version requires you to have one real Internet IP address for every host on your network.

1 to 1

The term *1 to 1* refers to the NAT translation between two hosts when static NAT is configured. There's a one-to-one translation from the inside local to the inside global.

Overloading

This is the most popular type of NAT configuration. Overloading really is a form of dynamic NAT that maps multiple unregistered IP addresses to a single registered IP address (many-to-one) by using different source ports. It is also known as *Port Address Translation (PAT)*, which is also commonly referred to as NAT Overload. PAT allows you to permit thousands of users to connect to the Internet using only one real global IP address. NAT Overload is the real reason we haven't run out of valid IP addresses on the Internet.

Source Addressing

In Figure 5.3, you can see host 10.1.1.1 sending an Internet-bound packet to the border router configured with NAT. The router identifies the source IP address as an inside local IP address destined for an outside network, translates the source IP address in the packet, and documents the translation in the NAT table.

FIGURE 5.3   Basic NAT translation

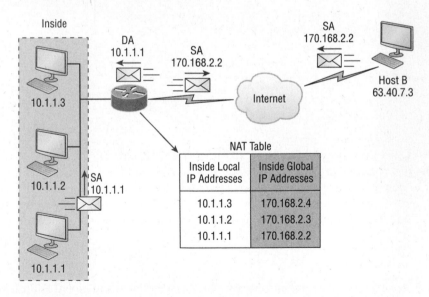

The packet is sent to the outside interface with the new translated source address. The external host returns the packet to the destination host and the NAT router translates the inside global IP address back to the inside local IP address using the NAT table.

One Way NAT

With one-way NAT (PAT), all inside hosts get translated to one single IP address, hence the term *overloading*. Again, the reason we've just run out of available global IP addresses on the Internet is because of overloading (PAT).

Take a look at the NAT table in Figure 5.4. In addition to the inside local IP address and inside global IP address, we now have port numbers. These port numbers help the router identify which host should receive the return traffic. The router uses the source port number from each host to differentiate the traffic from each of them. Notice that the packet has a destination port number of 80 when it leaves the router, and the HTTP server sends back the data with a destination port number of 1026, in this example. This allows the NAT translation router to differentiate between hosts in the NAT table and then translate the destination IP address back to the inside local address.

FIGURE 5.4   NAT overloading example (PAT)

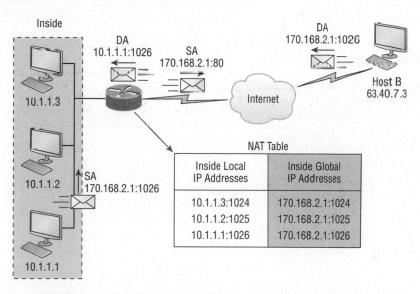

Port numbers are used at the Transport layer to identify the local host in this example. If we had to use real global IP addresses to identify the source hosts, that's called *static NAT*, and we would run out of addresses. PAT allows us to use the Transport layer to identify the hosts, which in turn allows us to theoretically use up to about 65,000 hosts with only one real IP address!

Exam Essentials

Remember the three methods of NAT.   The three types are static, dynamic, and overloading; the latter is also called PAT.

Understand static NAT.   This type of NAT is designed to allow one-to-one mapping between local and global addresses.

Understand dynamic NAT.   This version gives you the ability to map a range of unregistered IP addresses to a registered IP address from a pool of registered IP addresses.

Understand overloading.   Overloading really is a form of dynamic NAT that maps multiple unregistered IP addresses to a single registered IP address (many-to-one) by using different ports. It's also known as PAT.

Configure and Verify NAT for Given Network Requirements

In the following sections, I'll explain the configurations for NAT and NAT Overload (PAT).

Static NAT Configuration

Here is an example of a basic static NAT configuration:

```
ip nat inside source static 10.1.1.1 170.46.2.2
!
interface Ethernet0
 ip address 10.1.1.10 255.255.255.0
 ip nat inside
!
interface Serial0
 ip address 170.46.2.1 255.255.255.0
 ip nat outside
!
```

In the preceding router output, the ip nat inside source command identifies which IP addresses will be translated. In this configuration example, the ip nat inside source command configures a static translation between the inside local IP address 10.1.1.1 to the outside global IP address 170.46.2.2.

Scrolling farther down in the configuration, we find an `ip nat` command under each interface. The `ip nat inside` command identifies that interface as the inside interface. The `ip nat outside` command identifies that interface as the outside interface. When you look back at the `ip nat inside source` command, you can see that the command is referencing the inside interface as the source, or starting point, of the translation. You could also use the command like this: `ip nat outside source`. This option indicates that the interface you designated as the outside interface should become the source, or starting point, for the translation.

Dynamic NAT Configuration

Dynamic NAT really means we have a pool of addresses that we'll use to provide real IP addresses to a group of users on the inside. Because we don't use port numbers, we must have real IP addresses for every user who's trying to get outside the local network simultaneously.

Here is a sample output of a dynamic NAT configuration:

```
ip nat pool todd 170.168.2.3 170.168.2.254
    netmask 255.255.255.0
ip nat inside source list 1 pool todd
!
interface Ethernet0
 ip address 10.1.1.10 255.255.255.0
 ip nat inside
!
interface Serial0
 ip address 170.168.2.1 255.255.255.0
 ip nat outside
!
access-list 1 permit 10.1.1.0 0.0.0.255
!
```

The `ip nat inside source list 1 pool todd` command tells the router to translate IP addresses that match `access-list 1` to an address found in the IP NAT pool named todd. The ACL isn't there to filter traffic for security reasons by permitting or denying traffic. In this case, it's there to select or designate what we often call interesting traffic. When interesting traffic has been matched with the access list, it's pulled into the NAT process to be translated. This is actually a common use for access lists, which aren't always just stuck with the dull job of just blocking traffic at an interface!

The command `ip nat pool todd 170.168.2.3 192.168.2.254 netmask 255.255.255.0` creates a pool of addresses that will be distributed to the specific hosts that require global addresses. When troubleshooting NAT for Cisco exams, always check this pool to confirm that there are enough addresses in it to provide translation for all the inside hosts. Last, check to make sure the pool names match exactly on both lines, remembering that they are case sensitive; if they don't match, the pool won't work!

PAT (Overloading) Configuration

This last example shows how to configure inside global address overloading. This is the typical form of NAT that we would use today. It's actually now rare to use static or dynamic NAT unless it is for something like statically mapping a server, for example.

Here is a sample output of a PAT configuration:

```
ip nat pool globalnet 170.168.2.1 170.168.2.1 netmask 255.255.255.0
ip nat inside source list 1 pool globalnet overload
!
interface Ethernet0/0
 ip address 10.1.1.10 255.255.255.0
 ip nat inside
!
interface Serial0/0
 ip address 170.168.2.1 255.255.255.0
 ip nat outside
!
access-list 1 permit 10.1.1.0 0.0.0.255
```

The nice thing about PAT is that these are the only differences between this configuration and the previous dynamic NAT configuration:

- Our pool of addresses has shrunk to only one IP address.
- We included the overload keyword at the end of our ip nat inside source command.

The key factor to see in the example is that the one IP address that's in the pool for us to use is the IP address of the outside interface. This is perfect if you are configuring NAT Overload for yourself at home or for a small office that has only one IP address from your ISP. You could, however, use an additional address such as 170.168.2.2 if you had that address available to you as well, and doing that could prove very helpful in a very large implementation where you've got such an abundance of simultaneously active internal users that you need to have more than one overloaded IP address on the outside!

Simple Verification of NAT

Once you've chosen and configured the type of NAT you're going to run, you must be able to verify your configuration.

To see basic IP address translation information, use the following command:

```
Router#show ip nat translations
```

When looking at the IP NAT translations, you may see many translations from the same host to the corresponding host at the destination. Understand that this is typical when there are many connections to the same server.

You can also verify your NAT configuration via the debug ip nat command. This output will show the sending address, the translation, and the destination address on each debug line:

Router#**debug ip nat**

To clear your NAT entries from the translation table, use the clear ip nat translation command, and if you want to clear all entries from the NAT table, just use an asterisk (*) at the end of the command.

Cisco's NAT gives you some serious power—and it does so without much effort because the configurations are really pretty simple. But we all know nothing's perfect, so in case something goes wrong, you can figure out some of the more common culprits by running through this list of potential causes:

- Check the dynamic pools. Are they composed of the right scope of addresses?
- Check to see if any dynamic pools overlap.
- Check to see if the addresses used for static mapping and those in the dynamic pools overlap.
- Ensure that your access lists specify the correct addresses for translation.
- Make sure there aren't any addresses left out that need to be there, and ensure that none are included that shouldn't be.
- Check to make sure you've got both the inside and outside interfaces delimited properly.

A key thing to keep in mind is that one of the most common problems with a new NAT configuration often isn't specific to NAT at all—it usually involves a routing blooper. So, because you're changing a source or destination address in a packet, make sure your router still knows what to do with the new address after the translation!

Exam Essentials

Understand the static NAT configuration.   The configuration for static NAT is as follows:

```
ip nat inside source static 10.1.1.1 170.46.2.2
!
interface Ethernet0
 ip address 10.1.1.10 255.255.255.0
 ip nat inside
!
interface Serial0
 ip address 170.46.2.1 255.255.255.0
 ip nat outside
!
```

Understand the dynamic NAT configuration.   Here is the configuration for dynamic NAT:

```
ip nat pool todd 170.168.2.3 170.168.2.254
    netmask 255.255.255.0
ip nat inside source list 1 pool todd
!
interface Ethernet0
 ip address 10.1.1.10 255.255.255.0
 ip nat inside
!
interface Serial0
 ip address 170.168.2.1 255.255.255.0
 ip nat outside
!
access-list 1 permit 10.1.1.0 0.0.0.255
!
```

Understand the NAT Overload (PAT) configuration.   NAT Overload, also known as PAT, is configured as follows:

```
ip nat pool globalnet 170.168.2.1 170.168.2.1 netmask 255.255.255.0
ip nat inside source list 1 pool globalnet overload
!
interface Ethernet0/0
 ip address 10.1.1.10 255.255.255.0
 ip nat inside
!
interface Serial0/0
 ip address 170.168.2.1 255.255.255.0
 ip nat outside
!
access-list 1 permit 10.1.1.0 0.0.0.255
```

Understand how to verify NAT and PAT configurations.   To see basic IP address translation information, use the following command:

```
Router#show ip nat translations
```

You can also verify your NAT configuration via the debug ip nat command. This output will show the sending address, the translation, and the destination address on each debug line:

```
Router#debug ip nat
```

To clear your NAT entries from the translation table, use the clear ip nat translation command, and if you want to clear all entries from the NAT table, just use an asterisk (*) at the end of the command.

Configure and Verify NTP as a Client

Network Time Protocol (NTP) provides the time to all your network devices. To be more precise, NTP synchronizes clocks of computer systems over packet-switched, variable-latency data networks.

Typically you'll have an NTP server that connects through the Internet to an atomic clock. The time can then be synchronized through the network to keep all routers, switches, servers, and so on, receiving the same time information.

Correct network time within the network is important:

- Correct time allows the tracking of events in the network in the correct order.

- Clock synchronization is critical for the correct interpretation of events within the syslog data.

- Clock synchronization is critical for digital certificates.

Making sure all your devices have the correct time is especially helpful when it comes to your routers and switches, for looking at logs regarding security issues or other maintenance issues. Routers and switches issue log messages when different events take place—for example, when an interface goes down and then comes back up. As you already know, all messages generated by the IOS go only to the console port by default. However, as shown in Figure 5.5, those console messages can be directed to a syslog server.

FIGURE 5.5   Sending console messages to a syslog server

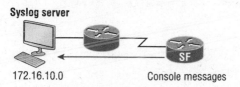

172.16.10.0   Console messages

A syslog server saves copies of console messages and can time-stamp them so you can view them at a later time. This is actually rather easy to do. Here would be the configuration on the SF router:

```
SF(config)#logging host 172.16.10.1
SF(config)#service timestamps log datetime msec
```

Now all the console messages will be stored in one location that you can view at your convenience.

To make sure all devices are synchronized with the same time information, we'll configure our devices to receive the accurate time information from a centralized server, as shown in Figure 5.6:

```
SF(config)#ntp server 172.16.10.1 version 4
```

FIGURE 5.6   Synchronizing time information

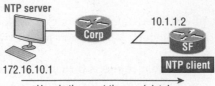

Here is the exact time and date!

Just use that one simple command on all your devices and each network device on your network will then have the same exact time and date information. You can then rest assured that your time stamps are accurate. You can also make your router or switch be an NTP server with the ntp master command.

To verify our VTP client is receiving clocking information, we use the following commands:

```
SF#sh ntp ?
  associations  NTP associations
  status        NTP status  status     VTP domain status
```

```
SF#sh ntp status
Clock is unsynchronized, stratum 16, no reference clock
nominal freq is 119.2092 Hz, actual freq is 119.2092 Hz, precision is 2**18
reference time is 00000000.00000000 (00:00:00.000 UTC Mon Jan 1 1900)
clock offset is 0.0000 msec, root delay is 0.00 msec
S1#sh ntp associations
```

```
address     ref clock      st  when  poll reach  delay  offset    disp
~172.16.10.1  0.0.0.0          16   -    64   0    0.0    0.00   16000.
* master (synced), # master (unsynced), + selected, - candidate, ~ configured
```

You can see in the example that the NTP client in SF is not synchronized with the server by using the show ntp status command. The stratum value is a number from 1 to 15, and a lower stratum value indicates a higher NTP priority; 16 means there is no clocking received.

Exam Essentials

Understand how to configure and verify NTP configurations on a Cisco device.   To configure NTP, use the ntp server command:

```
Router(config)#ntp server 172.16.10.1 version 4
```

To verify NTP, use the show ntp status command:

```
Router(config)#ntp server 172.16.10.1 version 4
```

Recognize High Availability (FHRP)

Redundancy is critical in small and large networks. I will now go over how to integrate redundancy and load-balancing features into your network. I am going to cover Virtual Router Redundancy Protocol (VRRP), Hot Standby Router Protocol (HSRP), and Gateway Load Balancing Protocol (GLBP), which are all known as first hop redundancy protocols.

If you're wondering how you can possibly configure a client to send data off its local link when its default gateway router has gone down, you've targeted a key issue because the answer is that usually you can't! Most host operating systems just don't allow you to change data routing.

IPv4 hosts can only be configured with one default gateway. This will cause a problem if there is a simple failure in the network. Figure 5.7 shows the inadequacies of IPv4 of being able to configure only one default gateway on a device.

FIGURE 5.7   Default gateway

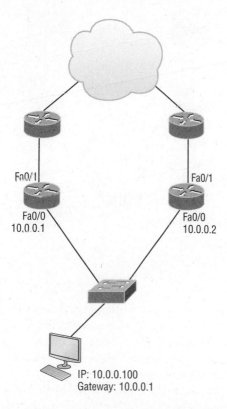

Is there another way to use the second active router? There is a feature that's enabled by default on Cisco routers called Proxy Address Resolution Protocol (Proxy ARP). Proxy ARP enables hosts, which have no knowledge of routing options, to obtain the MAC address of a gateway router that can forward packets for them.

You can see how this happens in Figure 5.8. If a Proxy ARP–enabled router receives an ARP request for an IP address that it knows isn't on the same subnet as the requesting host, it will respond with an ARP reply packet to the host. The router will give its own local MAC address—the MAC address of its interface on the host's subnet—as the destination MAC address for the IP address that the host is seeking to be resolved. After receiving the destination MAC address, the host will then send all the packets to the router, not knowing that what it sees as the destination host is really a router. The router will then forward the packets toward the intended host.

FIGURE 5.8   Proxy ARP

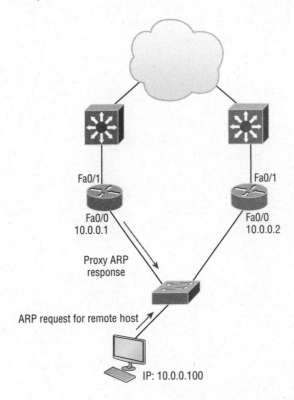

So with Proxy ARP, the host device sends traffic as if the destination device were located on its own network segment. If the router that responded to the ARP request fails, the source host continues to send packets for that destination to the same MAC address. But because they're being sent to a failed router, the packets will be sent to the other router that is also responding to ARP requests for remote hosts.

After the time-out period on the host, the proxy ARP MAC address ages out of the ARP cache. The host can then make a new ARP request for the destination and get the address of another proxy ARP router. Still, keep in mind that the host cannot send packets off of its subnet during the failover time.

VRRP

Virtual Router Redundancy Protocol (VRRP) allows a group of routers to form a single virtual router. In an HSRP or VRRP group, one router is elected to handle all requests sent to the virtual IP address. With HSRP, this is the active router. An HSRP group has one active router, at least one standby router, and many listening routers. A VRRP group has one master router and one or more backup routers and is the open standard implementation of HSRP.

Comparing VRRP and HSRP

With VRRP, LAN workstations are configured with the address of the virtual router as their default gateway, just as they are with HSRP, but VRRP differs from HSRP in these important ways:

- VRRP is an IEEE standard (RFC 2338) for router redundancy; HSRP is a Cisco proprietary protocol.
- The virtual router that represents a group of routers is known as a VRRP group.
- The active router is referred to as the master virtual router.
- The master virtual router may have the same IP address as the virtual router group.
- Multiple routers can function as backup routers.
- VRRP is supported on Ethernet, Fast Ethernet, and Gigabit Ethernet interfaces as well as on MultiProtocol Label Switching (MPLS) virtual private networks (VPNs) and VLANs.

VRRP Redundancy Characteristics

VRRP has some unique features:

- VRRP provides redundancy for the real IP address of a router or for a virtual IP address shared among the VRRP group members.
- If a real IP address is used, the router with that address becomes the master.
- If a virtual IP address is used, the master is the router with the highest priority.
- A VRRP group has one master router and one or more backup routers.
- The master router uses VRRP messages to inform group members of its status.
- VRRP allows load sharing across more than one virtual router.

HSRP

Hot Standby Router Protocol (HSRP) is a Cisco proprietary protocol that can be run on most, but not all, of Cisco's router and multilayer switch models. It defines a standby group, and each standby group that you define includes the following routers:

- Active router
- Standby router

- Virtual router
- Any other routers that maybe attached to the subnet

The problem with HSRP is that only one router is active and two or more routers just sit there in standby mode and won't be used unless a failure occurs.

Figure 5.9 shows how only one router is used at a time in an HSRP group.

FIGURE 5.9 HSRP active and standby routers

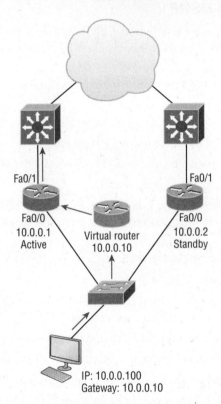

The standby group will always have at least two routers participating in it. The primary players in the group are the one active router and one standby router that communicate to each other using multicast Hello messages. The Hello messages provide all of the required communication for the routers. The Hello messages contain information required to accomplish the election that determines the active and standby router positions. They also hold the key to the failover process. If the standby router stops receiving Hello packets from the active router, it then takes over the active router role, as shown in Figure 5.10.

A virtual router in an HSRP group has a virtual IP address and a virtual MAC address. With HSRP, you create a totally new, made-up MAC address in addition to the IP address.

The HSRP MAC address has only one variable piece in it. The first 24 bits still identify the vendor who manufactured the device (the organizationally unique identifier, or OUI).

The next 16 bits in the address tells us that the MAC address is a well-known HSRP MAC address. Finally, the last 8 bits of the address are the hexadecimal representation of the HSRP group number.

FIGURE 5.10   An example of HSRP active and standby routers swapping interfaces

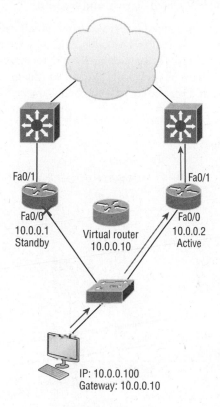

Here is an example of what an HSRP MAC address would look like:

`0000.0c07.ac0a`

This address can be broken down as follows:

- The first 24 bits (0000.0c) represent the vendor ID of the address; in the case of HSRP being a Cisco protocol, the ID is assigned to Cisco.

- The next 16 bits (07.ac) represent the well-known HSRP ID. This part of the address was assigned by Cisco in the protocol, so it's always easy to recognize that this address is for use with HSRP.

- The last 8 bits (0a) are the only variable bits and represent the HSRP group number that you assign. In this case, the group number is 10 and converted to hexadecimal when placed in the MAC address, where it becomes the 0a that you see.

You can see this MAC address added to the ARP cache of every router in the HSRP group. There will be the translation from the IP address to the MAC address as well as the interface on which it's located.

HSRP timers are very important to HSRP function because they ensure communication between the routers, and if something goes wrong, they allow the standby router to take over. The HSRP timers include hello, hold, active, and standby:

Hello timer The hello timer is the defined interval during which each of the routers send out Hello messages. Their default interval is 3 seconds, and they identify the state that each router is in. This is important because the particular state determines the specific role of each router and, as a result, the actions each will take within the group. Figure 5.11 shows the Hello messages being sent, and the router uses the hello timer to keep network flowing in case of a failure.

FIGURE 5.11 HSRP Hellos

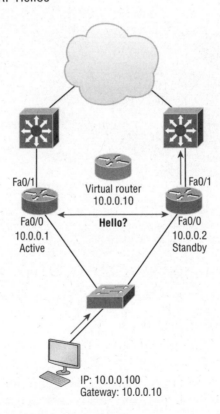

Hold timer The hold timer specifies the interval the standby router uses to determine whether the active router is offline or out of communication. By default, the hold timer is 10 seconds, roughly three times the default for the hello timer. By setting the hold timer at three times the hello timer, you ensure that the standby router doesn't take over the active role every time there's a short break in communication.

Active timer   The active timer monitors the state of the active router. The timer resets each time a router in the standby group receives a Hello packet from the active router. This timer expires based on the hold time value that's set in the corresponding field of the HSRP hello message.

Standby timer   The standby timer is used to monitor the state of the standby router. The timer resets anytime a router in the standby group receives a Hello packet from the standby router and expires based on the hold time value that's set in the respective Hello packet.

Group Roles

Each of the routers in the standby group has a specific function and role to fulfill. The three main roles are virtual router, active router, and standby router. Additional routers can also be included in the group.

Virtual router   As its name implies, the virtual router is not a physical entity. It defines the role that's held by one of the physical routers. The physical router that communicates as the virtual router is the current active router. The virtual router is nothing more than a separate IP address and MAC address to which packets are sent.

Active router   The active router is the physical router that receives data sent to the virtual router address and routes it onward to its various destinations. As I mentioned, this router accepts all the data sent to the MAC address of the virtual router in addition to the data that's been sent to its own physical MAC address. The active router processes the data that's being forwarded and will also answer any ARP requests destined for the virtual router's IP address.

Standby router   The standby router is the backup to the active router. Its job is to monitor the status of the HSRP group and quickly take over packet-forwarding responsibilities if the active router fails or loses communication. Both the active and standby routers transmit Hello messages to inform all other routers in the group of their role and status.

Other routers   An HSRP group can include additional routers, which are members of the group but don't take the primary role of either active or standby states. These routers monitor the Hello messages sent by the active and standby routers to ensure that an active and standby router exists for the HSRP group that they belong to. They will forward data that's specifically addressed to their own IP addresses, but they will never forward data addressed to the virtual router unless elected to the active or standby state. These routers send "speak" messages based on the hello timer interval that inform other routers of their position in an election.

GLBP

HSRP and VRRP provide gateway resiliency with per-subnet load balancing. The upstream bandwidth of the standby members of the redundancy group isn't used while the devices are in standby mode.

Only the active routers in HSRP and VRRP groups forward traffic for the virtual MAC. Resources associated with the standby router are not fully utilized. Some load balancing can be accomplished with these protocols through the creation of multiple groups and through the assignment of multiple default gateways, but be warned—these configurations create an administrative burden and are inefficient for today's networks!

Cisco designed a proprietary load-balancing protocol, Gateway Load Balancing Protocol (GLBP), to allow automatic selection and simultaneous use of multiple available gateways as well as permitting automatic failover between those gateways. GLBP takes an active/active approach on a per-subnet basis to support first-hop (default router) traffic when implemented with two routers on the same LAN. Multiple routers share the load of frames that, from a client perspective, are sent to a single default gateway address, as shown in Figure 5.12.

FIGURE 5.12   Gateway Load Balancing Protocol (GLBP)

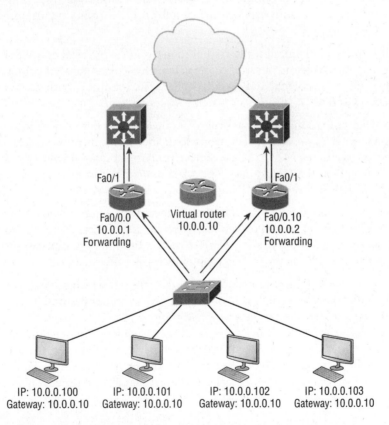

With GLBP, resources can be fully utilized without the administrative hassle of configuring multiple groups and managing multiple default gateway configurations as required when working with HSRP and VRRP.

GLBP essentially provides clients with the following functions:

- An active virtual gateway (AVG)
- An active virtual forwarder (AVF)

It also allows members of the group to communicate with each other through Hello messages sent every 3 seconds to the multicast address 224.0.0.102, User Datagram Protocol (UDP) port 3222.

Let me explain the AVG and AVF:

GLBP AVG   Members of a GLBP group elect one gateway to be the AVG for that group. Other group members provide backup for the AVG in the event that the AVG becomes unavailable. The AVG assigns a different virtual MAC address to each member of the GLBP group.

GLBP AVF   Each gateway assumes responsibility for forwarding packets that are sent to the virtual MAC address assigned to that gateway by the AVG. These gateways are known as AVFs for their virtual MAC address.

GLBP provides upstream load sharing by utilizing the redundant uplinks simultaneously. It uses link capacity efficiently, thus providing solid peak-load traffic coverage. By making use of multiple available paths upstream from the routers or layer 3 switches running GLBP, you can also reduce output queues. GLBP supports the following features:

Load sharing   You can configure GLBP so that traffic from LAN clients is shared by multiple routers. As the name suggests, load sharing distributes the traffic load more evenly among available routers.

Multiple virtual routers   GLBP supports up to 1,024 virtual routers as GLBP groups on each router's physical interface and up to four virtual forwarders per group.

Preemption   Preempt means "to replace with something considered to be of greater value or priority." The redundancy scheme of GLBP allows us to preempt an AVG with a higher-priority backup virtual gateway that has become available. Forwarder preemption works in a similar way, except that it's based upon weighting instead of priority and is enabled by default. One router can take over another router only during an election, and preemption is the only way to force an election when a device hasn't gone down.

Efficient resource utilization   GLBP makes it possible for any router in a group to serve as a backup, which eliminates the need for a dedicated backup router because all available routers can support network traffic.

Remember that only a single path is used with HSRP or VRRP, while other resources are idle unless you've got multiple groups and gateways configured. This means that a single path can be subjected to higher output queue rates during peak times, leading to lower performance caused by higher jitter rates. The good news is that we can mitigate the impact of jitter with GLBP because with it, more upstream bandwidth is available and additional upstream paths are used.

GLBP permits automatic selection and simultaneous use of all available gateways in the group. The members of a GLBP group elect one gateway to be the AVG for that group, and other members of the group provide backup for the AVG if it becomes unavailable. The AVG assigns a virtual MAC address to each member of the GLBP group. All routers become AVFs for frames addressed to that specific virtual MAC address. And as clients send ARP requests for the address of the default gateway, the AVG sends these virtual MAC addresses in the ARP replies. Don't forget that a GLBP group can have up to four members.

GLBP automatically manages the virtual MAC address assignment, determines who handles the forwarding, and ensures that each host has a reliable forwarding path if failures to gateways or tracked interfaces occur. Also, when failures do occur, the load-balancing ratio is adjusted among the remaining AVFs so that resources are used in the most efficient way.

These two steps will really help clarify how GLBP balances traffic using the round-robin algorithm:

1. When a client sends an ARP message for the gateway IP address, the AVG returns the virtual MAC address of one of the AVFs.

2. When a second client sends an ARP message, the AVG returns the next virtual MAC address from the list.

So having resolved a different MAC address for the default gateway, each client will send its routed traffic to separate routers even though they both have the same default gateway address configured. Remember that each GLBP router will be the designated AVF for the specific virtual MAC address that's been assigned to it.

Exam Essentials

Remember the three first hop redundancy protocols (FHRPs).   HSRP, VVRP and GLBP are all FHRPs, with HSRP and GLBP being Cisco proprietary protocols.

Remember how load balancing works with HSRP and GLBP.   HSRP load-balances per VLANs with trunk links and GLBP can perform per-host load balancing.

Remember how to verify HSRP and GLBP.   Use the show standby command with HSRP and show glbp with GLBP.

Configure and Verify Syslog

Reading system messages from a switch's or router's internal buffer is the most popular and efficient method of seeing what's going on with your network at a particular time. The best way is to log messages to a syslog server, which stores messages from you and can even time-stamp and sequence them for you, and it's easy to set up and configure!

Syslog allows you to display, sort. and even search messages, all of which makes it a really great troubleshooting tool. The search feature is especially powerful because you can use keywords and even severity levels. The server can email administrators based on the severity level of the message.

Network devices can be configured to generate a syslog message and forward it to various destinations. These four examples are popular ways to gather messages from Cisco devices:

- Logging buffer (on by default)
- Console line (on by default)
- Terminal lines (using the terminal monitor command)
- Syslog server

All system messages and debug output generated by the IOS go out only the console port by default and are also logged in buffers in RAM. Cisco routers aren't exactly shy about sending messages! To send a message to the VTY lines, use the terminal monitor command. In the following example, I'll also add a small configuration needed for syslog.

By default, we'd see something like this on our console line:

```
*Oct 21 17:33:50.565: %LINK-5-CHANGED: Interface FastEthernet0/0, changed
state to administratively down
*Oct 21 17:33:51.565: %LINEPROTO-5-UPDOWN: Line protocol on Interface
FastEthernet0/0, changed state to down
```

The Cisco router would send a general format version of the message to the syslog server that would be formatted something like this:

```
Seq no:timestamp: %facility-severity-MNEMONIC:description
```

The system message format can be broken down in this way:

seq no This stamp logs messages with a sequence number, but not by default. If you want this output, you've got to configure to get it.

timestamp Data and time of the message or event, which again will show up only if configured.

facility The facility to which the message refers.

severity A single-digit code from 0 to 7 that indicates the severity of the message.

MNEMONIC Text string that uniquely describes the message.

description Text string containing detailed information about the event being reported.

The severity levels, from the most severe to the least severe, are explained in Table 5.3.

TABLE 5.3 Severity levels

Severity Level	Explanation
Emergency (severity 0)	System is unusable.
Alert (severity 1)	Immediate action is needed.
Critical (severity 2)	Critical condition.
Error (severity 3)	Error condition.
Warning (severity 4)	Warning condition.
Notification (severity 5)	Normal but significant condition.
Information (severity 6)	Normal information message.
Debugging (severity 7)	Debugging message.

Utilize Syslog Output

Cisco devices send all log messages of the severity level you've chosen to the console. They'll also go to the buffer, and both happen by default. You can disable and enable these features with the following commands:

```
Router(config)#logging ?
  Hostname or A.B.C.D  IP address of the logging host
  buffered             Set buffered logging parameters
  buginf               Enable buginf logging for debugging
  cns-events           Set CNS Event logging level
  console              Set console logging parameters
  count                Count every log message and timestamp last occurrence
  esm                  Set ESM filter restrictions
  exception            Limit size of exception flush output
  facility             Facility parameter for syslog messages
  filter               Specify logging filter
  history              Configure syslog history table
  host                 Set syslog server IP address and parameters
  monitor              Set terminal line (monitor) logging parameters
  on                   Enable logging to all enabled destinations
  origin-id            Add origin ID to syslog messages
  queue-limit          Set logger message queue size
```

```
   rate-limit          Set messages per second limit
   reload              Set reload logging level
   server-arp          Enable sending ARP requests for syslog servers when
                       first configured
   source-interface    Specify interface for source address in logging
                       transactions
   trap                Set syslog server logging level
   userinfo            Enable logging of user info on privileged mode enabling
```

```
Router(config)#logging console
Router(config)#logging buffered
```

If you want to disable the defaults, use the following commands:

```
Router(config)#no logging console
Router(config)#no logging buffered
```

You can see the buffers with the show logging command here:

```
Router#sh logging
Syslog logging: enabled (11 messages dropped, 1 messages rate-limited,
                0 flushes, 0 overruns, xml disabled, filtering disabled)
   Console logging: level debugging, 29 messages logged, xml disabled,
                    filtering disabled
   Monitor logging: level debugging, 0 messages logged, xml disabled,
                    filtering disabled
   Buffer logging: level debugging, 1 messages logged, xml disabled,
                   filtering disabled
   Logging Exception size (4096 bytes)
   Count and timestamp logging messages: disabled
No active filter modules.

   Trap logging: level informational, 33 message lines logged

Log Buffer (4096 bytes):
*Jun 21 23:09:37.822: %SYS-5-CONFIG_I: Configured from console by console
Router#
```

A syslog server saves copies of console messages and can time-stamp them for viewing at a later time, as shown in Figure 5.13. This is actually pretty easy to configure, and here's how doing that would look on the SF router:

```
SF(config)#logging 172.16.10.1
SF(config)#service timestamps log datetime msec
```

FIGURE 5.13   Messages sent to a syslog server

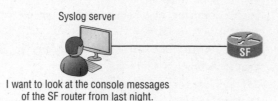

Syslog server

I want to look at the console messages
of the SF router from last night.

Console messages will be stored in one location to be viewed at your convenience!

We can limit the amount of messages sent to the syslog server, based on severity with the following command:

```
SF(config)#logging trap ?
  <0-7>          Logging severity level
  alerts         Immediate action needed        (severity=1)
  critical       Critical conditions            (severity=2)
  debugging      Debugging messages             (severity=7)
  emergencies    System is unusable             (severity=0)
  errors         Error conditions               (severity=3)
  informational  Informational messages         (severity=6)
  notifications  Normal but significant conditions (severity=5)
  warnings       Warning conditions             (severity=4)
  <cr>
SF(config)#logging trap warnings
```

Notice that we can use either the number or the actual severity level name—and they are in alphabetical order, not severity order. With severity level 4, I'll receive messages for levels 0 through 4.

You can configure the router to use sequence numbers:

```
SF(config)#no service timestamps
SF(config)#service sequence-numbers
SF(config)#^Z
000038: %SYS-5-CONFIG_I: Configured from console by console
```

When you exit configuration mode, the router will send a message like the one shown in the preceding code lines. Without the time-stamps enabled, you'll no longer see a time and date, but you will see a sequence number:

```
Sequence number: 000038
Facility: %SYS
Severity level: 5
MNEMONIC: CONFIG_I
Description: Configured from console by console
```

Exam Essentials

Understand the use of the syslog feature. The syslog feature is a great tool for trouble-shooting network issues. System messages can be forwarded to several destinations.

Understand how to configure and verify syslog To enable the syslog feature on a Cisco device, use the logging command:

```
Router(config)#logging console
Router(config)#logging buffered
```

To verify the syslog feature on a Cisco device, use the show logging command:

```
Router#sh logging
Syslog logging: enabled (11 messages dropped, 1 messages rate-limited,
                0 flushes, 0 overruns, xml disabled, filtering disabled)
    Console logging: level debugging, 29 messages logged, xml disabled,
                filtering disabled
    Monitor logging: level debugging, 0 messages logged, xml disabled,
                filtering disabled
    Buffer logging: level debugging, 1 messages logged, xml disabled,
                filtering disabled
    Logging Exception size (4096 bytes)
    Count and timestamp logging messages: disabled
No active filter modules.

    Trap logging: level informational, 33 message lines logged

Log Buffer (4096 bytes):
*Jun 21 23:09:37.822: %SYS-5-CONFIG_I: Configured from console by console
Router#
```

Describe SNMP v2 & v3

SNMP is an Application layer protocol that provides a message format for agents on a variety of devices to communicate with network management stations (NMSs). These agents send messages to the NMS, which either reads or writes information in the database stored on the NMS called a management information base (MIB).

The NMS periodically queries or polls the SNMP agent on a device to gather and analyze statistics via GET messages. End devices running SNMP agents would send an SNMP trap to the NMS if a problem occurs. This is demonstrated in Figure 5.14.

FIGURE 5.14 SNMP GET and TRAP messages

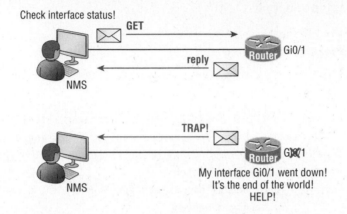

Admins can also use SNMP to provide some configuration to agents as well, called SET messages. In addition to polling to obtain statistics, SNMP can be used for analyzing information and compiling the results in a report or even a graph. Thresholds can be used to trigger a notification process when exceeded. Graphing tools are used to monitor the CPU statistics of Cisco devices like a core router. The CPU should be monitored continuously, and the NMS can graph the statistics. Notification will be sent when any threshold you've set has been exceeded.

Here are the differences in SNMPv2c and SNMPv3 messages:

SNMPv2c Supports plaintext authentication with MD5 or SHA with no encryption but provides GET BULK, which is a way to gather many types of information at once and minimize the number of GET requests. It offers a more detailed error message reporting method, but it's not more secure than v1, and it uses UDP even though it can be configured to use TCP.

SNMPv3 Supports strong authentication with MD5 or SHA-1, providing confidentiality (encryption) and data integrity of messages via DES or DES-256 encryption between agents and managers. GET BULK is a supported feature of SNMPv3, and this version uses TCP.

Management Information Base (MIB)

A management information base (MIB) is a collection of information that's organized hierarchically and can be accessed by protocols like SNMP. RFCs define some common public variables, but most organizations define their own private branches along with basic SNMP standards. Organizational IDs (OIDs) are laid out as a tree with different levels assigned by different organizations, with top-level MIB OIDs belonging to various standards organizations.

Vendors assign private branches in their own products. Take a look at Cisco's OIDs, which are described in words or numbers to locate a particular variable in the tree, as shown in Figure 5.15.

FIGURE 5.15   Cisco's MIB OIDs

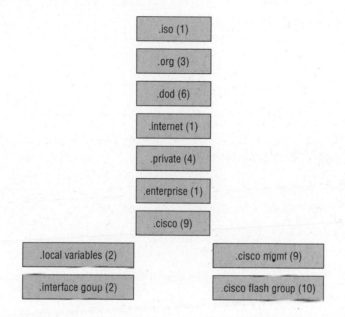

Using CPU as an example, it's a key thing to check at least every 5 minutes.

Here's the command from an NMS prompt on a Linux box running the SNMP application:

```
[14:11][admin@nms]$ snmpget -v2c -c community 192.168.10.12
.1.3.6.1.4.1.9.2.1.58.0
SNMPv2-SMI::enterprises.9.2.1.58.0=INTEGER: 19
```

You must specify the version, the correct community string, the IP address of the network device you're querying, plus the OID number. The community string will authenticate your access to the MIB database so the NMS can access the switch. The community string definition on the NMS must match at least one of the three community string definitions on the network devices.

Exam Essentials

Remember the differences between SNMPv2 and SNMPv3.   SNMPv2 uses UDP but can use TCP; however, v2 still sends data to the network management station (NMS) in clear text. SNMPv3 uses TCP and authenticates users, plus you can use ACLs in the SNMP strings to protect the NMS from unauthorized use.

Review Questions

1. Which device will send the ARP replies to clients with GLBP?

   A. The HRSP active router

   B. The router with the highest IP address

   C. The AVR

   D. The VRRP router

   E. The passive listening router

2. Which of the following needs to be added to the following configuration to enable PAT?

   ```
   ip nat pool Corp 198.18.41.129 198.18.41.134 netmask 255.255.255.248
   access-list 1 permit 192.168.76.64 0.0.0.31
   ```

   A. `ip nat pool inside overload`

   B. `ip nat inside source list 1 pool Corp overload`

   C. `ip nat pool outside overload`

   D. `ip nat pool Corp 198.41.129 net 255.255.255.0 overload`

3. Which SNMP version provides authentication, data integrity, and encryption?

   A. SNMPv1

   B. SNMPv2

   C. SNMPv3

   D. SNMPv4

   E. SNMPv6

4. Which statements are true in regard to both HSRP and GLBP? (Choose two.)

   A. VRRP should always be used instead of HSRP and GLBP if possible.

   B. HSRP is proprietary, and GLBP should be used with multiple vendors.

   C. HSRP can load-balance based on VLANs for which they are active.

   D. GLBP can have multiple forwarders with the same subnet/VLAN.

   E. HSRP can load-balance on the same LAN.

5. You need to configure all your routers and switches so they synchronize their clocks from one time source. What command will you type for each device?

   A. `clock synchronization` *ip_address*

   B. `ntp master` *ip_address*

   C. `sync ntp` *ip_address*

   D. `ntp server` *ip_address* `version` *number*

6. Which command would you place on an interface connected to the Internet?

    A. ip nat inside

    B. ip nat outside

    C. ip outside global

    D. ip inside local

7. Which router command will enable a host to receive its IP address, subnet mask, and default gateway from a DHCP server on a remote LAN?

    A. ip server *ip_address*

    B. ip dhcp server *ip_address*

    C. ip helper-address *ip_address*

    D. ip server-helper *ip_address*

8. What two commands can you use to verify your NTP client? (Choose two.)

    A. show ntp server

    B. show ntp status

    C. show vtp status

    D. show ntp associations

    E. show clock source

9. What is the default lease time when configuring DHCP on a Cisco router?

    A. 24 hours

    B. 18 hours

    C. 12 hours

    D. 6 hours

10. If you want to exclude certain IP addresses from being issued to hosts such as servers or printers by a router configured with DHCP, what command can you use?

    A. Router(config-dhcp)#**ip exclude address ip addresses**

    B. Router(config)#**dhcp exclude address ip addresses**

    C. Router(config-dhcp)#**ip dhcp-exclude address ip addresses**

    D. Router(config)#**ip dhcp excluded-address ip addresses**

Chapter

6

Network Device Security

THE FOLLOWING CCNA ROUTING AND SWITCHING EXAM OBJECTIVES ARE COVERED IN THIS CHAPTER:

✓ **Configure and verify network device security features such as.**

- Device password security
- Enable secret vs enable
- Transport
- Disable telnet
- SSH
- VTYs
- Physical security
- Service password
- Describe external authentication methods

✓ **Configure and verify Switch Port Security features such as.**

- Sticky MAC
- MAC address limitation
- Static/dynamic
- Violation modes
  - Err disable
  - Shutdown
- Protect restrict
- Shutdown unused ports
- Err-disable recovery

- Assign unused ports to an unused VLAN
- Setting native VLAN to other than VLAN 1

✓ **Configure and verify ACLs to filter network traffic.**

✓ **Configure and verify ACLs to limit telnet and SSH access to the router.**

In this chapter, I'll cover some of the security features available on Cisco devices, such as password security, Telnet, and SSH, and how to secure a device with various passwords. I'll also go over port security on a Cisco switch and how to use an access control list to filter network traffic and limit Telnet and SSH access to a router.

Configure and Verify Network Device Security Features

Security is a vital part of computer networks today. In the following sections, I'll go over some of the security features that are available and how you can prevent unauthorized use or access to your routers and switches.

Device Password Security

There are five passwords you'll need to secure your Cisco routers: console, auxiliary, telnet (VTY), enable password, and enable secret. The enable secret and enable password are the ones used to set the password for securing privileged mode. Once the enable commands are set, users will be prompted for a password. The other three are used to configure a password when user mode is accessed through the console port, through the auxiliary port, or via Telnet.

Enable Secret vs. Enable Password

The enable password or the enable secret password is used to secure privileged exec mode on a router or switch. The big difference is that the enable password is configured in clear text and can be viewed by using the show running-config command. The enable secret command uses a variation of an MD5 hash algorithm to encrypt the password.

```
Router#show running-config
Building configuration...
```

```
 -- Output omitted --
hostname Router
!
!
!
enable secret 5 $1$mERr$V5ujdIM9bTB/I.ipB0gkJ0
enable password password
!
```

You set the enable passwords from global configuration mode like this:

```
Todd(config)#enable ?
 last-resort Define enable action if no TACACS servers
            respond
 password   Assign the privileged level password
 secret     Assign the privileged level secret
 use-tacacs Use TACACS to check enable passwords
```

The following list describes the enable password parameters:

last-resort   Allows you to enter the router even if you set up authentication through a TACACS server and it's not available. It won't be used if the TACACS server is working.

password   Sets the enable password on older, pre-10.3 systems and is never used if an enable secret is set.

secret   The newer, encrypted password that overrides the enable password if it has been set.

use-tacacs   Tells the router to authenticate through a TACACS server. It comes in really handy when you have lots of routers because changing the password on a multitude of them can be insanely tedious. It's much easier to simply go through the TACACS server and change the password only once!

Here's an example that shows how to set the enable passwords:

```
Todd(config)#enable secret todd
Todd(config)#enable password todd
The enable password you have chosen is the same as your
  enable secret. This is not recommended. Re-enter the
  enable password.
```

If you try to set the enable secret and enable passwords the same, the router will give you a polite warning to change the second password.

Transport

The transport feature is used when you want to control remote access to a router or switch, such as, for example, when you're using Telnet or SSH.

```
Router(config-line)#transport ?
  input   Define which protocols to use when connecting to the terminal server
  output  Define which protocols to use for outgoing connections


Router(config-line)#transport input ?
  all     All protocols
  none    No protocols
  ssh     TCP/IP SSH protocol
  telnet  TCP/IP Telnet protocol
```

Disable Telnet

Telnet is a great tool to manage routers and switches from a remote location. However, it has its faults. Telnet by itself sends commands in clear text. If security is a major concern in your network, you can disable Telnet by enabling SSH as the only transport input.

SSH

Secure Shell (SSH) is the preferred method of accessing a router or switch instead of Telnet because it creates a more secure session. The Telnet application uses an unencrypted data stream, but SSH uses encryption keys to send data so your username and password aren't sent in clear text.

Here are the steps for setting up SSH:

1. Set your hostname:

   ```
   Router(config)#hostname Todd
   ```

2. Set the domain name—both the hostname and domain name are required for the encryption keys to be generated:

   ```
   Todd(config)#ip domain-name Lammle.com
   ```

3. Set the username to allow SSH client access:

   ```
   Todd(config)#username Todd password Lammle
   ```

4. Generate the encryption keys for securing the session:

```
Todd(config)#crypto key generate rsa
The name for the keys will be: Todd.Lammle.com
Choose the size of the key modulus in the range of 360 to
4096 for your General Purpose Keys. Choosing a key modulus
Greater than 512 may take a few minutes.


How many bits in the modulus [512]: 1024
% Generating 1024 bit RSA keys, keys will be non-exportable...
[OK] (elapsed time was 6 seconds)


Todd(config)#
1d14h: %SSH-5-ENABLED: SSH 1.99 has been enabled*June 24
19:25:30.035: %SSH-5-ENABLED: SSH 1.99 has been enabled
```

5. Enable SSH version 2 on the router—not mandatory, but strongly suggested:

```
Todd(config)#ip ssh version 2
```

6. Connect to the VTY lines of the switch:

```
Todd(config)#line vty 0 15
```

7. Configure your access protocols:

```
Todd(config-line)#transport input ?
  all     All protocols
  none    No protocols
  ssh     TCP/IP SSH protocol
  telnet  TCP/IP Telnet protocol
```

Beware of this next line, and make sure you never use it in production because it's a horrendous security risk:

```
Todd(config-line)#transport input all
```

I recommend using the next line to secure your VTY lines with SSH:

```
Todd(config-line)#transport input ssh ?
  telnet  TCP/IP Telnet protocol
  <cr>
```

You can use Telnet when a situation arises that specifically calls for it. If you want to go with Telnet as well, here's how you do that:

```
Todd(config-line)#transport input ssh telnet
```

Know that if you don't use the keyword telnet at the end of the command string, then only SSH will work on the device. You can go with either, just as long as you understand that SSH is way more secure than Telnet.

VTYs

To set the user-mode password for Telnet access into the router or switch, use the line vty command. IOS switches typically have 16 lines, but routers running the Enterprise edition have considerably more. The best way to find out how many lines you have is to use that handy question mark like this:

```
Todd(config-line)#line vty 0 ?
% Unrecognized command
Todd(config-line)#exit
Todd(config)#line vty 0 ?
  <1-15>  Last Line number
  <cr>
Todd(config)#line vty 0 15
Todd(config-line)#password telnet
Todd(config-line)#login
```

This output clearly shows that you cannot get help from your (config-line)# prompt. You must go back to global config mode in order to use the question mark (?).

If you try to telnet into a device that doesn't have a VTY password set, you'll receive an error saying the connection has been refused because the password isn't set:

```
Todd#telnet SwitchB
Trying SwitchB (10.0.0.1)…Open


Password required, but none set
[Connection to SwitchB closed by foreign host]
Todd#
```

You can get around this and tell the switch to allow Telnet connections without a password by using the no login command:

```
SwitchB(config-line)#line vty 0 15
SwitchB(config-line)#no login
```

WARNING   I definitely do not recommend using the no login command to allow Telnet connections without a password, unless you're in a testing or classroom environment. In a production network, always set your VTY password!

After your IOS devices are configured with an IP address, you can use the Telnet program to configure and check your routers instead of having to use a console cable. You can use the Telnet program by typing **telnet** from any command prompt (DOS or Cisco).

Physical Security

Physical security is your first line of defense when it comes to device security. Access to your routers and switches should be limited to authorized personnel only. Without physical security measures in place, devices can be disabled, altered, or even stolen!

Service Password

Because only the enable secret password is encrypted by default, you'll need to manually configure the user-mode and enable passwords for encryption.

Notice that you can see all the passwords except the enable secret when performing a show running-config on a switch:

```
Todd#sh running-config
Building configuration...

Current configuration : 1020 bytes
!
! Last configuration change at 00:03:11 UTC Mon Mar 1 1993
!
version 15.0
no service pad
service timestamps debug datetime msec
service timestamps log datetime msec
no service password-encryption
!
hostname Todd
!
enable secret 4 ykw.3/tgsOuy9.6qmgG/EeYOYgBvfX4v.S8UNA9Rddg
enable password todd
!
[output cut]
```

To manually encrypt your passwords, use the service password-encryption command. Here's how:

```
Todd#config t
Todd(config)#service password-encryption
Todd(config)#exit
Todd#show run
Building configuration...
!
!
enable secret 4 ykw.3/tgsOuy9.6qmgG/EeYOYgBvfX4v.S8UNA9Rddg
enable password 7 1506040800
!
[output cut]
!
!
line con 0
 password 7 050809013243420C
 login
line vty 0 4
 password 7 06120A2D424B1D
 login
line vty 5 15
 password 7 06120A2D424B1D
 login
!
end
Todd#config t
Todd(config)#no service password-encryption
Todd(config)#^Z
Todd#
```

Describe External Authentication Methods

Using an external method of securing your network devices is an alternative way of providing security for your network. With the use of a TACACS+ server, access to all of your network devices is authenticated through one process, so you don't have to manually configure each device with user-mode and privileged-mode passwords.

Exam Essentials

Differentiate the enable password and enable secret password.   Both of these passwords are used to gain access into privileged mode. However, the enable secret password is newer and is always encrypted by default. Also, if you set the enable password and then set the enable secret, only the enable secret will be used.

Set the enable secret on a router.   To set the enable secret, you use the global config command enable secret. Do not use enable secret password password or you will set your password to password password. Here is an example:

```
enable
config t
enable secret todd
```

Set the Telnet password on a router.   To set the Telnet password, the sequence is as follows:

```
enable
config t
  line vty 0 4
    password todd
    login
```

Describe the advantages of using Secure Shell and list its requirements.   Secure Shell (SSH) uses encrypted keys to send data so that usernames and passwords are not sent in the clear. It requires that a hostname and domain name be configured and that encryption keys be generated.

Configure and Verify Switch Port Security Features

It's not a good thing to have your switches available for anyone to just plug into and play around with. We worry about wireless security; switch security is just as much important, if not more.

All ports are enabled by default, so we need to make sure there's no access to unused switch ports!

But just how do we actually prevent someone from simply plugging a host into one of our switch ports—or worse, adding a hub, switch, or access point into the Ethernet jack in their office? By default, MAC addresses will just dynamically appear in your MAC forward/filter database, and you can stop them in their tracks by using port security!

A secured switch port can associate anywhere from 1 to 8,192 MAC addresses. You can choose to allow the switch to learn these values dynamically, or you can set static addresses for each port using the `switchport port-security mac-address` *mac-address* command.

```
S3#config t
S3(config)#int range f0/3-4
S3(config-if-range)#switchport mode access
S3(config-if-range)#switchport port-security
S3(config-if-range)#do show port-security int f0/3
Port Security               : Enabled
Port Status                 : Secure-down
Violation Mode              : Shutdown
Aging Time                  : 0 mins
Aging Type                  : Absolute
SecureStatic Address Aging  : Disabled
Maximum MAC Addresses       : 1
Total MAC Addresses         : 0
Configured MAC Addresses    : 0
Sticky MAC Addresses        : 0
Last Source Address:Vlan    : 0000.0000.0000:0
Security Violation Count    : 0
```

The first command sets the mode of the ports to "access" ports. These ports must be access or trunk ports to enable port security. By using the command `switchport port-security` on the interface, I've enabled port security with a maximum MAC address of 1 and violation of shutdown. These are the defaults, and you can see them in the highlighted output of the `show port-security int f0/3` command in the preceding code.

Port security is enabled, as displayed on the first line, but the second line shows Secure-down because I haven't connected my hosts into the ports yet. Once I do, the status will show Secure-up and would become Secure-shutdown if a violation occurs.

It's very important to remember that you can set parameters for port security but it won't work until you enable port security at the interface level. Notice the output for port F0/6:

```
S3#config t
S3(config)#int range f0/6
S3(config-if-range)#switchport mode access
S3(config-if-range)#switchport port-security violation restrict
S3(config-if-range)#do show port-security int f0/6
Port Security               : Disabled
Port Status                 : Secure-up
Violation Mode              : restrict
[output cut]
```

Port Fa0/6 has been configured with a violation of shutdown, but the first line shows that port security has not been enabled on the port yet. Remember, you must use this command at interface level to enable port security on a port:

```
S3(config-if-range)#switchport port-security
```

Verify your configuration with the following commands:

```
S3#show port-security
S3#show port-security int fa0/3
S3#show running-config
```

Sticky MAC

With the sticky command, you can provide static MAC address security without having to type in absolutely everyone's MAC address on the network. Figure 6.1 shows two hosts connected to the single switch port Fa0/3 via either a hub or an access point (AP).

FIGURE 6.1   Port security on a switch port restricts port access by MAC address.

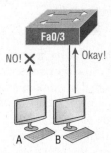

Port Fa0/3 is configured to observe and allow only certain MAC addresses to associate with the specific port, so in this example, Host A is denied access but Host B is allowed to associate with the port.

By using port security, you can limit the number of MAC addresses that can be assigned dynamically to a port, set static MAC addresses.

MAC Address Limitation

You can limit the number of MAC addresses on a switchport by using the maximum command.

In the following example, the first two MAC addresses coming into the port are configured as static addresses and will be placed in the running-config, but when a third address tried to connect, the port would shut down immediately.

```
Switch(config-if)#switchport port-security maximum 2
Switch(config-if)#switchport port-security violation shutdown
```

Static/Dynamic

When configuring port security, you can manually configure a static MAC address on a switchport, or the switch can learn the MAC address dynamically.

To add a static MAC entry, use these commands:

```
Switch(config-if)#switchport port-security
Switch(config-if)#switchport port-security violation restrict
Switch(config-if)#switchport port-security mac-address aa.bb.cc.dd.ee.ff
```

To configure the switch to learn a MAC address dynamically, use the sticky command:

```
Switch(config-if)#switchport port-security mac-address sticky
```

Violation Modes

Most Cisco switches ship with their ports in desirable mode, which means that those ports will desire to trunk when sensing that another switch has just been connected.

When configuring security on switch ports, there are several options to choose from when a violation occurs on a particular port.

```
Switch(config-if)#switchport port-security violation ?
   protect    Security violation protect mode
   restrict   Security violation restrict mode
   shutdown   Security violation shutdown mode
```

Err Disable

When you configure port security with the violation shutdown command and a violation has occurred, the port is put into err disabled mode. To re-enable the port, an administrator must manually enable the port with the no shutdown command.

Shutdown

The shutdown command is used with the port-security violation command:

```
Switch(config-if)#switchport port-security violation shutdown
Switch(config-if)#
```

When a violation on the switchport occurs, the switch will put the port into err disabled mode, and the port must be re-enabled manually.

Protect Restrict

There are two other modes you can use instead of just shutting down the port. When you use the restrict and protect modes, another host can connect up to the maximum MAC addresses allowed, but after the maximum has been met, all frames will just be dropped and the port won't be shut down. Additionally, both the restrict mode and shutdown violation mode alert you via SNMP that a violation has occurred on a port.

Shutdown Unused Ports

One of the easiest methods of securing ports on a switch is to disable them manually with the shutdown command. The switchport is unusable until an administrator manually re-enables the port.

```
Switch(config-if)#shutdown
Switch#show running-config
Building configuration...


 -- output omitted --
!
interface FastEthernet0/1
!
interface FastEthernet0/2
 shutdown
!
```

Interface Fa0/2 has been disabled manually.

Err Disable Recovery

In the event a switchport has been disabled because of a security violation, the switchport must be re-enabled manually.

```
Switch(config-if)#no shutdown
Switch#show running-config
Building configuration...


 -- output omitted --
!
interface FastEthernet0/1
```

```
!
interface FastEthernet0/2
!
```

Interface Fa0/2 is now operational.

Assign Unused Ports to an Unused VLAN

By default, all ports on a Cisco switch are enabled and ready to be used. Another method for securing switchports is to assign them to an unused VLAN. When you do this, hosts connected to the switchport will be unable to communicate with other devices on the LAN. Remember, VLANs create a separate broadcast domain, and in order to communicate outside of that particular VLAN, inter-VLAN routing must also be configured.

Setting Native VLAN to Other than VLAN 1

To manage a Cisco switch remotely, you must configure an IP address on the management VLAN. Telnet, SSH, SNMP, and so on, all need an IP address in order to communicate with the switch through the network (in-band). The IP address is configured with what is called the management VLAN interface—a routed interface on every Cisco switch and called interface VLAN 1. This management interface can be changed, and Cisco recommends that you change it to a different management interface for security purposes.

When you have multiple switches and multiple VLANs in your network, trunk ports use the native VLAN to send all untagged traffic. The native VLAN allows the trunks to accept information that was received without any VLAN identification or frame tag.

To change the native VLAN, use the following command:

```
S1(config)#int f0/15
S1(config-if)#switchport trunk native vlan ?
  <1-4094>  VLAN ID of the native VLAN when this port is in trunking mode
S1(config)#switchport trunk native vlan 4
```

Exam Essentials

Understand the reason for port security.   Port security restricts access to a switch based on MAC addresses.

Know the command to enable port security.   To enable port security on a port, you must first make sure the port is an access port and then use the switchport port-security command at the interface level. You can set the port security parameters before or after enabling port security.

Know the commands to verify port security.   To verify port security, use the show port-security, show port-security interface interface, and show running-config commands.

Configure and Verify ACLs to Filter Network Traffic

An *access control list* (ACL) is essentially a list of conditions that categorize packets, and they really come in handy when you need to exercise control over network traffic. An ACL would be your tool of choice for decision making in these situations.

One of the most common and easiest-to-understand uses of access lists is to filter unwanted packets when implementing security policies.

There are three important rules for comparing a packet with an access list:

- The packet is always compared with each line of the access list in sequential order—it will always start with the first line of the access list, move on to line 2, then line 3, and so on.

- The packet is compared with lines of the access list only until a match is made. Once it matches the condition on a line of the access list, the packet is acted upon and no further comparisons take place.

- There is an implicit "deny" at the end of each access list—this means that if a packet doesn't match the condition on any of the lines in the access list, the packet will be discarded.

Each of these rules has some powerful implications when filtering IP packets with access lists, so keep in mind that creating effective access lists definitely takes some practice.

There are three main types of access lists:

Standard access lists   These access lists use only the source IP address in an IP packet as the condition test. All decisions are made based on the source IP address. This means that standard access lists basically permit or deny an entire suite of protocols. They don't distinguish between any of the many types of IP traffic such as Web, Telnet, UDP, and so on.

Extended access lists   Extended access lists can evaluate many of the other fields in the layer 3 and layer 4 headers of an IP packet. They can evaluate source and destination IP addresses, the Protocol field in the Network layer header, and the port number at the Transport layer header. This gives extended access lists the ability to make much more granular decisions when controlling traffic.

Named access lists   *Named access lists* are either standard or extended and not actually a distinct type. I'm just distinguishing them because they're created and referred to differently than standard and extended access lists are, but they're still functionally the same.

Once you create an access list, it's not really going to do anything until you apply it. Yes, they're there on the router, but they're inactive until you tell that router what to do with them. To use an access list as a packet filter, you need to apply it to an interface on the router where you want the traffic filtered. And you've got to specify which direction of traffic you want the access list applied to.

By specifying the direction of traffic, you can and must use different access lists for inbound and outbound traffic on a single interface:

Inbound access lists   When an access list is applied to inbound packets on an interface, those packets are processed through the access list before being routed to the outbound interface. Any packets that are denied won't be routed because they're discarded before the routing process is invoked.

Outbound access lists   When an access list is applied to outbound packets on an interface, packets are routed to the outbound interface and then processed through the access list before being queued.

There are some general guidelines that you should keep in mind when creating and implementing access lists on a router:

- You can assign only one access list per interface per protocol per direction. This means that when applying IP access lists, you can have only one inbound access list and one outbound access list per interface.

- Organize your access lists so that the more specific tests are at the top.

- Anytime a new entry is added to the access list, it will be placed at the bottom of the list, which is why I highly recommend using a text editor for access lists.

- You can't remove one line from an access list. If you try to do this, you will remove the entire list. This is why it's best to copy the access list to a text editor before trying to edit the list. The only exception is when you're using named access lists.

    You can edit, add, or delete a single line from a named access list.

- Unless your access list ends with a permit any command, all packets will be discarded if they do not meet any of the list's tests. This means every list should have at least one permit statement or it will deny all traffic.

- Create access lists and then apply them to an interface. Any access list applied to an interface without access-list test statements present will not filter traffic.

- Access lists are designed to filter traffic going through the router. They will not filter traffic that has originated from the router.

- Place IP standard access lists as close to the destination as possible. This is the reason we don't really want to use standard access lists in our networks. You can't put a standard access list close to the source host or network because you can only filter based on source address and all destinations would be affected as a result.

- Place IP extended access lists as close to the source as possible. Since extended access lists can filter on very specific addresses and protocols, you don't want your traffic to traverse the entire network just to be denied. By placing this list as close to the source address as possible, you can filter traffic before it uses up precious bandwidth.

Standard IP access lists filter network traffic by examining the source IP address in a packet. You create a *standard IP access list* by using the access-list numbers 1–99 or in the expanded range of 1300–1999 because the type of ACL is generally differentiated using a number. Based on the number used when the access list is created, the router knows which type of syntax to expect as the list is entered. By using numbers 1–99 or 1300–1999, you're telling the router that you want to create a standard IP access list, so the router will expect syntax specifying only the source IP address in the test lines.

The following output displays a good example of the many access-list number ranges that you can use to filter traffic on your network. The IOS version delimits the protocols you can specify access for:

```
Corp(config)#access-list ?
  <1-99>           IP standard access list
  <100-199>        IP extended access list
  <1000-1099>      IPX SAP access list
  <1100-1199>      Extended 48-bit MAC address access list
  <1200-1299>      IPX summary address access list
  <1300-1999>      IP standard access list (expanded range)
  <200-299>        Protocol type-code access list
  <2000-2699>      IP extended access list (expanded range)
  <300-399>        DECnet access list
  <600-699>        Appletalk access list
  <700-799>        48-bit MAC address access list
  <800-899>        IPX standard access list
  <900-999>        IPX extended access list
  dynamic-extended Extend the dynamic ACL absolute timer
  rate-limit       Simple rate-limit specific access list
```

Here is the syntax used when creating a standard IP access list:

```
Corp(config)#access-list 10 ?
  deny    Specify packets to reject
  permit  Specify packets to forward
  remark  Access list entry comment
```

By using the access-list numbers 1–99 or 1300–1999, you're telling the router that you want to create a standard IP access list, which means you can only filter on source IP address.

Once you've chosen the access-list number, you need to decide whether you're creating a permit or deny statement:

```
Corp(config)#access-list 10 deny ?
  Hostname or A.B.C.D  Address to match
  any                  Any source host
  host                 A single host address
```

The next step is more detailed because there are three options available in it:

1. The first option is to use the permit, deny, or any parameter to permit, deny, or any source host or network.

2. The second choice is to use an IP address to specify either a single host or a range of them.

3. The last option is to use the host command to specify a specific host only.

The any command is pretty obvious—any source address matches the statement, so every packet compared against this line will match. The host command is relatively simple too:

```
Corp(config)#access-list 10 deny host ?
  Hostname or A.B.C.D  Host address
Corp(config)#access-list 10 deny host 172.16.30.2
```

This tells the list to deny any packets from host 172.16.30.2. The default parameter is host. In other words, if you type **access-list 10 deny 172.16.30.2**, the router assumes you mean host 172.16.30.2 and that's exactly how it will show in your running-config.

You can specify either a particular host or a range of hosts, and it's known as wildcard masking. In fact, to specify any range of hosts, you must use wildcard masking in the access list.

Wildcards are used with access lists to specify an individual host, a network, or a specific range of a network or networks. The block sizes you learned in Chapter 3 are used to specify a range of addresses key to understanding wildcards:

```
172.16.30.5 0.0.0.0
```

The four zeros represent each octet of the address. Whenever a zero is present, it indicates that octet in the address must match the corresponding reference octet exactly. To specify that an octet can be any value, use the value 255. Here's an example of how a /24 subnet is specified with a wildcard mask:

```
172.16.30.0 0.0.0.255
```

This tells the router to match up the first three octets exactly, but the fourth octet can be any value.

If you want to specify only a small range of subnets, this is where block sizes come in. You have to specify the range of values in a block size, so you can't choose to specify 20 networks. You can specify only the exact amount that the block size value allows. This means that the range would have to be either 16 or 32, but not 20.

In Figure 6.2, a router has three LAN connections and one WAN connection to the Internet. Users on the Sales LAN should not have access to the Finance LAN, but they should be able to access the Internet and the marketing department files. The Marketing LAN needs to access the Finance LAN for application services.

FIGURE 6.2   Standard IP access list example with three LANs and a WAN connection

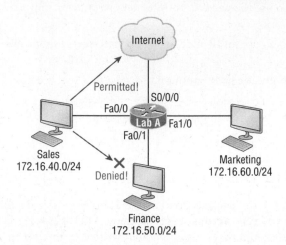

The following standard IP access list is configured on the router:

```
Lab_A#config t
Lab_A(config)#access-list 10 deny 172.16.40.0 0.0.0.255
Lab_A(config)#access-list 10 permit any
```

It's very important to remember that the any command is the same thing as saying the following using wildcard masking:

```
Lab_A(config)#access-list 10 permit 0.0.0.0 255.255.255.255
```

Since the wildcard mask says that none of the octets are to be evaluated, every address matches the test condition, so this is functionally doing the same as using the any keyword.

At this point, the access list is configured to deny source addresses from the Sales LAN to the Finance LAN and to allow everyone else. But remember, no action will be taken until the access list is applied on an interface in a specific direction!

This access list is configured on the Fa0/1 interface as an outbound list:

```
Lab_A(config)#int fa0/1
Lab_A(config-if)#ip access-group 10 out
```

Doing this completely stops traffic from 172.16.40.0 from getting out FastEthernet0/1. It has no effect on the hosts from the Sales LAN accessing the Marketing LAN and the Internet because traffic to those destinations doesn't go through interface Fa0/1. Any packet trying to exit out Fa0/1 will have to go through the access list first.

Using an *extended access list* allow us to specify source and destination addresses as well as the protocol and port number that identify the upper-layer protocol or application. An extended ACL is just what we need to affectively allow users access to a physical LAN while denying them access to specific hosts—even specific services on those hosts!

The extended access-list range is from 100 to 199 and 2000–2699 range.

After choosing a number in the extended range, you decide what type of list entry to make. For this example, I'm going to use a deny list entry:

```
Corp(config)#access-list 110 ?
  deny     Specify packets to reject
  dynamic  Specify a DYNAMIC list of PERMITs or DENYs
  permit   Specify packets to forward
  remark   Access list entry comment
```

And once you've chosen the type of ACL, you need to select a protocol field entry:

```
Corp(config)#access-list 110 deny ?
  <0-255>  An IP protocol number
  ahp      Authentication Header Protocol
  eigrp    Cisco's EIGRP routing protocol
  esp      Encapsulation Security Payload
  gre      Cisco's GRE tunneling
  icmp     Internet Control Message Protocol
  igmp     Internet Gateway Message Protocol
  ip       Any Internet Protocol
  ipinip   IP in IP tunneling
  nos      KA9Q NOS compatible IP over IP tunneling
  ospf     OSPF routing protocol
  pcp      Payload Compression Protocol
  pim      Protocol Independent Multicast
  tcp      Transmission Control Protocol
  udp      User Datagram Protocol
```

 If you want to filter by Application layer protocol, you have to choose the appropriate layer 4 transport protocol after the permit or deny statement. For example, to filter Telnet or FTP, choose TCP since both Telnet and FTP use TCP at the Transport layer. Selecting IP wouldn't allow you to specify a particular Application protocol later and filter based on only source and destination addresses.

Filter an Application layer protocol that uses TCP by selecting TCP as the protocol and indicating the specific destination TCP port at the end of the line. Next, you'll be prompted for the source IP address of the host or network. I'll choose the any command to allow any source address:

```
Corp(config)#access-list 110 deny tcp ?
  A.B.C.D  Source address
```

```
any      Any source host
host     A single source host
```

After you've selected the source address, you can then choose the specific destination address:

```
Corp(config)#access-list 110 deny tcp any ?
  A.B.C.D  Destination address
  any      Any destination host
  eq       Match only packets on a given port number
  gt       Match only packets with a greater port number
  host     A single destination host
  lt       Match only packets with a lower port number
  neq      Match only packets not on a given port number
  range    Match only packets in the range of port numbers
```

In this output, you can see that any source IP address that has a destination IP address of 172.16.30.2 has been denied:

```
Corp(config)#access-list 110 deny tcp any host 172.16.30.2 ?
  ack          Match on the ACK bit
  dscp         Match packets with given dscp value
  eq           Match only packets on a given port number
  established  Match established connections
  fin          Match on the FIN bit
  fragments    Check non-initial fragments
  gt           Match only packets with a greater port number
  log          Log matches against this entry
  log-input    Log matches against this entry, including input interface
  lt           Match only packets with a lower port number
  neq          Match only packets not on a given port number
  precedence   Match packets with given precedence value
  psh          Match on the PSH bit
  range        Match only packets in the range of port numbers
  rst          Match on the RST bit
  syn          Match on the SYN bit
  time-range   Specify a time-range
  tos          Match packets with given TOS value
  urg          Match on the URG bit
  <cr>
```

Once you have the destination host addresses in place, you just need to specify the type of service to deny using the equal to option, entered as eq. The following help screen reveals the options available now. You can choose a port number or use the application name:

```
Corp(config)#access-list 110 deny tcp any host 172.16.30.2 eq ?
  <0-65535>     Port number
  bgp           Border Gateway Protocol (179)
  chargen       Character generator (19)
  cmd           Remote commands (rcmd, 514)
  daytime       Daytime (13)
  discard       Discard (9)
  domain        Domain Name Service (53)
  drip          Dynamic Routing Information Protocol (3949)
  echo          Echo (7)
  exec          Exec (rsh, 512)
  finger        Finger (79)
  ftp           File Transfer Protocol (21)
  ftp-data      FTP data connections (20)
  gopher        Gopher (70)
  hostname      NIC hostname server (101)
  ident         Ident Protocol (113)
  irc           Internet Relay Chat (194)
  klogin        Kerberos login (543)
  kshell        Kerberos shell (544)
  login         Login (rlogin, 513)
  lpd           Printer service (515)
  nntp          Network News Transport Protocol (119)
  pim-auto-rp   PIM Auto-RP (496)
  pop2          Post Office Protocol v2 (109)
  pop3          Post Office Protocol v3 (110)
  smtp          Simple Mail Transport Protocol (25)
  sunrpc        Sun Remote Procedure Call (111)
  syslog        Syslog (514)
  tacacs        TAC Access Control System (49)
  talk          Talk (517)
  telnet        Telnet (23)
  time          Time (37)
  uucp          Unix-to-Unix Copy Program (540)
  whois         Nicname (43)
  www           World Wide Web (HTTP, 80)
```

Okay—now let's block Telnet (port 23) to host 172.16.30.2 only. If the users want to use FTP, fine—that's allowed. The `log` command is used to log messages every time the access-list entry is hit.

Here's our result:

```
Corp(config)#access-list 110 deny tcp any host 172.16.30.2 eq 23 log
```

This line says to deny any source host trying to telnet to destination host 172.16.30.2. Keep in mind that the next line is an implicit deny by default. If you apply this access list to an interface, you might as well just shut the interface down because by default, there's an implicit deny `all` at the end of every access list. So we've got to follow up the access list with the following command:

```
Corp(config)#access-list 110 permit ip any any
```

The IP in this line is important because it will permit the IP stack. If TCP was used instead of IP in this line, then UDP would all be denied. Remember, the 0.0.0.0 255.255.255.255 is the same command as any, so the command could also look like this:

```
Corp(config)#access-list 110 permit ip 0.0.0.0 255.255.255.255
0.0.0.0 255.255.255.255
```

But if you did this, when you looked at the running-config, the commands would be replaced with the any any. I like efficiency, so I'll just use the any command because it requires less typing.

As always, once our access list is created, we must apply it to an interface with the same command used for the IP standard list:

```
Corp(config-if)#ip access-group 110 in
```

Or this:

```
Corp(config-if)#ip access-group 110 out
```

Named access lists are just another way to create standard and extended access lists. In medium to large enterprises, managing ACLs can become a real hassle over time! A handy way to make things easier is to copy the access list to a text editor, edit the list, and then paste the new list back into the router, which works pretty well. It's really common to think things like, "What if I find a problem with the new list and need to back out of the change?"

Named access lists allow us to use names for creating and applying either standard or extended access lists. There's really nothing new or different about these ACLs aside from being readily identifiable in a way that makes sense to humans, but there are some subtle changes to the syntax. So let's re-create the standard access list we created earlier for our test network in Figure 6.2 using a named access list:

```
Lab_A#config t
Lab_A(config)# ip access-list ?
  extended    Extended Access List
```

```
log-update  Control access list log updates
logging     Control access list logging
resequence  Resequence Access List
standard    Standard Access List
```

Notice that I started by typing **ip access-list**, not **access-list**. Doing this allows me to enter a named access list. Next, I'll need to specify it as a standard access list:

```
Lab_A(config)#ip access-list standard ?
  <1-99>       Standard IP access-list number
  <1300-1999>  Standard IP access-list number (expanded range)
  WORD         Access-list name
```

```
Lab_A(config)#ip access-list standard BlockSales
Lab_A(config-std-nacl)#
```

I've specified a standard access list, and then I added the name *BlockSales*. I definitely could've used a number for a standard access list, but instead, I chose to use a nice, clear descriptive name. And notice that after entering the name, I hit Enter and the router prompt changed. This confirms that I'm now in named access list configuration mode and that I'm entering the named access list:

```
Lab_A(config-std-nacl)#?
Standard Access List configuration commands:
  default  Set a command to its defaults
  deny     Specify packets to reject
  exit     Exit from access-list configuration mode
  no       Negate a command or set its defaults
  permit   Specify packets to forward
```

```
Lab_A(config-std-nacl)#deny 172.16.40.0 0.0.0.255
Lab_A(config-std-nacl)#permit any
Lab_A(config-std-nacl)#exit
Lab_A(config)#^Z
Lab_A#
```

Okay—so I've entered the access list and then exited configuration mode. Next, I'll take a look at the running configuration to verify that the access list is indeed in the router:

```
Lab_A#sh running-config | begin ip access
ip access-list standard BlockSales
 deny   172.16.40.0 0.0.0.255
 permit any
!
```

And there it is: the BlockSales access list has truly been created and is in the running-config of the router. Next, I'll need to apply the access list to the correct interface:

```
Lab_A#config t
Lab_A(config)#int fa0/1
Lab_A(config-if)#ip access-group BlockSales out
```

Clear skies! At this point, we've re-created the work done earlier using a named access list. Where named ACLs really shine is that they allow us to insert, delete, or edit a single line.

The remark keyword is really important because it arms you with the ability to include comments—remarks—regarding the entries you've made in both your IP standard and extended ACLs. Remarks are very cool because they efficiently increase your ability to examine and understand your ACLs to superhero level! Without them, you'd be caught in a quagmire of potentially meaningless numbers without anything to help you recall what all those numbers mean.

Even though you have the option of placing your remarks either before or after a permit or deny statement, I totally recommend that you choose to position them consistently so you don't get confused about which remark is relevant to a specific permit or deny statement.

To get this going for both standard and extended ACLs, just use the access-list *access-list number* remark *remark* global configuration command like this:

```
R2#config t
R2(config)#access-list 110 remark Permit Bob from Sales Only To Finance
R2(config)#access-list 110 permit ip host 172.16.40.1 172.16.50.0 0.0.0.255
R2(config)#access-list 110 deny ip 172.16.40.0 0.0.0.255 172.16.50.0 0.0.0.255
R2(config)#ip access-list extended No_Telnet
R2(config-ext-nacl)#remark Deny all of Sales from Telnetting to Marketing
R2(config-ext-nacl)#deny tcp 172.16.40.0 0.0.0.255 172.16.60.0 0.0.0.255 eq 23
R2(config-ext-nacl)#permit ip any any
R2(config-ext-nacl)#do show run
[output cut]
!
ip access-list extended No_Telnet
 remark Stop all of Sales from Telnetting to Marketing
 deny   tcp 172.16.40.0 0.0.0.255 172.16.60.0 0.0.0.255 eq telnet
 permit ip any any
!
access-list 110 remark Permit Bob from Sales Only To Finance
access-list 110 permit ip host 172.16.40.1 172.16.50.0 0.0.0.255
access-list 110 deny    ip 172.16.40.0 0.0.0.255 172.16.50.0 0.0.0.255
access-list 110 permit ip any any
!
```

I was able to add a remark to both an extended list and a named access list. Keep in mind that you cannot see these remarks in the output of the show access-list command; they only show up in the running-config.

It's always good to be able to verify a router's configuration. Table 6.1 lists the commands that we can use to achieve that.

TABLE 6.1 Commands used to verify access-list configuration

Command	Effect
show access-list	Displays all access lists and their parameters configured on the router. Also shows statistics about how many times the line either permitted or denied a packet. This command does not show you which interface the list is applied on.
show access-list 110	Reveals only the parameters for access list 110. Again, this command will not reveal the specific interface the list is set on.
show ip access-list	Shows only the IP access lists configured on the router.
show ip interface	Displays which interfaces have access lists set on them.
show running-config	Shows the access lists and the specific interfaces that have ACLs applied on them.

We've already used the show running config command to verify that a named access list was in the router, so now let's take a look at the output from some of the other commands.

The show access-list command will list all ACLs on the router, whether they're applied to an interface or not:

```
Lab_A#show access-list
Standard IP access list 10
    10 deny    172.16.40.0, wildcard bits 0.0.0.255
    20 permit any
Standard IP access list BlockSales
    10 deny    172.16.40.0, wildcard bits 0.0.0.255
    20 permit any
Extended IP access list 110
    10 deny tcp any host 172.16.30.5 eq ftp
    20 deny tcp any host 172.16.30.5 eq telnet
    30 permit ip any any
```

```
     40 permit tcp host 192.168.177.2 host 172.22.89.26 eq www
     50 deny tcp any host 172.22.89.26 eq www
Lab_A#
```

First, notice that access list 10 as well as both of our named access lists appear on this list—remember, my extended named ACL was named 110! Second, notice that even though I entered actual numbers for TCP ports in access list 110, the show command gives us the protocol names rather than TCP ports for serious clarity.

The best part is those numbers on the left side: 10, 20, 30, and so on. Those are called sequence numbers, and they allow us to edit our named ACL. Here's an example where I added a line into the named extended ACL 110:

```
Lab_A (config)#ip access-list extended 110
Lab_A (config-ext-nacl)#21 deny udp any host 172.16.30.5 eq 69
Lab_A#show access-list
[output cut]
Extended IP access list 110
     10 deny tcp any host 172.16.30.5 eq ftp
     20 deny tcp any host 172.16.30.5 eq telnet
     21 deny udp any host 172.16.30.5 eq tftp
     30 permit ip any any
     40 permit tcp host 192.168.177.2 host 172.22.89.26 eq www
     50 deny tcp any host 172.22.89.26 eq www
```

You can see that I added line 21. I could have deleted a line or edited an existing line as well—very nice!

Here's the output of the show ip interface command:

```
Lab_A#show ip interface fa0/1
FastEthernet0/1 is up, line protocol is up
  Internet address is 172.16.30.1/24
  Broadcast address is 255.255.255.255
  Address determined by non-volatile memory
  MTU is 1500 bytes
  Helper address is not set
  Directed broadcast forwarding is disabled
  Outgoing access list is 110
  Inbound access list is not set
  Proxy ARP is enabled
  Security level is default
  Split horizon is enabled
[output cut]
```

Be sure to notice the bold line indicating that the outgoing list on this interface is 110, yet the inbound access list isn't set. What happened to BlockSales? I had configured that outbound on Fa0/1! That's true, I did, but I configured my extended named ACL 110 and applied it to Fa0/1 as well. You can't have two lists on the same interface, in the same direction.

And as I've already mentioned, you can use the show running-config command to see any and all access lists.

Exam Essentials

Remember the standard and extended IP access-list number ranges.   The number ranges you can use to configure a standard IP access list are 1–99 and 1300–1999. The number ranges for an extended IP access list are 100–199 and 2000–2699.

Understand the term *implicit deny*.   At the end of every access list is an *implicit deny*. What this means is that if a packet does not match any of the lines in the access list, it will be discarded. Also, if you have nothing but deny statements in your list, the list will not permit any packets.

Understand the standard IP access-list configuration command.   To configure a standard IP access list, use the access-list numbers 1–99 or 1300–1999 in global configuration mode. Choose permit or deny, and then choose the source IP address you want to filter.

Understand the extended IP access-list configuration command.   To configure an extended IP access list, use the access-list numbers 100–199 or 2000–2699 in global configuration mode. Choose permit or deny, the Network layer protocol field, the source IP address you want to filter on, the destination address you want to filter on, and finally, the Transport layer port number if TCP or UDP has been specified as the protocol.

Remember the command to verify an access list on a router interface.   To see whether an access list is set on an interface and in which direction it is filtering, use the show ip interface command. This command will not show you the contents of the access list, merely which access lists are applied on the interface.

Remember the command to verify the access-list configuration.   To see the configured access lists on your router, use the show access-list command. This command will not show you which interfaces have an access list set.

Configure and Verify ACLs to Limit Telnet and SSH Access to the Router

Trying to stop users from telnetting or trying to SSH to a router is really challenging because any active interface on a router is fair game for VTY/SSH access. Creating an extended IP ACL that limits access to every IP address on the router may sound like a solution, but if you did that, you'd have to apply it inbound on every interface, which really wouldn't scale well if you happen to have dozens, even hundreds, of interfaces. You can use a standard IP access list to control access to the VTY lines themselves.

When you apply an access list to the VTY lines, you don't need to specify the protocol since access to the VTY already implies terminal access via the Telnet or SSH protocols. You also don't need to specify a destination address because it really doesn't matter which interface address the user used as a target for the Telnet session. All you really need control of is where the user is coming from, which is betrayed by their source IP address.

You need to do these two things to make this happen:

1. Create a standard IP access list that permits only the host or hosts you want to be able to telnet into the routers.

2. Apply the access list to the VTY line with the access-class in command.

Here, I'm allowing only host 172.16.10.3 to telnet into a router:

```
Lab_A(config)#access-list 50 permit host 172.16.10.3
Lab_A(config)#line vty 0 4
Lab_A(config-line)#access-class 50 in
```

Because of the implied deny any at the end of the list, the ACL stops any host from telnetting into the router except the host 172.16.10.3, regardless of the individual IP address on the router being used as a target. It's a good idea to include an admin subnet address as the source instead of a single host, but the reason I demonstrated this was to show you how to create security on your VTY lines without adding latency to your router.

When you put the access-class in command on the VTY lines, only packets trying to telnet into the router will be checked and compared, providing easy-to-configure yet solid security for your router!

To verify your access-list configuration, issue the show running-config command or the show access-lists command.

Exam Essentials

Remember the command to configure an access list to deny Telnet and SSH access.   Create a standard IP access list that permits only the host or hosts you want to be able to telnet into the routers. Apply the access list to the VTY line with the access-class in command.

Remember the command to verify the access-list configuration.   To see the configured access lists on your router, use the show access-list command. This command will not show you which interfaces have an access list set.

Review Questions

1. Which two of the following commands are required when configuring SSH on your router? (Choose two.)

    A. enable secret *password*

    B. exec-timeout 0 0

    C. ip domain-name *name*

    D. username *name* password *password*

    E. ip ssh version 2

2. Which of the following commands sets the privileged-mode password to *Cisco* and encrypts the password?

    A. enable secret password Cisco

    B. enable secret cisco

    C. enable secret Cisco

    D. enable password Cisco

3. You try to telnet into SF from router Corp and receive this message:

    ```
    Corp#telnet SF
    Trying SF (10.0.0.1)…Open


    Password required, but none set
    [Connection to SF closed by foreign host]
    Corp#
    ```

    Which of the following sequences will address this problem correctly?

    A. Corp(config)#line console 0

    Corp (config-line)#password password

    Corp (config-line)#login

    B. SF (config)#line console 0

    SF(config-line)#enable secret password

    SF(config-line)#login

    C. Corp(config)#line vty 0 4

    Corp (config-line)#password password

    Corp (config-line)#login

    D. SF (config)#line vty 0 4

    SF(config-line)#password password

    SF(config-line)#login

4. Which command in the following configuration is a prerequisite for the other commands to function?

```
S3#config t
S(config)#int fa0/3
S3(config-if#switchport port-security
S3(config-if#switchport port-security maximum 3
S3(config-if#switchport port-security violation restrict
S3(config-if#Switchport mode-security aging time 10
```

   A. `switchport mode-security aging time 10`

   B. `switchport port-security`

   C. `switchport port-security maximum 3`

   D. `switchport port-security violation restrict`

5. Which two of the following switch port violation modes will alert you via SNMP that a violation has occurred on a port?

   A. Restrict

   B. Protect

   C. Shutdown

   D. Err-disable

6. Which Cisco IOS command is used to verify the port security configuration of a switch port?

   A. `show interfaces port-security`

   B. `show port-security interface`

   C. `show ip interface`

   D. `show interfaces switchport`

7. Write the command required to disable the port if a security violation occurs. Write only the command and not the prompt.

8. Which of the following statements is false when a packet is being compared to an access list?

   A. It's always compared with each line of the access list in sequential order.

   B. Once the packet matches the condition on a line of the access list, the packet is acted upon and no further comparisons take place.

   C. There is an implicit "deny" at the end of each access list.

   D. Until all lines have been analyzed, the comparison is not over.

9. You need to create an access list that will prevent hosts in the network range of 192.168.160.0 to 192.168.191.0. Which of the following lists will you use?

   A. `access-list 10 deny 192.168.160.0 255.255.224.0`

   B. `access-list 10 deny 192.168.160.0 0.0.191.255`

   C. `access-list 10 deny 192.168.160.0 0.0.31.255`

   D. `access-list 10 deny 192.168.0.0 0.0.31.255`

10. You have created a named access list called BlockSales. Which of the following is a valid command for applying this to packets trying to enter interface Fa0/0 of your router?

   A. `(config)#ip access-group 110 in`

   B. `(config-if)#ip access-group 110 in`

   C. `(config-if)#ip access-group BlockSales in`

   D. `(config-if)#BlockSales ip access-list in`

Chapter

7

Troubleshooting

THE FOLLOWING CCNA ROUTING AND SWITCHING EXAM OBJECTIVES ARE COVERED IN THIS CHAPTER:

- ✓ Identify and correct common network problems.

- ✓ Utilize netflow data.

- ✓ Troubleshoot and correct common problems associated with IP addressing and host configurations.

- ✓ Troubleshoot and Resolve VLAN problems.
  - identify that VLANs are configured
  - port membership correct
  - IP address configured

- ✓ Troubleshoot and Resolve trunking problems on Cisco switches.
  - correct trunk states
  - correct encapsulation configured
  - correct vlans allowed

- ✓ Troubleshoot and Resolve Spanning Tree operation issues.
  - root switch
  - priority
  - mode is correct
  - port states

- ✓ Troubleshoot and Resolve routing issues.
  - routing is enabled
  - routing table is correct
  - correct path selection

✓ **Troubleshoot and Resolve OSPF problems.**

- neighbor adjacencies
- Hello and Dead timers
- OSPF area
- Interface MTU
- Network types
- Neighbor states
- OSPF topology database

✓ **Troubleshoot and Resolve EIGRP problems.**

- neighbor adjancies
- AS number
- Load balancing
- Split horizon

✓ **Troubleshoot and Resolve interVLAN routing problems.**

- Connectivity
- Encapsulation
- Subnet
- Native VLAN
- Port mode trunk status

✓ **Troubleshoot and Resolve ACL issues.**

- Statistics
- Permitted networks
- Direction
- Interface

✓ **Troubleshoot and Resolve WAN implementation issues.**

- Serial interfaces
- PPP
- Frame relay

✓ **Troubleshoot and Resolve Layer 1 problems.**

- Framing

- CRC

- Runts

- Giants

- Dropped packets

- Late collision

- Input / Output errors

✓ **Monitor NetFlow statistics.**

✓ **Troubleshoot etherchannel problems.**

In this chapter, I will cover some of the troubleshooting methods on the various technologies used with Cisco routers and switches. Learning how to identify and correct network problems is essential in today's networks and an integral part of the Cisco exam objectives.

Identify and Correct Common Network Problems

What would you say to someone who called you saying they weren't able to get to a server on a remote network? What's the first thing you would have this user do, besides reboot Windows? Ping is a great place to start because the Ping program is a great tool for finding out if a device is alive on the network with a simple ICMP echo request and echo reply. But being able to ping the host as well as the server doesn't guarantee that all is well in the network! Keep in mind that there's more to the Ping program than just being used as a quick and simple testing protocol.

Let's use Figure 7.1 as basis to run through a troubleshooting scenario.

FIGURE 7.1 Troubleshooting scenario

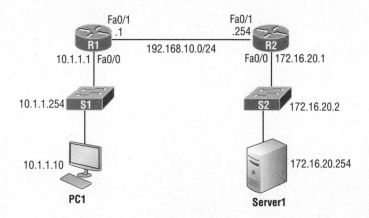

In this scenario, a manager calls you and says that he cannot log in to Server1 from PC1. Your job is to find out why and fix it. The Cisco objectives are clear on the troubleshooting steps you need to take when a problem has been reported:

1. Check the cables to find out if there's a faulty cable or interface in the mix and verify the interface's statistics.

2. Make sure that devices are determining the correct path from the source to the destination. Manipulate the routing information if needed.

3. Verify that the default gateway is correct.

4. Verify that name resolution settings are correct.

5. Verify that there are no *access control lists (ACLs)* blocking traffic.

In order to effectively troubleshoot this problem, we'll narrow down the possibilities by process of elimination. We'll start with PC1 and verify that it's configured correctly and also that IP is working correctly.

There are four steps for checking the PC1 configuration:

1. Test that the local IP stack is working by pinging the loopback address.

2. Test that the local IP stack is talking to the Data Link layer (LAN driver) by pinging the local IP address.

3. Test that the host is working on the LAN by pinging the default gateway.

4. Test that the host can get to remote networks by pinging remote Server1.

Let's check out the PC1 configuration by using the ipconfig command:

```
C:\Users\Todd Lammle>ipconfig

Windows IP Configuration

Ethernet adapter Local Area Connection:

   Connection-specific DNS Suffix  . : localdomain
   Link-local IPv6 Address . . . . . : fe80::64e3:76a2:541f:ebcb%11
   IPv4 Address. . . . . . . . . . . : 10.1.1.10
   Subnet Mask . . . . . . . . . . . : 255.255.255.0
   Default Gateway . . . . . . . . . : 10.1.1.1
```

We can also check the route table on the host with the route print command to see if it truly does know the default gateway:

```
C:\Users\Todd Lammle>route print
[output cut]
IPv4 Route Table
===========================================================================
Active Routes:
Network Destination        Netmask          Gateway       Interface  Metric
```

```
        0.0.0.0              0.0.0.0        10.1.1.10          10.1.1.1 10
[output cut]
```

Between the output of the ipconfig and the route print command, we can be assured that the hosts are aware of the correct default gateway.

> For the Cisco exam, it's extremely important to be able to check and verify the default gateway on a host and that this address matches the router's interface!

So, let's verify that the local IP stack is initialized by pinging the loopback address now:

```
C:\Users\Todd Lammle>ping 127.0.0.1

Pinging 127.0.0.1 with 32 bytes of data:
Reply from 127.0.0.1: bytes=32 time<1ms TTL=128
Reply from 127.0.0.1: bytes=32 time<1ms TTL=128
Reply from 127.0.0.1: bytes=32 time<1ms TTL=128
Reply from 127.0.0.1: bytes=32 time<1ms TTL=128

Ping statistics for 127.0.0.1:
    Packets: Sent = 4, Received = 4, Lost = 0 (0% loss),
Approximate round trip times in milli-seconds:
    Minimum = 0ms, Maximum = 0ms, Average = 0ms
```

This output confirms the IP address and configured default gateway of the host as well as the fact that the local IP stack is working. Our next move is to verify that the IP stack is talking to the LAN driver by pinging the host's own IP address:

```
C:\Users\Todd Lammle>ping 10.1.1.10

Pinging 10.1.1.10 with 32 bytes of data:
Reply from 10.1.1.10: bytes=32 time<1ms TTL=128
Reply from 10.1.1.10: bytes=32 time<1ms TTL=128
Reply from 10.1.1.10: bytes=32 time<1ms TTL=128
Reply from 10.1.1.10: bytes=32 time<1ms TTL=128

Ping statistics for 10.1.1.10:
    Packets: Sent = 4, Received = 4, Lost = 0 (0% loss),
Approximate round trip times in milli-seconds:
    Minimum = 0ms, Maximum = 0ms, Average = 0ms
```

And now that we know the local stack is solid and the IP stack is communicating with the LAN driver, it's time to check our local LAN connectivity by pinging the default gateway:

```
C:\Users\Todd Lammle>ping 10.1.1.1

Pinging 10.1.1.1 with 32 bytes of data:
Reply from 10.1.1.1: bytes=32 time<1ms TTL=128
Reply from 10.1.1.1: bytes=32 time<1ms TTL=128
Reply from 10.1.1.1: bytes=32 time<1ms TTL=128
Reply from 10.1.1.1: bytes=32 time<1ms TTL=128

Ping statistics for 10.1.1.1:
    Packets: Sent = 4, Received = 4, Lost = 0 (0% loss),
Approximate round trip times in milli-seconds:
    Minimum = 0ms, Maximum = 0ms, Average = 0ms
```

Looking good! I'd say our host is in good shape. Let's try to ping the remote server next to see if our host is actually getting off the local LAN to communicate remotely:

```
C:\Users\Todd Lammle>ping 172.16.20.254

Pinging 172.16.20.254 with 32 bytes of data:
Request timed out.
Request timed out.
Request timed out.
Request timed out.

Ping statistics for 172.16.20.254:
    Packets: Sent = 4, Received = 0, Lost = 4 (100% loss),
```

Well, looks like we've confirmed local connectivity but not remote connectivity, so we're going to have to dig deeper to isolate our problem. But first and just as important, it's key to make note of what we can rule out at this point:

1. The PC is configured with the correct IP address and the local IP stack is working.

2. The default gateway is configured correctly and the PC's default gateway configuration matches the router interface IP address.

3. The local switch is working because we can ping through the switch to the router.

4. We don't have a local LAN issue, meaning our Physical layer is good because we can ping the router. If we couldn't ping the router, we would need to verify our physical cables and interfaces.

Let's see if we can narrow the problem down further using the `traceroute` command:

```
C:\Users\Todd Lammle>tracert 172.16.20.254

Tracing route to 172.16.20.254 over a maximum of 30 hops

  1    1 ms    1 ms    <1 ms   10.1.1.1
  2    *       *       *       Request timed out.
  3    *       *       *       Request timed out.
```

Well, we didn't get beyond our default gateway, so let's go over to R2 and see if we can talk locally to the server:

```
R2#ping 172.16.20.254

Pinging 172.16.20.254 with 32 bytes of data:
Reply from 172.16.20.254: bytes=32 time<1ms TTL=128
Reply from 172.16.20.254: bytes=32 time<1ms TTL=128
Reply from 172.16.20.254: bytes=32 time<1ms TTL=128
Reply from 172.16.20.254: bytes=32 time<1ms TTL=128

Ping statistics for 172.16.20.254:
    Packets: Sent = 4, Received = 0, Lost = 4 (100% loss),
```

Okay, we just eliminated a local LAN problem by connecting to Server1 from the R2 router, so we're good there. Let's summarize what we know so far:

1. PC1 is configured correctly.

2. The switch located on the 10.1.1.0 LAN is working.

3. PC1's default gateway is correctly configured.

4. R2 can communicate with the server, so we don't have a remote LAN issue.

But something is clearly still wrong, so what should we check now? Now would be a great time to verify the Server1 IP configuration and make sure the default gateway is configured correctly. Let's take a look:

```
C:\Users\Server1>ipconfig

Windows IP Configuration

Ethernet adapter Local Area Connection:

   Connection-specific DNS Suffix  . : localdomain
   Link-local IPv6 Address . . . . . : fe80::7723:76a2:e73c:2acb%11
```

```
    IPv4 Address. . . . . . . . . . : 172.16.20.254
    Subnet Mask . . . . . . . . . . : 255.255.255.0
    Default Gateway . . . . . . . . : 172.16.20.1
```

Okay—the Server1 configuration looks good and the R2 router can ping the server, so it seems that the server's local LAN is solid, the local switch is working, and there are no cable or interface issues. But let's zoom in on interface Fa0/0 on R2 and talk about what to expect if there were errors on this interface:

```
R2#sh int fa0/0
FastEthernet0/0 is up, line protocol is up
[output cut]
  Full-duplex, 100Mb/s, 100BaseTX/FX
  ARP type: ARPA, ARP Timeout 04:00:00
  Last input 00:00:05, output 00:00:01, output hang never
  Last clearing of "show interface" counters never
  Input queue: 0/75/0/0 (size/max/drops/flushes); Total output drops: 0
  Queueing strategy: fifo
  Output queue: 0/40 (size/max)
  5 minute input rate 0 bits/sec, 0 packets/sec
  5 minute output rate 0 bits/sec, 0 packets/sec
     1325 packets input, 157823 bytes
     Received 1157 broadcasts (0 IP multicasts)
     0 runts, 0 giants, 0 throttles
     0 input errors, 0 CRC, 0 frame, 0 overrun, 0 ignored
     0 watchdog
     0 input packets with dribble condition detected
     2294 packets output, 244630 bytes, 0 underruns
     0 output errors, 0 collisions, 3 interface resets
     347 unknown protocol drops
     0 babbles, 0 late collision, 0 deferred
     4 lost carrier, 0 no carrier
     0 output buffer failures, 0 output buffers swapped out
```

You've got to be able to analyze interface statistics to find problems if they exist. Here is a list of the issues to look for using the output above:

Speed and duplex settings   Good to know is that the most common cause of interface errors is due to a mismatched duplex mode between two ends of an Ethernet link. This is why it's so important to make sure that the switch and its hosts (PCs, router interfaces, etc.) have the same speed setting. If not, they just won't connect. And if they have mismatched duplex setting, you'll receive a legion of errors, which cause nasty performance issues, intermittent connectivity—even total loss of communication!

Using autonegotiation for speed and duplex is a very common practice and it's enabled by default. But if this fails for some reason, you'll have to set the configuration manually like this:

```
Switch(config)#int gi0/1
Switch(config-if)#speed ?
  10    Force 10 Mbps operation
  100   Force 100 Mbps operation
  1000  Force 1000 Mbps operation
  auto  Enable AUTO speed configuration
Switch(config-if)#speed 1000
Switch(config-if)#duplex ?
  auto  Enable AUTO duplex configuration
  full  Force full duplex operation
  half  Force half-duplex operation
Switch(config-if)#duplex full
```

If you have a duplex mismatch, a telling sign is that the late collision counter will increment.

Input queue drops   If the input queue drops counter increments, this signifies that more traffic is being delivered to the router than it can process. If this is consistently high, try to determine exactly when these counters are increasing and how the events relate to CPU usage. You'll see the ignored and throttle counters increment as well.

Output queue drops   This counter indicates that packets were dropped due to interface congestion, leading to packet drops and queuing delays. When this occurs, applications like VoIP will experience performance issues. If you observe this constantly incrementing, consider QoS.

Input errors   Input errors often indicate high errors such as CRCs. This can point to cabling problems, hardware issues, or duplex mismatches.

Output errors   This is the total number of frames that the port tried to transmit when an issue such as a collision occurred.

We're going to move on in our troubleshooting process of elimination progression by analyzing the routers' actual configurations. Here's R1's routing table:

```
R1>sh ip route
[output cut]
Gateway of last resort is 192.168.10.254 to network 0.0.0.0

S*    0.0.0.0/0 [1/0] via 192.168.10.254
      10.0.0.0/8 is variably subnetted, 2 subnets, 2 masks
C         10.1.1.0/24 is directly connected, FastEthernet0/0
L         10.1.1.1/32 is directly connected, FastEthernet0/0
      192.168.10.0/24 is variably subnetted, 2 subnets, 2 masks
```

```
C        192.168.10.0/24 is directly connected, FastEthernet0/1
L        192.168.10.1/32 is directly connected, FastEthernet0/1
```

This actually looks pretty good! Both of our directly connected networks are in the table and we can confirm that we have a default route going to the R2 router. So now let's verify the connectivity to R2 from R1:

```
R1>sh ip int brief
Interface               IP-Address      OK? Method Status               Protocol
FastEthernet0/0         10.1.1.1        YES manual up                        up
FastEthernet0/1         192.168.10.1    YES manual up                        up
Serial0/0/0             unassigned      YES unset  administratively down down
Serial0/1/0             unassigned      YES unset  administratively down down
R1>ping 192.168.10.254
Type escape sequence to abort.
Sending 5, 100-byte ICMP Echos to 192.168.10.254, timeout is 2 seconds:
!!!!!
Success rate is 100 percent (5/5), round-trip min/avg/max = 1/2/4 ms
```

This looks great too! Our interfaces are correctly configured with the right IP address and the Physical and Data Link layers are up. By the way, I also tested layer 3 connectivity by pinging the R2 Fa0/1 interface.

Since everything looks good so far, our next step is to check into the status of R2's interfaces:

```
R2>sh ip int brief
Interface               IP-Address      OK? Method Status               Protocol
FastEthernet0/0         172.16.20.1     YES manual up                        up
FastEthernet0/1         192.168.10.254  YES manual up                        up
R2>ping 192.168.10.1
Type escape sequence to abort.
Sending 5, 100-byte ICMP Echos to 192.168.10.1, timeout is 2 seconds:
!!!!!
Success rate is 100 percent (5/5), round-trip min/avg/max = 1/2/4 ms
```

Well, everything still checks out at this point. The IP addresses are correct and the Physical and Data link layers are up. I also tested the layer 3 connectivity with a ping to R1, so we're all good so far. We'll examine the routing table next:

```
R2>sh ip route
[output cut]
Gateway of last resort is not set

     10.0.0.0/24 is subnetted, 1 subnets
```

```
S        10.1.1.0 is directly connected, FastEthernet0/0
      172.16.0.0/16 is variably subnetted, 2 subnets, 2 masks
C        172.16.20.0/24 is directly connected, FastEthernet0/0
L        172.16.20.1/32 is directly connected, FastEthernet0/0
      192.168.10.0/24 is variably subnetted, 2 subnets, 2 masks
C        192.168.10.0/24 is directly connected, FastEthernet0/1
L        192.168.10.254/32 is directly connected, FastEthernet0/1
```

Okay—we can see that all our local interfaces are in the table, as well as a static route to the 10.1.1.0 network. But do you see the problem? Look closely at the static route. The route was entered with an exit interface of Fa0/0, and the path to the 10.1.1.0 network is out Fa0/1! Aha! We've found our problem! Let's fix R2:

```
R2#config t
R2(config)#no ip route 10.1.1.0 255.255.255.0 fa0/0
R2(config)#ip route 10.1.1.0 255.255.255.0 192.168.10.1
```

That should do it; let's verify from PC1.

```
C:\Users\Todd Lammle>ping 172.16.20.254

Pinging 172.16.20.254 with 32 bytes of data:
Reply from 172.16.20.254: bytes=32 time<1ms TTL=128
Reply from 172.16.20.254: bytes=32 time<1ms TTL=128
Reply from 172.16.20.254: bytes=32 time<1ms TTL=128
Reply from 172.16.20.254: bytes=32 time<1ms TTL=128

Ping statistics for 172.16.20.254
    Packets: Sent = 4, Received = 4, Lost = 0 (0% loss),
Approximate round trip times in milli-seconds:
    Minimum = 0ms, Maximum = 0ms, Average = 0ms
```

Our snag appears to be solved, but just to make sure, we really need to verify with a higher-level protocol like Telnet:

```
C:\Users\Todd Lammle>telnet 172.16.20.254
Connecting To 172.16.20.254...Could not open connection to the host, on port 23:
 Connect failed
```

Okay, that's not good! We can ping to Server1, but we can't telnet to it. In the past, I've verified that telnetting to this server worked, but it's still possible that we have a failure on the server side. To find out, let's verify our network first, starting at R1:

```
R1>ping 172.16.20.254
Type escape sequence to abort.
```

```
Sending 5, 100-byte ICMP Echos to 172.16.20.254, timeout is 2 seconds:
!!!!!
Success rate is 100 percent (5/5), round-trip min/avg/max = 1/1/4 ms
R1>telnet 172.16.20.254
Trying 172.16.20.254 ...
% Destination unreachable; gateway or host down
```

This is some pretty ominous output! Let's try R2 and see what happens:

```
R2#telnet 172.16.20.254
Trying 172.16.20.254 ... Open

User Access Verification

Password:
```

Oh my—I can ping the server from a remote network, but I can't telnet to it, but the local router can! These factors eliminate my server being a problem since I can telnet to the server when I'm on the local LAN.

And we know we don't have a routing problem because we fixed that already. So what's next? Let's check to see if there's an ACL on R2:

```
R2>sh access-lists
Extended IP access list 110
    10 permit icmp any any (20 matches)
```

Seriously? What a loopy access list to have on a router! This ridiculous list permits ICMP, but that's it. It denies everything except ICMP due to the implicit deny ip any any at the end of every ACL. But before we uncork the champagne, we need to see if this foolish list has been applied to our interfaces on R2 to confirm that this is really our problem:

```
R2>sh ip int fa0/0
FastEthernet0/0 is up, line protocol is up
  Internet address is 172.16.20.1/24
  Broadcast address is 255.255.255.255
  Address determined by setup command
  MTU is 1500 bytes
  Helper address is not set
  Directed broadcast forwarding is disabled
  Outgoing access list is 110
  Inbound  access list is not set
```

There it is—that's our problem all right! In case you're wondering why R2 could telnet to Server1, it's because an ACL filters only packets trying to go through the router—not packets generated at the router. Let's get to work and fix this:

```
R2#config t
R2(config)#no access-list 110
```

I just verified that I can telnet from PC1 to Server1, but let's try telnetting from R1 again:

```
R1#telnet 172.16.20.254
Trying 172.16.20.254 ... Open

User Access Verification

Password:
```

Nice—looks like we're set, but what about using the name?

```
R1#telnet Server1
Translating "Server1"...domain server (255.255.255.255)

% Bad IP address or host name
```

Well, we're not all set just yet. Let's fix R1 so that it can provide name resolution:

```
R1(config)#ip host Server1 172.16.20.254
R1(config)#^Z
R1#telnet Server1
Trying Server1 (172.16.20.254)... Open

User Access Verification

Password:
```

Great—things are looking good from the router, but if the customer can't telnet to the remote host using the name, we've got to check the DNS server to confirm connectivity and for the correct entry for the server. Another option would be to configure the local host table manually on PC1.

The last thing to do is to check the server to see if it's responding to HTTP requests via the telnet command, believe it or not! Here's an example:

```
R1#telnet 172.16.20.254 80
Trying 172.16.20.254, 80 ... Open
```

Yes—finally! Server1 is responding to requests on port 80 so we're in the clear.

Exam Essentials

Remember the Cisco steps in troubleshooting a network.   There are five steps you need to take when a problem has been reported:

1. Check the cables to find out if there's faulty cable or interface in the mix and verify the interface's statistics.
2. Make sure that devices are determining the correct path from the source to the destination. Manipulate the routing information if needed.
3. Verify that the default gateway is correct.
4. Verify that name resolution settings are correct.
5. Verify that there are no ACLs blocking traffic.

Utilize Netflow Data

NetFlow enables near real-time visualization and analysis of recorded and aggregated flow data. You can specify the router, the aggregation scheme, and the time interval for when you want to view and then retrieve the relevant data and sort it into bar charts, pie charts, and so on. The components used with NetFlow include a router enabled with NetFlow and a NetFlow collector.

Service providers use NetFlow to do the following:

- Efficiently measure who is using network service and for which purpose.
- Perform accounting and charge back according to the resource utilizing level.
- Use the measured information for more effective network planning so that resource allocation and deployment are well aligned with customer requirements.
- Use the information to better structure and customize the set of available applications and services to meet user needs and customer service requirements.

There are different types of analyzers available to gather NetFlow statistics and analyze the traffic on your network by showing the following:

- Major users of the network, meaning top talkers, top listeners, top protocols, and so on.
- Websites that are routinely visited, plus what's been downloaded.
- Who's generating the most traffic and using excessive bandwidth.
- Descriptions of bandwidth needs for an application as well as your available bandwidth.

NetFlow is built around TCP/IP communication for statistical record keeping using the concept of a flow. A flow is a unidirectional stream of packets between a source and destination host or system. With an understanding of TCP/IP, NetFlow is using socket information, meaning source and destination IP addresses and source and destination port numbers. There are a few more fields that NetFlow uses. Here is a list of commonly used NetFlow flows:

- Source IP address
- Destination IP address
- Source port number
- Destination port number
- Layer 3 protocol field
- Type of Service (ToS) marking
- Input logical interface

The first four fields are the sockets used between the source and destination host, which identify the application. The protocol field identifies the data the packet is carrying, and ToS in the IPv4 header describes how QoS rules are applied to the packets in the flow. If a packet has a key field that's different from another packet, it's considered to belong to another flow. The three values that must be the same within a sequence of packets for NetFlow to consider them a network flow are the source IP address, the ingress interface, and the destination IP address. NetFlow is configured on the router's interfaces. In order to track IPv4 traffic, the flow monitor component can be applied to an interface.

Using NetFlow provides the following benefits:

- Network, application, and user monitoring
- Security analysis
- Accounting/billing

To verify NetFlow, you need to verify that the correct interfaces in the correct direction have been configured, starting with the show ip flow interface command:

```
SF#sh ip flow interface
FastEthernet0/0
  ip flow ingress
  ip flow egress
```

The correct interface of Fast Ethernet 0/0 is configured with the ingress and egress command. Now check the export parameters via the show ip flow export command:

```
SF#sh ip flow export
Flow export v9 is enabled for main cache
  Exporting flows to 172.16.20.254 (9996) 172.16.20.254 (9996)
  Exporting using source interface Loopback0
  Version 9 flow records
  43 flows exported in 15 udp datagrams
[output cut]
```

Notice that the destination port is 9996. This is the Cisco default port number on which the NetFlow collectors listen for NetFlow packets. I can use the sh ip cache flow command to verify my flows by examining the information stored on a router directly, which will show that I'm actually collecting packets.

```
SF#sh ip cache flow
IP packet size distribution (161 total packets):
[output cut]
IP Flow Switching Cache, 278544 bytes
  1 active, 4095 inactive, 1 added
  215 ager polls, 0 flow alloc failures
  Active flows timeout in 30 minutes
  Inactive flows timeout in 15 seconds
IP Sub Flow Cache, 21640 bytes
  1 active, 1023 inactive, 1 added, 1 added to flow
  0 alloc failures, 0 force free
  1 chunk, 1 chunk added
  last clearing of statistics never
Protocol        Total   Flows   Packets Bytes Packets Active(Sec) Idle(Sec)
--------        Flows   /Sec    /Flow   /Pkt  /Sec    /Flow       /Flow
TCP-Telnet      14      0.0     19      58    0.1     6.5         11.7
TCP-WWW         8       0.0     9       108   0.1     2.5         1.7
SrcIf        SrcIPaddress   DstIf     DstIPaddress    Pr SrcP DstP  Pkts
Fa0/0        172.16.10.1    gig0/1    255.255.255.255 11 0044 0050  161
```

You can see that packets are truly being received—1161 so far—and the bottom lines show that the router is collecting flow for Telnet and HTTP. You can also see the source interface, source IP, destination interface, and source and destination ports in hex (50 is 80 in hex). It's important to remember that the show ip cache flow command provides a summary of the NetFlow statistics, including which protocols are in use.

Exam Essentials

Understand what Cisco's NetFlow is used for.   Cisco IOS NetFlow efficiently provides a key set of services for IP applications, including network traffic accounting for baselining, usage-based network billing for consumers of network services, network design and planning, general network security, and DoS and DDoS monitoring capabilities as well as general network monitoring.

Remember the benefits of NetFlow.   Some of the benefits to using NetFlow are network, application, and user monitoring; security analysis; and accounting/billing.

Troubleshoot and Correct Common Problems Associated with IP Addressing and Host Configurations

Running into trouble now and then in networking is a given, so being able to troubleshoot IP addressing is clearly a vital skill. You can usually fix an IP network regardless of whether you're on site or at home!

I'm going to show you the "Cisco way" of troubleshooting IP addressing. Let's use Figure 7.2 as an example of your basic IP trouble—poor Sally can't log in to the Windows server.

FIGURE 7.2   Basic IP troubleshooting

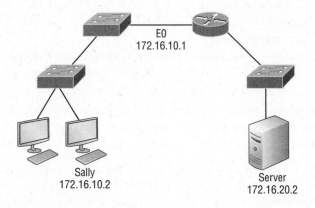

Here are the four troubleshooting steps Cisco recommends:

1. Open a Command window and ping 127.0.0.1. This is the diagnostic, or loopback, address, and if you get a successful ping, your IP stack is considered initialized. If it fails, then you have an IP stack failure and need to reinstall TCP/IP on the host.

```
C:\>ping 127.0.0.1
Pinging 127.0.0.1 with 32 bytes of data:
Reply from 127.0.0.1: bytes=32 time<1ms TTL=128
Reply from 127.0.0.1: bytes=32 time<1ms TTL=128
Reply from 127.0.0.1: bytes=32 time<1ms TTL=128
Reply from 127.0.0.1: bytes=32 time<1ms TTL=128
Ping statistics for 127.0.0.1:
    Packets: Sent = 4, Received = 4, Lost = 0 (0% loss),
Approximate round trip times in milli-seconds:
    Minimum = 0ms, Maximum = 0ms, Average = 0ms
```

2. From the Command window, ping the IP address of the local host (we'll assume correct configuration here, but always check the IP configuration too!). If that's successful, your network interface card (NIC) is functioning. If it fails, there is a problem with the NIC. Success here doesn't just mean that a cable is plugged into the NIC, only that the IP protocol stack on the host can communicate to the NIC via the LAN driver.

```
C:\>ping 172.16.10.2
Pinging 172.16.10.2 with 32 bytes of data:
Reply from 172.16.10.2: bytes=32 time<1ms TTL=128
Reply from 172.16.10.2: bytes=32 time<1ms TTL=128
Reply from 172.16.10.2: bytes=32 time<1ms TTL=128
Reply from 172.16.10.2: bytes=32 time<1ms TTL=128
Ping statistics for 172.16.10.2:
    Packets: Sent = 4, Received = 4, Lost = 0 (0% loss),
Approximate round trip times in milli-seconds:
    Minimum = 0ms, Maximum = 0ms, Average = 0ms
```

3. From the CMD window, ping the default gateway (router). If the ping works, it means that the NIC is plugged into the network and can communicate on the local network. If it fails, you have a local physical network problem that could be anywhere from the NIC to the router.

```
C:\>ping 172.16.10.1
Pinging 172.16.10.1 with 32 bytes of data:
Reply from 172.16.10.1: bytes=32 time<1ms TTL=128
Reply from 172.16.10.1: bytes=32 time<1ms TTL=128
Reply from 172.16.10.1: bytes=32 time<1ms TTL=128
Reply from 172.16.10.1: bytes=32 time<1ms TTL=128
Ping statistics for 172.16.10.1:
    Packets: Sent = 4, Received = 4, Lost = 0 (0% loss),
Approximate round trip times in milli-seconds:
    Minimum = 0ms, Maximum = 0ms, Average = 0ms
```

4. If steps 1 through 3 were successful, try to ping the remote server. If that works, then you know that you have IP communication between the local host and the remote server. You also know that the remote physical network is working.

```
C:\>ping 172.16.20.2
Pinging 172.16.20.2 with 32 bytes of data:
Reply from 172.16.20.2: bytes=32 time<1ms TTL=128
Reply from 172.16.20.2: bytes=32 time<1ms TTL=128
Reply from 172.16.20.2: bytes=32 time<1ms TTL=128
Reply from 172.16.20.2: bytes=32 time<1ms TTL=128
```

```
Ping statistics for 172.16.20.2:
    Packets: Sent = 4, Received = 4, Lost = 0 (0% loss),
Approximate round trip times in milli-seconds:
    Minimum = 0ms, Maximum = 0ms, Average = 0ms
```

If the user still can't communicate with the server after steps 1 through 4 have been completed successfully, you probably have some type of name resolution problem and need to check your Domain Name System (DNS) settings. But if the ping to the remote server fails, then you know you have some type of remote physical network problem and need to go to the server and work through steps 1 through 3 until you find the snag.

Here are some basic commands that you can use to help troubleshoot your network from both a PC and a Cisco router. Keep in mind that though these commands may do the same thing, they're implemented differently.

ping   Uses ICMP echo requests and replies to test if a node IP stack is initialized and alive on the network.

traceroute   Displays the list of routers on a path to a network destination by using TTL time-outs and ICMP error messages. This command will not work from a command prompt.

tracert   Same function as traceroute, but it's a Microsoft Windows command and will not work on a Cisco router.

arp -a   Displays IP-to-MAC-address mappings on a Windows PC.

show ip arp   Same function as arp -a, but displays the ARP table on a Cisco router. Like the commands traceroute and tracert, arp -a and show ip arp are not interchangeable between DOS and Cisco IOS.

ipconfig /all   Used only from a Windows command prompt; shows you the PC network configuration.

Once you've gone through all these steps and, if necessary, used the appropriate commands, what do you do when you find a problem? How do you go about fixing an IP address configuration error? Time to cover the next step—determining and fixing the issue at hand!

It's common for a host, router, or other network device to be configured with the wrong IP address, subnet mask, or default gateway. Because this happens way too often, you must know how to find and fix IP address configuration errors.

A good way to start is to draw out the network and IP addressing scheme.

Once you have your network accurately drawn out, including the IP addressing scheme, you need to verify each host's IP address, mask, and default gateway address to establish the problem. Of course, this is assuming that you don't have a Physical layer problem.

Look at the example illustrated in Figure 7.3. A user in the sales department calls and tells you that she can't get to ServerA in the marketing department. You ask her if she can get to ServerB in the marketing department, but she doesn't know because she doesn't have rights to log on to that server. What do you do?

First, guide your user through the four troubleshooting steps you learned earlier in this section. Steps 1 through 3 work, but step 4 fails. By looking at the figure, can you determine the problem? Look for clues in the network drawing. First, the WAN link between the Lab_A router and the Lab_B router shows the mask as a /27. You should already know that this mask is 255.255.255.224 and determine that all networks are using this mask. The network address is 192.168.1.0. What are our valid subnets and hosts? 256 – 224 = 32, so this makes our subnets 0, 32, 64, 96, 128, etc. So, by looking at the figure, you can see that subnet 32 is being used by the sales department. The WAN link is using subnet 96, and the marketing department is using subnet 64.

FIGURE 7.3 IP address problem

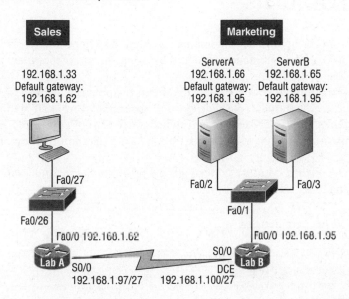

Now you've got to establish what the valid host ranges are for each subnet. You should now be able to easily determine the subnet address, broadcast addresses, and valid host ranges. The valid hosts for the Sales LAN are 33 through 62, and the broadcast address is 63 because the next subnet is 64, right? For the Marketing LAN, the valid hosts are 65 through 94 (broadcast 95), and for the WAN link, 97 through 126 (broadcast 127). By closely examining the figure, you can determine that the default gateway on the Lab_B router is incorrect. That address is the broadcast address for subnet 64, so there's no way it could be a valid host!

Exam Essentials

Understand the troubleshooting tools that you can use from your host and a Cisco router. The ping 127.0.0.1 command tests your local IP stack, and tracert is a Windows command to track the path a packet takes through an internetwork to a destination. Cisco routers use the command traceroute, or just trace for short. Don't confuse the Windows and Cisco commands. Although they produce the same output, they don't work from the same prompts. The command ipconfig /all will display your PC network configuration from a DOS prompt, and arp -a (again from a DOS prompt) will display IP-to-MAC-address mapping on a Windows PC.

Troubleshoot and Resolve VLAN Problems

VLANs are used to break up broadcast domains in a layer 2 switched network. We assign ports on a switch into a VLAN broadcast domain by using the switchport access vlan command.

The access port carries traffic for a single VLAN that the port is a member of. If members of one VLAN want to communicate with members in the same VLAN that are located on a different switch, then a port between the two switches needs to be configured either to be a member of this single VLAN or as a trunk link, which passes information on all VLANs by default.

We're going to use Figure 7.4 as we go through the procedures for troubleshooting VLAN and trunking.

FIGURE 7.4   VLAN connectivity

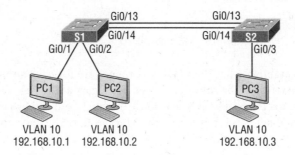

Identify That VLANs Are Configured

A manager calls and says they can't communicate with the new Sales team member that just connected to the network. How would you proceed to solve this issue? Well, because the Sales hosts are in VLAN 10, we'll begin by verifying that our databases on both switches are correct.

Use the show vlan or show vlan brief command to check if the expected VLAN is actually in the database. Here's a look at the VLAN database on S1:

```
S1#sh vlan

VLAN Name                             Status    Ports
---- -------------------------------- --------- -------------------------------
1    default                          active    Gi0/3, Gi0/4, Gi0/5, Gi0/6
                                                Gi0/7, Gi0/8, Gi0/9, Gi0/10
                                                Gi0/11, Gi0/12, Gi0/13, Gi0/14
                                                Gi0/15, Gi0/16, Gi0/17, Gi0/18
                                                Gi0/19, Gi0/20, Gi0/21, Gi0/22
                                                Gi0/23, Gi0/24, Gi0/25, Gi0/26
                                                Gi0/27, Gi0/28
10   Sales                            active    Gi0/1, Gi0/2
20   Accounting                       active
26   Automation10                     active
27   VLAN0027                         active
30   Engineering                      active
170  VLAN0170                         active
501  Private501                       active
502  Private500                       active
[output cut]
```

This output shows that VLAN 10 is in the local database and that Gi0/1 and Gi0/2 are associated with VLAN 10.

Port Membership Correct

Verify the content addressable memory (CAM) with the show mac address-table command:

```
S1#sh mac address-table
          Mac Address Table
-------------------------------------------

Vlan    Mac Address       Type        Ports
----    -----------       --------    -----
 All    0100.0ccc.cccc    STATIC      CPU
[output cut]
   1    000d.2830.2f00    DYNAMIC     Gi0/24
   1    0021.1c91.0d8d    DYNAMIC     Gi0/13
   1    0021.1c91.0d8e    DYNAMIC     Gi0/14
   1    b414.89d9.1882    DYNAMIC     Gi0/17
```

```
    1     b414.89d9.1883    DYNAMIC    Gi0/18
    1     ecc8.8202.8282    DYNAMIC    Gi0/15
    1     ecc8.8202.8283    DYNAMIC    Gi0/16
   10     001a.2f55.c9e8    DYNAMIC    Gi0/1
   10     001b.d40a.0538    DYNAMIC    Gi0/2
Total Mac Addresses for this criterion: 29
```

Your switch will show quite a few MAC addresses assigned to the CPU at the top of the output; they are used by the switch to manage the ports. The very first MAC address listed is the base MAC address of the switch and used by STP in the bridge ID. In the preceding output, we can see that there is a MAC address associated with VLAN 10 and that it was dynamically learned. We can also establish that this MAC address is associated to Gi0/1.

IP Address Configured

VLAN 1 is typically the administrative VLAN on a Cisco switch. Configuring an IP address on VLAN 1 allows the switch to be managed from a remote location.

```
2960#config t
2960(config)#int vlan 1
2960(config-if)#ip address 192.168.10.2 255.255.255.0
2960(config-if)#no shutdown
2960(config-if)#exit
2960(config)#ip default-gateway 192.168.10.1
```

You have to execute a no shutdown on the VLAN interface and set the ip default-gateway address to the router.

Exam Essentials

Understand the methods to view the VLANs that are configured on a switch.   The show vlan or show vlan brief command will display any VLANs that are configured on the switch.

Understand how to determine what ports on a switch are assigned to specific VLANs. The show mac address-table command will display what ports are associated with specific MAC addresses.

Understand how to assign an IP address to the management VLAN on a switch.   To configure an IP address on a switch for remote management purposes, assign an IP address on interface VLAN 1. Remember to issue the no shutdown command to enable the interface.

```
2960#config t
2960(config)#int vlan 1
```

```
2960(config-if)#ip address 192.168.10.2 255.255.255.0
2960(config-if)#no shutdown
```

Troubleshoot and Resolve Trunking Problems on Cisco Switches

In this part of the chapter, I'll cover trunking problems in a switched network. I'll go over the different trunking states, the encapsulation types, and how to allow the correct VLANs across a trunk link.

VLAN identification is what switches use to keep track of all those frames as they're traversing a switch fabric. It's how switches identify which frames belong to which VLANs, and there's more than one trunking method.

Inter-Switch Link (ISL) is a way of explicitly tagging VLAN information onto an Ethernet frame. This tagging information allows VLANs to be multiplexed over a trunk link through an external encapsulation method. This allows the switch to identify the VLAN membership of a frame received over the trunked link.

By running ISL, you can interconnect multiple switches and still maintain VLAN information as traffic travels between switches on trunk links. ISL functions at layer 2 by encapsulating a data frame with a new header and by performing a new cyclic redundancy check (CRC).

Of note is that ISL is proprietary to Cisco switches and it's used for Fast Ethernet and Gigabit Ethernet links only.

IEEE 802.1q was created by the IEEE as a standard method of frame tagging. It actually inserts a field into the frame to identify the VLAN. If you're trunking between a Cisco switched link and a different brand of switch, you've got to use 802.1q for the trunk to work.

Unlike ISL, which encapsulates the frame with control information, 802.1q inserts an 802.1q field along with tag control information.

Correct Trunk States

Different options are available when configuring a switch interface:

switchport mode dynamic auto   This mode makes the interface able to convert the link to a trunk link. The interface becomes a trunk interface if the neighboring interface is set to trunk or desirable mode. The default is dynamic auto on a lot of Cisco switches, but that default trunk method is changing to dynamic desirable on most new models.

switchport mode dynamic desirable   This one makes the interface actively attempt to convert the link to a trunk link. The interface becomes a trunk interface if the neighboring interface is set to trunk, desirable, or auto mode. I used to see this mode as the default on some switches, but not any longer. This is now the default switch port mode for all Ethernet interfaces on all new Cisco switches.

switchport mode trunk   Puts the interface into permanent trunking mode and negotiates to convert the neighboring link into a trunk link. The interface becomes a trunk interface even if the neighboring interface isn't a trunk interface.

switchport nonegotiate   This prevents the interface from generating Dynamic Trunking Protocol (DTP) frames. You can use this command only when the interface switchport mode is access or trunk. You must manually configure the neighboring interface as a trunk interface to establish a trunk link.

Correct Encapsulation Configured

The 2960 switch runs only the IEEE 802.1q encapsulation method. To configure trunking on a Fast Ethernet port, use the interface command switchport mode trunk. It's a bit different on a 3560 switch.

The following switch output shows the trunk configuration on interfaces Fa0/15–18 as set to trunk:

```
S1(config)#int range f0/15-18
S1(config-if-range)#switchport trunk encapsulation dot1q
S1(config-if-range)#switchport mode trunk
```

If you have a switch that only runs the 802.1q encapsulation method, then you wouldn't use the encapsulation command as I did in the preceding output. Let's check out our trunk ports now:

```
S1(config-if-range)#do sh int f0/15 swi
Name: Fa0/15
Switchport: Enabled
Administrative Mode: trunk
Operational Mode: trunk
Administrative Trunking Encapsulation: dot1q
Operational Trunking Encapsulation: dot1q
Negotiation of Trunking: On
Access Mode VLAN: 1 (default)
Trunking Native Mode VLAN: 1 (default)
Administrative Native VLAN tagging: enabled
Voice VLAN: none
```

Notice that port Fa0/15 is a trunk and running 802.1q. Let's take another look:

```
S1(config-if-range)#do sh int trunk
Port       Mode         Encapsulation   Status      Native vlan
Fa0/15     on           802.1q          trunking    1
Fa0/16     on           802.1q          trunking    1
Fa0/17     on           802.1q          trunking    1
```

```
Fa0/18        on              802.1q        trunking      1
Port          Vlans allowed on trunk
Fa0/15        1-4094
Fa0/16        1-4094
Fa0/17        1-4094
Fa0/18        1-4094
```

Take note of the fact that ports 15–18 are now in the trunk mode of on and the encapsulation is now 802.1q instead of the negotiated ISL.

Correct VLANs Allowed

By default, all VLANs are allowed across trunk links. This can be changed to allow only certain VLAN traffic across.

```
S1#sh int trunk
[output cut]
Port          Vlans allowed on trunk
Fa0/15        1-4094
Fa0/16        1-4094
Fa0/17        1-4094
Fa0/18        1-4094
S1(config)#int f0/15
S1(config-if)#switchport trunk allowed vlan 4,6,12,15
S1(config-if)#do show int trunk
[output cut]
Port          Vlans allowed on trunk
Fa0/15        4,6,12,15
Fa0/16        1-4094
Fa0/17        1-4094
Fa0/18        1-4094
```

The preceding command affected the trunk link configured on S1 port F0/15, causing it to drop all traffic sent and received for VLANs 4, 6, 12, and 15. You can try to remove VLAN 1 on a trunk link, but it will still send and receive management like CDP and DTP.

Exam Essentials

Know the different port states for trunking ports.   Switchport mode dynamic auto, switchport mode dynamic desirable, switchport mode trunk, and switchport nonegotiate are the available port states for trunk links.

Understand the encapsulation methods on switchports. Cisco 2960 switches only support the IEEE 802.1q encapsulation. When you issue the command switchport mode trunk, the switchport uses the IEE 802.1q encapsulation. Cisco 3560 switches support the IEEE 802.1q and the Cisco proprietary ISL encapsulation.

Know how to determine what VLANs are allowed across a trunk link. The command show interface trunk will display what ports are configured for trunking and the encapsulation method for each one.

Troubleshoot and Resolve Spanning Tree Operation Issues

Troubleshooting spanning tree operations is critical in switched networks. Not only do you want to avoid losing connectivity in your LAN, you also want to ensure that your switches are operating efficiently!

Root Switch

The root switch, commonly just referred to as a *root bridge*, is the bridge with the lowest and, therefore, the best bridge ID. The switches within the STP network elect a root bridge, which becomes the focal point in the network. All other decisions in the network, like which ports on the non-root bridges should be blocked or put in forwarding mode, are made from the perspective of the root bridge, and once it has been elected, all other bridges must create a single path to it. The port with the best path to the root bridge is called the root port.

To verify our root bridge on a Cisco switch, just use the command show spanning-tree. From its output, we can determine our root bridge, priorities, root ports, and designated and blocking/discarding ports.

Figure 7.5 shows the network we'll work with in this section.

FIGURE 7.5 Our simple three-switch network

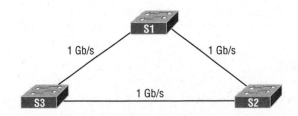

Let's start by taking a look at the output from S1:

```
S1#sh spanning-tree vlan 1
VLAN0001
  Spanning tree enabled protocol ieee
  Root ID    Priority    32769
             Address     0001.42A7.A603
             This bridge is the root
             Hello Time  2 sec  Max Age 20 sec  Forward Delay 15 sec

  Bridge ID  Priority    32769  (priority 32768 sys-id-ext 1)
             Address     0001.42A7.A603 him
             Hello Time  2 sec  Max Age 20 sec  Forward Delay 15 sec
             Aging Time  20

Interface        Role Sts Cost      Prio.Nbr Type
---------------- ---- --- --------- -------- --------------------------------
Gi1/1            Desg FWD 4         128.25   P2p
Gi1/2            Desg FWD 4         128.26   P2p
```

Looking at the root ID, it's easy to see that S3 isn't the root bridge, because the MAC addresses of the root bridge and this bridge are different and there is a root port. But the output tells us it's a cost of 4 to get to the root bridge and also that it's located out port 26 of the switch (Gi1/2). This tells us that the root bridge is one Gigabit Ethernet link away.

Priority

The bridge ID is how STP keeps track of all the switches in the network. It's determined by a combination of the bridge priority, which is 32,768 by default on all Cisco switches, and the base MAC address. The bridge with the lowest bridge ID becomes the root bridge in the network. Once the root bridge is established, every other switch must make a single path to it. Most networks benefit by forcing a specific bridge or switch to be the root bridge by setting its bridge priority lower than the default value.

You can change the priority on a switch to force it to become the root bridge using the following command:

```
S2(config)#spanning-tree vlan 2 priority 16384
```

You can set the priority to any value from 0 through 61,440 in increments of 4,096. Setting it to zero (0) means that the switch will always be a root as long as it has a lower MAC address than another switch that also has its bridge ID set to 0. If you want to set a switch to be the root bridge for every VLAN in your network, then you have to change the priority for each VLAN, with 0 being the lowest priority you can use.

Mode Is Correct

Switch ports are most often in either the blocking or forwarding state. A forwarding port is typically the one that's been determined to have the lowest (best) cost to the root bridge. But when and if the network experiences a topology change due to a failed link or because someone has added in a new switch, you'll see the ports on a switch transitioning through listening and learning states.

Blocking ports is a strategy for preventing network loops. Once a switch determines the best path to the root bridge for its root port and any designated ports, all other redundant ports will be in blocking mode. Blocked ports can still receive BPDUs—they just don't send out any frames.

If a switch determines that a blocked port should become the designated or root port because of a topology change, it will go into listening mode and check all BPDUs it receives to make sure it won't create a loop once the port moves into forwarding mode.

Port States

The ports on a bridge or switch running IEEE 802.1d STP can transition through five different states:

Disabled (technically, not a transition state)   A port in the administratively disabled state doesn't participate in frame forwarding or STP. A port in the disabled state is virtually nonoperational.

Blocking   As I mentioned, a blocked port won't forward frames; it just listens to BPDUs. The purpose of the blocking state is to prevent the use of looped paths. All ports are in blocking state by default when the switch is powered up.

Listening   This port listens to BPDUs to make sure no loops occur on the network before passing data frames. A port in listening state prepares to forward data frames without populating the MAC address table.

Learning   The switch port listens to BPDUs and learns all the paths in the switched network. A port in learning state populates the MAC address table but still doesn't forward data frames. Forward delay refers to the time it takes to transition a port from listening to learning mode, or from learning to forwarding mode, which is set to 15 seconds by default and can be seen in the show spanning-tree output.

Forwarding   This port sends and receives all data frames on the bridged port. If the port is still a designated or root port at the end of the learning state, it will enter the forwarding state.

Exam Essentials

Remember the states of STP.   A port in the disabled state is virtually nonoperational. The purpose of the blocking state is to prevent the use of looped paths. A port in listening state prepares to forward data frames without populating the MAC address table. A port in learning state populates the MAC address table but doesn't forward data frames. A port in forwarding state sends and receives all data frames on the bridged port.

Troubleshoot and Resolve Routing Issues

I'll now cover some of the troubleshooting methods to use when you're using routing protocols. As you know, routing protocols include RIP, EIGRP, and OSPF. Using these simple troubleshooting tips will help you tremendously on the job site and the testing site!

Routing Is Enabled

One of the best tools to determine which routing protocol is being used, or if a routing protocol is even configured on a router, is show ip protocols.

This command will show you a wealth of information such as which protocol (if any) is running on the router, the metrics used, the networks the protocol has learned, and its administrative distance (trustworthiness of the route).

Take a look at this router output:

```
R1#show ip protocols

Routing Protocol is "eigrp  10 "
  Outgoing update filter list for all interfaces is not set
  Incoming update filter list for all interfaces is not set
  Default networks flagged in outgoing updates
  Default networks accepted from incoming updates
  EIGRP metric weight K1=1, K2=0, K3=1, K4=0, K5=0
  EIGRP maximum hopcount 100
  EIGRP maximum metric variance 1
Redistributing: eigrp 10
  Automatic network summarization is not in effect
  Maximum path: 4
  Routing for Networks:
     10.0.0.0
     192.168.36.0
     192.168.60.0
     192.168.77.0
  Routing Information Sources:
    Gateway         Distance      Last Update
    192.168.77.34   90            54465
  Distance: internal 90 external 170
R1#
```

In this output, we see that EIGRP is running, its AS is 10, what networks it has learned, and its administrative distances.

Routing Table Is Correct

Troubleshooting network problems and connectivity problems can be tedious. How can you tell if remote networks are known by your router? The show ip route will display what networks your router knows about.

```
R1#show ip route
Codes: C - connected, S - static, I - IGRP, R - RIP, M - mobile, B - BGP
       D - EIGRP, EX - EIGRP external, O - OSPF, IA - OSPF inter area
       N1 - OSPF NSSA external type 1, N2 - OSPF NSSA external type 2
       E1 - OSPF external type 1, E2 - OSPF external type 2, E - EGP
       i - IS-IS, L1 - IS-IS level-1, L2 - IS-IS level-2, ia - IS-IS inter area
       * - candidate default, U - per-user static route, o - ODR
       P - periodic downloaded static route

Gateway of last resort is not set

     10.0.0.0/24 is subnetted, 1 subnets
C       10.10.10.0 is directly connected, FastEthernet0/0
     192.168.60.0/29 is subnetted, 2 subnets
D       192.168.60.64 [90/30720] via 192.168.77.34, 00:07:37, FastEthernet0/1
D       192.168.60.80 [90/284160] via 192.168.77.34, 00:07:37, FastEthernet0/1
     192.168.77.0/30 is subnetted, 1 subnets
C       192.168.77.32 is directly connected, FastEthernet0/1
R1#
```

In this output, the section at the top gives us an explanation of what the router has learned about networks. The letter C tells us we are directly connected to another router, what network is being used, and what interface it learned the network on. The letter D tells us that EIGRP is the routing protocol being run, what networks it has learned, and what interfaces the networks were learned on.

Correct Path Selection

Large networks can be difficult to troubleshoot. Learning how a router chooses which route it will use when using routing protocols or manual configurations can be very helpful to you. Knowing how the routing table is built can help you troubleshoot routing problems.

The following is used by the router when it builds the routing table:

- Administrative distance. This measures the trustworthiness of the route learned.
- Metric. This measures the best path to a given destination.
- Prefix length.

When a router receives routing information from its neighbors, it chooses the best path to any given destination and installs this path into the routing table. Table 7.1 shows the default administrative distances.

TABLE 7.1 Default administrative distances

Routing Source	Default AD
Connected	0
Static	1
EIGRP	90
IGRP	100
OSPF	110
RIP	120

Routes with the lowest administrative distance are added to the routing table. If multiple routes have the same administrative distance, the router will use metrics to determine which route has the best path. The path with the lowest metric will be selected for entry into the routing table.

In the case where multiple paths are available to route a packet to a destination, the router will also use the prefix length. The path with the longest prefix length will be used to route the packet.

In this example, there are three entries in the routing table.

```
Router#show ip route
  ....
  D   192.168.60.0/26 [90/25789217] via 192.168.77.1
  R   192.168.60.0/24 [120/4] via 192.168.78.1
  O   192.168.60.0/19 [110/229840] via 192.168.79.1
```

If a packet arrives on a router interface destined for 192.168.32.1, the packet is directed toward 192.168.77.1 because 192.168.32.1 falls within the 192.168.32.0/26 network (192.168.32.0 to 192.168.32.63). It also falls within the other two routes available, but the 192.168.32.0/26 has the longest prefix within the routing table (26 bits versus 24 or 19 bits).

Exam Essentials

Understand how to determine if a routing protocol is running on a router.   The command `show ip protocols` will display what routing protocol (if any) is running on the router.

Understand how to determine what routes are being used on a router.   The command `show ip route` will display what routes are being used by the router to forward packets to known destination networks.

Understand how to determine the best path a router will use to route packets to remote networks.   Routers use administrative distance, metrics, and prefix length to insert the best route into the routing table.

Know the routing protocol administrative distances.   Directly connected routes have an administrative distance (AD) of 0, static routes have an AD of 1, EIGRP is 90, IGRP is 100, OSPF is 110, and RIP is 120.

Troubleshoot and Resolve OSPF Problems

Next, we'll focus on troubleshooting OSPF. Table 7.2 lists various show commands that can be used to monitor and troubleshoot OSPF.

TABLE 7.2   OSPF verification commands

Command	Provides the following
`show ip ospf neighbor`	Verifies your OSPF-enabled interfaces
`show ip ospf interface`	Displays OSPF-related information on an OSPF-enabled interface
`show ip protocols`	Verifies the OSPF process ID and that OSPF is enabled on the router

Command	Provides the following
show ip route	Verifies the routing table, and displays any OSPF injected routes
show ip ospf database	Lists a summary of the LSAs in the database, with one line of output per LSA, organized by type

We use the show ip ospf command to display OSPF information for one or all OSPF processes running on the router. Information contained therein includes the router ID, area information, SPF statistics, and LSA timer information.

```
Corp#sh ip ospf
 Routing Process "ospf 1" with ID 1.1.1.1
 Supports only single TOS(TOS0) routes
 Supports opaque LSA
 It is an area border router
 SPF schedule delay 5 secs, Hold time between two SPFs 10 secs
 Minimum LSA interval 5 secs. Minimum LSA arrival 1 secs
 Number of external LSA 0. Checksum Sum 0x000000
 Number of opaque AS LSA 0. Checksum Sum 0x000000
 Number of DCbitless external and opaque AS LSA 0
 Number of DoNotAge external and opaque AS LSA 0
 Number of areas in this router is 3. 3 normal 0 stub 0 nssa
 External flood list length 0
    Area BACKBONE(0)
        Number of interfaces in this area is 2
        Area has no authentication
        SPF algorithm executed 19 times
        Area ranges are
        Number of LSA 7. Checksum Sum 0x0384d5
        Number of opaque link LSA 0. Checksum Sum 0x000000
        Number of DCbitless LSA 0
        Number of indication LSA 0
        Number of DoNotAge LSA 0
        Flood list length 0
    Area 1
        Number of interfaces in this area is 1
        Area has no authentication
        SPF algorithm executed 43 times
        Area ranges are
        Number of LSA 7. Checksum Sum 0x0435f8
```

```
            Number of opaque link LSA 0. Checksum Sum 0x000000
            Number of DCbitless LSA 0
            Number of indication LSA 0
            Number of DoNotAge LSA 0
            Flood list length 0
        Area 2
            Number of interfaces in this area is 1
            Area has no authentication
            SPF algorithm executed 38 times
            Area ranges are
            Number of LSA 7. Checksum Sum 0x0319ed
            Number of opaque link LSA 0. Checksum Sum 0x000000
            Number of DCbitless LSA 0
            Number of indication LSA 0
            Number of DoNotAge LSA 0
            Flood list length 0
```

Notice that most of the preceding information will not be displayed with this command output when using single-area OSPF. We have more displayed here because it's providing information about each area we've configured on this router.

The show ip ospf interface command displays all interface-related OSPF information. Data is displayed for all OSPF-enabled interfaces or for specified interfaces.

```
Router#sh ip ospf interface gi0/0
GigabitEthernet0/0 is up, line protocol is up
  Internet address is 10.10.10.1/24, Area 0
  Process ID 1, Router ID 1.1.1.1, Network Type BROADCAST, Cost: 1
  Transmit Delay is 1 sec, State DR, Priority 1
  Designated Router (ID) 1.1.1.1, Interface address 10.10.10.1
  No backup designated router on this network
  Timer intervals configured, Hello 10, Dead 40, Wait 40, Retransmit 5
    Hello due in 00:00:05
  Index 1/1, flood queue length 0
  Next 0x0(0)/0x0(0)
  Last flood scan length is 1, maximum is 1
  Last flood scan time is 0 msec, maximum is 0 msec
  Neighbor Count is 0, Adjacent neighbor count is 0
  Suppress hello for 0 neighbor(s)
```

Using the show ip ospf database command will give you information about the number of routers in the internetwork plus the neighboring router's ID. This is the topology database.

```
Router#sh ip ospf database
            OSPF Router with ID (1.1.1.1) (Process ID 1)
```

```
                  Router Link States (Area 0)

Link ID           ADV Router       Age       Seq#        Checksum Link count
1.1.1.1           1.1.1.1          196       0x8000001a 0x006d76 2

                  Summary Net Link States (Area 0)
Link ID           ADV Router       Age       Seq#        Checksum
172.16.10.0       1.1.1.1          182       0x80000095 0x00be04
172.16.10.4       1.1.1.1          177       0x80000096 0x009429
10.10.40.0        1.1.1.1          1166      0x80000091 0x00222b
10.10.50.0        1.1.1.1          1166      0x80000092 0x00b190
10.10.20.0        1.1.1.1          1114      0x80000093 0x00fa64
10.10.30.0        1.1.1.1          1114      0x80000094 0x008ac9

                  Router Link States (Area 1)

Link ID           ADV Router       Age       Seq#        Checksum Link count
1.1.1.1           1.1.1.1          1118      0x8000002a 0x00a59a 2
172.16.10.2       172.16.10.2      1119      0x80000031 0x00af47 4

                  Summary Net Link States (Area 1)
Link ID           ADV Router       Age       Seq#        Checksum
10.10.10.0        1.1.1.1          178       0x80000076 0x0021a5
10.10.11.0        1.1.1.1          178       0x80000077 0x0014b0
172.16.10.4       1.1.1.1          173       0x80000078 0x00d00b
10.10.40.0        1.1.1.1          1164      0x80000074 0x005c0e
10.10.50.0        1.1.1.1          1164      0x80000075 0x00eb73

                  Router Link States (Area 2)

Link ID           ADV Router       Age       Seq#        Checksum Link count
1.1.1.1           1.1.1.1          1119      0x8000002b 0x005cd6 2
172.16.10.6       172.16.10.6      1119      0x8000002d 0x0020a3 4

                  Summary Net Link States (Area 2)
Link ID           ADV Router       Age       Seq#        Checksum
10.10.10.0        1.1.1.1          179       0x8000007a 0x0019a9
10.10.11.0        1.1.1.1          179       0x8000007b 0x000cb4
172.16.10.0       1.1.1.1          179       0x8000007c 0x00f0ea
10.10.20.0        1.1.1.1          1104      0x80000078 0x003149
10.10.30.0        1.1.1.1          1104      0x80000079 0x00c0ae
Router#
```

Considering we have only eight networks configured in our internetwork, there's a huge amount of information in this database! You can see all the routers and the RID of each—the highest IP address related to individual routers. And each output under each area represents LSA type 1, indicating the area they're connected to.

Neighbor Adjacencies

The show ip ospf neighbor command is super useful because it summarizes the pertinent OSPF information regarding neighbors and their adjacency state. If a DR or BDR exists, that information will also be displayed. Here's a sample:

```
Router#sh ip ospf neighbor
Neighbor ID    Pri   State          Dead Time   Address        Interface
172.16.10.2      0   FULL/  -       00:00:34    172.16.10.2    Serial0/0/0
172.16.10.6      0   FULL/  -       00:00:31    172.16.10.6    Serial0/0/1
```

The reason that the Corp connections to SF and LA don't have a DR or BDR listed in the output is that by default, elections don't happen on point-to-point links and they show FULL/ - . But we can see that the Corp router is fully adjacent to all three routers from its output.

The output of this command shows the neighbor ID, which is the RID of the router. RIDs are based on highest IP address of any active interface when the OSPF process is started on the router.

Next we see the Pri field, which is the priority field that's set to 1 by default. Don't forget that on point-to-point links, elections don't happen, so the interface is set to 0 in this example. The state field shows Full/-, which means all routers are synchronized with their LSDB, and the /- means there is no election on this type of interface. The dead time is counting down, and if the router does not hear from its neighbor before this expires, the link will be considered down. The address is the actual address of the neighbor's interface connecting to the router.

Hello and Dead Timers

The period between Hello packets is the hello time, which is 10 seconds by default. The dead time is the length of time allotted for a Hello packet to be received before a neighbor is considered down—four times the Hello interval, unless otherwise configured.

OSPF Area

The OSPF area represents the area that the originating router interface belongs to. Single-area OSPF presents some serious scalability challenges, as shown in Figure 7.6.

Single-area OSPF design places all routers into a single OSPF area, which results in many LSAs being processed on every router. OSPF also allows us to take a large OSPF topology and break it down into multiple, more manageable areas, as illustrated in Figure 7.7.

FIGURE 7.6   OSPF single-area network: All routers flood the network with link-state information to all other routers within the same area.

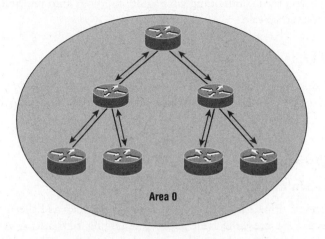

FIGURE 7.7   OSPF multi-area network: All routers flood the network only within their area.

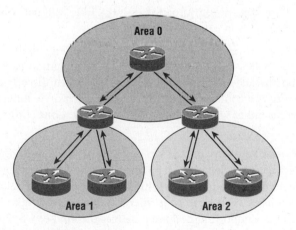

There are advantages with this hierarchical approach. First, routers that are internal to a defined area don't need to worry about having a link-state database for the entire network because they need one for only their own areas. This factor seriously reduces memory overhead! Second, routers that are internal to a defined area now have to recalculate their link-state database only when there's a topology change within their given area. Topology changes in one area won't cause global OSPF recalculations, further reducing processor overhead.

Finally, because routes can be summarized at area boundaries, the routing tables on each router don't need to be as huge as they would be in a single-area environment!

There is a catch: as you start subdividing your OSPF topology into multiple areas, the configuration gets more complex.

Interface MTU

Maximum transmission unit (MTU) is used to measure the size of packets on an interface. Although the default of 1,500 bytes can be manipulated for troubleshooting, it typically is left at the default.

Network Types

OSPF supports several different types of networks:

Broadcast (multi-access)   *Broadcast (multi-access) networks* such as Ethernet allow multiple devices to connect to or access the same network, enabling a *broadcast* ability in which a single packet is delivered to all nodes on the network. In OSPF, a DR and BDR must be elected for each broadcast multi-access network.

Nonbroadcast multi-access   *Nonbroadcast multi-access (NBMA)* networks are networks such as Frame Relay, X.25, and Asynchronous Transfer Mode (ATM). These types of networks allow for multi-access without broadcast ability like Ethernet. NBMA networks require special OSPF configuration to function properly.

Point-to-point   *Point-to-point* refers to a type of network topology made up of a direct connection between two routers that provides a single communication path. The point-to-point connection can be physical—for example, a serial cable that directly connects two routers—or logical, where two routers thousands of miles apart are connected by a circuit in a Frame Relay network. Either way, point-to-point configurations eliminate the need for DRs or BDRs.

Point-to-multipoint   *Point-to-multipoint* refers to a type of network topology made up of a series of connections between a single interface on one router and multiple destination routers. All interfaces on all routers share the point-to-multipoint connection and belong to the same network. Point-to-multipoint networks can be further classified according to whether they support broadcasts or not. This is important because it defines the kind of OSPF configurations you can deploy.

All of these terms play a critical role when you're trying to understand how OSPF actually works, so again, make sure you're familiar with each of them. Having these terms down will enable you to confidently place them in their proper context.

Exam Essentials

Know how OSPF routers become neighbors and/or adjacent. OSPF routers become neighbors when each router sees the other's Hello packets.

Be able to verify the operation of OSPF. There are many show commands that provide useful details on OSPF, and it is useful to be completely familiar with the output of each: show ip route, show ip ospf, show ip ospf database, show ip ospf interface, show ip ospf neighbor, and show ip protocols.

Troubleshoot and Resolve EIGRP Problems

EIGRP usually runs smoothly and is relatively low maintenance, but there are several commands you need to memorize for using on a router that can be super helpful when troubleshooting EIGRP. I'm going to demonstrate the tools you'll need to verify and troubleshoot EIGRP.

Table 7.3 contains all of the commands you need to know for verifying that EIGRP is functioning well and offers a brief description of what each command does.

TABLE 7.3   EIGRP troubleshooting commands

Command	Description/Function
show ip eigrp neighbors	Shows all EIGRP neighbors
show ip eigrp interfaces	Lists the interfaces on which the router has actually enabled EIGRP
show ip route eigrp	Shows EIGRP entries in the routing table
show ip eigrp topology	Shows entries in the EIGRP topology table
show ip eigrp traffic	Shows the packet count for EIGRP packets sent and received
show ip protocols	Shows information about the active protocol sessions

When troubleshooting an EIGRP problem, it's always a good idea to start by getting an accurate map of the network, and the best way to do that is by using the show ip eigrp neighbors command to find out who your directly connected neighbors are. This command shows all adjacent routers that share route information within a given AS. If neighbors are missing, check the configuration, AS number, and link status on both routers to verify that the protocol has been configured correctly.

```
Router#sh ip eigrp neighbors
IP-EIGRP neighbors for process 20
H    Address              Interface      Hold Uptime    SRTT   RTO  Q  Seq
                                         (sec)          (ms)       Cnt Num
1    172.16.10.2          Se0/0           11 03:54:25    1    200  0  127
0    172.16.10.6          Se0/1           11 04:14:47    1    200  0  2010
```

Here's a breakdown of the important information in the preceding output:

- H indicates the order in which the neighbor was discovered.

- Hold time in seconds is how long this router will wait for a Hello packet to arrive from a specific neighbor.

- The Uptime value indicates how long the neighbor relationship has been established.

- The SRTT field is the smooth round-trip timer and represents how long it takes to complete a round-trip from this router to its neighbor and back. This value delimits how long to wait after a multicast for a reply from this neighbor. The router will attempt to establish communication via unicasts if it doesn't receive a reply.

- The time between multicast attempts is specified by the Retransmission Time Out (RTO) field, which is based upon the SRTT values.

- The Q value tells us if there are any outstanding messages in the queue. We can make a mental note that there's a problem if we see consistently large values here!

- Finally, the Seq field shows the sequence number of the last update from that neighbor, which is used to maintain synchronization and avoid duplicate messages or their out-of-sequence processing.

Get the local status of your router by using the show ip eigrp interface command:

```
Router#sh ip eigrp interfaces
IP-EIGRP interfaces for process 20

                      Xmit Queue   Mean  Pacing Time   Multicast     Pending
Interface     Peers   Un/Reliable  SRTT  Un/Reliable   Flow Timer    Routes
Gi0/0          0       0/0          0      0/1           0             0
Se0/1          1       0/0          1      0/15          50            0
Se0/0          1       0/0          1      0/15          50            0
Gi0/1          0       0/0          0      0/1           0             0
```

```
Router#sh ip eigrp interface detail s0/0
IP-EIGRP interfaces for process 20

                     Xmit Queue   Mean   Pacing Time   Multicast    Pending
Interface     Peers  Un/Reliable  SRTT   Un/Reliable   Flow Timer   Routes
Se0/0         1      0/0          1      0/15          50           0
  Hello interval is 5 sec
  Next xmit serial <none>
  Un/reliable mcasts: 0/0  Un/reliable ucasts: 21/26
  Mcast exceptions: 0  CR packets: 0  ACKs suppressed: 9
  Retransmissions sent: 0  Out-of-sequence rcvd: 0
  Authentication mode is not set
```

The first command, show ip eigrp interfaces, lists all interfaces for which EIGRP is enabled as well as those the router is currently sending Hello messages to in an attempt to find new EIGRP neighbors. The show ip eigrp interface detail *interface* command lists more details per interface, including the local route's own Hello interval. You can use these commands to verify that all your interfaces are within the AS process used by EIGRP, but also note that the passive interfaces won't show up in these outputs. So be sure to also check to see if an interface has been configured as passive if not present in the outputs.

If all neighbors are present, then verify the routes learned. By executing the show ip route eigrp command, you're given a quick picture of the routes in the routing table. If a certain route doesn't appear in the routing table, you need to verify its source. If the source is functioning properly, then check the topology table.

The routing table looks like this:

```
D    192.168.10.0/24 [90/2172416] via 172.16.10.6, 02:29:09, Serial0/1
                     [90/2172416] via 172.16.10.2, 02:29:09, Serial0/0
     172.16.0.0/30 is subnetted, 2 subnets
C       172.16.10.4 is directly connected, Serial0/1
C       172.16.10.0 is directly connected, Serial0/0
     10.0.0.0/24 is subnetted, 6 subnets
C       10.10.10.0 is directly connected, Loopback0
C       10.10.11.0 is directly connected, Loopback1
D       10.10.20.0 [90/2300416] via 172.16.10.6, 02:29:09, Serial0/1
                   [90/2297856] via 172.16.10.2, 02:29:10, Serial0/0
D       10.10.30.0 [90/2300416] via 172.16.10.6, 02:29:10, Serial0/1
                   [90/2297856] via 172.16.10.2, 02:29:10, Serial0/0
D       10.10.40.0 [90/2297856] via 172.16.10.6, 02:29:10, Serial0/1
                   [90/2300416] via 172.16.10.2, 02:29:10, Serial0/0
D       10.10.50.0 [90/2297856] via 172.16.10.6, 02:29:11, Serial0/1
                   [90/2300416] via 172.16.10.2, 02:29:11, Serial0/0
```

You can see here that most EIGRP routes are referenced with a *D* and that their administrative distance is 90. Remember that the [90/2300416] represents advertised distance/feasible distance (AD/FD), and in the preceding output, EIGRP is performing equal- and unequal-cost load balancing between two links to our remote networks.

We can get the topology table displayed for us via the show ip eigrp topology command. If the route is in the topology table but not in the routing table, it's a pretty safe assumption that there's a problem between the topology database and the routing table.

The topology table looks like this:

```
P 10.10.10.0/24, 1 successors, FD is 128256
        via Connected, GigabitEthernet0/0
P 10.10.11.0/24, 1 successors, FD is 128256
        via Connected, GigabitEthernet0/1
P 10.10.20.0/24, 1 successors, FD is 2297856
        via 172.16.10.2 (2297856/128256), Serial0/0
        via 172.16.10.6 (2300416/156160), Serial0/1
P 10.10.30.0/24, 1 successors, FD is 2297856
        via 172.16.10.2 (2297856/128256), Serial0/0
        via 172.16.10.6 (2300416/156160), Serial0/1
P 10.10.40.0/24, 1 successors, FD is 2297856
        via 172.16.10.6 (2297856/128256), Serial0/1
        via 172.16.10.2 (2300416/156160), Serial0/0
P 10.10.50.0/24, 1 successors, FD is 2297856
        via 172.16.10.6 (2297856/128256), Serial0/1
        via 172.16.10.2 (2300416/156160), Serial0/0
P 192.168.10.0/24, 2 successors, FD is 2172416
        via 172.16.10.2 (2172416/28160), Serial0/0
        via 172.16.10.6 (2172416/28160), Serial0/1
P 172.16.10.4/30, 1 successors, FD is 2169856
        via Connected, Serial0/1
P 172.16.10.0/30, 1 successors, FD is 2169856
        via Connected, Serial0/0
```

Notice that every route in this output is preceded by a *P*, which shows that these routes are in a *passive state*. This is good because routes in the active state indicate that the router has lost its path to this network and is searching for a replacement. Each entry also reveals the feasible distance, or FD, to each remote network as well as the next-hop neighbor through which packets will travel to this destination. Each entry also has two numbers in brackets, with the first indicating the feasible distance and the second, the advertised distance to a remote network.

The command show ip eigrp traffic enables us to see if updates are being sent. If the counters for EIGRP input and output packets don't increase, it means that no EIGRP information is being sent between peers. The following output indicates that the router is experiencing normal traffic:

```
Router#show ip eigrp traffic
IP-EIGRP Traffic Statistics for process 200
  Hellos sent/received: 2208/2310
  Updates sent/received: 184/183
  Queries sent/received: 17/4
  Replies sent/received: 4/18
  Acks sent/received: 62/65
  Input queue high water mark 2, 0 drops
```

And we can't forget the always useful troubleshooting command show ip protocols. Here's the output:

```
Routing Protocol is "eigrp 20"
  Outgoing update filter list for all interfaces is not set
  Incoming update filter list for all interfaces is not set
  Default networks flagged in outgoing updates
  Default networks accepted from incoming updates
  EIGRP metric weight K1=1, K2=0, K3=1, K4=0, K5=0
  EIGRP maximum hopcount 100
  EIGRP maximum metric variance 2
  Redistributing: eigrp 20
  EIGRP NSF-aware route hold timer is 240s
  Automatic network summarization is not in effect
  Maximum path: 4
  Routing for Networks:
    10.0.0.0
    172.16.0.0
  Routing Information Sources:
    Gateway         Distance      Last Update
    (this router)        90       04:23:51
  . 172.16.10.6          90       02:30:48
    172.16.10.2          90       02:30:48
  Distance: internal 90 external 170
```

In this output, we can see that EIGRP is enabled for autonomous system 20 and that the K values are set to their defaults. The variance is 2, so only equal- and unequal-cost load balancing is happening here. Automatic summarization has been turned off. We can also see that EIGRP is advertising two classful networks and that it sees two neighbors.

The show ip eigrp events command displays a log of every EIGRP event: when routes are injected and removed from the routing table and when EIGRP adjacencies are reset or fail. This information is so helpful in determining if there are routing instabilities in the network! Be advised that this command can result in quite a flood of information even for really simple configurations like ours. To demonstrate, here's the output:

```
Router#show ip eigrp events
Event information for AS 20:
1    22:24:24.258 Metric set: 172.16.10.0/30 2169856
2    22:24:24.258 FC sat rdbmet/succmet: 2169856 0
3    22:24:24.258 FC sat nh/ndbmet: 0.0.0.0 2169856
4    22:24:24.258 Find FS: 172.16.10.0/30 2169856
5    22:24:24.258 Metric set: 172.16.10.4/30 2169856
6    22:24:24.258 FC sat rdbmet/succmet: 2169856 0
7    22:24:24.258 FC sat nh/ndbmet: 0.0.0.0 2169856
8    22:24:24.258 Find FS: 172.16.10.4/30 2169856
9    22:24:24.258 Metric set: 192.168.10.0/24 2172416
10   22:24:24.258 Route install: 192.168.10.0/24 172.16.10.2
11   22:24:24.258 Route install: 192.168.10.0/24 172.16.10.6
12   22:24:24.254 FC sat rdbmet/succmet: 2172416 28160
13   22:24:24.254 FC sat nh/ndbmet: 172.16.10.6 2172416
14   22:24:24.254 Find FS: 192.168.10.0/24 2172416
15   22:24:24.254 Metric set: 10.10.50.0/24 2297856
16   22:24:24.254 Route install: 10.10.50.0/24 172.16.10.6
17   22:24:24.254 FC sat rdbmet/succmet: 2297856 128256
18   22:24:24.254 FC sat nh/ndbmet: 172.16.10.6 2297856
19   22:24:24.254 Find FS: 10.10.50.0/24 2297856
20   22:24:24.254 Metric set: 10.10.40.0/24 2297856
21   22:24:24.254 Route install: 10.10.40.0/24 172.16.10.6
22   22:24:24.250 FC sat rdbmet/succmet: 2297856 128256
 --More--
```

Neighbor Adjacencies

Once you ensure that you have good connectivity between your routers using the ping or traceroute command, EIGRP neighborship is critical in your network. Here are some key things to look for if your routers have not formed an adjacency:

- Interfaces between the devices are down.
- The two routers have mismatching EIGRP autonomous system numbers.
- Proper interfaces are not enabled for the EIGRP process.
- An interface is configured as passive.

- The K values are mismatched.
- EIGRP authentication is misconfigured.

If the adjacency is up but you're not receiving remote network updates, there may be a routing problem, likely caused by these issues:

- The proper networks aren't being advertised under the EIGRP process.
- An access list is blocking the advertisements from remote networks.
- Automatic summary is causing confusion in your discontiguous network.

We'll use Figure 7.8 as our example network. The routers are preconfigured with IP addresses.

FIGURE 7.8   Troubleshooting scenario

A good place to start is by checking to see if we have an adjacency with show ip eigrp neighbors and show ip eigrp interfaces. It's also smart to see what information the show ip eigrp topology command reveals:

```
Corp#sh ip eigrp neighbors
IP-EIGRP neighbors for process 20
Corp#
```

```
Corp#sh ip eigrp interfaces
IP-EIGRP interfaces for process 20
```

		Xmit Queue	Mean	Pacing Time	Multicast	Pending
Interface	Peers	Un/Reliable	SRTT	Un/Reliable	Flow Timer	Routes
Se0/1	0	0/0	0	0/15	50	0
Fa0/0	0	0/0	0	0/1	0	0
Se0/0	0	0/0	0	0/15	50	0

```
Corp#sh ip eigrp top
IP-EIGRP Topology Table for AS(20)/ID(10.10.11.1)

Codes: P - Passive, A - Active, U - Update, Q - Query, R - Reply,
       r - reply Status, s - sia Status
```

```
P 10.1.1.0/24, 1 successors, FD is 28160
        via Connected, FastEthernet0/0
```

AS Number

Rule out layer 1, 2, or 3 issues between routers. If everything seems to be working between the routers except EIGRP, check the EIGRP configurations with the show ip protocols command:

```
Corp#sh ip protocols
Routing Protocol is "eigrp 20"
  Outgoing update filter list for all interfaces is not set
  Incoming update filter list for all interfaces is not set
  Default networks flagged in outgoing updates
  Default networks accepted from incoming updates
  EIGRP metric weight K1=1, K2=0, K3=1, K4=0, K5=0
  EIGRP maximum hopcount 100
  EIGRP maximum metric variance 2
  Redistributing: eigrp 20
  EIGRP NSF-aware route hold timer is 240s
  Automatic network summarization is in effect
  Maximum path: 4
  Routing for Networks:
    10.0.0.0
    172.16.0.0
    192.168.1.0
Passive Interface(s):
    FastEthernet0/1
  Routing Information Sources:
    Gateway         Distance      Last Update
    (this router)        90       20:51:48
    192.168.1.2          90       00:22:58
    172.16.10.6          90       01:58:46
    172.16.10.2          90       01:59:52
  Distance: internal 90 external 170
```

One of the first things to check when your routers are not forming adjacencies is to ensure that each of your EIGRP routers are in the same autonomous system. This output shows that AS 20 is being used.

Load Balancing

By default, EIGRP can provide equal-cost load balancing across up to 4 links. EIGRP can actually load-balance across up to 32 links with 15.0 code (equal or unequal), or, with the pre-15.0 code, up to 16 paths to remote networks with the following command:

```
Router(config)#router eigrp 10
Router(config-router)#maximum-paths ?
  <1-32>  Number of paths
```

To investigate load balancing issues in your routing table, use the show ip eigrp topology command:

```
Router#sh ip eigrp topology
IP-EIGRP Topology Table for AS(20)/ID(10.10.11.1)

Codes: P - Passive, A - Active, U - Update, Q - Query, R - Reply,
       r - reply Status, s - sia Status

P 10.10.10.0/24, 1 successors, FD is 128256
        via Connected, GigbitEthernet0/0
P 10.10.11.0/24, 1 successors, FD is 128256
        via Connected, GigbitEthernet0/1
P 10.10.20.0/24, 1 successors, FD is 2300416
        via 172.16.10.6 (2300416/156160), Serial0/1
        via 172.16.10.2 (3200000/128256), Serial0/0
P 10.10.30.0/24, 1 successors, FD is 2300416
        via 172.16.10.6 (2300416/156160), Serial0/1
        via 172.16.10.2 (3200000/128256), Serial0/0
P 10.10.40.0/24, 1 successors, FD is 2297856
        via 172.16.10.6 (2297856/128256), Serial0/1
        via 172.16.10.2 (3202560/156160), Serial0/0
P 10.10.50.0/24, 1 successors, FD is 2297856
        via 172.16.10.6 (2297856/128256), Serial0/1
        via 172.16.10.2 (3202560/156160), Serial0/0
P 192.168.10.0/24, 1 successors, FD is 2172416
        via 172.16.10.6 (2172416/28160), Serial0/1
        via 172.16.10.2 (3074560/28160), Serial0/0
P 172.16.10.4/30, 1 successors, FD is 2169856
        via Connected, Serial0/1
P 172.16.10.0/30, 1 successors, FD is 3072000
        via Connected, Serial0/0
```

There are two paths to the 192.168.10.0/24 network, but it's using the next hop of 172.16.10.6 because of the feasible distance (FD). The advertised distance between two routers is 28,160, but the cost to get to each router via the WAN link is the same. This means the FD is not the same, meaning we're not load-balancing by default.

Both WAN links are a T1, so this should have load-balanced by default, but EIGRP has determined that it costs more to go through one router than through another. Since EIGRP uses bandwidth and delay of the line to determine the best path, use the show interfaces command:

```
Router#sh int s0/0
Serial0/0 is up, line protocol is up
  Hardware is PowerQUICC Serial
  Description: <<Connection to CR1>>
  Internet address is 172.16.10.1/30
  MTU 1500 bytes, BW 1000 Kbit, DLY 20000 usec,
     reliability 255/255, txload 1/255, rxload 1/255
  Encapsulation HDLC, loopback not set Keepalive set (10 sec)

Router#sh int s0/1
Serial0/1 is up, line protocol is up
  Hardware is PowerQUICC Serial
  Internet address is 172.16.10.5/30
  MTU 1500 bytes, BW 1544 Kbit, DLY 20000 usec,
     reliability 255/255, txload 1/255, rxload 1/255
  Encapsulation HDLC, loopback not set Keepalive set (10 sec)
```

EIGRP uses the following statistics to determine the metrics to a next-hop router: MTU, bandwidth, delay, reliability, and load, with bandwidth and delay enabled by default. The bandwidth on the serial0/0 interface is set to 1,000 Kbit, which is not the default bandwidth. Serial0/1 is set to the default bandwidth of 1,544 Kbit.

Set the bandwidth back to the default on the s0/0 interface and it should start load-balancing to the 192.168.10.0 network. Use the no bandwidth command to set it back to its default of 1.544 Mbps:

```
Router(config)#int s0/0
Router(config-if)#no bandwidth
Router(config-if)#^Z
```

Split Horizon

Split horizon is enabled on interfaces by default, which means that if a route update is received on an interface from a neighbor router, this interface will not advertise those networks back out to the neighbor router who sent them. Use the show ip interface *interface* command:

```
Router#sh ip int s0/0
Serial0/0 is up, line protocol is up
  Internet address is 172.16.10.1/24
  Broadcast address is 255.255.255.255
  Address determined by setup command
  MTU is 1500 bytes
  Helper address is not set
  Directed broadcast forwarding is disabled
  Multicast reserved groups joined: 224.0.0.10
  Outgoing access list is not set
  Inbound  access list is not set
  Proxy ARP is enabled
  Local Proxy ARP is disabled
  Security level is default
  Split horizon is enabled
[output cut]
```

Most of the time it's more helpful than harmful, but let's look at the internetwork in Figure 7.9.

Notice that the SF and NY routers are each advertising their routes to the Corp router. Look what the Corp router sends back to each router in Figure 7.10.

The Corp router is not advertising back out the advertised networks that it received on each interface. This is saving the SF and NY routers from receiving the incorrect route information that they could possibly get to their own network through the Corp router.

This can cause problems. It seems reasonable not to send misinformation back to an originating router. You'll see this create a problem on point-to-multipoint links, such as Frame Relay, when multiple remote routers connect to a single interface at the Corp location. We can use logical interfaces, called subinterfaces, to solve the split horizon issue on a point-to-multipoint interface.

FIGURE 7.9   Split horizon in action, part 1

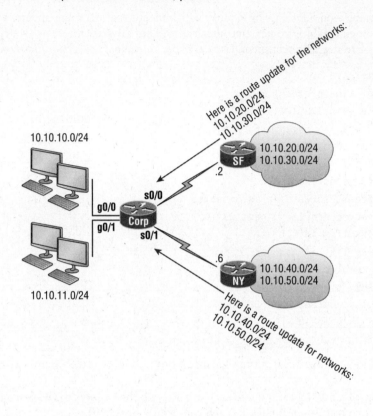

FIGURE 7.10   Split horizon in action, part 2

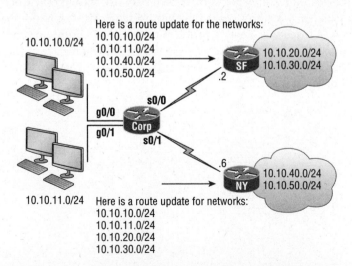

Exam Essentials

Know how to verify EIGRP operation. Know all of the EIGRP show commands and be familiar with their output and the interpretation of the main components of their output.

Be able to read an EIGRP topology table. Understand which are successors, which are feasible successors, and which routes will become successors if the main successor fails.

You must be able to troubleshoot EIGRP Go through the EIGRP troubleshooting scenario and make sure you understand to look for the AS number, ACLs, passive interfaces, variance, and other factors.

Be able to read an EIGRP neighbor table. Understand the output of the show ip eigrp neighbor command.

Troubleshoot and Resolve InterVLAN Routing Problems

The most common problem in computer networks is connectivity. In the following sections, I'll address what you can do to resolve connectivity issues as well as encapsulation errors and subnet, VLAN, and trunking problems with inter-VLAN routing.

Connectivity

VLANs are used to break up broadcast domains in a layer 2 switched network. We assign ports on a switch into a VLAN broadcast domain by using the switchport access vlan command.

The access port carries traffic for a single VLAN that the port is a member of. If members of one VLAN want to communicate with members in the same VLAN that are located on a different switch, then a port between the two switches needs to be either configured to be a member of this single VLAN or configured as a trunk link, which passes information on all VLANs by default.

We're going to use Figure 7.11 as a reference as we go through the procedures for troubleshooting VLAN and trunking.

A couple key times to troubleshoot VLANs are when and if you lose connectivity between hosts and when you're configuring new hosts into a VLAN but they're not working.

Here are the steps we'll follow to troubleshoot VLANs:

1. Verify the VLAN database on all your switches.

2. Verify your MAC address table.

3. Verify that your port VLAN assignments are configured correctly.

FIGURE 7.11   VLAN connectivity

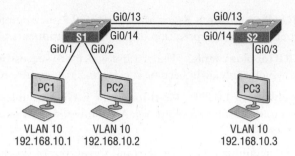

And here's a list of the commands we'll be using in this section:

```
Show vlan
Show mac address-table
Show interfaces interface switchport
switchport access vlan vlan
```

A manager calls and says they can't communicate with the new Sales team member who just connected to the network. The Sales hosts are in VLAN 10. First we'll verify that our databases on both switches are correct.

Use the show vlan or show vlan brief command to check if the expected VLAN is actually in the database.

S1#show vlan

```
VLAN Name                             Status    Ports
---- -------------------------------- --------- -------------------------------
1    default                          active    Gi0/3, Gi0/4, Gi0/5, Gi0/6
                                                Gi0/7, Gi0/8, Gi0/9, Gi0/10
                                                Gi0/11, Gi0/12, Gi0/13, Gi0/14
                                                Gi0/15, Gi0/16, Gi0/17, Gi0/18
                                                Gi0/19, Gi0/20, Gi0/21, Gi0/22
                                                Gi0/23, Gi0/24, Gi0/25, Gi0/26
                                                Gi0/27, Gi0/28
10   Sales                            active    Gi0/1, Gi0/2
20   Accounting                       active
26   Automation10                     active
27   VLAN0027                         active
30   Engineering                      active
170  VLAN0170                         active
501  Private501                       active
502  Private500                       active
[output cut]
```

This output shows that VLAN 10 is in the local database and that Gi0/1 and Gi0/2 are associated to VLAN 10.

Verify the CAM with the show mac address-table command:

```
S1#show mac address-table
          Mac Address Table
-------------------------------------------

Vlan    Mac Address       Type       Ports
----    -----------       --------   -----
 All    0100.0ccc.cccc    STATIC     CPU
[output cut]
   1    000d.2830.2f00    DYNAMIC    Gi0/24
   1    0021.1c91.0d8d    DYNAMIC    Gi0/13
   1    0021.1c91.0d8e    DYNAMIC    Gi0/14
   1    b414.89d9.1882    DYNAMIC    Gi0/17
   1    b414.89d9.1883    DYNAMIC    Gi0/18
   1    ecc8.8202.8282    DYNAMIC    Gi0/15
   1    ecc8.8202.8283    DYNAMIC    Gi0/16
  10    001a.2f55.c9e8    DYNAMIC    Gi0/1
  10    001b.d40a.0538    DYNAMIC    Gi0/2
Total Mac Addresses for this criterion: 29
```

The switch will show quite a few MAC addresses assigned to the CPU at the top of the output, which are used by the switch to manage the ports. The very first MAC address listed is your base MAC address of the switch and used by STP in the bridge ID. In the preceding output, we can see that there is a MAC address associated with VLAN 10 and that it was dynamically learned. We can also establish that this MAC address is associated to Gi0/1. S1 looks really good!

Let's take a look at S2 now. First, let's confirm that port PC3 is connected and check its configuration. Use the command show interfaces *interface* switchport command to do that:

```
S2#sh interfaces gi0/3 switchport
Name: Gi0/3
Switchport: Enabled
Administrative Mode: dynamic desirable
Operational Mode: static access
Administrative Trunking Encapsulation: negotiate
Operational Trunking Encapsulation: native
Negotiation of Trunking: On
Access Mode VLAN: 10 (Inactive)
Trunking Native Mode VLAN: 1 (default)
[output cut]
```

We can see that the port is enabled and that it's set to dynamic desirable. This means that if it connects to another Cisco switch, it will desire to trunk on that link. But keep in mind that we're using it as an access port, which is confirmed by the operational mode of static access. At the end of the output, the text shows Access Mode VLAN: 10 (Inactive). This is not a good thing! Let's examine S2's CAM and see what we find out:

```
S2#sh mac address-table
          Mac Address Table
-------------------------------------------

Vlan    Mac Address       Type        Ports
----    -----------       --------    -----
All     0100.0ccc.cccc    STATIC      CPU
[output cut]
   1    001b.d40a.0538    DYNAMIC     Gi0/13
   1    0021.1bee.a70d    DYNAMIC     Gi0/13
   1    b414.89d9.1884    DYNAMIC     Gi0/17
   1    b414.89d9.1885    DYNAMIC     Gi0/18
   1    ecc8.8202.8285    DYNAMIC     Gi0/16
Total Mac Addresses for this criterion: 26
```

Referring back to Figure 7.11, we can see that the host is connected to Gi0/3. The problem here is that we don't see a MAC address dynamically associated to Gi0/3 in the MAC address table. So what do we know so far that can help us? First, we can see that Gi0/3 is configured into VLAN 10 but that VLAN is inactive. Second, the host off of Gi0/3 doesn't appear in the CAM table. Next, take a look at the VLAN database:

```
S2#show vlan brief

VLAN Name                             Status     Ports
---- -------------------------------- ---------  -------------------------------
1    default                          active     Gi0/1, Gi0/2, Gi0/4, Gi0/5
                                                 Gi0/6, Gi0/7, Gi0/8, Gi0/9
                                                 Gi0/10, Gi0/11, Gi0/12, Gi0/13
                                                 Gi0/14, Gi0/15, Gi0/16, Gi0/17
                                                 Gi0/18, Gi0/19, Gi0/20, Gi0/21
                                                 Gi0/22, Gi0/23, Gi0/24, Gi0/25
                                                 Gi0/26, Gi0/27, Gi0/28

26   Automation10                     active
27   VLAN0027                         active
30   Engineering                      active
170  VLAN0170                         active
[output cut]
```

Look at that: there is no VLAN 10 in the database! Clearly that's the problem, but also an easy one to fix by simply creating the VLAN in the database:

```
S2#config t
S2(config)#vlan 10
S2(config-vlan)#name Sales
```

That's all there is to it. Now let's check the CAM again:

```
S2#sh mac address-table
        Mac Address Table
-------------------------------------------

Vlan    Mac Address       Type        Ports
----    -----------       --------    -----
 All    0100.0ccc.cccc    STATIC      CPU
[output cut]
   1    0021.1bee.a70d    DYNAMIC     Gi0/13
  10    001a.6c46.9b09    DYNAMIC     Gi0/3
Total Mac Addresses for this criterion: 22
```

We're good to go—the MAC address off of Gi0/3 shows in the MAC address table configured into VLAN 10.

If the port had been assigned to the wrong VLAN, it would have used the switch access vlan command to correct the VLAN membership. Here's an example of how to do that:

```
S2#config t
S2(config)#int gi0/3
S2(config-if)#switchport access vlan 10
S2(config-if)#do sh vlan
```

```
VLAN Name                             Status    Ports
---- -------------------------------- --------- -------------------------------
1    default                          active    Gi0/1, Gi0/2, Gi0/4, Gi0/5
                                                Gi0/6, Gi0/7, Gi0/8, Gi0/9
                                                Gi0/10, Gi0/11, Gi0/12, Gi0/13
                                                Gi0/14, Gi0/15, Gi0/16, Gi0/17
                                                Gi0/18, Gi0/19, Gi0/20, Gi0/21
                                                Gi0/22, Gi0/23, Gi0/24, Gi0/25
                                                Gi0/26, Gi0/27, Gi0/28
10   Sales                            active    Gi0/3
```

We can see that our port Gi0/3 is in the VLAN 10 membership. Now let's try to ping from PC1 to PC3:

```
PC1#ping 192.168.10.3
Type escape sequence to abort.
Sending 5, 100-byte ICMP Echos to 192.168.10.3, timeout is 2 seconds:
.....
Success rate is 0 percent (0/5)
```

No luck, so let's see if PC1 can ping PC2:

```
PC1#ping 192.168.10.2
Type escape sequence to abort.
Sending 5, 100-byte ICMP Echos to 192.168.10.2, timeout is 2 seconds:
!!!!!
Success rate is 100 percent (5/5), round-trip min/avg/max = 1/2/4 ms
PC1#
```

That worked! I can ping a host connected to the same switch, which is a member of the same VLAN, but I can't ping to a host on another switch that's a member of VLAN 10. To get to the bottom of this, let's quickly summarize what we've learned so far:

1. We know that the VLAN database is now correct on each switch.

2. The MAC address table shows the ARP entries for each host as well as a connection to each switch.

3. We've verified that our VLAN memberships are now correct on all the ports we're using.

But since we still can't ping to a host on another switch, we need to start checking out the connections between our switches.

Encapsulation

One of the issues you need to be aware of, as well as check for, is the frame tagging method. Some switches run 802.1q, and some run both 802.1q and ISL (Inter-Switch Link routing), so be sure the tagging method is compatible among all of your switches.

Set one side of each link to dynamic auto and the switch will trunk with a port set to desirable or on:

```
S2(config)#int gi0/13
S2(config-if)#switchport mode dynamic desirable
23:11:37: %LINEPROTO-5-UPDOWN: Line protocol on Interface GigabitEthernet0/13,
changed state to down
23:11:37: %LINEPROTO-5-UPDOWN: Line protocol on Interface Vlan1, changed state
to down
```

```
23:11:40: %LINEPROTO-5-UPDOWN: Line protocol on Interface GigabitEthernet0/13,
changed state to up
23:12:10: %LINEPROTO-5-UPDOWN: Line protocol on Interface Vlan1, changed state
to up

S2(config-if)#do show int trunk

Port        Mode        Encapsulation Status       Native vlan
Gi0/13      desirable   n-isl         trunking     1
[output cut]
```

With one side in auto and the other now in desirable, DTPs will be exchanged and they will trunk. Notice in the preceding output that the mode of S2's Gi0/13 link is desirable and that the switches actually negotiated ISL as a trunk encapsulation! Don't forget to notice the native VLAN.

Subnet

When you create VLANs, you're given the ability to create smaller broadcast domains within a layer 2 switched internetwork by assigning different ports on the switch to service different subnetworks. A VLAN is treated like its own subnet or broadcast domain, meaning that frames broadcast onto the network are only switched between the ports logically grouped within the same VLAN.

Figure 7.12 shows how we would create a router on a stick using a router's physical interface by creating logical interfaces—one for each VLAN.

FIGURE 7.12   A router creates logical interfaces.

We have one physical interface divided into multiple subinterfaces, with one subnet assigned per VLAN, each subinterface being the default gateway address for each VLAN/subnet. An encapsulation identifier must be assigned to each subinterface to define the VLAN ID of that subinterface.

Instead of using an external router interface for each VLAN, or an external router on a stick, we can configure logical interfaces on the backplane of the layer 3 switch; this is called inter-VLAN routing (IVR), and it's configured with a switched virtual interface (SVI). Figure 7.13 shows how hosts see these virtual interfaces.

It appears there's a router present, but there is no physical router present as there was when we used router on a stick. The IVR process takes little effort and is easy to implement, which makes it very cool! Plus, it's a lot more efficient for inter-VLAN routing than an external router is. To implement IVR on a multilayer switch, we just need to create logical interfaces in the switch configuration for each VLAN.

FIGURE 7.13   With IVR, routing runs on the backplane of the switch, and it appears to the hosts that a router is present.

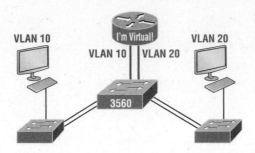

When it comes to troubleshooting subnets with inter-VLAN routing, remember that each VLAN is one subnet. Check connectivity between the switches and the subinterface of the router or layer 3 switch, and ensure that the correct encapsulation method is used.

Native VLAN

VLANs can be set up to span across multiple switches. When frames travel between switches, they are tagged with a particular VLAN ID and sent down a trunk port. Trunk ports support tagged and untagged traffic simultaneously if you're using 802.1q trunking. The trunk port is assigned a default port VLAN ID (PVID) for a VLAN upon which all untagged traffic will travel. This VLAN is also called the native VLAN and is always VLAN 1 by default. Take a look at Figure 7.14.

Similarly, any untagged or tagged traffic with a NULL (unassigned) VLAN ID is assumed to belong to the VLAN with the port default PVID. Again, this would be VLAN 1 by default. A packet with a VLAN ID equal to the outgoing port native VLAN is sent untagged and can communicate to only hosts or devices in that same VLAN. All other VLAN traffic has to be sent with a VLAN tag to communicate within a particular VLAN that corresponds with that tag.

Port Mode Trunk Status

When you lose connectivity between hosts in the same VLAN that are located on different switches, Cisco refers to this as *VLAN leaking*.

These are the steps we'll take to troubleshoot VLANs:

1. Verify that the interface configuration is set to the correct trunk parameters.

2. Verify that the ports are configured correctly.

3. Verify the native VLAN on each switch.

The show vlan command will only show you access ports. It will not display trunk ports. We can use the show interfaces *interface* switchport command to verify this as well:

```
S1#sho interfaces gi0/13 switchport
Name: Gi0/13
Switchport: Enabled
Administrative Mode: dynamic auto
Operational Mode: static access
Administrative Trunking Encapsulation: negotiate
Operational Trunking Encapsulation: native
Negotiation of Trunking: On
Access Mode VLAN: 1 (default)
Trunking Native Mode VLAN: 1 (default)
```

FIGURE 7.14   VLANs can span multiple switches by using trunk links, which carry traffic for multiple VLANs.

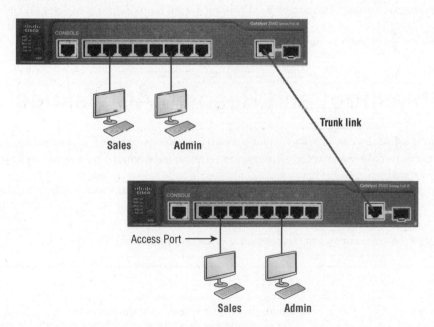

This output tells us that interface Gi0/13 is in mode dynamic auto. But its operational mode is static access, meaning it's not a trunk port. We can look closer at its trunking capabilities with the show interfaces *interface* trunk command:

```
S1#sh interfaces gi0/1 trunk
```

```
Port        Mode        Encapsulation  Status         Native vlan
Gi0/1       auto        negotiate      not-trunking   1
[output cut]
```

Sure enough—the port is not trunking. Notice that we can see that native VLAN is set to VLAN 1, which is the default native VLAN. This means that VLAN 1 is the default VLAN for untagged traffic.

Exam Essentials

Remember how to test for connectivity issues within a network.   Ping, Traceroute, and Telnet are excellent tools to test for connectivity within a network.

Understand the encapsulation methods used in inter-VLAN routing.   Cisco routers and switches support the IEEE 802.1q or the Cisco proprietary ISL encapsulation.

Understand the importance of subnets, native VLANs, and how to check the status of trunk ports on a switch.   Remember that when creating VLANs on a switch, you're also creating a separate subnet. The native VLAN is used with trunked ports to send tagged and untagged traffic to their perspective VLAN hosts. The command show interface trunk will display the ports on a switch when trunking is configured.

Troubleshoot and Resolve ACL Issues

Troubleshooting ACLs can be tricky, and depending on the complexity, it can be time consuming. In this part of the chapter, I will go over some troubleshooting methods to help resolve issues with ACLs.

To start troubleshooting ACLs, it's good to know what configurations are on the router. Table 7.4 lists some of the commands you can use to verify them.

TABLE 7.4   Commands used to verify access list configuration

Command	Effect
show access-list	Displays all access lists configured on the router and their parameters. Also shows statistics about how many times the line either permitted or denied a packet. This command does not show you which interface the list is applied on.

Command	Effect
show access-list 110	Reveals only the parameters for access list 110. Again, this command will not reveal the specific interface the list is set on.
show ip access-list	Shows only the IP access lists configured on the router.
show ip interface	Displays which interfaces have access lists set on them.
show running-config	Shows the access lists and the specific interfaces that have ACLs applied on them.

The show access-list command will list all ACLs on the router, whether they're applied to an interface or not:

```
Lab_A#show access-list
Standard IP access list 10
    10 deny    172.16.40.0, wildcard bits 0.0.0.255
    20 permit any
Standard IP access list BlockSales
    10 deny    172.16.40.0, wildcard bits 0.0.0.255
    20 permit any
Extended IP access list 110
    10 deny tcp any host 172.16.30.5 eq ftp
    20 deny tcp any host 172.16.30.5 eq telnet
    30 permit ip any any
    40 permit tcp host 192.168.177.2 host 172.22.89.26 eq www
    50 deny tcp any host 172.22.89.26 eq www
Lab_A#
```

Here's the output of the show ip interface command:

```
Lab_A#show ip interface fa0/1
FastEthernet0/1 is up, line protocol is up
   Internet address is 172.16.30.1/24
   Broadcast address is 255.255.255.255
   Address determined by non-volatile memory
   MTU is 1500 bytes
   Helper address is not set
   Directed broadcast forwarding is disabled
   Outgoing access list is 110
   Inbound access list is not set
```

```
    Proxy ARP is enabled
    Security level is default
    Split horizon is enabled
[output cut]
```

Be sure to notice the bold line indicating that the outgoing list on this interface is 110.

Statistics

To view the statistics of the number of times a line was permitted or denied, use the show access-list command:

```
Lab_A#show access-list
Extended IP access list 110
    10 deny tcp any host 172.16.30.5 eq ftp
    20 deny tcp any host 172.16.30.5 eq telnet (10 matches)
    30 permit ip any any
    40 permit tcp host 192.168.177.2 host 172.22.89.26 eq www
    50 deny tcp any host 172.22.89.26 eq www
Lab_A#
```

In this example, 10 attempts were made to telnet into a host with the IP of 172.16.30.5

Permitted Networks

When configuring ACLs, you have the option to permit a specific host, or you can permit specific hosts within a network. This is accomplished with the wildcard mask.

Wildcards are used with access lists to specify an individual host, a network, or a specific range of a network or networks. Block sizes are used to specify a range of addresses.

Wildcards are used with the host or network address to tell the router a range of available addresses to filter. To specify a host, the address would look like this:

```
172.16.30.5 0.0.0.0
```

The four zeros represent each octet of the address. Whenever a zero is present, it indicates that octet in the address must match the corresponding reference octet exactly. To specify that an octet can be any value, use the value 255. Here's an example of how a /24 subnet is specified with a wildcard mask:

```
172.16.30.0 0.0.0.255
```

This tells the router to match up the first three octets exactly, but the fourth octet can be any value.

Direction

There are some general access-list guidelines that you should keep in mind when creating and implementing access lists on a router:

You can assign only one access list per interface per protocol per direction. This means that when applying IP access lists, you can have only one inbound access list and one outbound access list per interface.

Interface

Here is an example of configuring an ACL on a router interface:

```
Lab_A#config t
Lab_A(config)#access-list 10 deny 172.16.40.0 0.0.0.255
Lab_A(config)#access-list 10 permit any
Lab_A(config)#int fa0/1
Lab_A(config-if)#ip access-group 10 out
```

Any packet trying to exit out Fa0/1 will have to go through the access list first. If there were an inbound list placed on Fa0/0, then any packet trying to enter interface Fa0/0 would have to go through the access list before being routed to an exit interface.

Exam Essentials

Remember the command to verify an access list on a router interface.   To see whether an access list is set on an interface and in which direction it is filtering, use the show ip interface command. This command will not show you the contents of the access list, merely which access lists are applied on the interface.

Remember the command to verify the access list configuration.   To see the configured access lists on your router, use the show access-list command. This command will not show you which interfaces have an access list set.

Troubleshoot and Resolve WAN Implementation Issues

Cisco supports several different wide area network (WAN) protocols that allow your local LAN to connect to other local LANs outside of your network.

WANs can use a number of different connection types available on the market today. Figure 7.15 shows the different WAN connection types that can be used to connect your LANs (made up of data terminal equipment, or DTE) together over the data (data communication equipment (DCE) network.

FIGURE 7.15   WAN connection types

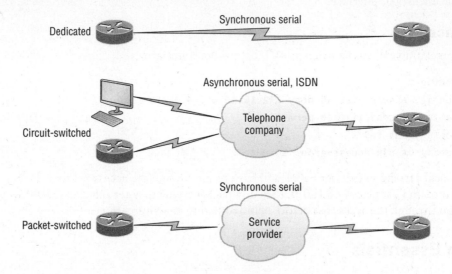

Here's an overview of each of these connections:

Dedicated (leased lines)   These are usually referred to as a *point-to-point* or dedicated connection. A *leased line* is a pre-established WAN communications path that goes from the CPE through the DCE switch, then over to the CPE of the remote site. The CPE enables DTE networks to communicate at any time with no cumbersome setup procedures to muddle through before transmitting data.

Circuit switching   When you hear the term *circuit switching*, think phone call. The big advantage is cost; most plain old telephone service (POTS) and ISDN dial-up connections are not flat rate, which is their advantage over dedicated lines. No data can transfer before an end-to-end connection is established. Circuit switching uses dial-up modems or ISDN and is used for low-bandwidth data transfers.

Packet switching   This is a WAN switching method that allows you to share bandwidth with other companies to save money. Packet switching will only really work for you if your data transfers are bursty, not continuous; think of a highway, where you can only go as fast as the traffic—packet switching is the same thing. Frame Relay and X.25 are packet-switching technologies with speeds that can range from 56 Kbps up to T3 (45 Mbps).

Serial Interfaces

Cisco supports many layer 2 WAN encapsulations on its serial interfaces, including HDLC, PPP, and Frame Relay. You can view them via the encapsulation ? command from any serial interface, but understand that the output you'll get can vary based upon the specific IOS version you're running:

```
Corp#config t
Corp(config)#int s0/0/0
Corp(config-if)#encapsulation ?
  atm-dxi      ATM-DXI encapsulation
  frame-relay  Frame Relay networks
  hdlc         Serial HDLC synchronous
  lapb         LAPB (X.25 Level 2)
  ppp          Point-to-Point protocol
  smds         Switched Megabit Data Service (SMDS)
  x25          X.25
```

If I had other types of interfaces on my router, I would have a different set of encapsulation options. Don't forget, you can't configure an Ethernet encapsulation on a serial interface or vice versa!

PPP

There are several things to consider when troubleshooting PPP on serial interfaces.

To verify that PPP encapsulation is enabled, take a look at a non-production network serial link in Figure 7.16.

FIGURE 7.16   PPP authentication example

Pod1R1   Pod1R2

hostname Pod1R1   hostname Pod1R2
username Pod1R2 password cisco   username Pod1R1 password cisco
interface serial 0   interface serial 0
ip address 10.0.1.1 255.255.255.0   ip address 10.0.1.2 255.255.255.0
encapsulation ppp   encapsulation ppp
clock rate 64000   bandwidth 512
bandwidth 512   ppp authentication chap
ppp authentication chap

You can start verifying the configuration with the show `interface` command like this:

```
Pod1R1#sh int s0/0
Serial0/0 is up, line protocol is up
  Hardware is PowerQUICC Serial
  Internet address is 10.0.1.1/24
  MTU 1500 bytes, BW 1544 Kbit, DLY 20000 usec,
      reliability 239/255, txload 1/255, rxload 1/255
  Encapsulation PPP
  loopback not set
  Keepalive set (10 sec)
  LCP Open
  Open: IPCP, CDPCP
[output cut]
```

The first line of output is important because it tells us that serial 0/0 is up/up. Notice that the interface encapsulation is PPP and that LCP is open. This means that it has negotiated the session establishment and all is well.

Take a look at the configurations in Figure 7.17.

FIGURE 7.17   Failed PPP authentication

Pod1R1   Pod1R2

hostname Pod1R1   hostname Pod1R2
username Pod1R2 password Cisco   username Pod1R1 password cisco
interface serial 0   interface serial 0
ip address 10.0.1.1 255.255.255.0   ip address 10.0.1.2 255.255.255.0
clock rate 64000   bandwidth 512
bandwidth 512   encapsulation ppp
encapsulation ppp   ppp authentication chap
ppp authentication chap

In this example, authentication will fail because of mismatched passwords. Usernames and passwords are case sensitive.

Take a look at the show `interface` command:

```
Pod1R1#sh int s0/0
Serial0/0 is up, line protocol is down
  Hardware is PowerQUICC Serial
  Internet address is 10.0.1.1/24
```

```
MTU 1500 bytes, BW 1544 Kbit, DLY 20000 usec,
    reliability 243/255, txload 1/255, rxload 1/255
Encapsulation PPP, loopback not set
Keepalive set (10 sec)
LCP Closed
Closed: IPCP, CDPCP
```

The first line of output shows us Serial0/0 is up and line protocol is down. This is because there are no keepalives coming from the remote router. Also notice that the LCP and NCP (IPCP, CDPCP) are closed because the authentication failed.

Debugging PPP Authentication

To display the CHAP authentication process as it occurs between two routers in the network, just use the command debug ppp authentication.

If your PPP encapsulation and authentication are set up correctly on both routers and your usernames and passwords are all good, then the debug ppp authentication command will display the results of the process, which is known as a three-way handshake.

If the password is wrong as they were previously in the PPP authentication failure example, the results would be displayed as a failure.

PPP with CHAP authentication is a three-way authentication, and if the username and passwords aren't configured exactly the way they should be, then the authentication will fail and the link will go down.

Mismatched WAN Encapsulations

If you have a point-to-point link but the encapsulations aren't the same, the link will never come up. The following router output shows if one link is configured with PPP and the other one is configured with HDLC.

```
Pod1R1#sh int s0/0
Serial0/0 is up, line protocol is down
  Hardware is PowerQUICC Serial
  Internet address is 10.0.1.1/24
  MTU 1500 bytes, BW 1544 Kbit, DLY 20000 usec,
    reliability 254/255, txload 1/255, rxload 1/255
  Encapsulation PPP, loopback not set
  Keepalive set (10 sec)
  LCP REQsent
Closed: IPCP, CDPCP
```

The serial interface is up/down and LCP is sending requests but will never receive any responses because router Pod1R2 is using the HDLC encapsulation. To fix this problem, you would have to go to router Pod1R2 and configure the PPP encapsulation on the serial interface.

You can set a Cisco serial interface back to the default of HDLC with the `no encapsulation` command:

```
Router(config)#int s0/0
Router(config-if)#no encapsulation
*Feb 7 16:00:18.678:%LINEPROTO-5-UPDOWN: Line protocol on Interface Serial0/0,
changed state to up
```

The link came up because it now matches the encapsulation on the other end of the link!

Mismatched IP Addresses

Another thing to consider when troubleshooting serial interfaces is IP addresses. This can be tricky to troubleshoot. The interface will appear to be up, but no communication will occur if one of the two links is configured with the wrong IP address. Take a look at Figure 7.18.

FIGURE 7.18   Mismatched IP addresses

Pod1R1   Pod1R2

```
hostname Pod1R1                          hostname Pod1R2
username Pod1R2 password cisco           username Pod1R1 password cisco
interface serial 0                      interface serial 0
ip address 10.0.1.1 255.255.255.0       ip address 10.2.1.2 255.255.255.0
clock rate 64000                        bandwidth 512
bandwidth 512                           encapsulation ppp
encapsulation ppp                       ppp authentication chap
ppp authentication chap
```

Looking at the following output, the interface shows that serial0/0 is up, line protocol is up, but this will never work!

```
Pod1R1#sh int s0/0
Serial0/0 is up, line protocol is up
  Hardware is PowerQUICC Serial
  Internet address is 10.0.1.1/24
  MTU 1500 bytes, BW 1544 Kbit, DLY 20000 usec,
     reliability 255/255, txload 1/255, rxload 1/255
  Encapsulation PPP, loopback not set
  Keepalive set (10 sec)
  LCP Open
  Open: IPCP, CDPCP
```

For the Cisco exam, you need to be able to troubleshoot PPP from the routing table.

To find and fix these problems, you can also use the show running-config, show interfaces, or show ip interfaces brief command on each router, or you can use the show cdp neighbors detail command.

Frame Relay

Frame Relay was one of the most popular WAN services deployed over the past two decades because of cost. By default, Frame Relay is classified as a nonbroadcast multi-access (NBMA) network, meaning it doesn't send any broadcasts such as RIP updates across the network.

In addition, Frame Relay is considerably more complex than the simple leased-line networks like those that use the HDLC and PPP protocols. The leased-line networks are easy to conceptualize, but not so much when it comes to Frame Relay.

There are several commands you can use to troubleshoot Frame Relay. To view the available options, use the show frame ? command:

```
Corp>sho frame ?
end-to-end      Frame-relay end-to-end VC information
fragment        show frame relay fragmentation information
ip              show frame relay IP statistics
lapf            show frame relay lapf status/statistics
lmi             show frame relay lmi statistics
map             Frame-Relay map table
pvc             show frame relay pvc statistics
qos-autosense   show frame relay qos-autosense information
route           show frame relay route
svc             show frame relay SVC stuff
traffic         Frame-Relay protocol statistics
vofr            Show frame-relay VoFR statistics
```

The most common parameters for the show frame-relay command are lmi, pvc, and map.

The *show frame-relay lmi* Command

The show frame-relay lmi command will give you the LMI traffic statistics exchanged between the local router and the Frame Relay switch as shown here:

```
Corp#sh frame lmi

LMI Statistics for interface Serial0/0 (Frame Relay DTE)LMI TYPE = CISCO
  Invalid Unnumbered info 0      Invalid Prot Disc 0
  Invalid dummy Call Ref 0       Invalid Msg Type 0
```

```
Invalid Status Message 0        Invalid Lock Shift 0
Invalid Information ID 0        Invalid Report IE Len 0
Invalid Report Request 0       Invalid Keep IE Len 0
Num Status Enq. Sent 61         Num Status msgs Rcvd 0
Num Update Status Rcvd 0       Num Status Timeouts 60
```

The router output from the show frame-relay lmi command shows you any LMI errors, plus the LMI type.

The *show frame pvc* Command

The show frame pvc command shows you a list of all configured PVCs and DLCI numbers. It provides the status of each PVC connection and traffic statistics too. It will also give you the number of BECN, FECN, and DE packets sent and received on the router per PVC:

```
Corp#sho frame pvc

PVC Statistics for interface Serial0/0 (Frame Relay DTE)

DLCI = 102,DLCI USAGE = LOCAL,PVC STATUS =ACTIVE,
INTERFACE = Serial0/0.102
 input pkts 50977876    output pkts 41822892
  in bytes 3137403144
 out bytes 3408047602    dropped pkts 5
  in FECN pkts 0
 in BECN pkts 0      out FECN pkts 0    out BECN pkts 0
 in DE pkts 9393     out DE pkts 0
 pvc create time 7w3d, last time pvc status changed 7w3d

DLCI = 103,DLCI USAGE =LOCAL,PVC STATUS =ACTIVE,
INTERFACE = Serial0/0.103
 input pkts 30572401    output pkts 31139837
  in bytes 1797291100
 out bytes 3227181474    dropped pkts 5
  in FECN pkts 0
 in BECN pkts 0      out FECN pkts 0    out BECN pkts 0
 in DE pkts 28       out DE pkts 0
 pvc create time 7w3d, last time pvc status changed 7w3d
```

If you want to see information about only PVC 102, you can type the command **show frame-relay pvc 102**.

The *show interface* Command

The show interface command will check for LMI traffic. It displays information about the encapsulation, layer 2 and layer 3 information, and line protocol, DLCI, and LMI information:

```
Corp#sho int s0/0
Serial0/0 is up, line protocol is up
 Hardware is HD64570
 MTU 1500 bytes, BW 1544 Kbit, DLY 20000 usec, rely
  255/255, load 2/255
 Encapsulation FRAME-RELAY, loopback not set, keepalive
  set (10 sec)
 LMI enq sent 451751,LMI stat recvd 451750,LMI upd recvd
  164,DTE LMI up
 LMI enq recvd 0, LMI stat sent 0, LMI upd sent 0
 LMI DLCI 1023 LMI type is CISCO frame relay DTE
 Broadcast queue 0/64, broadcasts sent/dropped 0/0,
  interface broadcasts 839294
```

The default LMI type for Cisco routers is LMI DLCI 1023, and for ANSI and Q.933A, it is zero (0). If the LMI DLCI is neither of these two values, there are issues with the service provider.

The *show frame map* Command

The show frame map command displays the mappings from the Network layer to DLCI:

```
Corp#show frame map
Serial0/0.102 (up): ip 10.1.12.2 dlci 102(0x66,0x400),
              dynamic, broadcast,, status defined, active
Serial0/0.103 (up): ip 10.1.13.2 dlci 103(0x67,0x410),
              dynamic, broadcast,, status defined, active
```

If Network layer addresses are marked dynamic, it means they were resolved with the dynamic protocol Inverse ARP (IARP). After the DLCI number is listed, you can see some numbers in parentheses. The first one is 0x66, which is the hex equivalent for the DLCI number 102, used on serial 0/0.102. And the 0x67 is the hex for DLCI 103 used on serial 0/0.103. The second numbers, 0x400 and 0x410, are the DLCI numbers configured in the Frame Relay frame. They're different because of the way the bits are spread out in the frame.

The preceding output is telling the Corp router that to get to 10.1.12.2, use DLCI 102. To get to a router with IP address 10.1.13.2, use DLCI 103. The Corp router would never use a remote DLCI.

The *debug frame lmi* Command

The debug frame lmi command will show real-time output on the router consoles by default (as with any debug command). This will enable you to verify and troubleshoot the Frame Relay connection by helping you determine whether the router and switch are exchanging the correct LMI information as in this example:

```
Corp#debug frame-relay lmi
Serial3/1(in): Status, myseq 214
RT IE 1, length 1, type 0
KA IE 3, length 2, yourseq 214, myseq 214
PVC IE 0x7 , length 0x6 , dlci 130, status 0x2 , bw 0
Serial3/1(out): StEnq, myseq 215, yourseen 214, DTE up
datagramstart = 0x1959DF4, datagramsize = 13
FR encap = 0xFCF10309
00 75 01 01 01 03 02 D7 D6

Serial3/1(in): Status, myseq 215
RT IE 1, length 1, type 1
KA IE 3, length 2, yourseq 215, myseq 215
Serial3/1(out): StEnq, myseq 216, yourseen 215, DTE up
datagramstart = 0x1959DF4, datagramsize = 13
FR encap = 0xFCF10309
00 75 01 01 01 03 02 D8 D7
```

When you're troubleshooting serial encapsulation problems, there are two Frame Relay encapsulations: Cisco and IETF. Cisco is the default, and it means that you have a Cisco router on each end of the Frame Relay network. If you don't have a Cisco router on the remote end of your Frame Relay network, then you need to run the IETF encapsulation:

```
RouterA(config)#int s0
RouterA(config-if)#encapsulation frame-relay ?
  ietf  Use RFC1490 encapsulation
  <cr>
RouterA(config-if)#encapsulation frame-relay ietf
```

Verify that you're using the correct encapsulation, then check out your Frame Relay mappings. Take a look at Figure 7.19.

RouterA can't talk to RouterB across the Frame Relay network because you cannot use a remote DLCI to communicate with the Frame Relay switch; you must use *your* DLCI number! The mapping should have included DLCI 100 instead of DLCI 200.

Routing protocol problems can often be associated with Frame Relay. See if you can find a problem with the two configurations in Figure 7.20.

FIGURE 7.19   Frame Relay mappings

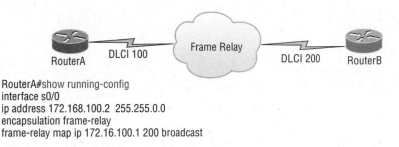

```
RouterA#show running-config
interface s0/0
ip address 172.168.100.2  255.255.0.0
encapsulation frame-relay
frame-relay map ip 172.16.100.1 200 broadcast
```

FIGURE 7.20   Frame Relay routing problems

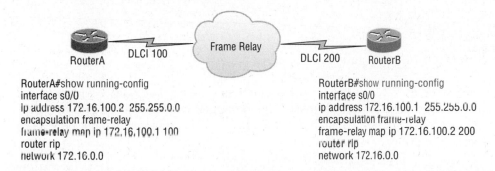

```
RouterA#show running-config
interface s0/0
ip address 172.16.100.2  255.255.0.0
encapsulation frame-relay
frame-relay map ip 172.16.100.1 100
router rip
network 172.16.0.0
```

```
RouterB#show running-config
interface s0/0
ip address 172.16.100.1  255.255.0.0
encapsulation frame-relay
frame-relay map ip 172.16.100.2 200
router rip
network 172.16.0.0
```

Remember, Frame Relay is a nonbroadcast multi-access (NBMA) network by default, meaning that it doesn't allow any broadcasts across the PVC. The mapping statements need to have the broadcast argument at the end of the line, so broadcasts such as RIP updates or multicasts to neighbors such as Hello packets can be sent across the PVC:

```
frame-relay map ip 172.16.100.1 100 broadcast
```

There may be problems with the routing protocols EIGRP and OSPF over Frame Relay as well. Take a look at Figure 7.21.

Frame Relay nonbroadcast multi-access (NBMA) networks won't allow broadcasts or multicasts, so an OSPF router will not attempt to dynamically discover any OSPF neighbors on the Frame Relay interface. This means that elections won't be allowed; you'd have to statically configure OSPF neighbors, plus the Corp router would need to be configured as a DR. With serial links, an NBMA network behaves like Ethernet and a DR is needed to exchange routing information. Only the Corp router can act as a DR because it would have the PVCs for all other routers. The easiest way to fix this is to use the command ip ospf network point-to-multipoint on all router Frame Relay interfaces—not just the Corp router, but all branches too!

FIGURE 7.21 Frame Relay OSPF routing problems

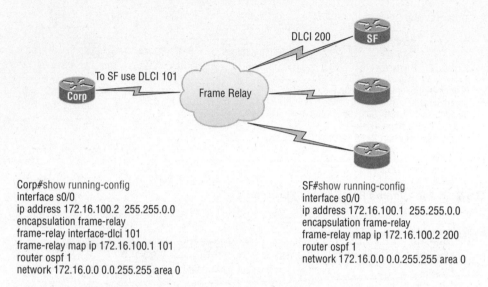

Corp#show running-config
interface s0/0
ip address 172.16.100.2 255.255.0.0
encapsulation frame-relay
frame-relay interface-dlci 101
frame-relay map ip 172.16.100.1 101
router ospf 1
network 172.16.0.0 0.0.255.255 area 0

SF#show running-config
interface s0/0
ip address 172.16.100.1 255.255.0.0
encapsulation frame-relay
frame-relay map ip 172.16.100.2 200
router ospf 1
network 172.16.0.0 0.0.255.255 area 0

Looking at Figure 7.22 you can see three remote sites connection to the Corp router with all routers running EIGRP. The hosts behind the Corp router can communicate with all hosts in all remote networks, but hosts in SF, LA, and NY cannot communicate with each other.

FIGURE 7.22 Frame Relay EIGRP routing problems

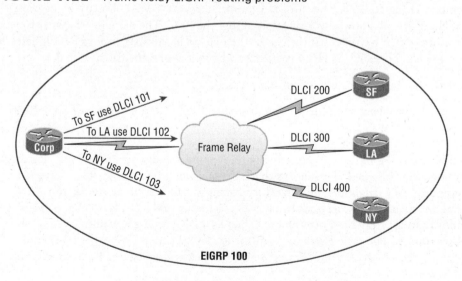

Look at the configuration of the Corp router:

```
interface Serial0/0
 ip address 192.168.10.1 255.255.255.0
 encapsulation frame-relay
frame-relay interface-dlci 101
frame-relay interface-dlci 102
frame-relay interface-dlci 103
!
```

Even though the configuration is correct, router updates are not being received because of the split horizon rule. This rules says you cannot advertise a network back out the same interface you received it on, which is the default configuration of all Cisco serial interfaces. This prevents the threat of network loops from occurring.

To solve this problem, you can use subinterfaces. By configuring the Corp router with subinterfaces, this solves the split horizon issues. Here's how to do a configuration:

1. Remove the `ip address` and `interface-dlci` commands from under the physical interface.

2. Create a subinterface (logical interface) for each PVC.

3. Design and implement a separate subnet (address space) for each subinterface.

4. Add the command `frame-relay interface-dlci` *dlci* under each subinterface.

```
interface Serial0/0
 no ip address (notice there is no IP address on the physical interface!)
 encapsulation frame-relay
 !
interface Serial0/0.101 point-to-point
 ip address 192.168.10.1 255.255.255.252
frame-relay interface-dlci 101
 !
interface Serial0/0.102 point-to-point
 ip address 192.168.10.5 255.255.255.252
frame-relay interface-dlci 102
 !
interface Serial0/0.103 point-to-point
 ip address 192.168.10.9 255.255.255.252
frame-relay interface-dlci 103
 !
```

Remember, there is no IP address under the physical interface, and each subinterface is a separate subnet or address space. Add the `frame-relay interface-dlci` command under each subinterface and the horizon issue is now resolved.

Exam Essentials

Remember the default serial encapsulation on Cisco routers.   Cisco routers use a proprietary High-Level Data-Link Control (HDLC) encapsulation on all their serial links by default.

Understand the different Frame Relay encapsulations.   Cisco uses two different Frame Relay encapsulation methods on its routers: Cisco and IETF. If you are using the Cisco encapsulation method, you are telling your router that a Cisco router is installed on the other side of the PVC. If you are using the IETF encapsulation, you are telling your router that a non-Cisco router is installed on the other side of the PVC.

Remember the commands for verifying and troubleshooting Frame Relay.   The show frame-relay lmi command will give you the LMI traffic statistics regarding LMI traffic exchanged between the local router and the Frame Relay switch. The show frame pvc command will list all configured PVCs and DLCI numbers.

Be able to troubleshoot a PPP link.   Understand that a PPP link between two routers will show up and a ping would even work between the router if the layer 3 addresses are wrong.

Remember the various types of serial WAN connections.   The serial WAN connections that are most widely used are HDLC, PPP, and Frame Relay.

Troubleshoot and Resolve Layer 1 Problems

In the following sections, I'll cover some basic commands that will help you resolve issues from layer 1 problems.

Verifying Your Network

The show running-config command would be the best way to verify your configuration, and show startup-config would be the best way to verify the configuration that'll be used the next time the router is reloaded.

Once you take a look at the running-config, if all appears well, you can verify your configuration with utilities like Ping and Telnet. Ping is a program that uses ICMP echo requests and replies. Ping sends a packet to a remote host, and if that host responds, you know that it's alive. Just because you can ping a Microsoft server does not mean you can log in! Ping is an awesome starting point for troubleshooting an internetwork.

You can ping with different protocols? Test this by typing **ping ?** at either the router user-mode or privileged-mode prompt:

```
Todd#ping ?
  WORD  Ping destination address or hostname
```

```
clns   CLNS echo
ip     IP echo
ipv6   IPv6 echo
tag    Tag encapsulated IP echo
<cr>
```

If you want to find a neighbor's Network layer address, either you go straight to the router or switch itself or you can type **show cdp entry * protocol** to get the Network layer addresses you need for pinging.

You can also use an extended ping to change the default variables, as shown here:

```
Todd#ping
Protocol [ip]:
Target IP address: 10.1.1.1
Repeat count [5]:
% A decimal number between 1 and 2147483647.
Repeat count [5]: 5000
Datagram size [100]:
% A decimal number between 36 and 18024.
Datagram size [100]: 1500
Timeout in seconds [2]:
Extended commands [n]: y
Source address or interface: FastEthernet 0/1
Source address or interface: Vlan 1
Type of service [0]:
Set DF bit in IP header? [no]:
Validate reply data? [no]:
Data pattern [0xABCD]:
Loose, Strict, Record, Timestamp, Verbose[none]:
Sweep range of sizes [n]:
Type escape sequence to abort.
Sending 5000, 1500-byte ICMP Echos to 10.1.1.1, timeout is 2 seconds:
Packet sent with a source address of 10.10.10.1
```

Notice that by using the question mark, I was able to determine that extended ping allows you to set the repeat count higher than the default of 5 and the datagram size larger. This raises the MTU and allows for a more accurate testing of throughput. The source interface is one last important piece of information I'll pull out of the output. You can choose which interface the ping is sourced from, which is really helpful in certain diagnostic situations. Using my switch to display the extended ping capabilities, I had to use my only routed port, which is named VLAN 1, by default.

Traceroute uses ICMP with IP time to live (TTL) time-outs to track the path a given packet takes through an internetwork. This is in contrast to Ping, which just finds the host and responds. Traceroute can also be used with multiple protocols. Check out this output:

```
Todd#traceroute ?
  WORD       Trace route to destination address or hostname
  aaa        Define trace options for AAA events/actions/errors
  appletalk  AppleTalk Trace
  clns       ISO CLNS Trace
  ip         IP Trace
  ipv6       IPv6 Trace
  ipx        IPX Trace
  mac        Trace Layer2 path between 2 endpoints
  oldvines   Vines Trace (Cisco)
  vines      Vines Trace (Banyan)
  <cr>
```

Telnet, FTP, and HTTP are really the best tools because they use IP at the Network layer and TCP at the Transport layer to create a session with a remote host. If you can telnet, ftp, or http into a device, you know that your IP connectivity just has to be solid!

```
Todd#telnet ?
  WORD IP address or hostname of a remote system
  <cr>
```

From the switch or router prompt, you just type a hostname or IP address and it will assume you want to telnet—you don't need to type the actual command, telnet.

Verifying Your Interfaces

Another way to verify your configuration is by typing show interface commands, the first of which is the show interface ? command. Doing this will reveal all the available interfaces to verify and configure.

The following output is from my freshly erased and rebooted 2811 router:

```
Router#sh int ?
  Async         Async interface
  BVI           Bridge-Group Virtual Interface
  CDMA-Ix       CDMA Ix interface
  CTunnel       CTunnel interface
  Dialer        Dialer interface
  FastEthernet  FastEthernet IEEE 802.3
  Loopback      Loopback interface
  MFR           Multilink Frame Relay bundle interface
```

```
Multilink          Multilink-group interface
Null               Null interface
Port-channel       Ethernet Channel of interfaces
Serial             Serial
Tunnel             Tunnel interface
Vif                PGM Multicast Host interface
Virtual-PPP        Virtual PPP interface
Virtual-Template   Virtual Template interface
Virtual-TokenRing  Virtual TokenRing
accounting         Show interface accounting
counters           Show interface counters
crb                Show interface routing/bridging info
dampening          Show interface dampening info
description        Show interface description
etherchannel       Show interface etherchannel information
irb                Show interface routing/bridging info
mac-accounting     Show interface MAC accounting info
mpls-exp           Show interface MPLS experimental accounting info
precedence         Show interface precedence accounting info
pruning            Show interface trunk VTP pruning information
rate-limit         Show interface rate-limit info
stats              Show interface packets & octets, in & out, by switching path
status             Show interface line status
summary            Show interface summary
switching          Show interface switching
switchport         Show interface switchport information
trunk              Show interface trunk information
|                  Output modifiers
<cr>
```

The only "real" physical interfaces are Fast Ethernet, Serial, and Async—the rest are all logical interfaces or commands you can use to verify with.

The next command is show interface fastethernet 0/0. It reveals the hardware address, logical address, and encapsulation method as well as statistics on collisions, as seen here:

```
Router#sh int f0/0
FastEthernet0/0 is up, line protocol is up
  Hardware is MV96340 Ethernet, address is 001a.2f55.c9e8 (bia 001a.2f55.c9e8)
  Internet address is 192.168.1.33/27
MTU 1500 bytes, BW 100000 Kbit, DLY 100 usec,
     reliability 255/255, txload 1/255, rxload 1/255
```

```
Encapsulation ARPA, loopback not set
Keepalive set (10 sec)
Auto-duplex, Auto Speed, 100BaseTX/FX
ARP type: ARPA, ARP Timeout 04:00:00
Last input never, output 00:02:07, output hang never
Last clearing of "show interface" counters never
Input queue: 0/75/0/0 (size/max/drops/flushes); Total output drops: 0
Queueing strategy: fifo
Output queue: 0/40 (size/max)
5 minute input rate 0 bits/sec, 0 packets/sec
5 minute output rate 0 bits/sec, 0 packets/sec
   0 packets input, 0 bytes
   Received 0 broadcasts, 0 runts, 0 giants, 0 throttles
   0 input errors, 0 CRC, 0 frame, 0 overrun, 0 ignored
   0 watchdog
   0 input packets with dribble condition detected
   16 packets output, 960 bytes, 0 underruns
   0 output errors, 0 collisions, 0 interface resets
   0 babbles, 0 late collision, 0 deferred
   0 lost carrier, 0 no carrier
   0 output buffer failures, 0 output buffers swapped out
Router#
```

The preceding interface is working and looks to be in good shape. The show interfaces command will show you if you're receiving errors on the interface, and it will also show you the maximum transmission unit (MTU). MTU is the maximum packet size allowed to transmit on that interface, bandwidth (BW) is for use with routing protocols, and 255/255 means that reliability is perfect! The load is 1/255, meaning no load.

Continuing through the output, can you figure out the bandwidth of the interface? Well, other than the easy giveaway of the interface being called a "FastEthernet" interface, we can see that the bandwidth is 100000 Kbit, which is 100,000,000. Kbit means to add three zeros, which is 100 Mbits per second, or Fast Ethernet. Gigabit would be 1,000,000 Kbits per second.

Be sure you don't miss the output errors and collisions, which show 0 in my output. If these numbers are increasing, then you have some sort of Physical or Data Link layer issue. Check your duplex! If you have one side as half-duplex and one at full-duplex, your interface will work, albeit really slow and those numbers will be increasing fast!

The most important statistic of the show interface command is the output of the line and Data Link protocol status. If the output reveals that FastEthernet 0/0 is up and the line protocol is up, then the interface is up and running:

```
Router#sh int fa0/0
FastEthernet0/0 is up, line protocol is up
```

The first parameter refers to the Physical layer, and it's up when it receives carrier detect. The second parameter refers to the Data Link layer, and it looks for keepalives from the connecting end. Keepalives are important because they're used between devices to make sure connectivity hasn't been dropped.

Here's an example of where your problem will often be found—on serial interfaces:

```
Router#sh int s0/0/0
Serial0/0 is up, line protocol is down
```

If you see that the line is up but the protocol is down, as displayed here, you're experiencing a clocking (keepalive) or framing problem—possibly an encapsulation mismatch. Check the keepalives on both ends to make sure they match. Make sure that the clock rate is set, if needed, and that the encapsulation type is equal on both ends. The preceding output tells us that there's a Data Link layer problem.

If you discover that both the line interface and the protocol are down, it's a cable or interface problem. The following output would indicate a Physical layer problem:

```
Router#sh int s0/0/0
Serial0/0 is down, line protocol is down
```

As you'll see next, if one end is administratively shut down, the remote end would present as down and down:

```
Router#sh int s0/0/0
Serial0/0 is administratively down, line protocol is down
```

To enable the interface, use the command no shutdown from interface configuration mode.

The next show interface serial 0/0/0 command demonstrates the serial line and the maximum transmission unit (MTU)—1,500 bytes by default. It also shows the default bandwidth (BW) on all Cisco serial links, which is 1.544 Kbps. This is used to determine the bandwidth of the line for routing protocols like EIGRP and OSPF. Another important configuration to notice is the keepalive, which is 10 seconds by default. Each router sends a keepalive message to its neighbor every 10 seconds, and if both routers aren't configured for the same keepalive time, it won't work! Check out this output:

```
Router#sh int s0/0/0
Serial0/0 is up, line protocol is up
 Hardware is HD64570
 MTU 1500 bytes, BW 1544 Kbit, DLY 20000 usec,
    reliability 255/255, txload 1/255, rxload 1/255
 Encapsulation HDLC, loopback not set, keepalive set
   (10 sec)
 Last input never, output never, output hang never
 Last clearing of "show interface" counters never
 Queueing strategy: fifo
```

```
Output queue 0/40, 0 drops; input queue 0/75, 0 drops
5 minute input rate 0 bits/sec, 0 packets/sec
5 minute output rate 0 bits/sec, 0 packets/sec
   0 packets input, 0 bytes, 0 no buffer
   Received 0 broadcasts, 0 runts, 0 giants, 0 throttles
   0 input errors, 0 CRC, 0 frame, 0 overrun, 0 ignored,
   0 abort
   0 packets output, 0 bytes, 0 underruns
   0 output errors, 0 collisions, 16 interface resets
   0 output buffer failures, 0 output buffers swapped out
   0 carrier transitions
   DCD=down DSR=down DTR=down RTS=down CTS=down
```

You can clear the counters on the interface by typing the command **clear counters**:

```
Router#clear counters ?
  Async            Async interface
  BVI              Bridge-Group Virtual Interface
  CTunnel          CTunnel interface
  Dialer           Dialer interface
  FastEthernet     FastEthernet IEEE 802.3
  Group-Async      Async Group interface
  Line             Terminal line
  Loopback         Loopback interface
  MFR              Multilink Frame Relay bundle interface
  Multilink        Multilink-group interface
  Null             Null interface
  Serial           Serial
  Tunnel           Tunnel interface
  Vif              PGM Multicast Host interface
  Virtual-Template Virtual Template interface
  Virtual-TokenRing Virtual TokenRing
  <cr>


Router#clear counters s0/0/0
Clear "show interface" counters on this interface
  [confirm][enter]
Router#
00:17:35: %CLEAR-5-COUNTERS: Clear counter on interface
  Serial0/0/0 by console
Router#
```

Finding where to start when troubleshooting an interface can be the difficult part, but certainly we'll look for the number of input errors and CRCs right away. Typically we'd see those statistics increase with a duplex error, but it could be another Physical layer issue such as the cable might be receiving excessive interference or the network interface cards might have a failure. Typically you can tell if it is interference when the CRC and input errors grow but the collision counters do not.

The next sections provide an overview of some of the output.

Framing

This output increments when frames received are of an illegal format or not complete. The output is typically incremented when a collision occurs.

CRC

At the end of each frame is a Frame Check Sequence (FCS) field that holds the answer to a cyclic redundancy check (CRC). If the receiving host's answer to the CRC does not match the sending host's answer, then a CRC error will occur.

Runts

These are frames that did not meet the minimum frame size requirement of 64 bytes. They are typically caused by collisions.

Giants

These are frames received on a host or switch interface that are larger than 1,518 bytes. Typically these are found when using 802.1q trunking on a switch port.

Dropped Packets

If the packet buffers are full, packets will be dropped. You see this increment along with the no buffer output. Typically, if the no buffer and ignored outputs are incrementing, you have some sort of broadcast storm on your LAN. This can be caused by a bad NIC or even a bad network design.

Late Collision

If all Ethernet specifications are followed during the cable install, all collisions should occur by the 64th byte of the frame. If a collision occurs after 64 bytes, the late collisions counter increments. This counter will increment on a duplex mismatched interface or if cable length exceeds specifications.

Input / Output Errors

Input errors are the total of many counters: runts, giants, no buffer, CRC, frame, overrun, and ignored counts. *Output errors* are the packets (frames) that the switch port tried to transmit but for which some problem occurred.

Verifying Interface Configuration

The show ip interface command will provide you with information regarding the layer 3 configurations of a router's interfaces:

```
Router#sh ip interface
FastEthernet0/0 is up, line protocol is up
  Internet address is 1.1.1.1/24
  Broadcast address is 255.255.255.255
  Address determined by setup command
  MTU is 1500 bytes
  Helper address is not set
  Directed broadcast forwarding is disabled
  Outgoing access list is not set
  Inbound  access list is not set
  Proxy ARP is enabled
  Security level is default
  Split horizon is enabled
[output cut]
```

The status of the interface, the IP address and mask, information on whether an access list is set on the interface, and basic IP information are all included in this output.

The show ip interface brief command is probably one of the best commands that you can ever use on a Cisco router. This command provides a quick overview of the router's interfaces, including the logical address and status:

```
Router#sh ip int brief
Interface          IP-Address     OK? Method Status                 Protocol
FastEthernet0/0    unassigned     YES unset  up                     up
FastEthernet0/1    unassigned     YES unset  up                     up
Serial0/0/0        unassigned     YES unset  up                     down
Serial0/0/1        unassigned     YES unset  administratively down  down
Serial0/1/0        unassigned     YES unset  administratively down  down
Serial0/2/0        unassigned     YES unset  administratively down  down
```

Remember, administratively down means that you need to type **no shutdown** in order to enable the interface. Notice that Serial0/0/0 is up/down, which means that the Physical layer is good and carrier detect is sensed but no keepalives are being received from the remote end. In a nonproduction network, like the one I am working with, this tells us the clock rate hasn't been set.

The show protocols command is also a really helpful command that you'd use in order to quickly see the status of layers 1 and 2 of each interface as well as the IP addresses used.

Here's a look at one of my production routers:

```
Router#sh protocols
Global values:
  Internet Protocol routing is enabled
Ethernet0/0 is administratively down, line protocol is down
Serial0/0 is up, line protocol is up
  Internet address is 100.30.31.5/24
Serial0/1 is administratively down, line protocol is down
Serial0/2 is up, line protocol is up
  Internet address is 100.50.31.2/24
Loopback0 is up, line protocol is up
  Internet address is 100.20.31.1/24
```

The show ip interface brief and show protocols commands provide the layer 1 and layer 2 statistics of an interface as well as the IP addresses.

The show controllers command displays information about the physical interface itself. It'll also give you the type of serial cable plugged into a serial port. Usually, this will only be a DTE cable that plugs into a type of data service unit (DSU).

```
Router#sh controllers serial 0/0
HD unit 0, idb = 0x1229E4, driver structure at 0x127E70
buffer size 1524 HD unit 0, V.35 DTE cable
```

```
Router#sh controllers serial 0/1
HD unit 1, idb = 0x12C174, driver structure at 0x131600
buffer size 1524 HD unit 1, V.35 DCE cable
```

Notice that serial 0/0 has a DTE cable, whereas the serial 0/1 connection has a DCE cable. Serial 0/1 would have to provide clocking with the clock rate command. Serial 0/0 would get its clocking from the DSU.

Let's look at this command again. In Figure 7.23, see the DTE/DCE cable between the two routers? Know that you will not see this in production networks!

Router R1 has a DTE connection, which is typically the default for all Cisco routers. Routers R1 and R2 can't communicate. Check out the output of the show controllers s0/0 command here:

```
R1#sh controllers serial 0/0
HD unit 0, idb = 0x1229E4, driver structure at 0x127E70
buffer size 1524 HD unit 0, V.35 DCE cable
```

FIGURE 7.23 Where do you configure clocking? Use the show controllers command on each router's serial interface to find out.

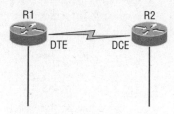

The show controllers s0/0 command reveals that the interface is a V.35 DCE cable. This means that R1 needs to provide clocking of the line to router R2. Basically, the wrong label is on the cable on the R1 router's serial interface. But if you add clocking on the R1 router's serial interface, the network should come right up.

Let's check out another issue, in Figure 7.24, that you can solve by using the show controllers command. Again, routers R1 and R2 can't communicate.

FIGURE 7.24 By looking at R1, the show controllers command reveals that R1 and R2 can't communicate.

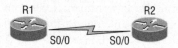

Here's the output of R1's show controllers s0/0 command and show ip interface s0/0:

```
R1#sh controllers s0/0
HD unit 0, idb = 0x1229E4, driver structure at 0x127E70
buffer size 1524 HD unit 0,
DTE V.35 clocks stopped
cpb = 0xE2, eda = 0x4140, cda = 0x4000
```

```
R1#sh ip interface s0/0
Serial0/0 is up, line protocol is down
  Internet address is 192.168.10.2/24
  Broadcast address is 255.255.255.255
```

If you use the show controllers command and the show ip interface command, you'll see that router R1 isn't receiving the clocking of the line. This network is a non-production network, so no CSU/DSU is connected to provide clocking for it. This means the DCE end of the cable will be providing the clock rate—in this case, the R2 router. The show ip interface indicates that the interface is up but the protocol is down, which means that no keepalives are being received from the far end. In this example, the likely culprit is the result of bad cable, or simply the lack of clocking.

Exam Essentials

Understand the use of the `ping` **command.**   The `ping` command is a very useful tool to verify connectivity between hosts or devices. The extended ping command gives you several variables to use when testing connectivity.

Understand the use of the `show ip interface` **and** `show ip interface brief` **commands.** The `show ip interface` command will provide you with information regarding the layer 3 configurations of a router's interfaces. The `show ip interface brief` command provides a quick overview of the router's interfaces, including the logical address and status.

Understand how to troubleshoot a serial link problem.   If you type **`show interface serial 0/0`** and see down, `line protocol is down`, this will be considered a Physical layer problem. If you see it as up, `line protocol is down`, then you have a Data Link layer problem.

Understand how to verify your router with the `show interfaces` **command.**   If you type **`show interfaces`**, you can view the statistics for the interfaces on the router, verify whether the interfaces are shut down, and see the IP address of each interface.

Monitor NetFlow Statistics

In this section, I'll go over Netflow and how you can gather some important statistics with it.

Cisco's Netflow is an application in that it helps manage and troubleshoot issues within your network. It does so by collecting information on IP traffic and providing network traffic accounting for baselining, usage-based network billing for consumers of network services, network design and planning, general network security, and DoS and DDoS monitoring capabilities as well as general network monitoring.

NetFlow is completely transparent to the users in the network, including all end stations and applications, and you don't need to run it on all your routers.

NetFlow enables near real-time visualization and analysis of recorded and aggregated flow data. You can specify the router, the aggregation scheme, and the time interval for when you want to view and then retrieve the relevant data and sort it into bar charts, pie charts, and so on. The components used with NetFlow include a router enabled with NetFlow and a NetFlow collector.

Service providers use NetFlow to do the following:

- Efficiently measure who is using network service and for which purpose
- Perform accounting and charging back according to the resource utilizing level
- Use measured information for more effective network planning so that resource allocation and deployment are well aligned with customer requirements
- Use the information to better structure and customize the set of available applications and services to meet user needs and customer service requirements

NetFlow is built around TCP/IP communication for statistical record keeping using the concept of a flow. A flow is a unidirectional stream of packets between a source and destination host or system. With an understanding of TCP/IP, you can figure out that NetFlow is using socket information, meaning source and destination IP addresses and source and destination port numbers. But there are a few more fields that NetFlow uses. Here is some of the most commonly used:

- Source IP address
- Destination IP address
- Source port number
- Destination port number
- Layer 3 protocol field
- Type of Service (ToS) marking
- Input logical interface

To verify NetFlow, ensure that the correct interfaces in the correct direction have been configured, starting with the show ip flow interface command like this:

```
SF#sh ip flow interface
FastEthernet0/0
  ip flow ingress
  ip flow egress
```

The correct interface of FastEthernet 0/0 is configured with the ingress and egress command. Now check the export parameters via the show ip flow export command:

```
SF#sh ip flow export
Flow export v9 is enabled for main cache
  Exporting flows to 172.16.20.254 (9996) 172.16.20.254 (9996)
  Exporting using source interface Loopback0
  Version 9 flow records
  43 flows exported in 15 udp datagrams
[output cut]
```

Notice that the destination port is 9996. This is the Cisco default port number on which the NetFlow collectors listen for NetFlow packets. I can use the sh ip cache flow command to verify my flows by examining the information stored on a router directly, which will show that I'm actually collecting packets:

```
SF#sh ip cache flow
IP packet size distribution (161 total packets):
[output cut]
IP Flow Switching Cache, 278544 bytes
  1 active, 4095 inactive, 1 added
```

```
    215 ager polls, 0 flow alloc failures
    Active flows timeout in 30 minutes
    Inactive flows timeout in 15 seconds
IP Sub Flow Cache, 21640 bytes
    1 active, 1023 inactive, 1 added, 1 added to flow
    0 alloc failures, 0 force free
    1 chunk, 1 chunk added
    last clearing of statistics never
Protocol        Total    Flows   Packets Bytes  Packets Active(Sec) Idle(Sec)
--------        Flows    /Sec    /Flow   /Pkt   /Sec    /Flow       /Flow
TCP-Telnet      14       0.0     19      58     0.1     6.5         11.7
TCP-WWW         8        0.0     9       108    0.1     2.5         1.7
SrcIf           SrcIPaddress     DstIf   DstIPaddress     Pr SrcP DstP  Pkts
Fa0/0           172.16.10.1      gig0/1  255.255.255.255  11 0044 0050  161
```

You can see that packets are being received—161 so far—and the bottom lines show that the router is collecting flow for Telnet and HTTP. You can also see the source interface, source IP, destination interface, and source and destination ports in hex (50 is 80 in hex). It's important to remember that the show ip cache flow command provides a summary of the NetFlow statistics, including which protocols are in use.

Exam Essentials

Understand what Cisco's NetFlow is used for. Cisco IOS NetFlow efficiently provides a key set of services for IP applications, including network traffic accounting for baselining, usage-based network billing for consumers of network services, network design and planning, general network security, and DoS and DDoS monitoring capabilities as well as general network monitoring.

Troubleshoot EtherChannel Problems

In this section, I'll cover some troubleshooting methods for solving EtherChannel problems within a network.

Ethernet networks have multiple links between devices. That provides redundancy and resiliency. In a switched network, STP will do its job of putting ports into blocking mode, and routers using EIGRP or OSPF could see these redundant links as individual ones.

EtherChannel is a port channel technology that was originally developed by Cisco as a switch-to-switch technique for grouping several Fast Ethernet or Gigabit Ethernet ports into one logical channel.

There is Cisco's version and the IEEE version of port channel negotiation protocols. Cisco's version is called Port Aggregation Protocol (PAgP), and the IEEE 802.3ad standard is called Link Aggregation Control Protocol (LACP). Both versions work equally well, but the way you configure each is slightly different. Both PAgP and LACP are negotiation protocols, and EtherChannel can actually be statically configured without PAgP or LACP. Still, it's better to use one of these protocols to help with compatibility issues as well as to manage link additions and failures between two switches.

Cisco EtherChannel allows us to bundle up to eight ports active between switches. The links must have the same speed, duplex setting, and VLAN configuration. You can't mix interface types and configurations into the same bundle.

Here are some of the terms to be familiar with:

Port channeling   Refers to combining two to eight Fast Ethernet or two Gigabit Ethernet ports together between two switches into one aggregated logical link to achieve more bandwidth and resiliency.

EtherChannel   Cisco's proprietary term for port channeling.

PAgP   This is a Cisco proprietary port channel negotiation protocol that aids in the automatic creation of EtherChannel links. All links in the bundle must match the same parameters (speed, duplex, VLAN info), and when PAgP identifies matched links, it groups the links into an EtherChannel. This is then added to STP as a single bridge port. At this point, PAgP's job is to send packets every 30 seconds to manage the link for consistency, any link additions and modifications, and failures.

LACP (802.3ad)   This has the exact same purpose as PAgP, but is nonproprietary so it can work between multi-vendor networks.

`channel-group`   This is a command on Ethernet interfaces used to add the specified interface to a single EtherChannel. The number following this command is the port channel ID.

`interface port-channel`   Here's a command that creates the bundled interface. Ports can be added to this interface with the `channel-group` command. Keep in mind that the interface number must match the group number.

To verify EtherChannel, start with the `show etherchannel port-channel` command to see information about a specific port channel interface:

```
S2#sh etherchannel port-channel
            Channel-group listing:
            ----------------------


Group: 1
----------
            Port-channels in the group:
            --------------------------
```

```
Port-channel: Po1     (Primary Aggregator)
------------


Age of the Port-channel   = 00d:00h:46m:49s
Logical slot/port     = 2/1      Number of ports = 2
GC                    = 0x00000000      HotStandBy port = null
Port state            = Port-channel
Protocol              =   LACP
Port Security         = Disabled

Ports in the Port-channel:

Index   Load   Port    EC state           No of bits
------+------+------+------------------+-----------
  0     00    Gig0/2   Active                0
  0     00    Gig0/1   Active                0
Time since last port bundled:     00d:00h:46m:47s    Gig0/1
S2#
```

Notice that we have one group and that we're running the IEEE LACP version of port channeling. We're in Active mode, and that Port-channel: Po1 interface has two physical interfaces. The heading Load is not the load over the interfaces; it's a hexadecimal value that decides which interface will be chosen to specify the flow of traffic.

The show etherchannel summary command displays one line of information per port channel:

```
S2#sh etherchannel summary
Flags:  D - down        P - in port-channel
        I - stand-alone s - suspended
        H - Hot-standby (LACP only)
        R - Layer3       S - Layer2
        U - in use       f - failed to allocate aggregator
        u - unsuitable for bundling
        w - waiting to be aggregated
        d - default port


Number of channel-groups in use: 1
Number of aggregators:          1

Group  Port-channel  Protocol     Ports
------+-------------+-----------+------------------------------------------------

1      Po1(SU)           LACP    Gig0/1(P) Gig0/2(P)
```

This command shows that we have one group, that we're running LACP, and that Gig0/1 (P) and Gig0/2 (P) means these ports are in port-channel mode. This command isn't really all that helpful unless you have multiple channel groups, but it does tell us our group is working well.

Exam Essentials

Understand what EtherChannel is and how to verify it.   EtherChannel allows you to bundle links to get more bandwidth instead of allowing STP to shut down redundant ports. You can configure Cisco's PAgP, or the IEEE version, LACP, by creating a port channel interface and assigning the port channel group number to the interfaces you are bundling. To verify the EtherChannel configurations, you can use the show etherchannel port-channel and show etherchannel summary commands.

Review Questions

1. Which of the following would put switch interfaces into EtherChannel port number 1, using LACP? (Choose two.)

   A. `Switch((config)#interface port-channel 1`

   B. `Switch((config)#channel-group 1 mode active`

   C. `(config-if)#Switch#interface port-channel 1`

   D. `Switch((config-if)#channel-group 1 mode active`

2. What is the most common cause of interface errors?

   A. Speed mismatch

   B. Duplex mismatch

   C. Buffer overflows

   D. Collisions between a dedicated switch port and a NIC

3. Which should you look for when troubleshooting an adjacency? (Choose four.)

   A. Verify the AS numbers.

   B. Verify that you have the proper interfaces enabled for EIGRP.

   C. Make sure there are no mismatched K values.

   D. Check your passive interface settings.

   E. Make sure your remote routers are not connected to the Internet.

   F. If authentication is configured, make sure all routers use different passwords.

4. Which command will show all the LSAs known to a router?

   A. `show ip ospf`

   B. `show ip ospf neighbor`

   C. `show ip ospf interface`

   D. `show ip ospf database`

5. Which of the following command options are displayed when you use the Router#**show frame-relay ?** command? (Choose three.)

   A. `dlci`

   B. `neighbors`

   C. `lmi`

   D. `pvc`

   E. `map`

6. What router command allows you to determine whether an IP access list is enabled on a particular interface?

    A. `show ip port`

    B. `show access-lists`

    C. `show ip interface`

    D. `show access-lists interface`

7. What is true of the following output?

```
S1#sh vlan

VLAN Name                     Status    Ports
---- -------------------- --------- -------------------------------
1    default              active    Fa0/1, Fa0/2, Fa0/3, Fa0/4
                                    Fa0/5, Fa0/6, Fa0/7, Fa0/8
                                    Fa0/9, Fa0/10, Fa0/11, Fa0/12
                                 Fa0/13, Fa0/14, Fa0/19, Fa0/20,
                                 Fa0/22, Fa0/23, Gi0/1, Gi0/2
2    Sales                active
3    Marketing                      Fa0/21
4    Accounting           active
[output cut]
```

    A. Interface Fa0/15 is a trunk port.

    B. Interface Fa0/17 is an access port.

    C. Interface Fa0/21 is a trunk port.

    D. VLAN 1 was populated manually.

8. Which command will show you whether a DTE or a DCE cable is plugged into serial 0/0 on your router's WAN port?

    A. `sh int s0/0`

    B. `sh int serial 0/0`

    C. `show controllers s 0/0`

    D. `show serial 0/0 controllers`

9. Which of the following are roles in STP? (Choose all that apply.)

   A. Blocking

   B. Discarding

   C. Root

   D. Non-designated

   E. Forwarding

   F. Designated

10. Which command enables you to view a summary of the NetFlow statistics of the protocols on a router?

   A. `show ip flow`

   B. `show ip cache flow`

   C. `show ip netflow`

   D. `show ip flow interface gi0/1`

Chapter

8

WAN Technologies

THE FOLLOWING CCNA ROUTING AND SWITCHING EXAM OBJECTIVES ARE COVERED IN THIS CHAPTER:

✓ **Configure and verify operation status of a Serial interface.**

✓ **Identify different WAN Technologies.**

- Metro Ethernet
- VSAT
- Cellular 3G / 4G
- MPLS
- T1 / E1
- ISDN
- DSL
- Frame relay
- Cable
- VPN

✓ **Configure and verify a basic WAN serial connection.**

✓ **Configure and verify a PPP connection between Cisco routers.**

✓ **Configure and verify Frame Relay on Cisco routers.**

✓ **Implement and troubleshoot PPPoE.**

✓ **Troubleshoot and Resolve WAN implementation issues.**

- Serial interfaces
- PPP
- Frame relay

The Cisco IOS supports a ton of different wide area network (WAN) protocols that help you extend your local LANs to other LANs at remote sites. Essential information exchange between disparate sites is vital these days! But even so, it wouldn't exactly be cost effective or efficient to install your own cable and connect all of your company's remote locations yourself, would it? A much better way to get this done is to just lease the existing installations that service providers already have in place.

This chapter will cover the various types of connections, technologies, and devices used in today's WANs. We'll also delve into how to implement and configure High-Level Data-Link Control (HDLC), Point-to-Point Protocol (PPP), and Frame Relay. I'll describe Point-to-Point Protocol over Ethernet (PPPoE), cable, digital subscriber line (DSL), MultiProtocol Label Switching (MPLS), and metro Ethernet plus last mile and long-range WAN technologies. I'll also introduce you to WAN security concepts, tunneling, and virtual private network basics.

Identify Different WAN Technologies

Cisco supports many layer 2 WAN encapsulations on its serial interfaces, including HDLC, PPP, and Frame Relay, which map to the CCNA R/S objectives. You can view them via the encapsulation ? command from any serial interface, but understand that the output you'll get can vary based upon the specific IOS version you're running:

```
Corp#config t
Corp(config)#int s0/0/0
Corp(config-if)#encapsulation ?
  atm-dxi      ATM-DXI encapsulation
  frame-relay  Frame Relay networks
  hdlc         Serial HDLC synchronous
  lapb         LAPB (X.25 Level 2)
  ppp          Point-to-Point protocol
  smds         Switched Megabit Data Service (SMDS)
  x25          X.25
```

I also want to point out that if I had other types of interfaces on my router, I would have a different set of encapsulation options. And never forget that you can't configure an Ethernet encapsulation on a serial interface or vice versa!

Common WAN Protocols

The most prominently known WAN protocols (and those covered in the latest CCNA Routing and Switching objectives) are HDLC, PPP, PPPoE, ATM, metro Ethernet, VSAT, cellular 3G/4G, MPLS, ISDN, DSL, ADSL, Frame Relay, and cable. Just so you know, the only WAN protocols you'll usually find configured on a serial interface are HDLC, PPP, and Frame Relay.

Here's an overview of these protocols:

Metro Ethernet   Metropolitan area Ethernet is a metropolitan area network (MAN) that's based on Ethernet standards and can connect a customer to a larger network and the Internet. If it's available, businesses can use metro Ethernet to connect their own offices together, which is another very cost-effective connection option. MPLS-based metro Ethernet networks use MPLS in the ISP by providing an Ethernet or fiber cable to the customer as a connection. From the customer, it leaves the Ethernet cable, jumps onto MPLS, and then Ethernet again on the remote side. This is a smart and thrifty solution that's very popular if you can get it in your area.

VSAT   Very Small Aperture Terminal (VSAT) can be used if you have many locations geographically spread out in a large area. VSAT uses a two-way satellite ground station with dishes available through many companies like Dish Network or Hughes and connects to satellites in geosynchronous orbit. A good example of where VSATs are a useful, cost-effective solution would be companies that use satellite communications to VSATs, like gasoline stations that have hundreds or thousands of locations spread out over the entire country. How could you connect them otherwise? Using leased lines would be cost prohibitive, and dial-ups would be way too slow and hard to manage. Instead, the signal from the satellite connects to many remote locations at once, which is much more cost effective and efficient!

Cellular 3G / 4G   Having a wireless hot spot in your pocket is pretty normal these days. If you have a pretty current cellular phone, then you can probably can gain access through your phone to the Internet. You can even get a 3G/4G card for an ISR router that's useful for a small remote office that's in the coverage area.

MPLS   *MultiProtocol Label Switching (MPLS)* is a data-carrying mechanism that emulates some properties of a circuit-switched network over a packet-switched network. MPLS is a switching mechanism that imposes labels (numbers) to packets and then uses the labels to forward the packets. The labels are assigned on the edge of the MPLS network, and the packets are forwarded inside the MPLS network based solely on the labels.

The labels usually correspond to a path to layer 3 destination addresses, which is on par with IP destination-based routing. MPLS was designed to support the forwarding of protocols other than TCP/IP. Because of this, label switching within the network is achieved the same way, irrespective of the layer 3 protocol. In larger networks, the result of MPLS labeling is that only the edge routers perform a routing lookup. All the core routers forward packets based on the labels, which makes forwarding the packets through the service provider network faster. This is a big reason most companies have replaced their Frame Relay networks with MPLS service today. Last, you can use Ethernet with MPLS to connect a WAN, and this is called Ethernet over MPLS, or EoMPLS.

ISDN   *Integrated Services Digital Network (ISDN)* is a set of digital services that transmit voice and data over existing phone lines. ISDN offers a cost-effective solution for remote users who need a higher-speed connection than analog POTS dial-up links can give them, and it's also a good choice to use as a backup link for other types of links, such as Frame Relay or T1 connections.

DSL   Digital subscriber line is a technology used by traditional telephone companies to deliver advanced services such as high-speed data and sometimes video over twisted-pair copper telephone wires. It typically has lower data-carrying capacity than fiber networks, and data speeds can be limited in range by line lengths and quality. Digital subscriber line is not a complete end-to-end solution but rather a Physical layer transmission technology like dial-up, cable, or wireless. DSL connections are deployed in the last mile of a local telephone network—the local loop. The connection is set up between a pair of DSL modems on either end of a copper wire located between the customer premises equipment (CPE) and the Digital Subscriber Line Access Multiplexer (DSLAM). A DSLAM is a device that is located at the provider's central office (CO) and concentrates connections from multiple DSL subscribers.

ADSL   *Asymmetrical DSL (ADSL)* supports both voice and data at the same time, but it was created to allot more bandwidth downstream than upstream because it's best for residential subscribers who usually need more downstream bandwidth for activities like downloading video, movies, music, online gaming, general surfing, and getting emails—some of which include sizeable attachments. ADSL will give you a downstream rate from 256 Kbps to 8 Mbps, but anything going upstream is only going to reach around 1.5 Mbps max.

Plain old telephone service (POTS) provides a channel for analog voice transmission and can transmit without a problem with ADSL over the same twisted-pair telephone line. Actually, depending on the type of ADSL, not just two but three information channels commonly utilize the same wiring simultaneously. This is why people can use a phone line and an ADSL connection at the same time and not affect either service.

Frame Relay   A packet-switched technology that made its debut in the early 1990s, *Frame Relay* is a high-performance Data Link and Physical layer specification. It's pretty much a successor to X.25, except that much of the technology in X.25 used to compensate for physical errors like noisy lines has been eliminated. An upside to Frame Relay is that it can be more cost effective than point-to-point links, plus it typically runs at speeds of 64 Kbps up to 45 Mbps (T3). Another Frame Relay benefit is that it provides features for dynamic bandwidth allocation and congestion control.

Cable   In a modern *hybrid fiber-coaxial (HFC)* network, typically 500 to 2,000 active data subscribers are connected to a certain cable network segment, all sharing the upstream and downstream bandwidth. HFC is a telecommunications industry term for a network that incorporates both optical fiber and coaxial cable to create a broadband network. The actual bandwidth for Internet service over a cable TV (CATV) line can be up to about 50 Mbps on the download path to the subscriber, with about 2.5 Mbps of bandwidth on the upload path. Typically users get an access speed from 10 Mbps to 30 Mbps. This data rate varies greatly throughout the United States and can be much, much higher today.

VPN

A *virtual private network (VPN)* allows the creation of private networks across the Internet, enabling privacy and tunneling of non-TCP/IP protocols. VPNs are used daily to give remote users and disjointed networks connectivity over a public medium like the Internet instead of using more expensive permanent means.

A VPN fits somewhere between a LAN and WAN, with the WAN often simulating a LAN link because your computer, on one LAN, connects to a different, remote LAN and uses its resources remotely. The key benefit of using VPNs is a big one—security!

Benefits of VPNs

The Cisco objectives cover the following information as benefits of VPNs:

Security VPNs can provide very good security by using advanced encryption and authentication protocols, which will help protect your network from unauthorized access. IPsec and SSL fall into this category. Secure Sockets Layer (SSL) is an encryption technology that is used with web browsers and has native SSL encryption, and SSL VPNs are known as Web VPNs. You can also use the Cisco AnyConnect SSL VPN client installed on your PC, as well as the Clientless Cisco SSL VPN, to provide an SSL VPN solution.

Cost savings By connecting the corporate remote offices to their closest Internet provider and then creating a VPN tunnel with encryption and authentication, you can gain a huge savings over opting for traditional leased point-to-point lines. This also permits higher bandwidth links and security, all for far less money than traditional connections.

Scalability VPNs scale very well to quickly bring up new offices or have mobile users connect securely while traveling or when connecting from home.

Compatibility with broadband technology For remote and traveling users and remote offices, any Internet access can provide a connection to the corporate VPN. This allows users to take advantage of the high-speed Internet access of DSL or cable modems.

VPN Categories

VPNs are categorized based upon the role they play in a business. There are three different categories of VPNs:

Remote access VPNs These allow remote users such as telecommuters to securely access the corporate network wherever and whenever they need to.

Site-to-site VPNs Also known as intranet VPNs, these allow a company to connect its remote sites to the corporate backbone securely over a public medium like the Internet instead of requiring more expensive WAN connections like Frame Relay.

Extranet VPNs These allow an organization's suppliers, partners, and customers to be connected to the corporate network in a limited way for business-to-business (B2B) communications.

Exam Essentials

Remember the various types of serial WAN connections.   The serial WAN connections that are most widely used are HDLC, PPP, and Frame Relay.

Understand the term *virtual private network*.   You need to understand why and how to use a VPN between two sites and the purpose that IPsec serves with VPNs.

Configure and Verify a Basic WAN Serial Connection

Cisco's HDLC is the default encapsulation used by Cisco routers over synchronous serial links. And Cisco's HDLC is proprietary, meaning it won't communicate with any other vendor's HDLC implementation. But don't give Cisco grief for it—*everyone's* HDLC implementation is proprietary. Figure 8.1 shows the Cisco HDLC format and how the Cisco HDLC format differs from other vendors' HDLC format.

FIGURE 8.1   Cisco's HDLC frame format. Each vendor's HDLC has a proprietary data field to support multiprotocol environments.

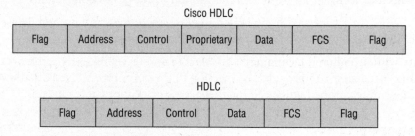

The reason every vendor has a proprietary HDLC encapsulation method is that each vendor has a different way for the HDLC protocol to encapsulate multiple Network layer protocols. If the vendors didn't have a way for HDLC to communicate the different layer 3 protocols, then HDLC would be able to operate in only a single layer 3 protocol environment. This proprietary header is placed in the data field of the HDLC encapsulation.

It's pretty simple to configure a serial interface if you're just going to connect two Cisco routers across a T1, for example. Figure 8.2 shows a point-to-point connection between two cities.

FIGURE 8.2   Configuring Cisco's HDLC proprietary WAN encapsulation

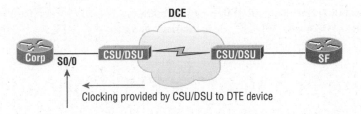

We can easily configure the routers with a basic IP address and then enable the interface. Assuming the link to the ISP is up, the routers will start communicating using the default Cisco HDLC encapsulation. Let's take a look at the Corp router configuration so you can see just how easy this can be:

```
Corp(config)#int s0/0
Corp(config-if)#ip address 172.16.10.1 255.255.255.252
Corp(config-if)#no shut


Corp#sh int s0/0
Serial0/0 is up, line protocol is up
  Hardware is PowerQUICC Serial
  Internet address is 172.16.10.1/30
  MTU 1500 bytes, BW 1544 Kbit, DLY 20000 usec,
      reliability 255/255, txload 1/255, rxload 1/255
  Encapsulation HDLC, loopback not set
  Keepalive set (10 sec)


Corp#sh run | begin interface Serial0/0
interface Serial0/0
 ip address 172.16.10.1 255.255.255.252
!
```

Note that all I did was add an IP address before I enabled the interface. Now, as long as the SF router is running the default serial encapsulation, this link will come up. Notice in the preceding output that the show interface command does show the encapsulation type of HDLC but the output of show running-config does not. This is important—remember that if you don't see an encapsulation type listed under a serial interface in the active configuration file, you know it's running the default encapsulation of Cisco HDLC.

Exam Essentials

Remember the default serial encapsulation on Cisco routers.   Cisco routers use a proprietary High-Level Data-Link Control (HDLC) encapsulation on all their serial links by default.

Configure and Verify a PPP Connection between Cisco Routers

Point-to-Point Protocol (PPP) is a Data Link layer protocol that can be used over either asynchronous serial (dial-up) or synchronous serial (ISDN) media. I'm going to demonstrate how to configure PPP between two directly connected Cisco routers with a serial link.

Configuring PPP on Cisco Routers

Configuring PPP encapsulation on an interface is really pretty straightforward. To configure it from the CLI, use these simple router commands:

```
Router#config t
Router(config)#int s0
Router(config-if)#encapsulation ppp
Router(config-if)#^Z
Router#
```

Of course, PPP encapsulation has to be enabled on both interfaces connected to a serial line in order to work, and there are several additional configuration options available to you via the ppp ? command.

Configuring PPP Authentication

After you configure your serial interface to support PPP encapsulation, you can then configure authentication using PPP between routers. But first, you must set the hostname of the router if it hasn't been set already. After that, you set the username and password for the remote router that will be connecting to your router, like this:

```
Router#config t
Router(config)#hostname RouterA
RouterA(config)#username RouterB password cisco
```

When using the username command, remember that the username is the hostname of the remote router that's connecting to your router. And it's case sensitive too. Also, the password on both routers must be the same. It's a plaintext password that you can see with a show run command, and you can encrypt the password by using the command service password-encryption. You must have a username and password configured for each remote system you plan to connect to. The remote routers must also be similarly configured with usernames and passwords.

Now, after you've set the hostname, usernames, and passwords, choose either CHAP or PAP as the authentication method:

```
RouterA#config t
RouterA(config)#int s0
RouterA(config-if)#ppp authentication chap pap
RouterA(config-if)#^Z
RouterA#
```

If both methods are configured on the same line as I've demonstrated here, then only the first method will be used during link negotiation. The second acts as a backup just in case the first method fails.

Verifying and Troubleshooting Serial Links

Okay—now that PPP encapsulation is enabled, you need to verify that it's up and running. First, let's take a look at a figure of a sample nonproduction network serial link. Figure 8.3 shows two routers connected with a point-to-point serial connection, with the DCE side on the Pod1R1 router.

FIGURE 8.3 PPP authentication example

Pod1R1   Pod1R2

```
hostname Pod1R1                          hostname Pod1R2
username Pod1R2 password cisco           username Pod1R1 password cisco
interface serial 0                       interface serial 0
ip address 10.0.1.1 255.255.255.0        ip address 10.0.1.2 255.255.255.0
encapsulation ppp                        encapsulation ppp
clock rate 64000                         bandwidth 512
bandwidth 512                            ppp authentication chap
ppp authentication chap
```

You can start verifying the configuration with the show interface command like this:

```
Pod1R1#sh int s0/0
Serial0/0 is up, line protocol is up
  Hardware is PowerQUICC Serial
  Internet address is 10.0.1.1/24
  MTU 1500 bytes, BW 1544 Kbit, DLY 20000 usec,
```

```
    reliability 239/255, txload 1/255, rxload 1/255
 Encapsulation PPP
 loopback not set
 Keepalive set (10 sec)
 LCP Open
 Open: IPCP, CDPCP
[output cut]
```

The first line of output is important because it tells us that serial 0/0 is up/up. Notice that the interface encapsulation is PPP and that LCP is open. This means that it has negotiated the session establishment and all is well. The last line tells us that NCP is listening for the protocols IP and CDP, shown with the NCP headers IPCP and CDPCP.

But what would you see if everything isn't so perfect? I'm going to type in the configuration shown in Figure 8.4 to find out.

FIGURE 8.4   Failed PPP authentication

Pod1R1   Pod1R2

hostname Pod1R1   hostname Pod1R2
username Pod1R2 password Cisco   username Pod1R1 password cisco
interface serial 0   interface serial 0
ip address 10.0.1.1 255.255.255.0   ip address 10.0.1.2 255.255.255.0
clock rate 64000   bandwidth 512
bandwidth 512   encapsulation ppp
encapsulation ppp   ppp authentication chap
ppp authentication chap

What's wrong here? Take a look at the usernames and passwords. Do you see the problem now? That's right, the C is capitalized on the Pod1R2 username command found in the configuration of router Pod1R1. This is wrong because the usernames and passwords are case sensitive. Now let's take a look at the show interface command and see what happens:

```
Pod1R1#sh int s0/0
Serial0/0 is up, line protocol is down
  Hardware is PowerQUICC Serial
  Internet address is 10.0.1.1/24
  MTU 1500 bytes, BW 1544 Kbit, DLY 20000 usec,
     reliability 243/255, txload 1/255, rxload 1/255
  Encapsulation PPP, loopback not set
  Keepalive set (10 sec)
```

```
LCP Closed
Closed: IPCP, CDPCP
```

First, notice that the first line of output shows us Serial0/0 is up and line protocol is down. This is because there are no keepalives coming from the remote router. The next thing I want you to notice is that the LCP and NCP are closed because the authentication failed.

Debugging PPP Authentication

To display the CHAP authentication process as it occurs between two routers in the network, just use the command debug ppp authentication.

If your PPP encapsulation and authentication are set up correctly on both routers and your usernames and passwords are all good, then the debug ppp authentication command will display an output that looks like the following output, which is called the three-way handshake:

```
d16h: Se0/0 PPP: Using default call direction
1d16h: Se0/0 PPP: Treating connection as a dedicated line
1d16h: Se0/0 CHAP: O CHALLENGE id 219 len 27 from "Pod1R1"
1d16h: Se0/0 CHAP: I CHALLENGE id 208 len 27 from "Pod1R2"
1d16h: Se0/0 CHAP: O RESPONSE id 208 len 27 from "Pod1R1"
1d16h: Se0/0 CHAP: I RESPONSE id 219 len 27 from "Pod1R2"
1d16h: Se0/0 CHAP: O SUCCESS id 219 len 4
1d16h: Se0/0 CHAP: I SUCCESS id 208 len 4
```

But if you have the password wrong as they were previously in the PPP authentication failure example back in Figure 8.4, the output would look something like this:

```
1d16h: Se0/0 PPP: Using default call direction
1d16h: Se0/0 PPP: Treating connection as a dedicated line
1d16h: %SYS-5-CONFIG_I: Configured from console by console
1d16h: Se0/0 CHAP: O CHALLENGE id 220 len 27 from "Pod1R1"
1d16h: Se0/0 CHAP: I CHALLENGE id 209 len 27 from "Pod1R2"
1d16h: Se0/0 CHAP: O RESPONSE id 209 len 27 from "Pod1R1"
1d16h: Se0/0 CHAP: I RESPONSE id 220 len 27 from "Pod1R2"
1d16h: Se0/0 CHAP: O FAILURE id 220 len 25 msg is "MD/DES compare failed"
```

PPP with CHAP authentication is a three-way authentication, and if the username and passwords aren't configured exactly the way they should be, then the authentication will fail and the link will go down.

Mismatched WAN Encapsulations

If you have a point-to-point link but the encapsulations aren't the same, the link will never come up. Figure 8.5 shows one link with PPP and one with HDLC.

FIGURE 8.5   Mismatched WAN encapsulations

Pod1R1   Pod1R2

hostname Pod1R1   hostname Pod1R2
username Pod1R2 password cisco   username Pod1R1 password cisco
interface serial 0   interface serial 0
ip address 10.0.1.1 255.255.255.0   ip address 10.0.1.2 255.255.255.0
clock rate 64000   bandwidth 512
bandwidth 512   encapsulation hdlc
encapsulation ppp

Look at router Pod1R1 in this output:

```
Pod1R1#sh int s0/0
Serial0/0 is up, line protocol is down
  Hardware is PowerQUICC Serial
  Internet address is 10.0.1.1/24
  MTU 1500 bytes, BW 1544 Kbit, DLY 20000 usec,
     reliability 254/255, txload 1/255, rxload 1/255
  Encapsulation PPP, loopback not set
  Keepalive set (10 sec)
  LCP REQsent
Closed: IPCP, CDPCP
```

The serial interface is up/down and LCP is sending requests but will never receive any responses because router Pod1R2 is using the HDLC encapsulation. To fix this problem, you would have to go to router Pod1R2 and configure the PPP encapsulation on the serial interface. One more thing: Even though the usernames are configured incorrectly, it doesn't matter because the command ppp authentication chap isn't used under the serial interface configuration. This means that the username command isn't relevant in this example.

You can set a Cisco serial interface back to the default of HDLC with the no encapsulation command like this:

```
Router(config)#int s0/0
Router(config-if)#no encapsulation
*Feb 7 16:00:18.678:%LINEPROTO-5-UPDOWN: Line protocol on Interface Serial0/0,
changed state to up
```

Notice the link came up because the encapsulation on both ends of the link match!

    Always remember that you just can't have PPP on one side and HDLC on the other—they don't get along!

Mismatched IP Addresses

A tricky problem to spot is if you have HDLC or PPP configured on your serial interface but your IP addresses are wrong. Things seem to be just fine because the interfaces will show that they are up. Take a look at Figure 8.6 and see if you can see what I mean—the two routers are connected with different subnets—router Pod1R1 with 10.0.1.1/24 and router Pod1R2 with 10.2.1.2/24.

FIGURE 8.6   Mismatched IP addresses

Pod1R1   Pod1R2

```
hostname Pod1R1                          hostname Pod1R2
username Pod1R2 password cisco           username Pod1R1 password cisco
interface serial 0                       interface serial 0
ip address 10.0.1.1  255.255.255.0       ip address 10.2.1.2  255.255.255.0
clock rate 64000                         bandwidth 512
bandwidth 512                            encapsulation ppp
encapsulation ppp                        ppp authentication chap
ppp authentication chap
```

This will never work. Let's take a look at the output:

```
Pod1R1#sh int s0/0
Serial0/0 is up, line protocol is up
  Hardware is PowerQUICC Serial
  Internet address is 10.0.1.1/24
  MTU 1500 bytes, BW 1544 Kbit, DLY 20000 usec,
     reliability 255/255, txload 1/255, rxload 1/255
  Encapsulation PPP, loopback not set
  Keepalive set (10 sec)
  LCP Open
  Open: IPCP, CDPCP
```

See that? The IP addresses between the routers are wrong but the link appears to be working just fine. This is because PPP, like HDLC and Frame Relay, is a layer 2 WAN encapsulation, so it doesn't care about IP addresses at all. So yes, the link is up, but you can't use IP across this link since it's misconfigured, or can you? Well, yes and no. If you try to ping you'll see that this actually works! This is a feature of PPP, but not HDLC or Frame Relay. But just because you can ping to an IP address that's not in the same subnet doesn't mean your network traffic and routing protocols will work. So be careful with this issue, especially when troubleshooting PPP links!

 For the Cisco objectives, you need to be able to troubleshoot PPP from the routing table.

To find and fix this problem, you can also use the show running-config, show interfaces, or show ip interfaces brief command on each router, or you can use the show cdp neighbors detail command:

```
Pod1R1#sh cdp neighbors detail
-------------------------
Device ID: Pod1R2
Entry address(es):
  IP address: 10.2.1.2
```

Since the layer 1 (Physical) and layer 2 (Data Link) are up/up, you can view and verify the directly connected neighbor's IP address and then solve your problem.

Exam Essentials

Be able to troubleshoot a PPP link. Understand that a PPP link between two routers will show up and a ping would even work between the router if the layer 3 addresses are wrong.

Remember the PPP Data Link layer protocols. The three Data Link layer protocols are Network Control Protocol (NCP), which defines the Network layer protocols; Link Control Protocol (LCP), a method of establishing, configuring, maintaining, and terminating the point-to-point connection; and High-Level Data-Link Control (HDLC), the MAC layer protocol that encapsulates the packets.

Configure and Verify Frame Relay on Cisco Routers

As a CCNA R/S, you'll be expected to understand the basics of the Frame Relay technology and also to be able to configure it in simple scenarios. First, understand that Frame Relay is a packet-switched technology. From everything you've learned so far, just telling you this should make you immediately realize several things about it:

- You won't be using the encapsulation hdlc or encapsulation ppp command to configure it.

- Frame Relay doesn't work like a point-to-point leased line even though it can be made to look and act like one.

- Frame Relay is usually less expensive than leased lines are, but there are some sacrifices required to net that savings.

So why do we use Frame Relay? Figure 8.7 will help you form a snapshot of what a network looked like before Frame Relay as a first step to answering this question.

FIGURE 8.7 Before Frame Relay was configured

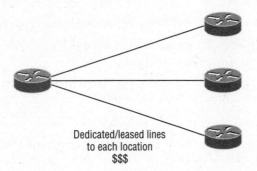

Dedicated/leased lines
to each location
$$$

Now check out Figure 8.8. You can see that there's now only one connection between the router and the Frame Relay switch. That right there saves some major cash!

FIGURE 8.8 After Frame Relay was configured

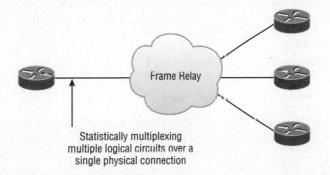

Statistically multiplexing
multiple logical circuits over a
single physical connection

Let's say you needed to add seven remote sites to be accessed from the corporate office but you have only one free serial port on your router—it's Frame Relay to the rescue! Of course, this also means that you now have a single point of failure, which is not so good. But Frame Relay was typically used to save money, not to make a network more resilient.

Frame Relay Bandwidth

Frame Relay provides a packet-switched network to lots of different customers at the same time, which is good because it spreads out the cost of the switches among many customers. But remember, Frame Relay is based on the assumption that those dependent on it will never need to transmit data constantly or simultaneously.

Frame Relay works by providing a portion of dedicated bandwidth to each user, and it also allows the user to exceed their guaranteed bandwidth if resources on the telco network happen to be available. So basically, Frame Relay providers allow customers to buy a lower amount of bandwidth than what they really use. There are two separate bandwidth specifications with Frame Relay:

Access rate   The maximum speed at which the Frame Relay interface can transmit.

CIR   The maximum bandwidth of data guaranteed to be delivered. It's the average amount that the service provider will allow you to transmit.

If these two values are equal, the Frame Relay connection will operate pretty much as a leased line would. But these values can also be set differently.

> The CIR is the rate, in bits per second, at which the Frame Relay switch agrees to transfer data.

Frame Relay Encapsulation Types

When configuring Frame Relay on Cisco routers, you need to specify it as an encapsulation on serial interfaces. And as I said earlier, you can't use HDLC or PPP with Frame Relay. When you configure Frame Relay, you must choose one of two encapsulation types: Cisco and IETF (Internet Engineering Task Force), as shown in the following output:

```
RouterA(config)#int s0
RouterA(config-if)#encapsulation frame-relay ?
  ietf  Use RFC1490 encapsulation
  <cr>
```

Unless you manually type in **ietf**, the default encapsulation option is Cisco, and predictably, it's what you want to go with when connecting two Cisco devices. You'd opt for the IETF-type encapsulation if you needed to connect a Cisco device to a non-Cisco device with Frame Relay. Whichever you choose, make sure the Frame Relay encapsulation is the same on both ends.

Virtual Circuits

Frame Relay operates using *virtual circuits* as opposed to the physical circuits that leased lines use. These virtual circuits are what link together the thousands of devices connected to the provider's "cloud." Frame Relay provides a virtual circuit between your two DTE devices, which makes them appear to be connected via an actual circuit. In reality, they're dumping their frames into a large, shared infrastructure. You never see the complexity of what's actually happening inside the cloud because you only have a virtual circuit.

And on top of all that, there are two types of virtual circuits—permanent and switched. Permanent virtual circuits (PVCs) are by far the most common type in use today. What *permanent* means here is that the telco creates the mappings inside its gear, and as long as you pay the bill, they'll remain in place.

Switched virtual circuits (SVCs) are more like a phone call. The virtual circuit is established when data needs to be transmitted. The virtual circuit is dismantled when the data transfer is complete.

Data Link Connection Identifiers (DLCIs)

Frame Relay PVCs are identified to DTE end devices by *Data Link Connection Identifiers (DLCIs)*. A Frame Relay service provider typically assigns DLCI values, which are used on Frame Relay interfaces to distinguish between different virtual circuits. Because many virtual circuits can be terminated on one multipoint Frame Relay interface, many DLCIs are often affiliated with it.

Inverse ARP (IARP) is used with DLCIs in a Frame Relay network, and it is somewhat similar to ARP in the fact that it maps a DLCI to an IP address—kind of like ARP does with MAC addresses to IP addresses. And even though you can't configure IARP, you can disable it. It runs on a Frame Relay router and maps the DLCI to an IP address for Frame Relay so it knows how to get to the IP address at the other end of the PVC. You can see IP-to-DLCI mappings with the show frame-relay map command.

Inverse ARP (IARP) is used to map a known DLCI to an IP address.

DLCIs are locally significant—global significance requires the entire network to use the Local Management Interface (LMI) extensions that offer global significance. This is why you'll mostly find global DLCIs only in private networks.

For a picture of why DLCIs are considered locally significant, take a look at Figure 8.9. In the figure, DLCI 100 is considered locally significant to RouterA and identifies the circuit to RouterB between RouterA and its ingress Frame Relay switch. DLCI 200 would identify this same circuit to RouterA between RouterB and its ingress Frame Relay switch.

FIGURE 8.9   DLCIs are local to your router. RouterA uses DLCI 100 to send data to RouterB.

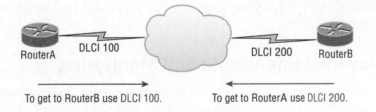

DLCI numbers that are used to identify a PVC are typically assigned by the provider and start at 16.

You configure a DLCI number to be applied to a subinterface like this:

```
RouterA(config-if)#frame-relay interface-dlci ?
  <16-1007> Define a DLCI as part of the current subinterface
RouterA(config-if)#frame-relay interface-dlci 16
```

DLCIs identify the logical circuit between the local router and a Frame Relay switch.

Local Management Interface (LMI)

Local Management Interface (LMI) is a signaling standard used between your router and the first Frame Relay switch it's connected to. It allows for passing information about the operation and status of the virtual circuit between the provider's network and the DTE (your router). It communicates information about the following:

Keepalives   These verify that data is flowing.

Multicasting   This is an optional extension of the LMI specification that permits the efficient distribution of routing information and ARP requests over a Frame Relay network. Multicasting uses the reserved DLCIs from 1019 through 1022.

Global addressing   This provides global significance to DLCIs, allowing the Frame Relay cloud to work exactly like a LAN. This has never been run in a production network to this day.

Status of virtual circuits   This provides DLCI status. The status inquiries and messages are used as keepalives when there is no regular LMI traffic to send.

But remember, LMI is not communication between your routers; it's communication between your router and the nearest Frame Relay switch. So it's entirely possible that the router on one end of a PVC is actively receiving LMI while the router on the other end of the PVC is not. And of course, PVCs won't work with one end down, which clarifies the local nature of LMI communications.

There are three different types of LMI message formats: Cisco, ANSI, and Q.933A. The different kinds in use depend on both the type and configuration of the telco's switching gear, so it's imperative that you configure your router for the correct format, which should be provided by the telco.

Frame Relay Implementation and Monitoring

There are a ton of Frame Relay commands and configuration options, but I'm going to zero in on the ones you really need to know when studying for the CCNA Routing and Switching exam. I'm going to start with one of the simplest configuration options—two routers with a single PVC between them.

Single Interface

Let's get started by looking at a simple example where we just want to connect two routers with a single PVC. Here's how that configuration would look:

```
RouterA#config t
RouterA(config)#int s0/0
RouterA(config-if)#encapsulation frame-relay
```

```
RouterA(config-if)#ip address 172.16.20.1 255.255.255.0
RouterA(config-if)#frame-relay lmi-type ansi
RouterA(config-if)#frame-relay interface-dlci 101
RouterA(config-if)#^Z
RouterA#
```

The first step is to specify the encapsulation as Frame Relay. Notice that since I didn't specify a particular encapsulation type—either Cisco or IETF—the Cisco default type was used. If the other router were non-Cisco, I would've specified IETF. Next, I assigned an IP address to the interface and then specified the LMI type of ANSI based on information provided by the telecommunications provider. Again, the default is Cisco. Finally, I added the DLCI of 101, which indicates the PVC we want to use and has been given to me by my ISP, assuming there's only one PVC on this physical interface.

That's all there is to it—if both sides are configured correctly, and the switch is working, the circuit will come up.

Subinterfaces

As I mentioned earlier, you can have multiple virtual circuits on a single serial interface and yet treat each as a separate interface. You can make this happen by creating *subinterfaces*. Think of a subinterface as a logical interface that's defined by the IOS software. Several subinterfaces will share a single hardware interface, yet for configuration purposes, they operate as if they were separate physical interfaces. This is known as multiplexing.

To configure a router in a Frame Relay network so it will avoid split horizon issues that will not permit certain routing updates, just configure a separate subinterface for each PVC, with a unique DLCI and subnet assigned to the subinterface.

You define subinterfaces using a command like int s0/0.*subinterface number*. First, you have to set the encapsulation on the physical serial interface, and then you can define the subinterfaces—generally one subinterface per PVC.

FIGURE 8.10   Configuring subinterfaces

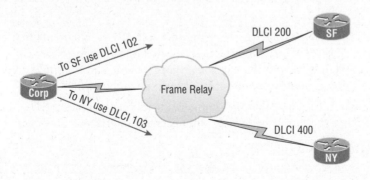

Here's an example, using Figure 8.10:

```
Corp(config)#int s0/0
Corp(config-if)#no shut
Corp(config-if)#encapsulation frame-relay
Corp(config-if)#int s0/0.?
  <0-4294967295>  Serial interface number
Corp(config-if)#int s0/0.102 ?
  multipoint       Treat as a multipoint link
  point-to-point  Treat as a point-to-point link
Corp(config-if)#int s0/0.102 point-to-point
Corp(config-subif)#ip address 10.1.12.1 255.255.255.0
Corp(config-subif)#frame-relay interface-dlci 102
Corp(config-subif)#int s0/0.103
Corp(config-subif)#ip address 10.1.13.1 255.255.255.0
Corp(config-subif)#frame-relay interface-dlci 103
```

Make sure you don't have an IP address under the physical interface if you have configured subinterfaces!

You can define a legion of subinterfaces on any given physical interface, but keep in mind that there are only about a thousand available DLCIs. In the preceding example, I chose to use subinterface 16 because that represents the DLCI number assigned to that PVC by the carrier. There are two types of subinterfaces:

Point-to-point   Used when a single virtual circuit connects one router to another. Each point-to-point subinterface requires its own subnet.

A point-to-point subinterface maps a single IP subnet per DLCI and addresses and resolves NBMA split horizon issues.

Multipoint   This is when the router is the center of a star of virtual circuits that are using a single subnet for all routers' serial interfaces connected to the Frame Relay cloud. You'll usually find this implemented with the hub router in this mode and the spoke routers in physical interface (always point-to-point) or point-to-point subinterface mode.

In the following output, notice that the subinterface number matches the DLCI number—not a requirement, but it seriously helps you administer the interfaces:

```
interface Serial0/0
 no ip address (don't configure an IP address on the physical interface!)
 no ip directed-broadcast
 encapsulation frame-relay
!
```

```
interface Serial0/0.102 point-to-point
 ip address 10.1.12.1 255.255.255.0
 no ip directed-broadcast
frame-relay interface-dlci 102
!
interface Serial0/0.103 point-to-point
 ip address 10.1.13.1 255.255.255.0
 no ip directed-broadcast
frame-relay interface-dlci 103
!
```

Notice also that there's no LMI type defined. This means that the routers are either running the Cisco default or using autodetect if you're running Cisco IOS version 11.2 or newer. I also want to point out that each interface maps to a single DLCI and is defined as a separate subnet. And remember—point-to-point subinterfaces solve split horizon issues as well!

Monitoring Frame Relay

Several commands are used frequently to check the status of your interfaces and PVCs once you have Frame Relay encapsulation set up and running. To list them, use the show frame ? command, as seen here:

```
Corp>sho frame ?
end-to-end    Frame-relay end-to-end VC information
fragment      show frame relay fragmentation information
ip            show frame relay IP statistics
lapf          show frame relay lapf status/statistics
lmi           show frame relay lmi statistics
map           Frame-Relay map table
pvc           show frame relay pvc statistics
qos-autosense show frame relay qos-autosense information
route         show frame relay route
svc           show frame relay SVC stuff
traffic       Frame-Relay protocol statistics
vofr          Show frame-relay VoFR statistics
```

The most common parameters that you view with the show frame-relay command are lmi, pvc, and map.

Now, let's take a look at the most frequently used commands and the information they provide.

The *show frame-relay lmi* Command

The show frame-relay lmi command will give you the LMI traffic statistics exchanged between the local router and the Frame Relay switch.

Here's an example:

```
Corp#sh frame lmi

LMI Statistics for interface Serial0/0 (Frame Relay DTE)LMI TYPE = CISCO
  Invalid Unnumbered info 0      Invalid Prot Disc 0
  Invalid dummy Call Ref 0       Invalid Msg Type 0
  Invalid Status Message 0       Invalid Lock Shift 0
  Invalid Information ID 0        Invalid Report IE Len 0
  Invalid Report Request 0       Invalid Keep IE Len 0
  Num Status Enq. Sent 61         Num Status msgs Rcvd 0
  Num Update Status Rcvd 0        Num Status Timeouts 60
```

The router output from the show frame-relay lmi command shows you any LMI errors, plus the LMI type. So, I have a question based on the output of the command. Is this Frame Relay network working? The answer is no because the router has sent 60 inquiries and has not received even one reply from the Frame Relay switch. If you see this, you need to call the provider because this is a Frame Relay switch configuration issue.

The *show frame pvc* Command

The show frame pvc command will present you with a list of all configured PVCs and DLCI numbers. It provides the status of each PVC connection and traffic statistics too. It will also give you the number of BECN, FECN, and DE packets sent and received on the router per PVC.

Here is an example:

```
Corp#sho frame pvc


PVC Statistics for interface Serial0/0 (Frame Relay DTE)


DLCI = 102,DLCI USAGE = LOCAL,PVC STATUS =ACTIVE,
INTERFACE = Serial0/0.102
 input pkts 50977876    output pkts 41822892
  in bytes 3137403144
 out bytes 3408047602   dropped pkts 5
  in FECN pkts 0
 in BECN pkts 0     out FECN pkts 0     out BECN pkts 0
 in DE pkts 9393    out DE pkts 0
 pvc create time 7w3d, last time pvc status changed 7w3d


DLCI = 103,DLCI USAGE =LOCAL,PVC STATUS =ACTIVE,
```

```
INTERFACE = Serial0/0.103
 input pkts 30572401    output pkts 31139837
  in bytes 1797291100
 out bytes 3227181474    dropped pkts 5
  in FECN pkts 0
 in BECN pkts 0        out FECN pkts 0        out BECN pkts 0
 in DE pkts 28        out DE pkts 0
 pvc create time 7w3d, last time pvc status changed 7w3d
```

If you want to see information about only PVC 102, you can type the command **show frame-relay pvc 102**. Let's take a closer look at the output of this one line:

```
DLCI = 102,DLCI USAGE = LOCAL,PVC STATUS =ACTIVE,
INTERFACE = Serial0/0.102
```

The PVC status field in the output of the show frame-relay pvc command reports the status of the PVC between the router and the Frame Relay switch. The switch (DCE) reports the status to the router (DTE) using the LMI protocol. There are three types of reported statuses:

ACTIVE   The switch is correctly programmed with the DLCI and there is a successful DTE-to-DTE circuit (router to router).

INACTIVE   The router is connected to the switch (DTE to DCE), but there's not a connection to the far-end router (DTE). This can be a router or switch configuration issue.

DELETED   The router (DTE) is configured for a DLCI that the switch (DCE) does not recognize or is not configured correctly.

The three LMI reported statuses are covered in the CCNA R/S objectives! Understand why you'd see each status.

The *show interface* Command

You can use the show interface command to check for LMI traffic. The show interface command displays information about the encapsulation as well as layer 2 and layer 3 information. It also displays line, protocol, DLCI, and LMI information. Check it out:

```
Corp#sho int s0/0
Serial0/0 is up, line protocol is up
 Hardware is HD64570
 MTU 1500 bytes, BW 1544 Kbit, DLY 20000 usec, rely
  255/255, load 2/255
 Encapsulation FRAME-RELAY, loopback not set, keepalive
  set (10 sec)
 LMI enq sent 451751,LMI stat recvd 451750,LMI upd recvd
```

```
 164,DTE LMI up
LMI enq recvd 0, LMI stat sent 0, LMI upd sent 0
LMI DLCI 1023 LMI type is CISCO frame relay DTE
Broadcast queue 0/64, broadcasts sent/dropped 0/0,
 interface broadcasts 839294
```

The LMI DLCI is used to define the type of LMI being used. If it happens to be 1023, it's the default LMI type for Cisco routers. If LMI DLCI is 0 (zero), then it's the ANSI LMI type (Q.933A uses 0 as well). If LMI DLCI is anything other than 0 or 1023, it's a 911—call your provider; they've got major issues!

The *show frame map* Command

The show frame map command displays the mappings from the Network layer to DLCI. Here's how that looks, using Figure 8.10:

```
Corp#show frame map
Serial0/0.102 (up): ip 10.1.12.2 dlci 102(0x66,0x400),
             dynamic, broadcast,, status defined, active
Serial0/0.103 (up): ip 10.1.13.2 dlci 103(0x67,0x410),
             dynamic, broadcast,, status defined, active
```

Notice that the Network layer addresses are marked dynamic, which means they were resolved with the dynamic protocol Inverse ARP (IARP). After the DLCI number is listed, you can see some numbers in parentheses. The first one is 0x66, which is the hex equivalent for the DLCI number 102, used on serial 0/0.102. And the 0x67 is the hex for DLCI 103 used on serial 0/0.103. The second numbers, 0x400 and 0x410, are the DLCI numbers configured in the Frame Relay frame. They're different because of the way the bits are spread out in the frame.

Again, looking at Figure 8.10, the preceding output is telling the Corp router that to get SF via 10.1.12.2, use DLCI 102. To get to the NY router via 10.1.13.2, use DLCI 103. The Corp router would never use a remote DLCI.

You must be able to find the DLCI number used to get to a remote site by using the show frame-relay map command.

The *debug frame lmi* Command

The debug frame lmi command will show real-time output on the router consoles by default (as with any debug command). The information this command gives you will enable you to verify and troubleshoot the Frame Relay connection by helping you determine whether the router and switch are exchanging the correct LMI information. Here's an example:

```
Corp#debug frame-relay lmi
Serial3/1(in): Status, myseq 214
RT IE 1, length 1, type 0
```

```
KA IE 3, length 2, yourseq 214, myseq 214
PVC IE 0x7 , length 0x6 , dlci 130, status 0x2 , bw 0
Serial3/1(out): StEnq, myseq 215, yourseen 214, DTE up
datagramstart = 0x1959DF4, datagramsize = 13
FR encap = 0xFCF10309
00 75 01 01 01 03 02 D7 D6


Serial3/1(in): Status, myseq 215
RT IE 1, length 1, type 1
KA IE 3, length 2, yourseq 215, myseq 215
Serial3/1(out): StEnq, myseq 216, yourseen 215, DTE up
datagramstart = 0x1959DF4, datagramsize = 13
FR encap = 0xFCF10309
00 75 01 01 01 03 02 D8 D7
```

Troubleshooting Frame Relay Networks

Troubleshooting Frame Relay networks isn't any harder than troubleshooting any other
type of network as long as you know what to look for. We'll go over some basic problems
that commonly occur in Frame Relay configuration and how to solve them.

First on the list are serial encapsulation problems. As you learned recently, there are two
Frame Relay encapsulations: Cisco and IETF. Cisco is the default, and it means that you have a
Cisco router on each end of the Frame Relay network. For this example, we'll use Figure 8.11.
If you don't have a Cisco router on the remote end of your Frame Relay network, then you
need to run the IETF encapsulation as shown here:

```
RouterA(config)#int s0
RouterA(config-if)#encapsulation frame-relay ?
  ietf  Use RFC1490 encapsulation
  <cr>
RouterA(config-if)#encapsulation frame-relay ietf
```

Once you verify that you're using the correct encapsulation, you then need to check out
your Frame Relay mappings.

So why can't RouterA talk to RouterB across the Frame Relay network in Figure 8.11?
To find that out, take a close look at the frame-relay map statement. See the problem now?
You cannot use a remote DLCI to communicate to the Frame Relay switch; you must use
your DLCI number! The mapping should have included DLCI 100 instead of DLCI 200.

Now that you know how to ensure that you have the correct Frame Relay encapsulation,
and that DLCIs are only locally significant, let's look into some routing protocol problems
that are often associated with Frame Relay. See if you can find a problem with the two configurations in Figure 8.12.

FIGURE 8.11   Frame Relay mappings

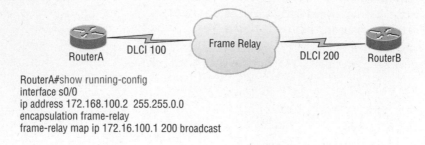

```
RouterA#show running-config
interface s0/0
ip address 172.168.100.2  255.255.0.0
encapsulation frame-relay
frame-relay map ip 172.16.100.1 200 broadcast
```

FIGURE 8.12   Frame Relay routing problems

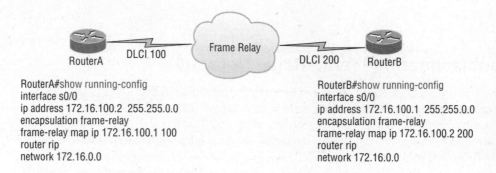

```
RouterA#show running-config
interface s0/0
ip address 172.16.100.2  255.255.0.0
encapsulation frame-relay
frame-relay map ip 172.16.100.1 100
router rip
network 172.16.0.0
```

```
RouterB#show running-config
interface s0/0
ip address 172.16.100.1  255.255.0.0
encapsulation frame-relay
frame-relay map ip 172.16.100.2 200
router rip
network 172.16.0.0
```

What's the problem? Frame Relay is a nonbroadcast multi-access (NBMA) network by default, meaning that it doesn't allow any broadcasts across the PVC. So, because the mapping statements do not have the broadcast argument at the end of the line, broadcasts such as RIP updates or multicasts to neighbors such as Hello packets won't be sent across the PVC. The correct line for RouterA would look like this:

```
frame-relay map ip 172.16.100.1 100 broadcast
```

But wait, do we even use RIP in our internetworks today? Maybe there are problems with the routing protocols EIGRP and OSPF over Frame Relay as well? Take a look at Figure 8.13 and see if you can spot a problem with the OSPF configuration.

Since Frame Relay NBMA networks won't allow broadcasts or multicasts, an OSPF router will not attempt to dynamically discover any OSPF neighbors on the Frame Relay interface. Also, since this means that elections won't be allowed, you'd have to statically configure OSPF neighbors, plus the Corp router would need to be configured as a DR. Even though these are serial links, an NBMA network behaves like Ethernet and a DR is needed to exchange routing information. Only the Corp router can act as a DR because it would have the PVCs for all other routers. But the easiest way to fix this problem is to use the command `ip ospf network point-to-multipoint` on all router Frame Relay interfaces—not just the Corp router, but all branches too!

Okay, this would solve the problem if you're running OSPF, but what if you're running EIGRP? In Figure 8.14 you can see three remote sites connected to the Corp router with all routers running EIGRP. The hosts behind the Corp router can communicate to all hosts in all remote networks, but hosts in SF, LA, and NY cannot communicate with each other.

FIGURE 8.13   Frame Relay OSPF routing problems

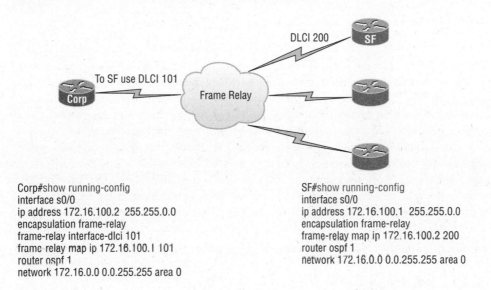

```
Corp#show running-config
interface s0/0
ip address 172.16.100.2  255.255.0.0
encapsulation frame-relay
frame-relay interface-dlci 101
frame relay map ip 172.16.100.1 101
router ospf 1
network 172.16.0.0 0.0.255.255 area 0
```

```
SF#show running-config
interface s0/0
ip address 172.16.100.1  255.255.0.0
encapsulation frame-relay
frame-relay map ip 172.16.100.2 200
router ospf 1
network 172.16.0.0 0.0.255.255 area 0
```

FIGURE 8.14   Frame Relay EIGRP routing problems

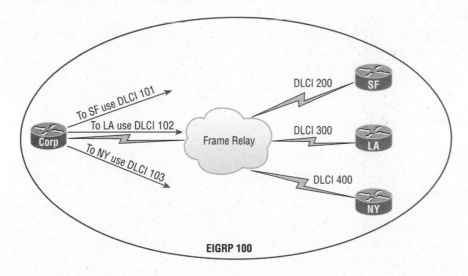

Let's take a look at the configuration of the Corp router now:

```
interface Serial0/0
 ip address 192.168.10.1 255.255.255.0
 encapsulation frame-relay
frame-relay interface-dlci 101
frame-relay interface-dlci 102
frame-relay interface-dlci 103
!
```

The Frame Relay network is all on one subnet, and the configuration looks good, so why can't hosts on the remote networks communicate with each other? Here's your answer: The SF router sends an EIGRP route update to the Corp router and the Corp router updates the local routing table with a route to SF's network. LA and NY do the same thing, and then each site's remote networks can communicate with the hosts behind the Corp router. However, when the Corp router sends route updates to the SF, LA, and NY routers, the updates don't include the other's routers remote network because of the split horizon rule. This rule says you cannot advertise a network back out the same interface you received it on, which is the default configuration of all Cisco serial interfaces. This prevents network loops from occurring.

We can solve this problem with subinterfaces. Take a look at the Corp router's new configuration with subinterfaces, which solves the split horizon issues. Here are the steps to take:

1. Remove the IP address and `interface-dlci` commands from under the physical interface.

2. Create a subinterface (logical interface) for each PVC.

3. Design and implement a separate subnet (address space) for each subinterface.

4. Add the command `frame-relay interface-dlci` *dlci* under each subinterface.

```
interface Serial0/0
 no ip address (notice there is no IP address on the physical interface!)
 encapsulation frame-relay
 !
interface Serial0/0.101 point-to-point
 ip address 192.168.10.1 255.255.255.252
frame-relay interface-dlci 101
 !
interface Serial0/0.102 point-to-point
 ip address 192.168.10.5 255.255.255.252
frame-relay interface-dlci 102
 !
interface Serial0/0.103 point-to-point
ip address 192.168.10.9 255.255.255.252
frame-relay interface-dlci 103
 !
```

Notice that there is no IP address under the physical interface, that each subinterface is a separate subnet or address space, and that I needed to add the `frame-relay interface-dlci` command under each subinterface. Our split horizon issue is now resolved.

Exam Essentials

Understand the different Frame Relay encapsulations.   Cisco uses two different Frame Relay encapsulation methods on its routers: Cisco and IETF. If you are using the Cisco encapsulation method, you are telling your router that a Cisco router is installed on the other side of the PVC. If you are using the IETF encapsulation, you are telling your router that a non-Cisco router is installed on the other side of the PVC.

Remember the commands for verifying and troubleshooting Frame Relay.   The show `frame-relay lmi` command will give you the LMI traffic statistics regarding LMI traffic exchanged between the local router and the Frame Relay switch. The show `frame pvc` command will list all configured PVCs and DLCI numbers.

Understand what the LMI is in Frame Relay.   The LMI is a signaling standard between a CPE device (router) and a frame-relay switch. The LMI is responsible for managing and maintaining the status between these devices. This also provides transmission keepalives to ensure that the PVC does not shut down because of inactivity.

Remember what the CIR is in Frame Relay.   The CIR is the rate, in bits per second, at which the provider of the Frame Relay switch agrees to transfer data.

Configure a Frame Relay connection.   The first step is to specify the encapsulation as Frame Relay. Next, assign an IP address to the interface. Next, specify an LMI type. Finally, add the Data Link Connection Identifier (DLCI).

Implement and Troubleshoot PPPoE

Used with ADSL services, Point-to-Point Protocol over Ethernet (PPPoE) encapsulates PPP frames in Ethernet frames and uses common PPP features like authentication, encryption, and compression. This is a tunneling protocol that layers IP and other protocols that run over PPP with the attributes of a PPP link so they can then be used to contact other Ethernet devices and initiate a point-to-point connection to transport IP packets.

Figure 8.15 displays typical usage of PPPoE over ADSL. As you can see, a PPP session is connected from the PC of the end user to the router and the subscriber PC IP address is assigned by the router via IPCP.

PPPoE is used to equip custom PPP-based software with the ability to deal with a connection that's not using a serial line and to be at home in a packet-oriented network environment like Ethernet. It also allows for a custom connection with login and password for Internet connection accounting. Another factor is that the opposite side of the link's IP address is given to it, and it's available only for the specific period that the PPPoE connection is open. This means that reusing IP addresses is dynamically permitted.

FIGURE 8.15 PPPoE with ADSL

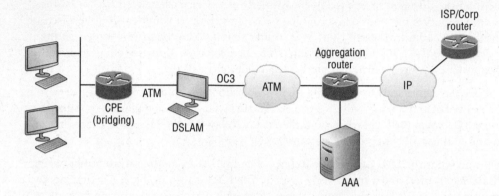

PPPoE has a discovery stage and a PPP session stage (see RFC 2516) that works like this: First, a host begins a PPPoE session, during which it has to execute a discovery process so it can choose the best server to meet the needs of the client machine's request. After that, it has to discover the Ethernet MAC address of the peer device and create a PPPoE session ID. So even though PPP creates a peer-to-peer relationship, the discovery part is innately a client-server relationship.

Exam Essentials

Understand the different features of PPPoE. PPPoE is a network protocol that encapsulates PPP frames inside Ethernet frames over a network and has features of PPP like authentication, encryption, and compression.

Review Questions

1. When setting up Frame Relay for point-to-point subinterfaces, which of the following must not be configured?

   A. The Frame Relay encapsulation on the physical interface

   B. The local DLCI on each subinterface

   C. An IP address on the physical interface

   D. The subinterface type as point-to-point

2. What does the following output tell you about why the serial link between the Corp router and the Remote router won't come up?

   ```
   Corp#sh int s0/0
   Serial0/0 is up, line protocol is down
     Hardware is PowerQUICC Serial
     Internet address is 10.0.1.1/24
     MTU 1500 bytes, BW 1544 Kbit, DLY 20000 usec,
        reliability 254/255, txload 1/255, rxload 1/255
     Encapsulation PPP, loopback not set


   Remote#sh int s0/0
   Serial0/0 is up, line protocol is down
     Hardware is PowerQUICC Serial
     Internet address is 10.0.1.2/24
     MTU 1500 bytes, BW 1544 Kbit, DLY 20000 usec,
        reliability 254/255, txload 1/255, rxload 1/255
     Encapsulation HDLC, loopback not set
   ```

   A. The serial cable is faulty.

   B. The IP addresses are not in the same subnet.

   C. The subnet masks are not correct.

   D. The keepalive settings are not correct.

   E. The layer 2 frame types are not compatible.

3. A default Frame Relay WAN is classified as what type of physical network?

   A. Point-to-point

   B. Broadcast multi-access

   C. Nonbroadcast multi-access

   D. Non-broadcast multipoint

4. You need to configure a router for a Frame Relay connection to a non-Cisco router. Which of the following commands will prepare the WAN interface of the router for this connection?

   A. `Router(config-if)#encapsulation frame-relay q933a`

   B. `Router(config-if)#encapsulation frame-relay ansi`

   C. `Router(config-if)#encapsulation frame-relay ietf`

   D. `Router(config-if)#encapsulation frame-relay cisco`

5. Which of the following are benefits of using a VPN in your internetwork? (Choose three.)

   A. Security

   B. Private high-bandwidth links

   C. Cost savings

   D. Incompatibility with broadband technologies

   E. Scalability

6. Which of the following describes the creation of private networks across the Internet, enabling privacy and tunneling of non-TCP/IP protocols?

   A. HDLC

   B. Cable

   C. VPN

   D. IPsec

   E. xDSL

7. Which of the following is true regarding WAN technologies? (Choose three.)

   A. You must use PPP on a link connecting two routers using a point-to-point lease line.

   B. You can use a T1 to connect a customer site to the ISP.

   C. You can use a T1 to connect a Frame Relay connection to the ISP.

   D. You can use Ethernet as a WAN service by using EoMPLS.

   E. When using an Ethernet WAN, you must configure the DLCI.

8. Which of the following encapsulates PPP frames in Ethernet frames and uses common PPP features like authentication, encryption, and compression?

   A. PPP

   B. PPPoA

   C. PPPoE

   D. Token Ring

9. Which encapsulations can be configured on a serial interface? (Choose three.)

    A. Ethernet

    B. Token Ring

    C. HDLC

    D. Frame Relay

    E. PPP

10. Which command is required for connectivity in a Frame Relay network if Inverse ARP is not operational?

    A. `frame-relay arp`

    B. `frame-relay map`

    C. `frame-relay interface-dci`

    D. `frame-relay lmi-type`

Appendix
A

Answers to Review Questions

Chapter 1: Operation of IP Data Networks

1. A. Fiber optic cables are the only ones that have a core surrounded by a material called cladding.

2. A. The device shown is a hub and hubs place all ports in the same broadcast domain and the same collision domain.

3. B. The Secure Shell (SSH) protocol sets up a secure session that's similar to Telnet over a standard TCP/IP connection and is employed for doing things like logging into systems, running programs on remote systems, and moving files from one system to another.

4. C, F. The switches are not used as either a default gateway or other destination. Switches have nothing to do with routing. It is very important to remember that the destination MAC address will always be the router's interface. The destination address of a frame, from HostA, will be the MAC address of the Fa0/0 interface of RouterA. The destination address of a packet will be the IP address of the network interface card (NIC) of the HTTPS server. The destination port number in the segment header will have a value of 443 (HTTPS).

5. B. The connection between the two switches requires a crossover and the connection from the hosts to the switches required a straight through.

6. A. Since the destination MAC address is different at each hop, it must keep changing. The IP address that is used for the routing process does not.

7. C. If a DHCP conflict is detected, either by the server sending a ping and getting a response or by a host using a gratuitous ARP (arp'ing for its own IP address and seeing if a host responds), then the server will hold that address and not use it again until it is fixed by an administrator.

8. B. The all-hub network at the bottom is one collision domain; the bridge network on top equals three collision domains. Add in the switch network of five collision domains—one for each switch port—and you get a total of nine.

9. C. This process involves looking up every destination in the routing table and finding the exit interface for every packet.

10. B. Address Resolution Protocol (ARP) is used to find the hardware address from a known IP address.

Chapter 2: LAN Switching Technologies

1. D. Hubs are not capable of providing a full-duplex connection.
2. B. The collision will invoke a backoff algorithm on all systems, not just the ones involved in the collision.
3. C. Once the IOS is loaded and up and running, the startup-config will be copied from NVRAM into RAM and from then on referred to as the running-config.
4. C, D. To configure SSH on your router, you need to set the username, the IP domain name, the local login, and the transport input SSH under the VTY lines and the crypto key command. SSH version 2 is suggested but not required.
5. B. The command traceroute (trace for short), which can be issued from user mode or privileged mode, is used to find the path a packet takes through an internetwork and will also show you where the packet stops because of an error on a router.
6. D. Since the question never mentioned anything about a suspended session, you can assume that the Telnet session is still open, and you would just type **exit** to close the session.
7. B. Gateway redundancy is not an issue addressed by STP.
8. B, C. Shutdown and protect mode will alert you via SNMP that a violation has occurred on a port.
9. D. Here's a list of ways VLANs simplify network management:
   - Network adds, moves, and changes are achieved with ease by just configuring a port into the appropriate VLAN.
   - A group of users that need an unusually high level of security can be put into its own VLAN so that users outside of the VLAN can't communicate with them.
   - As a logical grouping of users by function, VLANs can be considered independent from their physical or geographic locations.
   - VLANs greatly enhance network security if implemented correctly.
   - VLANs increase the number of broadcast domains while decreasing their size.
10. C. Unlike ISL, which encapsulates the frame with control information, 802.1q inserts an 802.1q field along with tag control information.

Chapter 3: IP Addressing (IPv4 / IPv6)

1. C. The loopback address with IPv4 is 127.0.0.1. With IPv6, that address is ::1.
2. A. The NDP neighbor advertisement (NA) contains the MAC address. A neighbor solicitation (NS) was initially sent asking for the MAC address.

3. C, D. Adjacencies and next-hop attributes now use link-local addresses, and OSPFv3 still uses multicast traffic to send its updates and acknowledgments with the addresses FF02::5 for OSPF routers and FF02::6 for OSPF designated routers. These are the replacements for 224.0.0.5 and 224.0.0.6, respectively.

4. C. Link-local addresses are meant for throwing together a temporary LAN for meetings or a small LAN that is not going to be routed but needs to share and access files and services locally.

5. C, D, E. OSPFv2 does not use the network command under global configuration mode, nor does it use wildcard masks as IPv4 does. However, they can both use the interface command to configure OSPF, both use a 32-bit RID, and both use LSAs.

6. C. A router solicitation is sent out using the all-routers multicast address of FF02::2. The router can send a router advertisement to all hosts using the FF02::1 multicast address.

7. B, D. To shorten the written length of an IPv6 address, successive fields of zeros may be replaced by double colons. In trying to shorten the address further, leading zeros may also be removed. Just as with IPv4, a single device's interface can have more than one address; with IPv6 there are more types of addresses and the same rule applies. There can be link-local, global unicast, multicast, and anycast addresses all assigned to the same interface.

8. B. This can be a hard question if you don't remember to invert the 7th bit! Always look for the 7th bit when studying for the Cisco exams. The EUI-64 autoconfiguration inserts an FF:FE in the middle of the 48-bit MAC address to create a unique IPv6 address.

9. B, C. If you verify your IP configuration on your host, you'll see that you have multiple IPv6 addresses, including a loopback address. The last 64 bits represent the dynamically created interface ID, and leading zeros are not mandatory in a 16-bit IPv6 field.

10. A. To enable OSPFv3, you enable the protocol at the interface level as with RIPng. The command string is `ipv6 ospf` *process-id* `area` *area-id*.

Chapter 4: IP Routing Technologies

1. C. Unlike ISL, which encapsulates the frame with control information, 802.1q inserts an 802.1q field along with tag control information.

2. D. Instead of using a router interface for each VLAN, you can use one Fast Ethernet interface and run ISL or 802.1q trunking. This allows all VLANs to communicate through one interface. Cisco calls this a "router on a stick."

3. B. The encapsulation command specifying the VLAN for the subinterface must be present under both subinterfaces.

4. A. The show ip ospf neighbor command displays all interface-related neighbor information. This output shows the DR and BDR (unless your router is the DR or BDR), the RID of all directly connected neighbors, and the IP address and name of the directly connected interface.

5. A, C. The process ID for OSPF on a router is only locally significant and used to identity a local OSPF database. You can use the same number on each router, or each router can have a different number. The numbers you can use are from 1 to 65,535. Don't get this confused with area numbers, which can be from 0 to 4.2 billion.

6. B, C. The distance-vector routing protocol sends its complete routing table out of all active interfaces at periodic time intervals. Link-state routing protocols send updates containing the state of their own links to all routers in the internetwork.

7. E. To copy the IOS to a backup host, which is stored in flash memory by default, use the copy flash tftp command.

8. C. Static routes have an administrative distance of 1 by default. Unless you change this, a static route will always be used over any other dynamically learned route. EIGRP has an administrative distance of 90, and RIP has an administrative distance of 120, by default.

9. B. To install a new license on an ISR2 router, use the license install *url* command.

10. D. When there is a change in the topology, the cache changes with it.

Chapter 5: IP Services

1. C. The active virtual router (AVR) responds with the virtual MAC addresses to the clients.

2. B. Once you create a pool for the inside locals to use to get out to the global Internet, you must configure the command to allow them access to the pool. The ip nat inside source list *number pool-name* overload command has the correct sequence for this question.

3. C. SNMPv3 supports strong authentication with MD5 or SHA-1, providing confidentiality (encryption) and data integrity of messages via DES or DES-256 encryption between agents and managers.

4. C, D. Both HSRP and GLBP are Cisco proprietary FHRPs, but only GLBP can load-balance between multiple forwarding routers on the same LAN.

5. D. To enable a device to be an NTP client, use the ntp server *IP_address* version version *number* command at global configuration mode.

6. B. You must configure your interfaces before NAT will provide any translations. On the outside network interfaces, you will use the command ip nat outside.

7. C. If you need to provide addresses from a DHCP server to hosts that aren't on the same LAN as the DHCP server, you can configure your router interface to relay or forward the DHCP client requests using the ip helper-address command. If you don't provide this service, your router would receive the DHCP client broadcast, promptly discard it, and the remote host would never receive an address.

8. B, D. You can verify your NTP client with the show ntp status and show ntp associations commands.

9. A. By default, Cisco routers come with a 24-hour lease time. This can be changed to a desired lease time.

10. D. In the pool of available addresses, you want to reserve addresses for hosts like the router interface, servers, printers. If you have a switch in the network, you will want to reserve an IP address for switch management (VLAN 1).

Chapter 6: Network Device Security

1. C, D. To configure SSH on your router, you need to set the username, the IP domain name, the login local command, and the transport input SSH under the VTY lines and the crypto key. SSH version 2 is suggested but not required.

2. C. The enable secret password is case sensitive, so the second option is wrong. To set the enable secret password, use the enable secret *password* command from global configuration mode. This password is automatically encrypted.

3. D. To allow a VTY (Telnet) session into your router, you must set the VTY password. Option C is wrong because it is setting the password on the wrong router. Notice that you have to set the password before you set the login command.

4. B. The switchport port-security command enables port security, which is a prerequisite for the other commands to function.

5. B, C. Shutdown and protect mode will alert you via SNMP that a violation has occurred on a port.

6. B. The show port-security interface command displays the current port security and status of a switch port.

7. switchport port-security violation shutdown This command is used to set the reaction of the switch to a port violation of shutdown.

8. D. It's compared with lines of the access list only until a match is made. Once the packet matches the condition on a line of the access list, the packet is acted upon and no further comparisons take place.

9. C. The range of 192.168.160.0 to 192.168.191.0 is a block size of 32. The network address is 192.168.160.0 and the mask would be 255.255.224.0, which for an access list must be a wildcard format of 0.0.31.255. The 31 is used for a block size of 32. The wildcard is always one less than the block size.

10. C. Using a named access list just replaces the number used when applying the list to the router's interface. `ip access-group BlockSales in` is correct.

Chapter 7: Troubleshooting

1. A, D. To configure EtherChannel, create the port channel from global configuration mode, and then assign the group number on each interface using the active mode to enable LACP.

2. B. The most common cause of interface errors is a mismatched duplex mode between two ends of an Ethernet link. If they have mismatched duplex setting, you'll receive a legion of errors, which cause nasty slow performance issues, intermittent connectivity, and massive collisions—even total loss of communication!

3. A, B, C, D. Here are the documented steps that Cisco says to check when you have an adjacency issue:

   - Interfaces between the devices are down.
   - The two routers have mismatching EIGRP autonomous system numbers.
   - Proper interfaces are not enabled for the EIGRP process.
   - An interface is configured as passive.
   - The K values are mismatched.
   - EIGRP authentication is misconfigured.

4. D. To see all LSAs a router has learned from its neighbors, you need to see the OSPF LSDB, and you can see this with the `show ip ospf database` command.

5. C, D, E. The `show frame-relay ?` command provides many options, but the options available in this question are `lmi`, `pvc`, and `map`.

6. C. Of the available choices, only the `show ip interface` command will tell you which interfaces have access lists applied. `show access-lists` will not show you which interfaces have an access list applied.

7. A. Ports Fa0/15–18 are not present in any VLANs. They are trunk ports.

8. C. The `show controllers serial 0/0` command will show you whether either a DTE or DCE cable is connected to the interface. If it is a DCE connection, you need to add clocking with the `clock rate` command.

9. A, C, D, E, F. The roles a switch port can play in STP are root, non-root, designated, non-designated, forwarding, and blocking. Discarding is used in RSTP.

10. B. The show ip cache flow command provides a summary of the NetFlow statistics, including which protocols are in use.

Chapter 8: WAN Technologies

1. C. It is very important to remember when studying the CCNA R/S exam objectives, and when configuring Frame Relay with point-to-point subinterfaces, that you do not put an IP address on the physical interface.

2. E. This is an easy question because the Remote router is using the default HDLC serial encapsulation and the Corp router is using the PPP serial encapsulation. You should go to the Remote router and set that encapsulation to PPP or change the Corp router back to the default of HDLC by typing **no encapsulation** under the interface.

3. C. Frame Relay, by default, is a nonbroadcast multi-access (NBMA) network, which means that broadcasts, such as RIP updates, will not be forwarded across the link by default.

4. C. If you have a Cisco router on one side of a Frame Relay network and a non-Cisco router on the other side, you would need to use the Frame Relay encapsulation type of IETF. The default is Cisco encapsulation, which means that a Cisco router must be on both sides of the Frame Relay PVC.

5. A, C, E. VPNs can provide very good security by using advanced encryption and authentication protocols, which will help protect your network from unauthorized access. By connecting the corporate remote offices to their closest Internet provider and then creating a VPN tunnel with encryption and authentication, you'll gain a huge savings over opting for traditional leased point-to-point lines. VPNs scale very well to quickly bring up new offices or have mobile users connect securely while traveling or when connecting from home. VPNs are very compatible with broadband technologies.

6. C. A VPN allows or describes the creation of private networks across the Internet, enabling privacy and tunneling of non-TCP/IP protocols. A VPN can be set up across any type of link.

7. B, C, D. This is just a basic WAN question to test your understanding of connections. PPP does not need to be used, so option A is not valid. You can use any type of connection to connect to a customer site, so option B is a valid answer. You can also use any type of connection to get to the Frame Relay switch, as long as the ISP supports it, and T1 is valid, so option C is okay. Ethernet as a WAN can be used with Ethernet over MPLS (EoMPLS); however, you don't need to configure a DLCI unless you're using Frame Relay, so E is not a valid answer for this question.

8. C. PPPoE encapsulates PPP frames in Ethernet frames and uses common PPP features like authentication, encryption, and compression. PPPoA is used for ATM.

9. C, D, E. Ethernet and Token Ring are LAN technologies and cannot be configured on a serial interface. PPP, HDLC, and Frame Relay are layer 2 WAN technologies that are typically configured on a serial interface.

10. B. If you have a router in your Frame Relay network that does not support IARP, you must create Frame Relay maps on your router, which provide known DLCI-to-IP-address mappings.

Appendix

B

About the Additional Study Tools

IN THIS APPENDIX:

✓ Additional study tools

✓ System requirements

✓ Using the study tools

✓ Troubleshooting

Additional Study Tools

The following sections are arranged by category and summarize the software and other goodies you'll find on the book's companion website. If you need help with installing the items, refer to the installation instructions in the "Using the Study Tools" section of this appendix.

The additional study tools can be found at www.sybex.com/go/ccnarsrg. Here, you will get instructions on how to download the files to your hard drive.

Test Engine

The files contain a test engine, which includes two practice exams.

Electronic Flashcards

These handy electronic flashcards are just what they sound like. One side contains a question, and the other side shows the answer.

PDF of Glossary of Terms

We have included an electronic version of the Glossary in .pdf format. You can view the electronic version of the Glossary with Adobe Reader.

Adobe Reader

We've also included a link to download the latest version of Adobe reader. For more information on Adobe Reader or to check for a newer version, visit Adobe's website at www.adobe.com/products/reader/.

System Requirements

Make sure your computer meets the minimum system requirements shown in the following list. If your computer doesn't match up to most of these requirements, you may have problems using the software and files. For the latest and greatest information, please refer to the ReadMe file located in the downloads.

- A PC running Windows XP or newer
- An Internet connection

Using the Study Tools

To install the items, follow these steps:

1. Download the .ZIP file to your hard drive, and unzip to an appropriate location. Instructions on where to download this file can be found here: www.sybex.com/go/ccnarsrg.

2. Click the Start.EXE file to open up the study tools file.

3. Read the license agreement, and then click the Accept button if you want to use the study tools.

The main interface appears. The interface allows you to access the content with just one or two clicks.

Troubleshooting

Wiley has attempted to provide programs that work on most computers with the minimum system requirements. Alas, your computer may differ, and some programs may not work properly for some reason.

The two likeliest problems are that you don't have enough memory (RAM) for the programs you want to use or you have other programs running that are affecting installation or running of a program. If you get an error message such as "Not enough memory" or "Setup cannot continue," try one or more of the following suggestions and then try using the software again:

Turn off any antivirus software running on your computer. Installation programs sometimes mimic virus activity and may make your computer incorrectly believe that it's being infected by a virus.

Close all running programs. The more programs you have running, the less memory is available to other programs. Installation programs typically update files and programs; so if you keep other programs running, installation may not work properly.

Have your local computer store add more RAM to your computer. This is, admittedly, a drastic and somewhat expensive step. However, adding more memory can really help the speed of your computer and allow more programs to run at the same time.

Customer Care

If you have trouble with the book's companion study tools, please call the Wiley Product Technical Support phone number at (800) 762-2974, or contact them at http://sybex.custhelp.com/.

Index

Note to the Reader: Throughout this index **boldfaced** page numbers indicate primary discussions of a topic. *Italicized* page numbers indicate illustrations.

Free Online Study Tools

Register on Sybex.com to gain access to a complete set of study tools to help you prepare for your CCNA Routing and Switching certification

Comprehensive Study Tool Package Includes:

- **Two Full-Length Practice Exams** to test your knowledge of the material

- **Electronic Flashcards** to reinforce your learning and give you that last-minute test prep before the exam

- **Searchable Glossary** gives you instant access to the key terms you'll need to know for the exam

Go to www.sybex.com/go/ccnarsrg to register and gain access to this comprehensive study tool package.